The Christian Peace Shelf

The Christian Peace Shelf is a selection of Herald Press books and pamphlets devoted to the promotion of Christian peace principles and their applications. The editor (appointed by the Mennonite Central Committee Peace Section) and an editorial board from the Brethren in Christ Church, the General Conference Mennonite Church, the Mennonite Brethren Church, and the Mennonite Church, represent the historic concern for peace within these constituencies.

FOR SERIOUS STUDY

Abrams, Ray H. *Preachers Present Arms* (1969). The involvement of the church in three modern wars.

Durland, William R. *No King But Caesar?* (1975). A Catholic lawyer looks at Christian violence.

Enz, Jacob J. *The Christian and Warfare* (1972). The roots of pacifism in the Old Testament.

Hershberger, Guy F. *War, Peace, and Nonresistance* (Third Edition, 1969). A classic comprehensive work on nonresistance in faith and history.

Hornus, Jean-Michael. *It Is Not Lawful for Me to Fight* (1980). Early Christian attitudes toward war, violence, and the state.

Kaufman, Donald D. *What Belongs to Caesar?* (1969). Basic arguments against voluntary payment of war taxes.

Lasserre, Jean. *War and the Gospel* (1962). An analysis of Scriptures related to the ethical problem of war.

Lind, Millard C. *Yahweh Is a Warrior* (1980). The theology of warfare in ancient Israel.

Ramseyer, Robert L. *Mission and the Peace Witness* (1979). Implications of the biblical peace testimony for the evangelizing mission of the church.

Sider, Ronald J. *Christ and Violence* (1979). A sweeping reappraisal of the church's teaching on violence.

Trocmé, André. *Jesus and the Nonviolent Revolution* (1973). The social and political relevance of Jesus.

Yoder, John H. *The Original Revolution* (1972). Essays on Christian pacifism.

_____ *Nevertheless* (1971). The varieties and shortcomings of Christian pacifism.

FOR EASY READING

Eller, Vernard. *War and Peace from Genesis to Revelation* (1981). Explores peace as a consistent theme developing throughout the Old and New Testaments.

Kaufman, Donald D. *The Tax Dilemma: Praying for Peace, Paying for War* (1978). Biblical, historical, and practical considerations on the war tax issue.

Kraybill, Donald B. *The Upside-Down Kingdom* (1978). A study of the synoptic gospels on affluence, war-making, status-seeking, and religious exclusivism.

Miller, John W. *The Christian Way* (1969). A guide to the Christian life based on the Sermon on the Mount.

Wenger, J. C. *The Way of Peace* (1977). A brief treatment on Christ's teachings and the way of peace through the centuries.

FOR CHILDREN

Bauman, Elizabeth Hershberger. *Coals of Fire* (1954). Stories of people who returned good for evil.

Moore, Ruth Nulton. *Peace Treaty* (1977). A historical novel involving the efforts of Moravian missionary Christian Frederick Post to bring peace to the Ohio Valley in 1758.

Smucker, Barbara Claassen. *Henry's Red Sea* (1955). The dramatic escape of 1,000 Russian Mennonites from Berlin following World War II.

WAR, PEACE, AND NONRESISTANCE

By

Guy Franklin Hershberger

A Christian Peace Shelf Selection

HERALD PRESS
Scottdale, Pennsylvania
Kitchener, Ontario

ACKNOWLEDGEMENTS

The author wishes to acknowledge the kindness of the publishers in granting permission to quote material from the following books to which they hold the copyright. R. H. Abrams, *Preachers Present Arms* (Round Table Press, New York); T. S. Eliot, *The Idea of a Christian Society* (Harcourt, Brace and Co., New York); A. E. Holt, *Christian Roots of Democracy in America* (The Friendship Press, New York); C. H. Hopkins, *The Rise. of the Social Gospel* (Yale University Press, New Haven, Conn.); S. B. Laughlin (Ed.), *Beyond Dilemmas: Quakers Look at Life* (J. B. Lippincott Co., Philadelphia); A. J. Muste, *Nonviolence in an Aggressive World* (Harper and Brothers, New York); Reinhold Niebuhr, *Moral Man and Immoral Society*, and *Christianity and Power Politics* (Charles Scribner's Sons, New York); R. Niebuhr, W. Pauck, and F. P. Miller, *The Church Against the World* (Willett, Clark and Co., Chicago); J. H. Oldham, *Church, Community and State* (Harper and Brothers, New York); Ira M. Price, *The Monuments of the Old Testament* (The Judson Press, Philadelphia); K. Shridharani, *My India, My America* (Duell, Sloan and Pearce, New York); K. Shridharani, *War Without Violence* (Harcourt, Brace and Co., New York); C. Henry Smith, *The Coming of the Russian Mennonites*, and *The Story of the Mennonites* (Mennonite Book Concern, Berne, Ind.); P. A. Sorokin, *The Crisis of Our Age* (E. P. Dutton and Co., New York); W. W. Sweet, *The Story of Religions in America* (Harper and Brothers, New York); Norman Thomas, *The Conscientious Objector in America* (The Viking Press, New York); J. W. Thompson, *Economic and Social History of the Middle Ages* (D. Appleton-Century Co., New York); W. W. Van Kirk, *Religion Renounces War*, and *Religion and the War of Tomorrow* (Willett, Clark and Co., Chicago); F. G. Villard, *W. L. Garrison on Nonresistance* (The Nation Press Co., New York); E. N. Wright, *Conscientious Objectors in the Civil War* (University of Pennsylvania Press, Philadelphia).

Foreword to the First Edition

The longfelt need for a comprehensive and authoritative work on nonresistance in Christian faith and history is ably met by the volume which now appears under the title, *War, Peace, and Nonresistance*. Its worth is enhanced by the fact that it adds to a clear presentation of the Biblical teachings on war and peace, not only a detailed report on the application of nonresistance in history and contemporary life chiefly as the Mennonites have practiced it, but also a sound analysis of the contrast between Biblical nonresistance and modern pacifism, together with practical suggestions for a vigorous program of nonresistant teaching and practice in the future. In scope, clarity, and thoroughness, in practical sense, in loyalty to the Scripture, and in ardor of personal commitment and appeal, the treatment is deeply satisfying. This volume should become the standard handbook in the field.

The preparation of the book was undertaken some years ago as a commission from the Peace Problems Committee of the Mennonite Church. Originally intended primarily as a student manual for younger groups, it developed into a systematic and extensive doctrinal and historical treatise. As such it meets a much larger need and renders a greater service. It is the hope of the Committee that it will not only clarify and deepen the convictions and fortify the living of Christians already committed to the nonresistant way of life, but that it will also be a convincing witness to all earnest seekers after God's way. This hope is intensified by the belief that the way of life involved in the practice of Christian nonresistance means vastly more than nonparticipation in war, seeing that it requires the unreserved practice of Christian love and a following in the steps of Jesus in the whole of life.

There is much challenge as well as inspiration in the nonresistant record of the Mennonites, who have constituted a brotherhood of peace from their very origin in Reformation times in Switzerland and Holland. But there is also much in the record, particularly in recent times, to stir the church out of dangerous complacency into aggressive and devoted action. *War, Peace, and Nonresistance* should be a valuable help to this end.

Throughout the Mennonite Church there will certainly be an almost universal endorsement of the author's final conclusions. On some of the intermediate points, however, there may be some disagreement, particularly concerning the difficult problem of war and peace in the Old Testament. This problem might have been quietly disposed of, and disagreement avoided, by the simple and truthful statement that God permitted under the old covenant what He forbade under the new. The author has chosen rather, in earnest inquiry, to seek to answer the question why the eternally holy and unchanging God did as He did. Some within the church maintain that under the old covenant the waging of war was in full accord with the will of God, but that the new covenant ordains the way of nonresistance and love which is taught by Christ and the apostles. The author has, by his study, been led to the conclusion that God's fundamental moral law is unchanging. Those who disagree with this answer will, we believe, appreciate the sincerity of the author in his endeavor to seek a truly Scriptural and reasonable solution, and will find stimulus to a fresh and critical examination of their own answers. It is apparent that differences concerning the question of Old Testament wars are not a matter of paramount importance, since both views agree on the New Testament teaching concerning the Christian's participation in war.

In giving the manuscript of *War, Peace, and Nonresistance* to the Herald Press for publication and the widest possible distribution, the Peace Problems Committee agreed with the Publishing Committee of the Mennonite Publication Board that responsibility for a final review of the manuscript should lie with Harold S. Bender and Paul Erb, the respective chairmen of the committees. The book as it now appears carries their wholehearted endorsement and commendation.

HAROLD S. BENDER, *Chairman*
Peace Problems Committee

Preface to the First Edition

Nonresistance is a Biblical principle, and a way of life, espoused by the Mennonites from the beginning of their history in the time of the Reformation. The present volume has been written in the hope that it may assist the Mennonite people themselves, as well as the general public, to a better understanding of their faith and life. An effort has been made to give a balanced treatment, including the Biblical foundations, the historical development, and the present state of the nonresistant faith, together with some suggestions for the future. Since many forms of pacifism exist today, an attempt has been made to analyze and classify these various types, and to show their relation to Biblical nonresistance.

In any discussion of the Scriptural basis of nonresistance the conclusions reached will depend in part on the author's view of the Scriptures themselves. It is an easy task to compile a list of Scriptures, especially from the Old Testament, which seem to indicate a divine approval of war. If these are taken as the norm of interpretation, and the remainder of the Bible is interpreted in the light of that norm, the conclusion will be a convincing case for war. This is the view of the fundamentalist militarists. The modernist pacifists, on the other hand, accept the ethical teachings of Jesus as the norm, not hesitating even to reject as unauthoritative any portion of Scripture which seems to be in conflict with that teaching. The neo-orthodox dualists, represented by Reinhold Neibuhr, recognize the nonresistant element in the teachings of Jesus; but since they also have a liberal view of the Scriptures, this teaching is not considered binding upon the Christian today. This view rejects popular pacifism, but considers pure New Testament nonresistance and "Christian militarism" to be supplementary to each other, the latter being the necessary solution for the political order, and the former serving as a witness to the pure Christian ethic.

The Mennonite view has always emphasized a covenant theology which recognizes a permission for war under the covenant of the Old Testament, and a prohibition of war under the covenant of the New Testament. It is the author's view that God has provided one fundamental moral law which has been and is valid for all time. This view holds that the Ten Commandments embody the essence of the moral law, and that the life and teachings of Jesus are its authoritative interpretation and fulfillment. This view begins with the premise that the commandment of love, and the injunction, "Thou shalt not kill," are part and parcel of God's fundamental moral law; and that the life and teachings of Christ are an authoritative endorsement, interpretation, and fulfillment of that command. It assumes that the lower standards of the Mosaic civil code represent a temporary concession on the part of God to the lowered moral state and the spiritual immaturity of that time; a concession made necessary by the sin of man, and not by the will of God.

The author desires to acknowledge his obligation to all who have assisted in any way in the preparation of this work. Goshen College kindly granted a sabbatical leave during the second semester of 1942-43 to provide time for writing. The manuscript was read by the Publishing Committee of the Mennonite Publication Board, as well as by the Peace Problems Committee which sponsored this work. Others who read the manuscript and gave helpful criticisms include John L. Horst, Chester K. Lehman, John R. Mumaw, P. H. Richert, Donovan E. Smucker, and Sanford C. Yoder. Carl Kreider gave helpful suggestions on Chapter XIII. Harold S. Bender and Paul Erb read the manuscript in its original form and again following its revision. My wife, Clara Hooley Hershberger, assisted in the task of proofreading. These friends have saved the author from many errors; those which remain must be charged to his account alone.

GUY F. HERSHBERGER

Goshen, Indiana
February 23, 1944

Preface to the Second Edition

More than eight years have passed since the first publication of this volume, and certain revisions seemed in order, making this third printing a revised edition. Chapters I to V remain as in the first edition with relatively little change. In Chapter III, however, a new section, "Nonresistance an Integral Part of the Gospel," has been added. A few lines have been added at the end of Chapter IV, pointing out the growth of nonresistance and pacifism within European and American Protestantism since the first World War. In Chapter V an attempt has been made to bring the statistical material up to date.

Chapters VI, VII, and IX of the first edition, treating the wartime experiences of the American Mennonites, have been condensed into Chapter VI of the revised edition. This seemed advisable, especially since the material in Chapter IX of the first edition is treated in great detail in the author's *The Mennonite Church in the Second World War,* published in 1951. Chapter VII of the revised edition contains some material from the original Chapter VIII, plus considerable new material, bringing the story of the recent world-wide Mennonite peace witness up to date. The revival of nonresistance among the Dutch and other European Mennonites, and the increasingly aggressive peace witness of the Mennonites throughout the world, made this revision especially necessary. The publication of John D. Unruh's *In the Name of Christ* (1952), a history of the Mennonite Central Committee, has made it possible to omit much of the relief history included in the original Chapter VIII.

Chapter VIII of the revised edition is Chapter X of the original, with some modification. Chapter IX is the original Chapter XI plus a condensation of Chapter XII. The latter contained a large amount of material illustrating the relation of Biblical nonresistance and modern pacifism as found in the American Civilian Public Service experiment. This detailed account of CPS seemed unnecessary in view of Melvin

PREFACE

Gingerich's *Service for Peace*, published in 1949. Chapter XI is the original Chapter XIV without change. Chapter X of the revised edition is the original Chapter XIII with a new title and a new approach: Instead of merely treating the implication of nonresistance for the problem of industrial conflict an attempt has been made to put the matter on a broader basis, showing the broader social implications of the Biblical doctrine of nonresistance. Chapter XII is the original Chapter XV with some additions. Three of the original twelve appendices have been omitted, and three new ones added. The selected bibliographies at the end of the various chapters have been slightly revised so as to include some significant new titles.

GUY F. HERSHBERGER

Goshen, Indiana
January 9, 1953

Preface to the Third Edition

War, Peace, and Nonresistance, first published in the midst of World War II, appeared in a second (revised) edition in 1953. The revisions at that time were chiefly three: (1) Those sections of the book treating wartime experience of the Mennonites were condensed, inasmuch as this story was now adequately told elsewhere. (2) The new world-wide Mennonite peace witness which was an outgrowth of the World War II experience was brought into focus. (3) In chapter 10 the social implications of Biblical nonresistance were outlined in broader perspective than in the first edition.

Except for a few minor changes the third edition is not an extensive revision. Three or four pages of chapter 7 bring the world-wide Mennonite peace witness up-to-date. A few statistics, particularly church membership figures, are updated. The select bibliographies at chapter ends include a few new titles of recent publication date. Four appendixes have been omitted and three new ones added, the latter being the most recent official statements of the Mennonite General Conference with respect to the Christian's relation to the state and the social implications of nonresistance. Other than this, the book remains as in the first and second editions.

It should be noted that the author's *The Way of the Cross in Human Relations,* published in 1958, attempts to do four things which go beyond what was attempted in *War, Peace, and Nonresistance:* (1) To examine more deeply the Scriptural and theological foundations of the Christian ethic, of what is here called the way of the cross. (2) To examine and evaluate more fully the response of Christians to the demands of that ethic through the centuries. (3) To explore more fully the social implications of the Christian ethic, the fuller meaning of the way of the cross, in modern life. (4) To view the whole in the perspective of New Testament eschatology.

Needless to say, despite whatever advance *The Way of the Cross in Human Relations* may represent, the author is happy to know that in the mind of the publisher *War, Peace, and*

PREFACE

Nonresistance has come to be accepted as a "classic" meriting continued publication. In a changing world, to be sure, abiding principles must ever find new and fresh applications to meet the needs of the changing times. But the important point is that the New Testament ethic constitutes a body of eternal principles which cannot change. And to the extent that these eternal principles are truly reflected in *War, Peace, and Nonresistance* the author trusts that the book can continue to have permanent value.

Were *War, Peace, and Nonresistance* written today for the first time, its treatment of pacifism and anti-pacifism, and of the social implications of the New Testament ethic, would no doubt come by a somewhat different approach than was the case in a day before anyone had heard of Martin Luther King, or had dreamed of American armies bogged down in a land war in far-off Vietnam. Even in *The Way of the Cross in Human Relations* neither the name of King nor that of Vietnam is to be found, so rapid is the change of our modern world—or so slow are authors in keeping up with the change.

But as changes come and go, and as nations and peoples rise and fall with the years, even more surely than these does the Lord of history rule over all, His eternal, immutable laws going on forever. It is the author's prayer, therefore, that *War, Peace, and Nonresistance,* despite its imperfections, may reflect these eternal laws with sufficient clarity to merit its continued use and perchance even future republication.

All Scripture quotations are from the King James Version, unless otherwise indicated.

Guy F. Hershberger

Goshen, Indiana
June 10, 1968

Contents

CONTENTS

CONTENTS

CONTENTS

xvi

1. War in Human History

War is a social conflict in which one party endeavors, with the use of force, to compel the submission of the other. It occurs in all kinds of social groups. Sometimes it is carried on between nations, sometimes between tribes. Religious wars have been common in certain periods of history. There are also wars between races, political parties, social classes, and even between families and individuals. Warfare is generally thought of as *armed* conflict, which results in the direct taking of human life. It should not be forgotten, however, that physical and armed force are not the only kinds of force. For a quarter of a century Gandhi directed an effective war for the independence of India, through the use of what he called "soul force." Gandhi's program of nonviolence was sometimes confused with nonresistance, but it was really a form of warfare, since its primary purpose was to bring about the submission of the opposition through compulsion.[1]

War and Material Civilization

War is as old as the human race. Its nominal causes may vary from time to time, but the fundamental cause remains the same. The Bible says that the first murderer sinned against God and then slew his brother.[2] The fundamental cause of war is sin. First there is disobedience in the heart against God. Warfare and murder then follow as the fruit of disobedience to the divine will. Like other forms of sin, warfare and murder have their consequences. When Cain committed his terrible deed he became a fugitive and a wanderer. The society in

[1] For a fuller discussion of Gandhi and nonviolence see Chapter IX.
[2] Gen. 4:5-8.

which he had formerly moved no longer trusted him, and he became an outcast.

In course of time, however, Cain and his descendants developed a society and a civilization of their own. Apparently it was a material civilization of some importance. The brief account in Genesis refers to dwellers in tents and dwellers in cities. There were flocks and herds, brass and iron tools, and musical instruments. But it was a worldly, secularized civilization which had turned against God. Its story begins with a murder and ends with a song of murder.[3] It is even possible that the very evil and worldliness of the Cainite civilization had something to do with the making of its material prosperity. The exclusion of spiritual interests allowed a concentration on secular affairs, resulting in a one-sided development of a worldly character. No doubt those who disregard the spiritual values of life and direct all their energies to secular pursuits frequently accomplish more in that direction than would be possible if they devoted the rightful part of their energies to the service of God and conducted their secular affairs on the basis of Christian principles.

At any rate, the growth of civilization to a high level is no guarantee against war. The two often go together, and either one may be a cause of the other. To be sure, war is also a destroyer of the cultural and spiritual elements in civilization, and if prolonged will destroy the material elements as well. But that war and the aggrandizement of material civilization often go hand in hand, there can be no doubt. The most destructive wars in history are being fought in our own age, with industry developed to the highest point known to man. This fact should have some meaning for the understanding of our own civilization. Might it be that future historians will describe our civilization not only as the most highly developed in industry, and the most destructive in warfare, but also as one of the most ungodly in its interests and the least appreciative of spiritual values? To say the least, the present world situation offers little comfort to the evolutionary view that

[3] Gen. 4:8, 23, 24.

warfare is primarily the work of primitive people recently emerged from a brute ancestry. Warfare is probably no more typical of so-called primitive peoples than it is of those who are supposedly civilized, and perhaps less so. History records much warfare among savage tribes, to be sure. But it has been suggested[4] that this practice among some tribes may be due to the influence of neighboring advanced civilizations which first plundered them for gold, slaves, and other forms of wealth. At any rate, the peoples of South Africa seem to have been relatively peaceful until the coming of the slave trade in modern times; and the American Indians likewise were generally peaceful before the civilized white man came with his guns, his ammunition, his trinkets, and his rum.

Wars in Ancient Times

Once a tribal people become warlike, however, they often provide no end of trouble for their more civilized neighbors. In ancient and medieval times, wars of plunder for the seizure of movable wealth were common. The cities and civilizations of the ancient Mediterranean were frequently raided by tribes of people from the hinterland. For centuries China was subject to raids by the tribes from Mongolia and Siberia. This type of warfare reached the height of its prevalence in the raids of the Huns, a barbarous Asiatic people who invaded Europe in the fifth century after Christ, and in the conquests of Genghis Khan, the Mongolian conqueror of the thirteenth century. Modern mechanical methods of warfare, however, have practically eliminated these tribal raids once so important in human history.

In ancient times numerous wars were fought also for the displacement of one people by another. In the third millennium B.C., Semitic peoples in large numbers moved into Mesopotamia, Arabia, and Syria in an effort to displace the earlier settlers and to make a home for themselves. In the second millennium the Aryans with a similar purpose moved into Asia

[4] A. Johnson, "War," *Encyclopedia of the Social Sciences* (New York, 1935), 15:331.

Minor, the Aegean region, Persia, and India. By the opening of the Christian era the Germanic peoples of northern Europe had begun a similar movement southward and westward which continued until the eighth and ninth centuries after Christ. From the eleventh to the seventeenth centuries the Turks from the East pressed into Asia Minor and southeastern Europe. Having as their purpose the displacement of entire populations, some of these wars were very brutal in character.

In ancient times wars were also frequently fought for the expansion of kingdoms and empires. Powerful monarchs endeavored to bring the surrounding territories under their control, and establish frontiers that would be secure against invasion. Frequently the result would be conflict with some other monarch who had similar ambitions. Assyria extended its borders northward and westward until it came into conflict with Egypt and with the Hittites in Asia Minor. As a result, the border warfare between Egypt and the Mesopotamian powers continued for centuries. In the sixth century B.C., the Persian Empire displaced the Assyrian and extended its way eastward to the Indus River and westward to include Egypt and Asia Minor. In the fourth century Alexander the Great held the position of world ruler for a brief time. Then in the third century B.C., ascendancy passed to the Romans, who began a new era of foreign conquest which continued into the Christian era, when the borders of the Empire were stabilized in Britain, on the Rhine, the Danube, the Caucasus, the Euphrates, Ethiopia, and the Sahara.

Whether the wars of ancient times were primarily for the seizure of movable wealth, or for the displacement of earlier settlers, or for the expansion of kingdoms and empires, the economic and financial motive was always present in some form or other. All of these wars were financed to a large extent by plunder taken in the conquest, and by the tribute exacted from the subjugated peoples. The taking of the plunder, and sometimes the exaction of the tribute, was the task of the conquering general, who frequently was tempted to use the wealth at his command for the overthrow of the monarch, thus seat-ing himself upon the throne. As a result, successful conquests by the general were often followed by internal revolts and struggles for power. In the Roman Republic such struggles were common, and continued long after the establishment of the Empire. Julius Caesar played an active part in such struggles in his day. Once the boundaries of the Empire were stabilized, therefore, the emperors were loath to extend them farther, lest the looting of new territories should provide rapacious generals with the means of disrupting the peace and order at home.

Wars in the Middle Ages

Ancient history comes to a close about A.D. 375. The following period, known as the Middle Ages, may be said to have closed by 1300. It begins with the migration of the German tribes and the disintegration of the Roman Empire in the West, and is characterized in turn by the growth of the feudal system, the revival of trade, the disintegration of the feudal system, and the beginnings of modern national states. The wars of this period were of less consequence than those of ancient times and, with a possible exception of the Crusades, were waged on a much smaller scale. As noted before, the Germanic migrations may be regarded as wars for the displacement of earlier settlers. And yet they did not result in the displacement or subjugation of large blocks of people, as did those of ancient times. They were rather infiltrations, the newcomers occupying the best lands in the old Empire, living side by side with the older populations, but often occupying positions of power and privilege, while the older population tilled the soil and rendered personal service to the new masters.

After the Germanic tribes had settled down, the flimsy kingdoms which they founded soon came to an end, and the feudal system took their place. Under this political system wars were local affairs, mainly efforts of feudal barons to extend their personal holdings, and the mass of the people had little interest in them. Toward the close of the eleventh century, however, came the Crusades, a series of wars in which the ambitious feudal nobility revived the idea of foreign conquest. The Crusades represent an awakening of the general social consciousness, in that the populace took a greater interest in the events of the time than was formerly the case. They were also in part a racial and religious conflict, in that the propaganda of the time played up the need for Christendom to destroy the wicked Turks, who were followers of Mohammed. But as in ancient times, the medieval wars, especially the Crusades, were also strongly motivated by economic factors. The warring knights of the West were lured by the wealth of the East more than they were impelled by a love for the church. This is especially true in the later Crusades, and even in the first Crusade Pope Urban II urged the Frankish warriors into the fray with these words:

> This land which you inhabit, shut in on all sides by the seas and surrounded by the mountain peaks, is too narrow for your large population; nor does it abound in wealth; and it furnishes scarcely food enough for its cultivators .... Let therefore hatred depart from among you, let your quarrels end, let wars cease, and let all dissensions and controversies slumber. Enter upon the road to the Holy Sepulchre; wrest that land from the wicked race, and subject it to yourselves. That land which as the Scripture says, "floweth with milk and honey," was given by God into the possession of the children of Israel.[5]

Wars in Modern Times

By 1300 the Middle Ages were coming to a close and the modern era was about to begin. In the centuries which followed, warfare retained all the basic causes and characteristics of former periods, although the immediate objectives and methods varied with the changing conditions of the time. The Crusades were over, but wars against the Turks continued until the close of the seventeenth century. Outstanding wars in the early modern period were those for the unification of national states which were just beginning to take form. The wars of Ferdinand and Isabella for the unification of Spain in the late fifteenth

---

[5] University of Pennsylvania, *Translations and Reprints from the Original Sources of European History* (Philadelphia, 1902), 1:2:6,7.

century are typical examples. Religious wars, between Protestants and Catholics especially, were important in the sixteenth and seventeenth centuries. But from the middle of the seventeenth century to near the close of the eighteenth, first place was taken by wars of rival dynastic powers (such as those of Louis XIV of France and the Hapsburg rulers of Austria) struggling for the mastery of continental Europe, and by wars for the domination of colonies, such as the Seven Years' War between England and France for the control of America and India. The French Revolution, a struggle for the overthrow of the old landed aristocracy by the rising middle class, began at the close of the eighteenth century.

Wars in the Nineteenth and Twentieth Centuries

During the first three quarters of the nineteenth century numerous wars were fought for national independence and unification. The American War of Independence had come in the late eighteenth century, and another for the preservation of the Union in the mid-nineteenth. Wars for the independence of the Spanish-American colonies were fought in the early nineteenth century. Italy and Germany were united by blood and iron at the middle of the same century. From 1830, through the century and beyond, there were numerous struggles for the independence of one or another of the subject states in the Balkans. Beginning about 1870 the western world entered a new era of imperialism. The growth of modern manufactures, the desire for foreign markets, and the need for raw materials, created a demand among the great powers of Europe, as well as in the United States and Japan, for colonies and commercial concessions in backward or undeveloped countries like China and Africa. This led to a series of imperialistic wars for the control of desired territories, such as the Sino-Japanese War in 1894-95, the Spanish-American War in 1898, the Boer War in South Africa in 1899, and the Russo-Japanese War in 1904-5. The European war of 1914-18 was the culmination of this series of wars. It grew out of the imperialistic and nationalistic rivalries of the great powers, and eventually it involved all of the major and many of the minor nations of the world so that it came to be called the World War. So great was its effect, and so far-reaching its consequences, that this war marked the end of an era.

The Rise of Modern Dictators

For a decade or more following 1918 the world outlook seemed more hopeful. Later events have shown, however, that surface appearances were misleading, that the settlements of the Versailles Treaty could not be permanent. Certain nations had suffered boundary and other changes to their disadvantage. Whether these changes were just or unjust, these nations, Germany in particular, were determined that they should not remain permanently. As a result of the war all the European countries experienced financial and other internal difficulties which in a number of cases brought on some kind of social and political revolution. The Communist party came to power in Russia in 1917, the Fascist party in Italy in 1922, and the Nazi regime in Germany in 1933. In each of these cases the government was controlled by a powerful personal dictator and a small group of associates bent on the correction of international wrongs, real or supposed, and anxious for the extension of their own political power.

This combination of circumstances caused many people to wonder whether the world was about to experience a revival of ancient civilization in its political and military aspects. Like the ancient monarchies, the new totalitarian states had a tendency toward absolutism in authority. Individual freedom was not tolerated. In education absolute uniformity was insisted upon. The church, if it existed at all, was subordinated to the state. In some cases men were actually or virtually taught to worship the state and its rulers. Under such a regime there is no place for the Scriptural injunction to "render . . . unto God the things that are God's." Caesar receives everything, the things which belong to himself and the things which belong to God as well. In such a state he who would obey God rather than men is not only thought of as a disloyal citizen, but he is often considered a rebel or traitor worthy of death.

In its beginning, at least, the second World War also resembled the wars of the ancient monarchies in a number of ways. It seemed to be a war of political aggrandizement, foreign conquest, and world empire. Weaker peoples and states were brought under the rule of the strong "monarch" who would consolidate all into one great empire surrounded by impregnable frontiers. The war also involved racial hatreds and a program for at least partial displacement of other peoples. The desire for economic power and leadership played a leading role, and there was even a certain amount of plunder and seizure of wealth in a modern form. By the close of the war it was clear that the imperialistic ambitions of the aggressors had not been realized. It was equally clear, however, that their defeat had not brought the end of dictatorship and the triumph of democracy and peace.

The Character of Modern Warfare

The most striking change which has come about in the recent history of warfare is the revolutionary character of its methods. Until recent times war was a relatively small-scale and inexpensive affair, both as to the number of men and the amount of materials involved. In ancient times it was the work of a small class of professional soldiers. The wars of the Middle Ages were carried on by the feudal and military aristocracy and their retainers, and the mass of the people had little interest in them. The small armies of early modern times consisted chiefly of voluntary mercenary soldiers, and the general population was little more concerned with them than were the common people of the Middle Ages. Toward the close of the eighteenth century, however, important changes were brought about, and with the coming of Napoleon in 1799 Europe was introduced for the first time to what was called the *levée en masse*. This meant that the entire people, not merely the ruling or military class, became direct participants in the war. In a short time the other European nations adopted the same principle. In the nineteenth century Prussia developed a system of universal compulsory military service which was soon copied by other nations; and today all the nations raise their armies by conscription.

Furthermore, in our machine age warfare has become a great industrial enterprise. Instead of a few simple hand tools of former times, a modern nation engaged in war requires hundreds of thousands of tanks and airplanes equipped with guns, ammunition and death-dealing bombs such as no one had dreamed of a few decades ago. Warfare on the sea requires airplanes and submarines and warships of every description, great and small. In the second World War the United States had under arms about 10,000,000 men. To feed and equip this vast array of armed forces, and to transport men and supplies overseas to the scene of battle, requires the full industrial strength of the entire nation. Modern warfare therefore becomes "total" warfare. The government assumes full command of the industrial resources of the entire nation. Factories are permitted to produce only the barest essentials for civilian consumption. Residential construction is suspended, except for the housing of war workers. Industry is "converted" to the manufacture of war materials, war transportation, and war supplies. Old factories are enlarged and new ones are constructed in order that the demands of war may be met. To accomplish this gigantic task the government's War Manpower Commission decides which occupations are essential in wartime and which are not. Men eligible for military service may be deferred if engaged in an essential industry; if not so engaged, they are inducted into the army. Thus, in modern warfare the nation's entire population is mobilized for war. All of the scientific resources and the intellectual energies of the nation are directed to the same end. Even quiet university campuses are converted into schools for the training of the armed forces. So completely is the entire nation mobilized for war that no one can escape its effect.

When the entire nation is organized for war the question of "morale" is of great importance. The mass of the people cannot support a war in the battlefield and in the factory unless they believe that the war is necessary for the welfare of the nation. Consequently governments at war resort to ingenious methods of propaganda to build up morale. All kinds of social pressure are resorted to in order that every citizen may be induced to perform his part. War propaganda always has a tendency to obscure and distort the facts, to arouse hatred, and otherwise to make it difficult for the citizen to think clearly and sanely on the issues at stake. Even when the propaganda is as truthful as it can be, the social pressures of wartime are so great that few people can resist them unless they have an unusually strong conviction that war is wrong. In wartime a mild opinion that peace is a good thing is not sufficient to make an individual a nonresistant Christian, for the propaganda and social pressures are so great that relatively few are able to resist them. It is this feature of modern warfare which makes it so much more vicious than that of earlier centuries. Until recently participation in any war was for the most part a voluntary matter. But today even the Christian who is thoroughly convinced that war is contrary to the will of God must frequently suffer if he would take his stand for what he believes is right.

An Age of Secularism

As suggested earlier in this chapter, ours is a secular, worldly civilization. Its energies are directed toward the achievement of material greatness. In the process, God has been largely forgotten. Our age is sadly lacking in an appreciation of spiritual values. The character of modern warfare is another illustration of this fact. This is reflected in the flimsy arguments advanced in the attempt to justify modern wars. The ancient monarchs prior to the Greeks and Romans do not seem to have made any attempt to justify their wars at all. Apparently they did not think of themselves as bound by moral or ethical restrictions. Theirs was frankly a materialistic outlook on life. The

Greeks and Romans, however, were somewhat restricted by moral considerations. They hesitated to declare war without being able to cite a list of grievances against the victim of their attack.

It is interesting, therefore, to follow the attitude of the Christian Church toward war, and to observe how the wars of Christendom have been justified. This will be discussed at greater length in Chapter IV. It should be mentioned at this point, however, that the early church was nonresistant. The compromise of the church with war began toward the close of the second century, and then after the church and state were united in the fourth century, warfare was more or less taken for granted. That the Christian conscience on this question remained much alive, however, is evident from Augustine's diligent efforts to show which are "just wars" and which are not just.[6]

In the Middle Ages the church tried to regulate warfare among the feudal nobility, insisting that one Christian prince should not wage war against another unless he had real grievances, and setting apart certain seasons when no war might be carried on at all. In modern times, however, the church has accomplished little for the prevention of war. It is generally agreed in modern Christendom that war is wrong, of course. Outside the so-called peace churches, however, the official creeds have not forbidden participation in war. Nations have waged war as they have seen fit and the churches have usually supported them, the ministry playing an active role in showing why this is the proper course to take.

In spite of the readiness of people to support war, however, it was popularly believed a generation ago that war would soon be a thing of the past. This belief was shared by many Christian people. The evolutionary view of society, and the progress of modern science and education, seemed to argue for a growing human enlightenment to the point where war would no longer be possible. This view, however, did not give sufficient consideration to the sinfulness of man and his need of redemp-

[6] See below, pp. 72-73.

tion. Furthermore, those modern students of society who are less influenced by the evolutionary idealism of the past century find little evidence in the scientific study of society itself for belief in an approaching warless world. Pitirim A. Sorokin, outstanding sociologist of our day, has shown that the curve of war in the history of the nations is at times upward and again downward, but he finds no evidence of a trend in a direction which points to the end of war. On the contrary, in the early 1920's he predicted that the twentieth century would be the bloodiest of all centuries in history to date, although believing that the present upward curve would in future centuries again recede. Sorokin's prediction was based on his belief that the present secular civilization of western society is disintegrating, and that such a period of disintegration and transition is always accompanied with much warfare.[7]

It is generally agreed that our present civilization is extremely sensate and materialistic, and many believe that for this reason it is in process of decay. As Wilhelm Pauck has said, since the Middle Ages a worldly, materialistic spirit has steadily drawn our western civilization away from God until today it "is disintegrating because it does not correspond to the divine . . . order of things."[8] In the mind of this writer there is no hope for the future until men become willing once more to heed the voice of the living God. With this every Christian lover of peace must agree. It is important, therefore, that the following two chapters of this book be devoted to a consideration of the Scriptural teaching on war and peace.

[7] P. A. Sorokin, *Contemporary Sociological Theories* (New York, 1928); *Social and Cultural Dynamics,* Vol. III (New York, 1937); *The Crisis of Our Age* (New York, 1941).
[8] H. R. Niebuhr, W. Pauck, and F. P. Miller, *The Church Against the World* (Chicago, 1935), 24.

SELECT BIBLIOGRAPHY

Alvin Johnson, "War," *Encyclopedia of the Social Sciences* (New York, 1935), is an excellent brief summary of war in human history. For a complete encyclopedic study of war, its history, character, and methods, see Quincy Wright, *A Study of War,* 2 vols. (Chicago, 1942). Alfred Vagts, *A History of Militarism* (New York, 1937), is a good historical survey of military science and tactics as well as the political and social influence of the military. The best sociological analysis of war, using a historical approach, is P. A. Sorokin, *Social and Cultural Dynamics,* Vol. III (New York, 1937). The same analysis in briefer form is found in Sorokin, *The Crisis of Our Age* (New York, 1941). H. Richard Niebuhur, Wilhelm Pauck, and Francis P. Miller, *The Church Against the World* (Chicago, 1935), is an able critique of the secularization of modern Christianity. Two recent books describing war in its historical and global perspectives are Lynn Montrose, *War Through the Ages* (Harper, 1960), and Theodore Ropp, *War in the Modern World* (Duke, 1959). Two dealing with the controlling influence of the military in national life are Bert Cochran, *The War System* (Macmillan, 1965), and John M. Swomley, *The Military Establishment* (Beacon, 1964).

2. Peace and War in the Old Testament

Christian nonresistance is a way of life in obedience to the will of God as revealed in Jesus Christ and in the holy Scriptures. It is true, of course, that Christians differ in their understanding of portions of the Scriptures, and particularly so with reference to the doctrine of nonresistance. This is due in part to the difference in moral teachings between the Old and the New Testaments. It is the writer's belief, however, that this difference between the two Testaments is frequently misunderstood; that the entire Scriptures correctly interpreted will show the Old and New Testaments to agree that the way of peace is God's way for His people at all times; that war and bloodshed were never intended to have a place in human conduct.

The Old and the New Covenants

In its historical aspect, the Bible is the story of God's dealings with the race from the beginning of human history to the time of Christ and the founding of the church. This revelation of God was a progressive one, consisting of two covenants, the one found in the Old Testament and the other in the New. We owe a great debt to the Anabaptists of the sixteenth century for their emphasis on this point. They stressed the fact that God through the prophet Jeremiah,[1] had promised a new covenant; that the writer to the Hebrews had declared the new covenant "a better covenant, which had been enacted upon better promises. For if that first covenant had been faultless, then would no place have been sought for a second."[2] A first reading of this passage brings something of a shock, for why should God

[1] Jer. 31:31-34.
[2] Heb. 8:6, 7 (ASV).

15

have given a faulty covenant to His people? It does not seem correct that a perfect and holy God should govern His people with an instrument which must later be set aside as imperfect. The idea of a covenant, however, implies a partnership between two parties, in this case between God and His people. Therefore one must conclude that if the old covenant was not perfect the cause of its imperfection lay on the side of the people and not with God.

When we examine the law of the Old Testament we find that it consists of three distinct parts: (1) The fundamental moral law as found in the Ten Commandments. (2) The civil law with its many ordinances designed for the needs of the people at the time when Moses gave them. (3) The ceremonial law, regulating the ritual and formal worship of God by Israel. Obedience to the fundamental moral law is God's requirement for meeting the high standard of His command: "Ye shall be holy: for I the Lord your God am holy."[3] This same standard is held up by Jesus when He says: "Be ye therefore perfect, even as your Father which is in heaven is perfect."[4] It was God's intention that human conduct should at all times be in full accord with this law of holiness and perfection, and before sin entered the world this intention was realized.

The fall of man, however, brought an important change in man's nature, with the result that human conduct descended to a lower level. The civil law of the Old Testament with its lower standards represents a concession on the part of God to the lowered moral state and the spiritual immaturity of the people of that time, a concession which was ended with the full revelation of the truth and power of God in Christ. The ceremonial law also provided a system of worship which looked forward to redemption through Christ, which would not have been necessary had it not been for the fact of sin. It is this concession in standards of conduct as found in the Mosaic civil law, together with the ceremonial worship for the atonement of sin, which constitutes the imperfect covenant of the Old

[3] Lev. 19:2.
[4] Matt. 5:48.

Testament. With the coming of Christ, however, sin is atoned for once for all, the concession to spiritual immaturity is removed, and human conduct is restored to its original place. Thus the perfect covenant of the New Testament restores human conduct to its rightful place where it was before the fall.

The Love of God in the Old and New Testaments

It is clear, therefore, that the way of holiness and perfection has been the will of God for His people at all times, and that any conduct short of this has been due to the sins of men. Even in the days of the old covenant it was God's will that His people should follow the way of peace and love, and had they been wholly obedient to God's will the wars and bloodshed of the Old Testament era would no doubt have been avoided.

An examination of the New Testament shows that under the new covenant the civil and ceremonial laws which constitute the old covenant were set aside, modified, or superseded. But the fundamental moral law was never changed. This is the same yesterday, today, and forever. Jesus referred to the Ten Commandments, implying that they were necessary for all time, and summed them up in two great laws: (1) "Thou shalt love the Lord thy God." (2) "Thou shalt love thy neighbour as thyself."[5] The central point in the law, therefore, is love: love for God and love for one's fellow men. This law of love is the foundation of the doctrine of nonresistance, and it is found in the Old Testament as well as in the New. The sixth commandment says: "Thou shalt not kill."[6] This commandment emphasizes the sacredness of human life and personality and is in full accord with the Apostle John of the new covenant who says: "Whosoever hateth his brother is a murderer: and ye know that no murderer hath eternal life abiding in him."[7] Jesus Christ also taught this way of love both by word and by example. Even in His death on the cross, in which He atoned

---

[5] Matt. 19:17-19 and Mark 12:30, 31. Jesus quotes Deut. 6:5 and Lev. 19:18.
[6] Ex. 20:13.
[7] I John 3:15.

for the sins of mankind, He demonstrated the law of love: "Christ also suffered for you, leaving you an example, that ye should follow his steps . . . who, when he was reviled, reviled not again; when he suffered, threatened not."[8]

When we examine the Scriptures we find many examples and admonitions of the way of love in the Old Testament as well as in the New. When there was strife between the herdsmen of Abraham and Lot, Abraham took the way of love and peacefully divided the land between them.[9] When the envious Philistines stopped Isaac's wells, Isaac did not take revenge, but in a Christlike spirit moved on to other grounds.[10] When Joseph was sold into Egypt by his jealous brothers, and after he rose to a position of second ruler in the land, he did not deal with them in the spirit of vengeance, but in the spirit of love returned good for evil.[11] In certain portions of the Old Testament God's people were commanded to exercise this way of love even toward their enemies. In the Book of Exodus we find this command: "If thou meet thine enemy's ox or his ass going astray, thou shalt surely bring it back to him again."[12] Proverbs says: "If thine enemy be hungry, give him bread to eat; and if he be thirsty, give him water to drink."[13] On one occasion, through a miracle at the hand of God, Elisha the prophet took a Syrian army captive and then in the spirit of love fed the men and sent them home.[14] From this evidence it is clear that the doctrine of love and nonresistance is found in the Old Testament as well as in the New.

The Wrath of God in the Old and New Testaments

At this point we must remind ourselves, however, that there is not only a *love* of God, but also a *wrath* of God. This doctrine of the wrath of God is likewise found in both the Old and the New Testaments. The Psalmist in the Old Testament, addressing Jehovah, says:

[8] I Pet. 2:21, 23 (ASV).
[9] Gen. 13:7-12.
[10] Gen. 26:12-33.
[11] Gen. 43—45.
[12] Ex. 23:4.
[13] Prov. 25:21.
[14] II Kings 6:8-23.

Thy hand will find out all thine enemies;
Thy right hand will find out those that hate thee.
Thou wilt make them as a fiery furnace in the time of thine
     anger:
Jehovah will swallow them up in His wrath,
And the fire shall devour them.[15]

The Apostle Paul in the New Testament speaks no less certainly of "the wrath of God . . . revealed from heaven against all ungodliness and unrighteousness of men, who hold the truth in unrighteousness."[16] God is a holy God, and His holiness can not tolerate sin. Therefore His wrath goes out against all sin and unrighteousness.

How the Wrath of God Works

Misunderstanding of the principle of nonresistance is sometimes due to a misunderstanding of two further questions: (1) How does God's wrath work? (2) Is the Christian an agent for the execution of God's wrath? We shall answer the two questions together as we proceed. The operation of God's wrath is graphically portrayed in the judgment scene of Matthew 25, where He rewards those who exercise love toward their fellow men and punishes those who manifest no love. From this account it is clear that there will be rewards and punishments in the future life and that it is God who administers them. It should be remembered, however, that not all rewards and punishments are reserved for the future. There are also rewards and punishments in this life, here and now. For the most part these consist simply of men reaping the natural consequences of their own conduct: "Be not deceived, God is not mocked: for whatsoever a man soweth, that shall he also reap."[17] This may be thought of as a sort of divine law of cause and effect which operates in human nature. If a man treats his neighbor with kindness, for example, the natural thing is for him to reap kindness in turn. If he manifests hatred and ill will, it is natural that he should reap these in turn.

[15] Ps. 21:8, 9 (ASV).   [16] Rom. 1:18.   [17] Gal. 6:7.

By this law of cause and effect, to a large extent, the deeds of men bring their own present reward or punishment. Even though God loves the sinner, and even though the Holy Spirit strives to bring him to God, if man deliberately chooses to continue in sin God will not, except in special cases, interfere with the law of cause and effect to prevent him from suffering for his sins. On the other hand, we should not think of the wrath of God as necessarily bringing a special immediate assignment of suffering to a given individual at a given point. This occurs in special cases, of course, but as a rule God allows the unrepentant sinner to have his way until in the course of human events he suffers the consequence of his own wrongdoing. That is, God punishes sin in this life by simply letting it go and allowing it to suffer its own consequences. He may, if occasion requires it, intervene in a special way, as when He prevented the hosts of Pharaoh from capturing the fleeing Israelites at the sea.[18] But ordinarily He does as Paul says in the Epistle to the Romans. He gives men "up unto a reprobate mind, to do those things which are not fitting,"[19] until eventually they reap what they have sown.

Human Vengeance Belongs to Sinful Society

It should also be remembered that under the law of cause and effect, that which comes as a consequence of, or punishment for, sin is frequently sin itself. The Book of Genesis tells the story of Cain and Abel. When Cain killed his brother, God said: "A fugitive and a vagabond shalt thou be in the earth."[20] From this Scripture it is sometimes assumed that God directly and personally drove Cain out of his home country to punish him. This is not an impossible interpretation. From the ac-

---

[18] Ex. 14:23-31.

[19] Rom. 1:28 (ASV).

[20] Gen. 4:12. The Hebrew original of the expression "thou shalt be" is the regular form for the simple future tense and is not necessarily imperative. The same is true in Gen. 9:6. It might be noted in passing that according to those who hold that God instituted capital punishment God should have ordered the execution of Cain. The fact that He did not do so, but intervened directly to save Cain's life, is a strong argument against the capital punishment theory.

count it seems more likely, however, that God used Cain's sinful fellow men to do the driving out. If this is the case, then God not only told Cain what his punishment would be, but also explained to him how the divine wrath works in a sinful society. Cain had chosen to commit murder and God now tells him that the natural consequence of his act would be that his sinful fellow men would not tolerate him any longer. If they had been true children of God they would have acted above the law of cause and effect, for they would have been governed by the fundamental moral law and would have returned good for evil. They would have manifested a spirit of nonresistance in the manner of those who "walk . . . after the Spirit."[21]

But since Cain's revengeful fellow men were sinners, they treated him in the way that is natural for the man who walks "after the flesh"[21] to treat an enemy, and they cast him out. If they could have laid hands on him, they would have put him to death.   Therefore, if he would save his life he must flee to the wilderness and live as a fugitive. No doubt the most direct divine intervention in the case of Cain was that intended, not to punish, but to save him from the consequences of his own act: "And Jehovah appointed a sign for Cain, lest any finding him should smite him."[22] God ordered no one to kill Cain but the natural consequence of Cain's deed in a sinful society was for men to cast him out and kill him, if they could lay hands on him. God is the author of the law of cause and effect, and this is the way it works in a society of sinful men. But we must remember that when this law operates, and as a result men punish the act of the murderer, they also sin in meting out the punishment. They are simply performing the normal function of members of a sinful society.

In Genesis 9:5, 6 this point is illustrated further. Here God says: "At the hand of every man's brother will I require the life of man. Whoso sheddeth man's blood, by man shall his blood be shed." That is, God requires every man to respect the life and personality of his fellow men. If a man violates this

21 Rom. 8:4.

22 Gen. 4:15 (ASV).

requirement he must suffer the consequences. Unless the murderer repents, it will mean punishment in the afterlife. But in any case, by the law of cause and effect, if a man commits murder the natural consequence will be for sinful members of his society to kill him. This is the normal way for God's disciplinary judgment to manifest itself in a sinful society, but it must be remembered that those members of society who take the murderer's life are also violating the fundamental moral law of God.

In this Scripture, however, some writers profess to find the divine establishment of government and the authorization of capital punishment. This interpretation is no doubt correct if we think of government with its powers of coercion as the logical and orderly working out of the divine law of cause and effect. That is, even a society of sinful men has found it necessary to deal with the offender in an orderly, organized manner.

We must remember, however, that in the Ten Commandments, and in the teachings of Christ, God has given the fundamental moral law for the Christian who is not ruled by the passions of the natural man. This fundamental moral law is above the law of cause and effect which operates in human nature, and it says: "Thou shalt not kill." Therefore he who takes a human life, even if he acts legally as an official of the state, is violating the will of God for His people. The avenger plays a part in the operation of the divine wrath which requires that men suffer the consequence of their own sin: but the act of human vengeance itself is in violation of God's fundamental moral law.[23]

The Christian Forbidden to Exercise Vengeance

The Christian is subject to this fundamental moral law which is made expressly binding upon him in the new covenant. For this reason the Christian cannot serve as an agent for the

[23] Some writers have argued that Ex. 20:13 refers only to murder as committed by the ordinary criminal, and not to legal killing by the state. According to this view the sixth commandment should be translated, "Thou shalt do no murder," using the words of Jesus in Matt. 19:18. There is nothing in the original Hebrew of Ex. 20:13,

execution of God's wrath. This prerogative belongs to God alone. Paul states this truth in a striking way when he says: "Avenge not yourselves, beloved, but give place unto the wrath of God: for it is written, Vengeance belongeth unto me; I will recompense, saith the Lord."[24] The New Testament in all its teachings holds firmly to this standard, and so does the fundamental moral law of the Old Testament. It is only the civil law of the old covenant that permits the lower level of vengeance and retaliation, and from the sayings of Jesus it seems clear that this permission was given only as a concession to the sinfulness and spiritual immaturity of Israel, its "hardness of heart."[25] Jesus also makes it clear that under the new covenant which He had come to establish the Christian is required to meet the higher standard. The lower standard of the imperfect former covenant is done away.

In the fifth chapter of Matthew, for example, Jesus deals with six specific moral questions: the taking of human life, adultery, divorce, the taking of oaths, revenge, and the attitude of the individual toward an enemy. He states the requirements of the civil code under the old covenant in regard to each of these issues and then, with the words, "Ye have heard that it was said by them of old time . . . but I say unto you," He sets aside the old requirement and in its place puts a new command on a level with the fundamental moral law.[26] In doing so Jesus declares His purpose to be the fulfillment of the moral law: "Think not that I came to destroy the law or the prophets:

---

however, which would suggest that there are two kinds of killing, one of which is right and the other wrong. This passage simply says, "Thou shalt not kill," and the only reasonable interpretation is that, according to the moral law, God's people are forbidden under all circumstances to take a human life.

[24] Rom. 12:19 (ASV). In Rom. 13:4 Paul calls the civil ruler "a revenger to execute wrath upon him that doeth evil." Here Paul is describing the function of the state in a sinful society for the carrying out of the law of cause and effect. The Christian dwells above this level, however, and lives according to the higher law of love. For a further discussion of Romans 13 see Chapter III.

[25] Matt. 19:8.

[26] In the first two cases, the taking of human life and the sin of adultery, Jesus quotes directly from the Ten Commandments. He does not change these commands in any way, however; but He does give them a meaning which was not given them under the civil law of the old covenant. Under the new covenant Jesus gives a new interpretation of these commands, bringing out the deeper meaning of God's fundamental moral law.

I came not to destroy, but to fulfil."[27] Thus by His Word of authority Jesus restores the standard of human conduct to its original high level.

The Anabaptists Stress the New Covenant

The early Swiss Anabaptists constantly stressed the idea that the new covenant was superior to the old. Pilgram Marpeck, their greatest theologian, said that the old covenant was only a shadow of the real covenant which came with Christ. In the old covenant there was a promise of spiritual blessings. Under the new covenant this promise is fulfilled. And with these blessings the Christian is expected to live according to the ethical teachings of the new covenant which has superseded the old. Under the old covenant, as found in the Mosaic code, Israel chastised its disobedient members with the sword and death, but the Christian Church under the new covenant may do so only with the Word of God and sword of the Spirit.

Today [there is] . . . another law, which is not a carnal law of ruling, or worldly, earthly judicial procedures as that of yesterday, but a . . . law or commandment of the Spirit—love and patience, which God "yesterday" promised and "today" for the first time wrote in the hearts . . . . Also that they should love all people, not merely their friends or dear ones, but also their enemies, and not to resist evil, as is clearly shown in Matt. 5, Luke 6, and Rom. 12. Also that one should not use carnal weapons against another; nor they against their enemies. Isa. 2, Micah 4, Matt. 5. All bodily, worldly, carnal earthly fighting, conflicts, and wars are annulled and abolished among them through such law. Psalms 4, 5, Hos. 2: Which law of love, Christ . . . then, as the present High Priest, Himself observed and thereby gave His followers a pattern to follow after.[28]

Other Anabaptist writers expressed similar views. In 1531 Hans Pfistermeyer challenged the state church leaders with the thought that "The New Testament is more perfect than the Old. . . . Christ has taught a higher and more perfect doctrine

---

[27] Matt. 5:17 (ASV).
[28] John C. Wenger, "The Theology of Pilgram Marpeck," *Mennonite Quarterly Review* (October, 1938), 12:241.

and made with His people a new covenant. In a theological debate at Frankenthal in the Palatinate in 1571 the Swiss Brethren said: "We believe that the New Testament surpasses the Old. So much of the Old Testament as is not irreconcilable with the doctrine of Christ, we accept. . . . If anything that is necessary for salvation and a godly life was not taught by Christ and the apostles but is contained in the Old Testament Scriptures, we desire to be shown."[29] And Menno Simons said: "All Scripture must be interpreted according to the spirit, teaching, walk and example of Christ and the apostles."[30]

Why Did God Permit War Under the Old Covenant

The question may fairly be asked: Why did God permit the lower standard of conduct in regard to retaliation and war under the old covenant? In particular, how do we explain the fact that God commanded Israel to go to war, even though Jesus Christ rejected warfare later on? Is Jesus contradicting God? Or why should God command Saul to destroy King Agag when His own fundamental moral law says, "Thou shalt not kill?" Does God contradict Himself? This difference between the standards of conduct of the two covenants is so great that some Christians have concluded that God from time to time changes His law for the conduct of men, for reasons beyond our knowledge. From this it has been argued that the question of the reason for the difference between the two standards of conduct should not be raised.

It should be remembered, however, that the Scriptures represent God as unchangeable in character and always the same. No reasonable interpretation of the Scriptures will suggest that something which is basically morally wrong at one time is basically right at another. The Epistle of James, which is full of moral instruction, says that with God there "is no variableness, neither shadow of turning."[31] In Malachi we find

---

[29] Quoted in John Horsch, *Mennonites in Europe* (Scottdale, Pa., 1942), 355, 356.
[30] *Ibid.*, 356.
[31] Jas. 1:17.

the words: "I am the Lord, I change not."[32] The writer to the
Hebrews speaks of "Jesus Christ the same yesterday, and to day,
and for ever."[33] Whenever we find a change in relationship between God and man it is due to a change in human character
and in the human will, and not to a change in the fundamental
character and will of God. In the beginning God created man
and called him "very good,"[34] but some time later, the Scriptures
say, "It repented the Lord that he had made man on the earth."[35]
This does not mean that God "repented" from an error, or that
He changed His character or His fundamental will, or that He
reversed His decision to create man and regretted His own
handiwork. It merely means that man, exercising his God-given
power of choice, had changed so that God had to deal with him
in a different way than He had originally intended. That is,
man is a free moral agent; if he chooses to be a saint God deals
with him as a saint, whereas if he chooses to be a sinner, God
deals with him as a sinner.

In the mind of the writer this fact gives the key for an understanding of the seeming difference between God's requirements under the old covenant and those under the new. Although God's basic will never changed, His "permissive will,"
to use an old-fashioned theological term, did change. That is,
it was not God's will that men should be sinners; but when they
chose to become sinners contrary to His will He permitted them
to do so and dealt with them accordingly. No doubt this is what
Paul means when he says, "The law . . . was added because of
transgressions."[36]

Two Levels of Humanity: Christian and Sub-Christian

The most reasonable answer to the question at hand would
seem to be that the moral law as found in the Ten Commandments is the true expression of God's basic will for all men,

---

[32] Mal. 3:6.

[33] Heb. 13:8.

[34] Gen. 1:31.

[35] Gen. 6:6.

[36] Gal. 3:19. This refers, not to the fundamental moral law, but to the civil and
ceremonial laws of the old covenant.

whether in the time of the Old Testament or of the New; it is His will now as it was "from the beginning," to use Jesus' own words. God has given man a free will, however, and when a man of his own choice repudiates the moral law, and deliberately follows the way of sin, he falls under the wrath of God and becomes subject to the law of cause and effect. From this point of view, therefore, there are two levels of humanity, which today would be called the Christian and the sub-Christian levels. It is God's will that all men should live on the Christian level where they will observe the higher law of love; but those men who reject God's will and choose to live on the sub-Christian level naturally must follow a different course, having repudiated the law of love. Their entire way of life is in conflict with the will of God. Yet God does not forsake them. As long as they reject His higher moral law He requires them to reap the consequences of their own evil. When a man on this lower level engages in theft, for example, another man, also acting on the sub-Christian level, although in a quite different category, arrests the thief and imprisons him. Neither of the two is conforming to the basic will of God, but when the first act occurs the second naturally follows. Therefore, in this secondary or indirect sense, God may be thought of as "commanding" the completion of the final link in the chain of circumstances which sinful man has deliberately begun to build. To change the figure, this might also be thought of as the permissive will, or the permissive command, of God for men of free will who have chosen to live on the sub-Christian level, and who have refused to obey God's basic will or His basic commands.

The Lower Standards of the Old Covenant Due to Israel's Sin

We can receive some light on this problem by reading what Jesus has to say about divorce. On one occasion He told the Pharisees: "He which made them *at the beginning* made them male and female . . . . For this cause shall a man . . . cleave to his wife: and they twain shall be one flesh. . . . What therefore God hath joined together, let not man put asunder." The

Pharisees replied by asking Jesus: "Why did Moses then command to give a writing of divorcement, and to put her away?" To this Jesus replied: "Moses because of the hardness of your hearts suffered you to put away your wives: *but from the beginning it was not so."*[37]

Here Jesus says that under God's basic and absolute moral law divorce is forbidden, and *in the beginning,* that is, before the fall, this was the rule. But when men sinned and descended to the "sub-Christian" level of life, divorce was permitted. It was *because of the hardness of their hearts* that God through Moses, permitted it. Here is an illustration of God's permissive command to a people on the sub-Christian level who had sinned by refusing to live by the higher law, in obedience to the real will of God. Nor is it possible to escape this conclusion by referring to the fact that Jesus says that "Moses . . . suffered you to put away your wives," for the law of divorce in Deuteronomy specifically authorized divorce: "He shall write her a bill of divorcement, and give it in her hand, and send her out of his house."[38] It is a clear case of law being given "because of transgressions."

The Old Testament provides other illustrations of the same principle. When the prophet Samuel grew old in years the people demanded a king. This was contrary to God's will and Samuel told them so. The people insisted, however, until God finally told Samuel to anoint a king, explaining that the people had not rejected Samuel, but God.[39] God even instructed Samuel how to proceed in selecting the king; and when Saul was selected, "Samuel said to all the people, See ye him whom the Lord hath chosen."[40] Here within the space of three chapters, the descent is made from the higher to the lower level. First God says it is not according to His will that Israel should have a king; then He tells Samuel to anoint a king; and finally God Himself chooses the man who is to be the king. That is, when Israel rejected the higher level, God gave the permissive com-

---

[37] Matt. 19:4-8. Italics are by the author.
[38] Deut. 24:1-4 (ASV).
[39] I Sam. 8:4-22.
[40] I Sam. 10:24.

mand for the lower level which they chose, with a warning, however, of the consequences they must suffer for so doing.

The sending of the twelve spies from Kadesh-barnea into Canaan is another illustration of this principle. God had brought Israel from Egypt through the Red Sea in a miraculous way. The law had been given at Sinai, and Israel had arrived at the very threshold of the promised land. Moses then spoke and said: "Behold, the Lord thy God hath set the land before thee: go up and possess it."[41] But instead of proceeding at once the people asked that spies be first sent into the land to examine it. The story in the Book of Numbers says God commanded Moses to send the spies,[42] but from Deuteronomy it is clear that the people had first requested this privilege after God had commanded them to march into the land and possess it.[43] Apparently this is another case of a law being added because the people transgressed and refused to follow God's original plan.

This seems all the more clear from what followed. After the spies returned from their investigation ten of them advised against going into the land because of the giants and the fortifications. Only Caleb and Joshua urged the people to obey the command of God, and when they did so the people rose up in rebellion against them. They threatened to remove Moses from office and elect a new captain to lead them back to Egypt. When Caleb and Joshua pleaded against this rash idea the people were ready to stone them and likely would have done so had God not interfered. So serious was this act of disobedience that God punished them by announcing that the possession of Canaan would be delayed until the end of forty years, when that generation would have passed away. As soon as the people heard this, they murmured and said they were going up at once, even though the day before they wanted to kill their good leaders for suggesting this. Moses warned them not to go: "Go not up, for the Lord is not among you."[44] But once more Israel "rebelled against the commandment of the Lord, and went presump-

---

[41] Deut. 1:21.
[42] Num. 13:1, 2.
[43] Deut. 1:22, 23.
[44] Num. 14:42.

tuously up into the hill," only to be attacked by a hostile tribe which chased them from Seir to Hormah, and inflicted great destruction.[45]

Old Testament Wars Due to Israel's Sin

The principal wars of the Old Testament were those fought by Israel in the effort to take possession of Canaan; and the story of Kadesh-barnea gives the key for an understanding of those wars. Undoubtedly, Israel's fightings were the consequence of her own sins, and contrary to the original intention of God. Exodus 20 gives us the story of the Ten Commandments, where the words, "Thou shalt not kill," occupy a prominent place in this fundamental moral law. Then Exodus 23, just a little later, is an instruction book for the approaching march to Canaan. This chapter contains some remarkable instructions, and some promises just as remarkable. The early portion deals with the treatment of enemies and reads almost like the Sermon on the Mount. "If thou meet thine enemy's ox or his ass going astray, thou shalt surely bring it back to him again. If thou see the ass of him that hateth thee lying under his burden, thou shalt forbear to leave him, thou shalt surely release it with him."[46]

Then, in speaking of the coming possession of Canaan, God says:

Behold, I send an Angel before thee, to keep thee in the way, and to bring thee into the place which I have prepared . . . . If thou shalt indeed obey his voice, and do all that I speak; then I will be an enemy unto thine enemies, and an adversary unto thine adversaries . . . . And I will send hornets before thee, which shall drive out the Hivite, the Canaanite, and the Hittite, from before thee. I will not drive them out from before thee in one year; lest the land become desolate, and the beast of the field multiply against thee. By little and little I will drive them out from before thee, until thou be increased, and inherit the land. And I will set thy bounds from the Red sea even unto the sea of the Philistines, and from the desert unto the river: for I will deliver the inhabitants of the land into your hand; and thou shalt drive them out before thee. Thou shalt make no covenant with them, nor with their gods. They shall not

---

[45] Deut. 1:43, 44.
[46] Ex. 23:4, 5 (ASV).

dwell in thy land, lest they make thee sin against me: for if thou serve their gods, it will surely be a snare unto thee.[47]

As Edward Yoder suggests, "This looks very much like a plan for the peaceful penetration of the land of Canaan under God's immediate leading and direction."[48] There are three essential points in the plan. First, God would remove the Canaanites by supernatural means. Second, the removal would be a gradual one, only as fast as Israel itself would be able to occupy the land through increase of its population. And third, the success of this program depended entirely on Israel keeping itself free from the wicked and depraved Canaanite tribes, morally, socially, and religiously. That is, strict obedience to God and the peaceful penetration of Canaan were to go together. Verse 31 of this passage, if taken alone, might seem to authorize war on Israel's part: "I will deliver the inhabitants of the land into your hand; and thou shalt drive them out before thee." This certainly does mean that as Israel moved into the land the former inhabitants were expected to leave; and in this sense Israel would "drive them out." But there is no mention here of armed force, and the tenor of the entire passage suggests that the driving out was to be accomplished without violence. God in His own way would provide the Canaanites with a motive to migrate as the new settlers approached.

This is altogether reasonable when we remember that God had only recently delivered Israel by supernatural means at the Red Sea. From the beginning Israel should have followed the principle: "Not by might, nor by power, but by my spirit, saith the Lord of hosts."[49] If God had saved Moses and His people from the mighty Pharaoh, why should He not do the same in the case of the puny Canaanite tribes? To this promise and condition God always attached a warning that disobedience would

[47] Ex. 23:20-33.

[48] Edward Yoder, "Wars in the Old Testament," *Gospel Herald* (July 18, 1940), 33:366. It has been argued against this interpretation that the passage does not say that God will not use war to drive out the enemy. But such an argument in favor of war merely because of the absence of a statement against war is unconvincing. The whole point is, *I, God*, will drive them out, but *you, man*, will not need to fight. Divine action will replace human action; miracle will replace war.

[49] Zech. 4:6.

bring disaster. "If ye walk contrary unto me, and will not hearken unto me . . . then will I also walk contrary unto you, and will punish you. . . . And I will bring a sword upon you . . . ."[50] Must we not conclude from this that Israel's experience with the sword as recorded in Joshua, Judges, and the books of Samuel, Kings, and Chronicles was simply the result of walking "contrary unto God"?

An examination of the record certainly shows that Israel's sins were great enough to warrant such a conclusion. Within a short time after receiving the Ten Commandments Israel sinned by worshiping the golden calf.[51] False worship was introduced by the offering of strange fire.[52] One man was guilty of blasphemy.[53] Israel murmured in criticism of its food and for other reasons.[54] Moses' own sister rebelled against him.[55] All these sins are mentioned prior to the disobedience and failure at Kadesh-barnea. Following that event we read of the rebellion under Korah, which God punished with a plague in which more than 14,000 people died.[56] A little later we find that the people began to mix with the Moabites in marriage and in worship even before the march into Canaan began.[57] After Israel had partially taken the land this practice continued in direct violation of God's command. Professor Ira M. Price describes this condition as follows:

> Peaceful proximity to the corrupt customs and worship of their neighbors was a subtle danger. It soon resulted in friendly commercial intercourse, in mixed marriages, in a kind of free and easy coalescence of manners and customs. The seductive religious rites and festivals of these new neighbors, appealing especially to the physical senses of Israel, soon made captives of the unwary conquerors, and won them over to the practices of the Canaanites. The debilitating effect of the new life in settled communities soon made havoc of the homely virtues of the sturdy nomads of the desert. The weakening of their moral and religious fiber made the territory of the Israelites a fair field for the ever-watchful and waiting enemies.

---

50 Lev. 26:21-25.   54 Num. 11.

51 Ex. 32.   55 Num. 12.

52 Lev. 10:1, 2.   56 Num. 16.

53 Lev. 24:10 ff.   57 Num. 25.

During the days of the judges, we find an incredibly corrupt condition of affairs (Judg. 19 to 21). The prevalence of priestly prostitution to the service of idols, of unspeakable crimes, kindled a flame of internal strife, in which Benjamin was almost exterminated. This state of things opened the door for new aggressions of the Philistines, who were not slow to see and improve their opportunity.[58]

The psalmist has given us a vivid description of the spiritual condition of Israel:

We have sinned . . . we have committed iniquity, we have done wickedly. Our fathers understood not thy wonders in Egypt. . . . They made a calf in Horeb, and worshipped the molten image. . . . Yea, they despised the pleasant land, they believed not his word: but murmured in their tents, and hearkened not unto the voice of the Lord. . . . They soon forgat his works; they waited not for his counsel; but lusted exceedingly in the wilderness, and tempted God in the heart. And he gave them their request; but sent leanness into their soul.[59]

When we look at this picture, do we need to wonder that God's plan for a peaceful possession of Canaan was not realized? If Israel lived on such a low moral and spiritual level, and if the tribes fought among themselves until one of them was almost exterminated, how could Israel be saved from fighting with the Canaanites? Certainly such a people were far from the nonresistant way of life. Israel's disobedient conduct and the nonresistant way of life simply do not go together. God's way of peace as required by the fundamental moral law could not be carried out until Israel was ready to repent from his sins and wholly follow the Lord. So in the meantime the law of cause and effect, of reaping what had been sown, had to have its way. The Israelites sinned and suffered the consequences of their own sin. They "lusted . . . in the wilderness," until God let them have their way; He "gave them up" to their lust, but "sent leanness into their soul," a leanness which could not measure up to the standards of the moral law.

The various Old Testament commands of God requiring

[58] Ira M. Price, *The Monuments and the Old Testament* (Philadelphia, 1925), 242-43, 245.   [59] Ps. 106.

killing, such as the commands to slay the Amalekites, to hew Agag to pieces, and to kill the giant Goliath, were permissive commands given to a sinful, lean-souled people who had chosen to live on the lower, "sub-Christian" level. It was God's will that Israel should possess the land of Canaan and since they refused to live the nonresistant way of life in taking it, choosing rather the way which leads to war, He gave the permissive command to take this way. But the permission was given only because Israel chose to live on the sub-Christian level. It is not God's plan that men should sin, but if they choose to sin He can still use them to carry out His eternal purposes. In a later day the prophet Isaiah proclaimed that God was sending the Assyrian as the instrument of His wrath to punish Judah for his sins: "O Assyria, rod of my anger, and staff of my fury!"[60] But the Assyrian was a greater sinner even than Judah while he was being used of God for this purpose, and in due time God scourged the Assyrian for his deeds.[61] The fact that God uses the "powers that be," according to Paul, as His ministers, "to execute wrath upon him that doeth evil,"[62] does not make these rulers and their conduct holy and righteous; they are still sinners.

No doubt it is the same in our age. Men spoke of God raising up Churchill, or Roosevelt, or Stalin to destroy Hitler. Perhaps He did. But who would say that God did not also use Hitler to punish the sins of other nations? While the sins of some nations may seem greater than those of others, surely all of the nations have sinned. Therefore perhaps God in His providence uses the nations to punish each other. But certainly all of them are sinning as they are being so used. In the same way God used a sinful warring Israel for the achievement of His purposes, and on occasion gave His permission for war to that end. But in following this course Israel's whole life was on a sub-Christian level in violation of God's fundamental moral law. The permissive commands of God were the result of Israel's sin.

---

[60] Isa. 10:5 (American translation).   [61] Isa. 10:26.   [62] Rom. 13:4.

Unless an understanding of God's dealing with men and nations down through history, such as the one which has been outlined above, is accepted, it is difficult to see how one can speak of God controlling and directing the affairs of the world, and having responsibility for the course of human history, without making Him the author of all the sins of human history. Of course a devout believer might take the position that he does not need to understand God's ways, and simply let the problem of war under the old covenant rest. In no case could he accept the position of the modernist who argues that the God of the Old Testament is not the same as the God of the New Testament, and that the Old Testament is simply to be ignored as not God's word.

No doubt all the provisions of the old covenant which are out of line with the standards of the new must be interpreted in the same way that the divorce law must be interpreted. Divorce, polygamy, the legal oath, retaliation, blood vengeance, capital punishment, warfare, and whatever Old Testament practices and elements in the Mosaic civil code Jesus set aside with His word of authority, had been permitted and authorized by God only because God's people had fallen into sin and rejected His way, so that they were unable to operate under the banner of love. Therefore, what Jesus did was not to contradict the program of God, but rather to restore the moral order among men to the place where God had originally placed it. Under the new covenant such authorized practices of the old code as were not in accord with the fundamental moral law had to be set aside, and were set aside by Jesus with His divine authority.

The Significance of the Old Testament Theocracy

It is sometimes suggested that the Old Testament wars and those provisions in the Mosaic code which are in conflict with the Sermon on the Mount, such as the use of force by the magistracy for the execution of justice, must be explained in terms of the Old Testament theocracy. It is argued that the state has a necessary place in society for the maintenance of law and order, and that to maintain such order the use of force is necessary. Therefore, since God authorized a merging of the civil and the religious affairs of Israel in a union of church and state, it must have been God's will that His people perform these necessary civil functions. From this it is argued that such exercise of force must have been basically right under the old covenant, even though it may not be so under the new covenant which provides a separation of church and state.

The answer to this would be that, from the viewpoint of Christian nonresistance, the use of force, whether by the military or by the civil magistracy, never was and is not now within the plan of God for His people. It is freely granted that these police functions are necessary in a society of sinful men; and in the course of human events, by the operation of the law of cause and effect, they will be exercised in such a society for the maintenance of order. As explained in Chapter III there is even a sense in which such magistrates and law enforcement officers are "ministers of God." But as explained elsewhere,[63] if these officials were wholly obedient to God's fundamental moral law they would be serving in some other capacity. The new covenant doctrine of nonresistance necessarily demands nonparticipation in those affairs of state which involve the use of force. And since the old covenant was an imperfect covenant, representing a concession to the sinfulness and spiritual immaturity of Israel, it must follow that the Old Testament union of the church with a state based on force was also such a concession. On the other hand, it must be remembered that if all of the Israelites had been wholly obedient to the Lord it would have been possible for the Old Testament theocracy to perform all of its necessary functions without the use of either the military or the civil police force, just as a society of nonresistant Christians, all of whom wholly followed the Lord, could do today. But, if such a Christian society were to be called a "state" it would certainly be a state altogether different from any that we know today; and it would also be quite different from that of Israel in the days of the old covenant.

[63] See below, pp. 240-242.

The Prophets Call Israel to Repentance and Peace

As we approach the later history of Israel, the fact grows increasingly clear that war was contrary to the basic will of God. When King David desired to build a temple for the worship of God he received a significant reply. God said to him: "Thou hast shed blood abundantly, and hast made great wars: thou shalt not build an house unto my name, because thou hast shed much blood upon the earth in my sight."[64] Here is a clear indication that warfare and the shedding of human blood were contrary to the will of God for His people. King David, great servant of God though he was, was nevertheless disqualified, because of his military career, for the high and holy task of building the temple where men would gather to worship the God of peace and love.

It is the writings of the prophets, however, that set forth most clearly in the Old Testament the true character of God's moral law. Even though these holy men were living under the old covenant, they were definitely knocking at the door of the new. Almost six hundred years before the time of Christ the prophet Ezekiel spoke of the hardness of Israel's heart, which he said must be done away: "I will give them one heart, and I will put a new spirit within you; and I will take the stony heart out of their flesh, and will give them an heart of flesh: that they may walk in my statutes, and keep mine ordinances, and do them: and they shall be my people, and I will be their God."[65]

The message of the prophet Isaiah is in the same vein. He presents a long catalogue of Israel's sins. They are rebellious.[66] They are "laden with iniquity, a seed of evil-doers, children that deal corruptly."[67] They are a people of unclean lips. Their head is sick and their heart is faint.[68] Their hands are full of blood. Their feet "make haste to shed innocent blood." "The way of peace they know not."[69] God had forsaken them because

---

[64] I Chron. 22:8.
[65] Ezek. 11:19, 20.
[66] Isa. 1:2.
[67] Isa. 1:4 (ASV).
[68] Isa. 6:5; 1:5.
[69] Isa. 1:15; 59:3, 7, 8.

they were idolators and warriors.[70] Had it not been for a small remnant they would have been like unto Sodom and Gomorrah.[71] How was the peaceful, nonresistant way of life possible among such a people? It could not exist in this state of affairs. But the time for a new manner of life was now approaching. The Messiah was soon to appear. The day of redemption was at hand. Though Israel like sheep had gone astray the Messiah would bear the iniquity of them all, and by His stripes they would be healed.[72]

Israel must be cleansed and purified: "Wash you, make you clean; put away the evil of your doings from before mine eyes; cease to do evil . . . . Come now, and let us reason together, saith the Lord: though your sins be as scarlet, they shall be as white as snow; though they be red like crimson, they shall be as wool."[73] In the new day of the Lord wars will be done away from among those who are washed in the blood of the Lamb: "And they shall beat their swords into plowshares, and their spears into pruning hooks: nation shall not lift up sword against nation, neither shall they learn war any more."[74] Or again: "All the armor of the armed man in the tumult, and the garments rolled in blood, shall be for burning, for fuel of fire. For unto us a child is born, unto us a son is given; and the government shall be upon his shoulder: and his name shall be called Wonderful, Counsellor, Mighty God, Everlasting Father, Prince of Peace."[75] This is the program of God for His people who have been redeemed from the sinful ways of backslidden Israel. This is the order of the new covenant to be inaugurated with the coming of the Messiah.[76]

Not all of the future events in God's program are clear, of course. Some Christians believe that at His second coming Christ will establish a literal kingdom upon the earth, in which only the redeemed will be present, and in which the peaceful

---

[70] Isa. 2:7, 8; 30:15-17; 31:1-3.
[71] Isa. 1:9.
[72] Isa. 53:5, 6.
[73] Isa. 1:16-18.
[74] Isa. 2:4.
[75] Isa. 9:5, 6 (ASV).
[76] It should be noted that this is the program for the redeemed, not for sinners.

state of affairs described in Isaiah will exist universally. Others do not believe that the Scriptures teach such a future kingdom. Whichever of these views in correct, there can be no question but that the peaceful, nonresistant way taught by Isaiah and Christ is intended for the everyday life of God's people, here and now. The redeemed of the Lord will indeed be required to turn their swords into plowshares, for then they will be able to do so because they will be born again of the Spirit of God. Of course, this manner of life will not be found in those who are not Christians. Until sin has been finally destroyed wars will continue. Even though nations do engage in war, however, the disciples of Christ are commanded to "follow his steps."[77]

Even in Isaiah's own day, though Israel lay between the hosts of Assyria on the one hand and those of Egypt on the other and in constant danger of invasion, especially from the East, the prophet makes it clear that it was not God's program that Israel should strike with the sword.

> Therefore thus saith the Lord, Jehovah of hosts, . . . be not afraid of the Assyrian, though he smite thee with the rod, and lift up his staff against thee, after the manner of Egypt. For yet a very little while, and . . . Jehovah of hosts will stir up against him a scourge . . . . And it shall come to pass in that day, that his burden shall depart from off thy shoulder, and his yoke from off thy neck . . . .[78]

Again and again Isaiah refers to the oppressor nations whom God will chastise, but Israel herself is not commanded to take up the sword against the enemy.[79] He warns Israel not to form a military alliance with Egypt; not to trust in horses and chariots; but to trust in the Lord. The Assyrian oppressor will be destroyed, but not by the sword of God's people. God in His own way will perform it.[80] And true to the word of the prophet, when King Sennacherib led the hosts of Assyria against Israel, Jehovah in His own way turned back the invader without the good King Hezekiah striking a single blow.[81] This deliverance

77 I Pet. 2:21.
78 Isa. 10:24-27 (ASV).
79 E.g., Isa. 13 and 16.
80 Isa. 30 and 31.
81 Isa. 37; II Kings 19.

is almost as remarkable as that at the Red Sea, and it would seem that Israel was just beginning once more to fit into the program and manner of life which God had planned for His people from the beginning, and which they had rejected in the days of Moses and those which followed.

The prophet Jeremiah, a century later, went even farther than Isaiah, and actually urged Judah to submit to the rule of Babylon: "Bring your necks under the yoke of the king of Babylon, and serve him and his people, and live."[82] Jeremiah made it clear that this nonresistant attitude toward the invader was according to the will of God: "Thus saith Jehovah, . . . the God of Israel: If thou wilt go forth unto the king of Babylon's princes, then thy soul shall live, and this city shall not be burned with fire; and thou shalt live, and thy house. But if thou wilt not go forth to the king of Babylon's princes, then shall this city be given into the hand of the Chaldeans, and they shall burn it with fire, and thou shalt not escape out of their hand."[83]

So nonresistant was Jeremiah in his attitude toward Babylon that his fellow Israelites charged him with treason and cast him into prison.[84] But the nonresistant prophet was misunderstood. Jeremiah was not guilty of treason; he was not disloyal to Judah. He knew that the Babylonian captivity was coming as a judgment from God upon the sins of Judah. For this reason it was useless for King Zedekiah to resist. What Judah needed was not resistance, but repentance from his sins.

Jeremiah does not stop, however, with his advice to surrender. The time was coming when Judah's punishment would be complete, and then he would be freed from captivity again. "Behold, I will turn again the captivity of Jacob's tents, and have compassion on his dwelling-places: and the city shall be builded upon its own hill, and the palace shall be inhabited after its own manner."[85] But the escape and return from captivity were also to be entirely without warfare on Judah's part. True, the warfare of wicked nations would have a part in the release from

[82] Jer. 27:12.
[83] Jer. 38:17, 18 (ASV).
[84] Jer. 37:13-15.
[85] Jer. 30:18 (ASV).

captivity: "Jehovah hath stirred up the spirit of the kings of the Medes: because his purpose is against Babylon, to destroy it: for it is the vengeance of Jehovah, the vengeance of his temple."[86] But God's people were not to fight. Isaiah says they were not even to flee, nor to go in haste: "For ye shall not go out in haste, neither shall ye go by flight: for Jehovah will go before you; and the God of Israel will be your rearward."[87]

Surely if the message of the prophets means anything it means that the day of warfare for God's people was over. The moral lapse represented by the harsh features of the Mosaic code could no longer be condoned, and the bloody wars of the days of the Judges were past. In the time of their ignorance God may have winked at Israel's inferior moral performance; out of mercy for a backslidden people He may have permitted it. But the day of redemption was now at hand, and under the new covenant which Christ at His coming would shortly establish God's people must walk in a newness of life in which warfare and strife can have no part.

[86] Jer. 51:11 (ASV).
[87] Isa. 52:12 (ASV).

SELECT BIBLIOGRAPHY

The most difficult problems relating to the doctrine of nonresistance are those found in the teachings of the Old Testament. A book with the traditional Calvinist view is Loraine Boettner, *The Christian Attitude Toward War* (Grand Rapids, Mich., 1940), who interprets the New Testament in the light of the Old. Since warfare is approved in the Old Testament, Boettner holds that it must be sanctioned in the New Testament as well. P. H. Richert, *A Brief Catechism on Difficult Scripture Passages and Involved Questions on the Use of the Sword* (Newton, Kans., n.d.), holds that in the Old Testament time God in some cases delegated the administration of vengeance to Israel, but that in the New Testament era He always reserves this prerogative to Himself. J. Irvin Lehman, *God and War* (Scottdale, Pa., 1942), holds that warfare in the Old Testa-was in accord with God's basic will; he also holds that in a future age God will again delegate the administration of vengeance to Christian people. For a treatise on the relation of the Old and New Testaments see John Horsch, *Mennonites in Europe* (Scottdale, Pa., 1942), chapter 42, and John C. Wenger, "The Theology of Pilgram Marpeck," *Mennonite Quarterly Review* (Goshen, Ind., October, 1938), 12:205-56. Treatments with an approach similar to that of the present author are Edward Yoder, *Must Christians Fight* (Akron, Pa., 1943), and "Wars in the Old Testament," *Gospel Herald* (Scottdale, Pa., July 18, 1940), also by Edward Yoder. A recent treatise on Christian pacifism, with a chapter on the Old Testament, is Culbert G. Rutenber, *The Dagger and the Cross* (New York, 1950). A Catholic pacifist view is presented by Johannes Ude, *Du Sollst Nicht Töten* (Dornbirn, Austria, 1948).

3. Nonresistance in the New Testament

The Old Testament prophets had declared that war and bloodshed were contrary to the will of God. The Gospels tell us of John the Baptist, who was "more than a prophet."[1] A prophet is one who proclaims the Word of God; but John was more than a prophet because he introduced Christ, the Word of God in person. Jesus the Christ, the incarnate God through whom all things were made, had come into the world with divine and absolute authority from heaven that all who receive Him might become the children of God.[2] It was He who inaugurated the new covenant in which the moral law is fulfilled and all human relations are restored to their rightful place.

The New Covenant and the Kingdom of God

The great mission of Christ was to bring men into the kingdom of God, to give them eternal life. When men came to inquire the way to eternal life He immediately referred them to the fundamental moral law, the Ten Commandments.[3] When they inquired further He explained that this law consists of two parts: "Thou shalt love the Lord thy God with all thy heart" and "Thou shalt love thy neighbour as thyself"[4]; and when they inquired still further He made it clear that this love which brings men into the kingdom of God can be received only by the power of God through the spiritual experience of regeneration.[5] If we love God and our fellow men it is because He first loved us, "and sent his Son to be the propitiation for our sins."[6]

---

[1] Matt. 11:9.
[2] John 1:1-12.
[3] Matt. 19:16-19.
[4] Matt. 22:37, 39.
[5] John 3:3.
[6] I John 4:10.

43

Christ, therefore, endorses the Ten Commandments and the law of love as the fundamental moral law, valid for all time, and it is through His grace and power that men are enabled to keep this law.

Just as clearly, however, does the New Testament also teach the wrath of God. We think at once of the judgment scene, where those who have no compassion for their hungry, cold, and naked brethren are condemned to everlasting punishment.[7] In one of Jesus' parables the tares which Satan sowed are allowed to grow with the wheat until the harvest when they are to be gathered and burned.[8] Woe is pronounced upon him who causes one of Christ's believing children to stumble and fall.[9] Punishment awaits those who do not have a heart of forgiveness toward their fellow men.[10] When Ananias and Sapphira lied to the Holy Spirit, they received immediate judgment at the hand of God.[11] The Apostle Paul refers to "the goodness and severity of God,"[12] declaring His wrath to be "revealed from heaven against all ungodliness and unrighteousness of men."[13] It is worthy of note, however, that nowhere in the New Testament are members of the kingdom of God given any part in the execution of God's wrath. Paul specifically says: "Avenge not yourselves, beloved, but give place unto the wrath of God: for it is written, Vengeance belongeth unto me; I will recompense, saith the Lord."[14] The holiness of God demands the punishment of sin, but punishment is the prerogative of God alone.

As was observed in Chapter II, Israel in the Old Testament did at times exercise vengeance, and the civil code of Moses contains a number of elements which are not in harmony with the fundamental moral law. Israel's feet were swift to shed blood and the way of peace they did not know.[15] It must be remembered, however, that this took place under the old covenant which was a concession to the sins of Israel. The old covenant

---

[7] Matt. 25:41-46.
[8] Matt. 13:30.
[9] Matt. 18:7.
[10] Matt. 18:35.
[11] Acts 5:5, 10.

[12] Rom. 11:22.
[13] Rom. 1:18.
[14] Rom. 12:19 (ASV).
[15] Rom. 3:15, 17.

was a concession to the hardness of men's hearts,[16] and therefore imperfect.[17] It was not God's original intention that men should exercise vengeance even in the days of the Old Testament, and if Israel had been wholly obedient unto the Lord no doubt her many wars could have been avoided. Neither should it be supposed that such obedience was impossible in the time of the old covenant. It is freely granted that since the coming of Christ men have more light than they had in the former time. Furthermore, Christ's redemptive work on the cross, and the coming of the Holy Spirit in a new way, constitute a source of greater power for holy living than that which was available to the men of the old covenant. But this does not mean that in the days of the Old Testament the power of God was insufficient for a holy life on the part of man. Even under the old covenant, if men came to God in true faith it was possible for them to have a spiritual experience as genuine, if not as full and as rich, as is that of the Christian today. The psalmist describes this experience in these words:

> Then I called on the name of the Lord:
>   "O Lord, I beseech thee, save my life!"
> Gracious is the Lord, and righteous;
>   our God is merciful.
> The Lord preserves the simple;
>   When I was brought low, he saved me.
> Return, O my soul, to your rest;
>   for the Lord has dealt bountifully with you.
>
> For thou hast delivered my soul from death,
>   my eyes from tears,
>   my feet from stumbling.[18]

Surely such an experience is evidence of sufficient power for holy living. The difficulty was that Israel as a nation did not avail itself of the power which was at hand, and this is the reason for the lower standards of the old covenant. Underlying both covenants is the fundamental moral law which is God's plan for human conduct, yesterday, today, and forever.[19] The

16 Matt. 19:8.   18 Ps. 116:4-8 (RSV).
17 Heb. 8:7; 10:1.   19 Matt. 5:17-19.

difference between the two is this, that whereas under the old covenant God made a concession to the hardness of men's hearts,[20] under the new covenant He gives His children a new heart so that they are able to accomplish that which men of a stony heart did not accomplish under the old covenant. The new covenant is better than the old because the consciences of men are now cleansed "from dead works to serve the living God."[21] The law of God is no longer written merely on tables of stone, or with ink, but by the Spirit of the living God into the very hearts of men.[22] The new and perfect covenant has invalidated the old imperfect one, and restored all conduct to the level of the fundamental moral law. The handwriting of ordinances as found in the ceremonial law is blotted out,[23] and the civil law of Moses is brought to an end that the moral law might be truly fulfilled.[24]

The man of the new covenant is saved by grace, and with the indwelling Spirit of God to direct his steps he is enabled to keep the moral law. In Christ he is a new creature; old things are passed away; all things are become new.[25] He is raised with Christ, and henceforth he walks in newness of life.[26] He is dead unto sin, and alive unto God; he is a servant of righteousness, obedient from the heart.[27] He is risen with Christ and seeks those things above. He has a heart of compassion, meekness, long-suffering, forgiveness; and the peace of God rules in his heart.[28] He walks in the light and has fellowship with God and his fellow Christians.[29] His life has been transformed by the power of God, hence he lives peaceably with all men. He does not avenge himself; he renders to no man evil for evil. If his enemy hungers he feeds him; he over-comes evil with good.[30] His life bears the fruit of the Spirit: love, joy, peace, long-suffering, kindness, goodness, faithfulness, meekness, self-control.[31] He knows that the salvation which "the prophets sought and searched diligently" is now at hand. Stirred with

[20] Matt. 19:8.

[21] Heb. 9:14.

[22] II Cor. 3:3.

[23] Col. 2:14.

[24] Matt. 5:17-48.

[25] II Cor. 5:17.

[26] Rom. 6:4.

[27] Rom. 6:11, 17, 18.

[28] Col. 3:1, 12-15.

[29] I John 1:6, 7.

[30] Rom. 12:2, 17-21.

[31] Gal. 5:22.

this thought, he girds up the loins of his mind to fashion himself after an "holy manner of living." He suffers gladly for the cause of Christ, because Christ also suffered, leaving an example that we should follow His steps.[32] This is the picture of the man of the new covenant as one finds it throughout the pages of the New Testament.

Christ the Author and Example of Nonresistance

Jesus Christ is the author of the new covenant, and those who are regenerated through Him are members of what He calls the kingdom of God. Christ Himself is the King and He invites men everywhere to submit to His rule. His is not a kingdom of earthly power, nor is the wrath of God manifest within it. It is a kingdom of love, characterized by the spirit of meekness: "Blessed are the meek: for they shall inherit the earth."[33] Christ Himself is the perfect example of love. Daily He walked, not after the flesh but after the Spirit. With Him the law of love was written, not on tables of stone but it was proclaimed in His every word and deed. Jesus frequently speaks of God as the loving heavenly Father who cares even for the birds of the field, and much more so for His children of faith.[34] God is likened to a shepherd who leaves the ninety and nine sheep safe in the fold and goes out into the wilderness to seek the one that is lost.[35] Or to the father who killed the fatted calf and made a great feast when his lost son returned home again.[36] Jesus calls Himself the good shepherd who willingly lays down his life for the sheep.[37]

The love of Jesus went out freely to all men; it knew no restrictions of race or nationality or of station in life. He healed the daughter of a Syrophoenician woman[38] and the son of a Roman centurion.[39] He revealed Himself to Nicodemus, a ruler in Israel,[40] and to the sinful woman of Samaria.[41] He

---

[32] I Pet. 1:10, 13, 14; 2:20, 21.
[33] Matt. 5:5.
[34] Matt. 6:26-30.
[35] Luke 15:3-7.
[36] Luke 15:11-32.
[37] John 10:11.
[38] Mark 7:25-30.
[39] Matt. 8:5-13.
[40] John 3:1-21.
[41] John 4:7-42.

loved the rich young man[42] and the humble Lazarus.[43] He ate with the outcast publicans that He might bring them into the kingdom.[44] By precept and example He taught His disciples to "heal the sick, raise the dead, cleanse the lepers, cast out demons."[45] He desired to gather the children of Jerusalem into His kingdom as a hen gathers her chickens under her wings,[46] and when they would not He wept with sorrow.[47]

Jesus kept the moral law perfectly. He never yielded to sin, and His life was one continuous demonstration of perfect love. The supreme expression of His love, however, is found in His death on the cross. Even though He was God, with authority to sit in judgment of sin, He chose rather to suffer death for the atonement of sin, that men might be redeemed. The sacrificial death on the cross was in complete harmony with the life of sacrifice which He had lived. His life and His death alike were motivated by a deep and burning love for sinful men. The manner in which Christ went to the cross is a perfect example of nonresistance. When the authorities came to arrest Him He made no attempt to resist, neither did He permit His friends to do so.[48] When He was unjustly accused at His trial He answered nothing, "insomuch that the governor marvelled greatly."[49] When He came to the place of crucifixion He was mocked and spat upon. They smote Him on the head. They crucified Him between two thieves. They railed on Him and wagged their heads. They challenged His deity and said, "If thou be the Son of God, come down from the cross."[50] But Christ's only reply was a prayer of love and mercy: "Father, forgive them; for they know not what they do."[51] In the words of Isaiah: "He was oppressed, yet when he was afflicted he opened not his mouth. As a lamb that is led to the slaughter, and as a sheep that before its shearers is dumb, so he opened not his mouth."[52] The life and death of Christ are a perfect example of love and nonresistance.

[42] Mark 10:17-22.
[43] John 11:1-46.
[44] Mark 2:15-17.
[45] Matt. 10:8 (ASV).
[46] Luke 13:34, 35.
[47] Luke 19:41.
[48] Matt. 26:47-52.
[49] Matt. 27:14.
[50] Matt. 27:27-44.
[51] Luke 23:34.
[52] Isa. 53:7 (ASV).

It is this Christ that bids us enter the kingdom of heaven and follow Him. When we do so we are "crucified with Christ" and it is no longer we that live, but "Christ living in us" that enables us to live the life set forth in the new covenant.[53] Peter admonishes Christians who suffer wrongfully to bear it with patience. In fact, this is the Christian's very calling: "For hereunto were ye called: because Christ also suffered for you, leaving you an example, that ye should follow his steps: who did no sin, neither was guile found in his mouth: who, when he was reviled, reviled not again; when he suffered, threatened not; but committed himself to him that judgeth righteously: who his own self bare our sins in his body upon the tree, that we, having died unto sins, might live unto righteousness."[54] Christ died not only that we might someday be saved in heaven. He also died that we might live unto righteousness here and now. He came to redeem men both from the guilt and the power of sin. Redemption is not only a passport to the glory world; it is power for righteous living and for a Christian testimony in this present sinful world. Righteousness is a fruit of redemption, and the man who is crucified with Christ must follow His steps.

Nonresistant Teaching in the New Testament

Many portions of the New Testament are devoted to specific instruction in what it means to follow Christ. Let us now direct our attention to those portions which deal with the principle of nonresistance in particular. In the introduction to the Sermon on the Mount, Jesus describes the members of His kingdom. They are poor in spirit, pure in heart, merciful, and meek. They hunger and thirst after righteousness; they are peacemakers; they suffer persecution for righteousness' sake.[55] Their prayer is that God's will might be done on earth as it is in heaven.[56] How different are these qualities from those so often manifested by Israel in the days of the old covenant! And

[53] Gal. 2:20.
[54] I Pet. 2:21-24 (ASV).
[55] Matt. 5:3-12.
[56] Matt. 6:10.

3

as these qualities of the Christian are different from those of backslidden Israel, so is his conduct different also.

In Matthew 5 Jesus definitely modifies the civil code of Moses because it does not measure up to the standards of the kingdom and of the fundamental moral law. Murder and adultery, for example, were a violation of the moral law, and the Mosaic code had recognized this fact by forbidding these sins. Israel's understanding of the moral law was not deep enough, however, for under the code of Moses this law was thought to have been kept if men merely abstained from overt acts of murder and adultery. Jesus says, however, that hatred and lust are as much a violation of the moral law as are the overt acts. Therefore under the new and perfect covenant men must be free from these as well.[57] Under the old covenant divorce and the legal oath had also been permitted, but since this permission was in violation of the moral law Jesus set it aside. Divorce and the oath, therefore, have no place under the new and perfect covenant.[58] Then Jesus comes to His explicit words on nonresistance where He says:

Ye have heard that it was said, An eye for an eye, and a tooth for a tooth: but I say unto you, Resist not him that is evil: but whosoever smiteth thee on thy right cheek, turn to him the other also. And if any man would go to law with thee, and take away thy coat, let him have thy cloak also. And whosoever shall compel thee to go one mile, go with him two.... Ye have heard that it was said, Thou shalt love thy neighbor, and hate thine enemy; but I say unto you, Love your enemies, and pray for them that persecute you.[59]

In this passage the emphasis is on love and forgiveness. Christian forgiveness knows no limit. On one occasion one of the disciples asked Jesus how often a brother should be forgiven if he continued to sin against him, and suggested seven times as a reasonable limit. But Jesus said: Not seven times, but seventy times seven.[60] Some people are willing enough to accept ready forgiveness as a proper method in the relationship of brethren.

[57] Matt. 5:21-30.
[58] Matt. 5:31-37.
[59] Matt. 5:38-44 (ASV).
[60] Matt. 18:21, 22.

But they question whether the nonresistant teachings of Jesus were meant to go beyond this realm. A careful examination of the passage from the Sermon on the Mount quoted above, however, will show that Jesus did mean to include much more than this. He specifically commands the Christian not to resist him that is evil. This "evil one" might conceivably be a brother gone astray, but just as likely it would be an ordinary man of the world who is an enemy. Jesus says to the Christians: Do not resist him; do not pay back to him in kind; deal with him in the spirit of love and so fulfill the fundamental moral law of God. "Whatsoever ye would that men should do to you, do ye even so to them: for this is the law and the prophets."[61]

Again, when Jesus set aside the civil law of eye for eye and tooth for tooth He was not speaking of personal retaliation, but of the ordinary legal method of avenging a wrong. Even the Mosaic code did not permit an individual who had lost a tooth to strike out the tooth of the offender personally. He must rather report the offense to the civil authorities and then the magistrates would administer punishment, which might consist of removing the offender's tooth. In Matthew 5:38, therefore, Jesus is saying that Christians must not appeal to the state for revenge against offenders. Also, the instruction to go a second mile refers to something more than personal relationships. Here, no doubt, Jesus was referring to the Roman practice of impressing subjects of the empire into some compulsory service, such as road building or courier duty. And Jesus says: Do not resist the Roman authorities in this demand, but submit; and rather than rebel, give two miles of service, even if only one is required.

The requirement of Jesus that the Christian love his enemy is in full accord with the words of Paul: "Avenge not yourselves, beloved, but give place unto the wrath of God: for it is written, Vengeance belongeth unto me; I will recompense, saith the Lord. But if thine enemy hunger, feed him; if he thirst, give him to drink. . . . Be not overcome of evil, but overcome evil

61 Matt. 7:12.

with good."[62] Throughout the New Testament there is a consistent emphasis on love and forgiveness, and a willingness to suffer for Christ. "Behold, I send you forth as sheep in the midst of wolves."[63] "And be not afraid of them that kill the body, . . . but rather fear him who is able to destroy both soul and body in hell."[64] Peter says: "If ye should suffer for righteousness' sake, blessed are ye."[65] Stephen, the evangelist, suffered a martyr's death; and even as he was being stoned he prayed that God would not lay this sin to the charge of those who killed him.[66] Paul was in prison many times, and suffered much for the faith that was in him; but the love of Christ constrained him to pursue his course consistently, even though in the end it meant his martyrdom also.

In the thirteenth chapter of I Corinthians Paul tells us that love "seeketh not its own."[67] When men fail to observe the principle of nonresistance it is frequently because they are seeking their own. Therefore it is not surprising to find much teaching in the New Testament on this major cause of strife and conflict. Paul says, "The love of money is a root of all kinds of evil."[68] In the same chapter he admonishes servants to have due regard for their masters and in another place he reminds the masters that they must treat their servants with love.[69] When the slave Onesimus was converted under the apostle's preaching, Paul sent him back to his master, "no longer as a servant," but as a beloved brother.[70] Among the early Christians at Jerusalem this love which "seeketh not its own" was so strong that the brethren "were of one heart and one soul," and even sold their possessions, and in the spirit of Christian love "had all things common."[71]

On one occasion Paul rebuked the Christians at Corinth for their failure in this matter of love. Strife had arisen among the Corinthians to the extent that they settled their difficulties in the civil courts of the state. But Paul says: "Dare any of you,

[62] Rom. 12:19-21 (ASV).
[63] Matt. 10:16.
[64] Matt. 10:28 (ASV).
[65] I Pet. 3:14 (ASV).
[66] Acts 7:60.

[67] I Cor. 13:5 (ASV).
[68] I Tim. 6:10 (ASV).
[69] Eph. 6:5-9.
[70] Philem. 16.
[71] Acts 4:32.

having a matter against his neighbor, go to law before the unrighteous, and not before the saints? . . . It is altogether a defect in you, that ye have lawsuits one with another. Why not rather take wrong? why not rather be defrauded?"[72] Here Paul says that Christians must deal with each other in the spirit of Christian love; if they do this they will have no need for unrighteous governments of this sinful world to settle their difficulties by means of force. To do so, in fact, would be a shame. The difficulty with the Corinthians was that in their relations each one was aiming at justice. But the New Testament way is to aim at love, not at justice. In aiming at justice the result is frequently a selfish struggle for power, position, or wealth. In aiming at love, however, the result is often justice as well as love. But even if this result does not follow, the Christian must continue to love anyway, for according to the teaching of Christ His disciples should be willing to suffer injustice rather than to forsake the way of love.

The Christian and the State

The state is an agency for the administration of justice with the aid of force, in an evil society, and it is not motivated by Christian love. Therefore the outlook of the New Testament is entirely unpolitical. It has nothing to say about how the affairs of state should be conducted. It does not suggest that the Christian should play any role in the state itself, and everywhere it assumes that he is not a part of the state. It simply recognizes the place of the state and the obligation of the Christian toward it. The Sermon on the Mount is not a piece of legislation for a secular state in a sinful society. It is a set of principles to govern the sons of the kingdom of heaven. And Jesus says this kingdom is "not of this world."[73] The Jews for the most part had a wrong idea of what the Messiah and His kingdom would be like. They were looking for a military leader who would overthrow the Roman conqueror and establish a political state of prestige and power. It seems that in His great temptation Jesus was actually

[72] I Cor. 6:1, 7 (ASV).
[73] John 18:36.

tempted to follow this course.[74] The power to do so was in His hand, if only He would renounce the plan of God and render obedience to Satan. But Jesus rejected the temptation and followed in the way of love and suffering, for which purpose He had come into the world. On another occasion the multitudes would have taken Jesus by force to make Him king, but again He refused.[75]

The function of the state is clearly stated in the New Testament. It is to maintain order in the evil society. Paul says: "Rulers are not a terror to good works, but to the evil." In this capacity the ruler is an agent of God for good.[76] Peter also says governors are sent of God "for the punishment of evildoers, and for the praise of them that do well."[77] In what sense, then, are rulers ministers of God? Only in the sense that in the operation of God's law of cause and effect in sinful human society, which requires that man suffer the consequence of his own evil, society has found it necessary to organize a state and appoint rulers with the power of coercion. When Paul wrote his epistle the Emperor Nero was on the Roman throne. Nero was one of the world's most wicked rulers and Paul certainly did not mean to teach that this wicked ruler was God's personal representative; or that Nero was ruling by a sort of divine right like that claimed by the kings of the seventeenth century.

Rulers of the state are ministers of God only in the sense that they help to bring evildoers to the consequence of their own evil, as required by God's law of cause and effect which operates in human society. The state is an instrument of society for the checking of its own evil, and frequently it uses one evil to check another. For this reason the ruler "beareth not the sword in vain." Like the Canaanite wars, the evil deeds of rulers may ultimately serve some divine purpose. Like Assyria of old, nations at war today may be used of God to punish the evil deeds, even of those who profess to be Christians. But these deeds of warfare are a violation of God's moral law, as were Israel's wars against Canaan. Certainly this was true of the Em-

74 Matt. 4:8-10.   76 Rom. 13:3, 4.
75 John 6:15.   77 I Pet. 2:14.

peror Nero of whom Paul wrote. What Romans 13 teaches is that rulers of states serve a divine purpose in checking evil, even though it be through sinful means. But this does not mean that God necessarily approves the deeds of rulers; in many cases He certainly does not. Nor does it make all rulers righteous and holy in God's sight.

What then should be the attitude of the Christian toward the state and its rulers? Paul makes it clear that he must have a general attitude of subordination. He must do nothing to hinder the state in its purpose. His own conduct must be righteous and not evil. He must be obedient to laws designed for the maintenance of order. He must pay taxes, and he must honor and respect those in authority. On another occasion Paul admonishes Christians to pray for kings and those in authority.[78] Peter likewise says they should "be subject to every ordinance of man for the Lord's sake: whether to the king, as supreme or unto governors."[79] Obedience to rulers, however, has a limit. It applies only in matters relating to the maintenance of order in the society of this world. The state may never encroach upon the sphere of the church. In faith, religion, and morals, the Christian must be in complete obedience to Christ; and if the requirements of the state in any way conflict with God's commands the Christian must do as John and Peter did when they said: "We must obey God rather than men."[80] This must certainly be the Christian's answer when the state requests him to violate God's moral law and the principle of nonresistance.

It is sometimes suggested that "subjection to the higher powers," as taught by Paul, involves an obligation to perform military service. But this interpretation would not have meant anything to the people to whom Paul was writing, because they were not required to serve in the Roman army. The military service which would have appealed most to them would have been one of rebellion against the Roman Empire. Therefore, "subjection to the higher powers" means primarily that the

78 I Tim. 2:1, 2
79 I Pet. 2:13, 14 (ASV).
80 Acts 5:29 (ASV).

Christian can have no part in a rebellion or revolution against the government in control. In Romans 13 Paul is teaching non-resistance, not an obligation to military service. A modern analogy might be found in the case of Christians in Norway, Denmark, or Czechoslovakia, under the rule of Hitler. Jesus would say in this case: Do not rebel against the foreign tyrant, but suffer in subjection rather than to violate the principle of nonresistance. This would indeed be a difficult situation for a nonresistant Christian. Rebellion would be a violation of the teachings of Christ; but submission to the tyrant's rule no doubt would also bring demands to violate these teachings through service in his army. Here again the Christian would need to obey God rather than men, and the result would be suffering, perhaps even death. This would be hard to endure, but it would be a true and genuine Christian martyrdom such as that suffered by many of the early Christians as well as by the Anabaptists of the sixteenth century. The disciple of Christ must always be ready to die for Him, if need be.

On one occasion Jesus was asked the question: "Is it lawful to give tribute unto Caesar, or not?" To this question He replied: "Render therefore unto Caesar the things that are Caesar's, and unto God the things that are God's."[81] This statement is also sometimes interpreted as an approval of military service for the Christian, because military service is supposed to be one of the "things that are Caesar's." But the situation here is almost precisely like that in Romans 13. Jesus' questioners were not men who would be interested in service in the Roman army. If anything, they would be interested in a military rebellion against the Roman authority. Therefore Jesus says, Give to Caesar that which is Caesar's. That is, do not rebel against him, not even to the extent of refusing to pay the tax. Here again Jesus is teaching nonresistance, not the opposite.

The way in which Jesus answered this question, however, shows that in His mind there is something much more important to the Christian than paying taxes to Caesar. In fact, He

---

[81] Matt. 22:17-21 (ASV).

did not answer the question at all; He simply said that Caesar should have what belongs to him. He does not even say that the tax belongs to Caesar, although this is implied. But the important part of the answer is the last part, where He says, "Render unto God the things that are God's." The meaning is something like this: Why yes, if the coin is Caesar's let him have that which belongs to him. But remember, there are some things which belong to God and be sure that you don't give any of these to Caesar. Jesus makes it clear that there is such a thing as a conflict between the demands of God and those of Caesar. This is a point which many people fail to catch. They think and speak as if there were no such thing as conflict between the requirements of God and those of Caesar. They assume that the demands of the state must always be obeyed; that they are not even open to question. Then they misinterpret the Bible in whatever way is necessary to make it agree with the government's demands. A friend of the writer has put it this way:

> To put my country and my God on an equal basis, to be equally obeyed, is . . . blasphemy. I know that "the powers that be" are ordained of God and are His ministers. But that includes Hitler. It applies particularly to Nero, who was even worse than Hitler. Are these too to be obeyed and acknowledged with equal authority with God? If so, why do we fight them? If the rulers of our country are the ministers of God in the sense that they have final authority over Christians, then so is Hitler, and you have God fighting God. The only possible interpretation of Romans 13 is that "the powers that be" are always to be obeyed except when obedience to them conflicts with obedience to God.[82]

Nonresistance Is for Our Time

Some people have attempted to minimize the conflict between God and Caesar by assigning the Sermon on the Mount and other peace teachings of Jesus to the millennium. As mentioned in the previous chapter, not all the events of the future are clear. Some Christians interpret the Scriptures to mean that at His second advent Christ is coming to establish a literal

[82] Letter of Carl M. Lehman to a friend, Dec. 9, 1942.

kingdom upon the earth; others that He is coming to judge the world, and that there will be no literal millennial reign. Whichever view is correct, however, the idea that the Sermon on the Mount is to be postponed to some future time is incompatible with a reasonable interpretation of the Scriptures, or of the millennium itself. If there is to be a literal millennium, all murder and hatred, conflict and strife, will surely be absent. There will be no enemies to love and no one to whom the other cheek needs to be turned; there will be no evil and no persecution. Therefore in the millennium there would not be any opportunity to apply these specific teachings, and much of the Sermon on the Mount would be meaningless.

Nowhere in the New Testament are Christians told to postpone obedience to some later time. John says, "Hereby we do know that we know him, if we keep his commandments. He that saith, I know him, and keepeth not his commandments, is a liar, and the truth is not in him. But whoso keepeth his word, in him verily is the love of God perfected."[83] Surely these words were meant for application here and now, not merely in some future age. In the Sermon on the Mount itself Jesus says, "Ye are the salt of the earth" and "Ye are the light of the world."[84] Certainly He is speaking of this present world, not some future one. It is also clear that the early Christians considered Jesus' words as instructions for literal observance in their own time. Paul's teaching on nonresistance in Romans 12 is as strong as that of Jesus. His teaching on litigation[85] is fully as explicit as is that of Jesus on the law of eye for eye and tooth for tooth. And the nonresistant teaching of Peter in his first epistle is equally strong.

Nonresistance an Integral Part of the Gospel

For some strange reason so-called Christians often tend to make a distinction between the Gospel and nonresistance, or between the Gospel and the ethical teachings of the New Testa-

---

[83] I John 2:3-5.
[84] Matt. 5:13, 14.
[85] I Cor. 6:1-7.

ment. They stress the importance of preaching the doctrine of salvation, the atoning work of Christ on the cross, and tell us this is the Gospel. Nonresistance and other ethical teachings of the New Testament, however, they seem to consider as of minor importance, meriting little or no attention; as though they were something apart from, or in addition to, the Gospel. How Christians can hold such a view is difficult to understand, for the New Testament itself makes no such distinction. Throughout the New Testament there is a close integration of the doctrine of salvation and the ethical teachings. The Pauline epistles are generally divided into two parts about equal in length, the first part stressing the doctrine of salvation, the latter part the practical and ethical teachings. According to Paul these two parts belong together, and neither one of them alone constitutes the Gospel.

In I Peter 2 the integration of nonresistance with the doctrine of salvation is most strikingly illustrated. Here Peter says that Christ "bare our sins in his own body on the tree, that we, being dead to sins, should live unto righteousness."[86] That is, the purpose of the atoning work on the cross is not merely to get us to heaven someday. It is to make us spiritually alive now, enabling us to live righteously in the present world. Of course, if we have this spiritual life we will be fit for heaven. Then Peter explains further what this means. He says that Christ in suffering for us left us an example that we should follow His steps *in the way of love and nonresistance,* "who, when he was reviled, reviled not again; when he suffered he threatened not."[87] That is, we as Christians are to manifest that same spirit of love and nonresistance which took Christ to the cross to die for the atonement of our sins.

In Philippians 2 this truth is further illustrated. Here Paul gives us perhaps the most profound statement in the entire New Testament concerning the humiliation, incarnation, and death of Christ, who although in the form of God "was made in the likeness of men . . . humbled himself, and became

[86] I Pet. 2:24.
[87] I Pet. 2:21-23.

obedient unto death, even the death of the cross."[88] Then this same Christ has also been exalted again so that all men should confess Him as Lord to the glory of God. Certainly nowhere in the Scriptures could one find a clearer statement than this concerning the deity of Christ, His incarnation, His death, and His present glorification. And yet the striking thing about this profound passage is that Paul introduced it at this point primarily as an illustration of the kind of spirit which must be manifested by the Christian who has been redeemed through the atoning work of Christ.

"Let this mind be in you, which was also in Christ Jesus," says Paul.[89] What sort of mind was in Christ Jesus? A humble, loving mind, which constrained Him, although God, to become human and to die upon the cross for the salvation of mankind. Then when Christians have the Christlike mind, what will they do? The answer is: They will "do all things without murmurings and disputings." They will "shine as lights," blameless and harmless, the sons of God, without rebuke, in the midst of a crooked and perverse nation."[90] What is the Gospel? It is the story of the redemptive work of Christ which makes men to be sons of God with a mind like that of Christ, constraining them to be humble, loving, blameless, harmless, peaceful, and nonresistant. All of this, and not a part of it, is the Gospel. The preacher who omits the doctrine of love and nonresistance from his sermons is not preaching the Gospel as it is given in the New Testament. Nonresistance is not something added to the Gospel. It is an integral part of the Gospel, and when it is omitted that which remains is something far less than the Gospel.

Disregarding the Truth a Serious Matter

In addition to this clear picture of the Gospel and of the Christian way of life we must also remember that the New Testament teaches the judgment of God upon sin. This judg-

[88] Phil. 2:7, 8.
[89] Phil. 2:5.
[90] Phil. 2:14, 15.

ment, moreover, seems to rest very heavily on those who have
come to a knowledge of the truth under the new covenant and
then deliberately reject it:

> For if we sin wilfully after that we have received the knowledge
> of the truth, there remaineth no more a sacrifice for sins, but a
> certain fearful expectation of judgment, and a fierceness of fire
> which shall devour the adversaries. A man that hath set at nought
> Moses' law dieth without compassion on the word of two or three
> witnesses; of how much sorer punishment, think ye, shall he be
> judged worthy, who hath trodden under foot the Son of God, and
> hath counted the blood of the covenant wherewith he was sanctified
> an unholy thing, and hath done despite unto the Spirit of grace? For
> we know him that said, Vengeance belongeth unto me, I will rec-
> compense. An again, The Lord shall judge his people. It is a
> fearful thing to fall into the hands of the living God.[91]

The seriousness of this matter was stated in a most forceful
manner during the days of the first World War by Maurice
Hess, a conscientious objector and a member of the Dunker
Church, at the time of his court-martial for refusing to bear
arms. In his testimony, Hess said:

> I do not believe that I am seeking martyrdom. As a young man,
> life and its hopes and freedom and opportunities for service are
> sweet to me. I want to go out into the world and make use of what
> little talent I may have acquired by long and laborious study.
> But I know that I dare not purchase these things at the price of
> eternal condemnation. I know the teaching of Christ, my Saviour.
> He taught us to resist not evil, to love our enemies, to bless them that
> curse us, and do good to them that hate us. Not only did He teach
> this, but He also practiced it in Gethsemane, before Pilate, and on
> Calvary. We would indeed be hypocrites and base traitors to our
> profession if we would be unwilling to bear the taunts and jeers of a
> sinful world, and its imprisonment, and torture or death, rather
> than to participate in war and military service. We know that obedi-
> ence to Christ will gain for us the glorious prize of eternal life. We
> cannot yield, we cannot compromise, we must suffer.[92]

In this chapter, and in the preceding one, it has been the
writer's view that the teaching of peace and nonresistance is

---

[91] Heb. 10:26-31 (ASV).
[92] Quoted in Norman Thomas, *The Conscientious Objector in America* (New York, 1923), 25, 26.

found in the Scriptures both of the Old and New Testaments; that the principle of nonresistance is an integral part of God's plan for His people; that it is a fruit of the Christian experience; and that the judgment of God rests upon those who disregard this teaching as much as it does upon those who neglect some other divine command. The attempt here has been to show by a fair and balanced treatment of the Scriptures that the nonresistant way of life is in accord with the whole tenor of the Gospel, and that it does not rest upon a few isolated passages. Obviously in such a brief treatment it is not possible to include comments on every passage bearing on the subject. It must also be recognized that there are a number of Biblical passages which present some difficulties of interpretation, such as the words of Jesus: "And he that hath no sword, let him sell his garment, and buy one."[93] A full treatment of these various passages would have made the present chapter too lengthy; and since in some cases the difficulty is due chiefly to a superficial understanding of the passages, their treatment would have involved a discussion of considerable matter not altogether relevant to the purpose of the present chapter. For this reason a discussion of certain difficult passages is included in appendix 2.

[93] Luke 22:36.

SELECT BIBLIOGRAPHY

The outstanding treatise on the New Testament peace teaching is G. H. C. Macgregor, *The New Testament Basis of Pacifism* (London, 1953). Although somewhat liberal in its interpretation of certain Scriptures and in its use of the term "redemption," it remains the best general treatment of the New Testament teaching. C. J. Cadoux, *The Early Christian Attitude to War* (London, 1919), has a chapter on the New Testament peace teaching. A helpful treatise is Ernest J. Bohn, *Christian Peace According to the New Testament Peace Teaching Outside the Gospels* (n.p., 1938). P. H. Richert, *A Brief Catechism on Difficult Scripture Passages and Involved Questions on the Use of the Sword* (Newton, Kans., n.d.), and Edward Yoder, *Must Christians Fight* (Akron, Pa., 1943), have much helpful material. A recent book challenging the nonresistant interpretation of the New Testament is Umphrey Lee, *The Historic Church and Modern Pacifism* (New York, 1943). Two helpful books from the Biblical nonresistant point of view are Hunter Beattie, *The Christian and War* (Philadelphia, 1942), and James D. Bales, *The Christian Conscientious Objector* (Berkeley, Calif.). Recent noteworthy books are: James R. Graham, *Strangers and Pilgrims* (Scottdale, Pa., 1951); C. G. Rutenber, *The Dagger and the Cross* (New York, 1950); Johannes Ude, *Du Sollst Nicht Töten* (Dornbirn, Austria, 1948); Daniel Parker, *Refus de la Guerre* (Le Chambon sur Lignon, Haute-Loire, France, 1949); Pierre Lorson, S. J., *Un Chretien Peutil etre Objecteur de Conscience?* (Paris, 1950); Charles E. Raven, *The Theological Basis of Christian Pacifism* (New York, 1951); Henry A. Fast, *Jesus and Human Conflict* (Herald Press, 1959); and Jean Lasserre, *War and the Gospel* (Scottdale, Pa., 1962). A helpful pamphlet is John A. Toews, *True Nonresistance Through Christ* (Winnipeg, 1955). A book treating the Biblical teaching on nonresistance in its broad social implications is Guy F. Hershberger, *The Way of the Cross in Human Relations* (Scottdale, Pa., 1958).

4. Peace, War, and the State in the History of the Church

This chapter is concerned with the nonresistant testimony of the church since the New Testament period. The Christian Church was founded under the rule of an authoritarian state. The Jews of that time desired to be free from this yoke, but the New Testament is clear in its teaching that Christians may not engage in political activity or in revolution to secure such freedom. They are admonished to be obedient to Caesar's rule. It should also be remembered that the earliest Christians, for the most part, were slaves and Jews and women, few if any of whom were eligible for political office or to serve as soldiers under the Roman government. Therefore, the matter of participation in the affairs of the Roman state was not an important practical question in the early church.

But what if Christianity should grow to the point where Gentiles, freemen, and Roman citizens in large numbers would be members of the church? Or what if soldiers and statesmen themselves should accept Christianity? This is precisely what happened by the fourth century, and then the question of political and military activity did become very important indeed. Would Roman statesmen and soldiers who became Christians renounce their profession? Would Christians who were legally eligible to hold public office, or to serve as soldiers, do so? If so, would they be true to the teachings of their Master? Would they Christianize the state, or would the affairs of state have a damaging effect on the life of the church? Where would the line of distinction be drawn between the kingdom of God and the kingdom of this world? We now proceed with an answer to these questions in a brief sketch of Christian history in its relation to peace, war, and the state.

The Early Church to A.D. *174*

It is quite clear that prior to about A.D. 174 it is impossible to speak of Christian soldiers. C. J. Cadoux, the best authority, says: "No Christian ever thought of enlisting in the army after his conversion until the reign of Marcus Aurelius (A. D. 161 to 180.)"[1] Cornelius[2] and the Philippian jailer[3] are two cases of men who were converted after they had been soldiers. Such cases are very rare during this early period, however, and the records do not tell us whether these men continued as soldiers after their baptism or not. The most reasonable presumption, however, would be that they did not.

The literature of the period between the writing of the New Testament and the year A.D. 174 also has little to say on the specific point of military service for Christians, evidently because the question seldom came up. The writings of this period are strongly nonresistant in their general tenor, however, so that it is quite unlikely that anyone remained both a soldier and a Christian for any length of time during this period. It is also significant that when the Romans besieged Jerusalem in the year A.D. 70, the Christians left the city and settled beyond the Jordan River in Perea. The records do not say positively that they did so because they believed it wrong to assist their fellow citizens in armed resistance, but this would seem to be a natural interpretation. At any rate "the flame of Jewish patriotism was extinct in the hearts of these Jerusalemite Christians."[4]

One of the early post-apostolic writings is the *Teaching of the Twelve Apostles*. This document, written early in the second century, possibly about A.D. 110 to 115, says: "Thou shalt not take evil counsel against thy neighbor. Thou shalt not hate any man."[5] Ignatius, writing to the Ephesians about

---

[1] C. J. Cadoux, *The Early Christian Attitude to War* (London, 1919), 17.
[2] Acts 10:1-48.
[3] Acts 16:19-24.
[4] Cadoux, *op. cit.,* 99.
[5] *Ante-Nicene Fathers* (Roberts and Donaldson, editors. New York, 1925). 7:378 (*Teaching of the Twelve Apostles, 2:6, 7*). This and the following quotations are taken directly from the *Ante-Nicene Fathers,* but follow closely the presentation of Cadoux and Heering.

the year 110, says: "Do not seek to avenge yourselves on those that injure you . . . . And let us imitate the Lord, 'who, when he was reviled, reviled not again'; when he was crucified, he answered not; 'when he suffered, he threatened not'; but prayed for his enemies."[6] About the same time Polycarp wrote the Philippians, urging obedience to the commandments of Christ, " 'not rendering evil for evil, or railing for railing,' or blow for blow, or cursing for cursing."[7] Justin Martyr, writing about A.D. 153, says: "We who were filled with war, and mutual slaughter, and every wickedness, have . . . changed our warlike weapons, our swords into ploughshares, and our spears into implements of tillage."[8] In 180 Athenagoras said: "We have learned not only not to return blow for blow, nor to go to law with those who plunder and rob us, but to those who smite us on one side of the face to offer the other side also, and to those who take away our coat to give likewise our cloak."[9] About the same time the pagan philosopher Celsus wrote against the Christians because they were not taking part in the civil government or serving as soldiers. He urges them "to help the king with all our might, and . . . to fight for him . . . and . . . lead an army along with him." Celsus argued, as some people do today that if everyone did as the nonresistant Christians did the Empire would be ruined.[10]

The Early Church A.D. 174 to 313

Beginning about the year A.D. 174, however, there were Christians in the Roman army. The first positive evidence of this is found in the writings of Tertullian, a leading church father, who opposed this new development with great vigor. He cites Jesus' command to Peter to put up his sword and then says: "Shall it be held lawful to make an occupation of the sword, when the Lord proclaims that he who uses the sword

---

[6] *Ibid.*, 1:54 (*Ignatius to Ephesians*, 10).
[7] *Ibid.*, 1:33 (*Polycarp to Philippians*, 2).
[8] *Ibid.*, 1:254 (*Dialogue*, 110).
[9] *Ibid.*, 2:129 (*Plea for the Christians*, 1).
[10] *Ibid.*, 4:667-68 (*Origen vs. Celsus*, 8:73).

shall perish by the sword? And shall the son of peace take part in the battle when it does not become him even to sue at law? And shall he apply the chain, and the prison, and the torture, and the punishment, who is not the avenger even of his own wrongs?" He admits a problem in the case of the man who is first a soldier and then becomes a Christian, but he says that in this case "there must be either an immediate abandonment of" military service "which has been the course with many," or the individual must suffer martyrdom.[11] From this passage it seems that previous to this many soldiers had quit their profession upon becoming Christians, and that Tertullian was condemning a new tendency not to do so.

One of the outstanding early church fathers was Origen. About the year 250 he wrote: "We have come in accordance with the counsels of Jesus to cut down our warlike and arrogant swords of argument into ploughshares, and we convert into sickles the spears we formerly used in fighting. For we no longer take 'sword against a nation,' nor do we learn 'any more to make war,' having become sons of peace for the sake of Jesus, who is our leader."[12] In another place Origen specifically states that Christians do not serve as soldiers or magistrates for the emperor.[13] He replied directly to the practical problem raised by the pagan Celsus who had said that if everyone refrained from military service as the Christians did the Empire would be ruined. He referred to the Scriptures and cited the miraculous escape of Israel from the hand of the Egyptians at the Red Sea. He was sure that in his own day God would save in an equally miraculous way any nation which would wholly obey the Lord in laying down its arms. He argued that Christians through their peaceful manner of life are a much greater help to the emperor than they would be if they served as soldiers or magistrates.

For men of God are assuredly the salt of the earth; they preserve the order of the world; and society is held together as long as the

11 *Ibid.*, 3:99, 100 (*De Corona*, 11).
12 *Ante-Nicene Fathers*, 4:558 (*Origen vs. Celsus*, 5:33). Cf. Cadoux, *op. cit.*, 130.
13 *Ibid.*, 4:668 (*Origen vs. Celsus*, 8:73-75).

salt is uncorrupted[14] . . . . And as we by our prayers vanquish all demons who stir up war, and lead to the violation of oaths, and disturb the peace, we in this way are much more helpful to the kings, than those who go into the fields to fight for them . . . . We do not indeed fight under him, although he require it; but we fight on his behalf, forming a special army—an army of piety—by offering our prayers to God . . . . Christians are benefactors of their country more than others. For they train up citizens, and inculcate piety to the Supreme Being; and they promote those whose lives in the smallest cities have been good and worthy, to a divine and heavenly city . . . . And it is not for the purpose of escaping public duties that Christians decline public offices, but that they may reserve themselves for a divine and more necessary service in the Church of God— for the salvation of men.[15]

Cyprian, Bishop of Carthage who died as a martyr in 258, said: "The whole earth is drenched in adversaries' blood, and if a murder is committed privately it is a crime, but if it happens with state authority, courage is the name for it." Christians "are not allowed to kill, but they must be ready to be put to death themselves," and "it is not permitted the guiltless to put even the guilty to death."[16] Lactantius of Bithynia writing in the early fourth century comments on the sixth commandment as follows: "When God forbids us to kill, he not only prohibits us from open violence . . . but he warns us against the commission of those things which are esteemed lawful among men. Thus it will be neither lawful for a just man to engage in warfare . . . . Therefore, with regard to this precept of God, there ought to be no exception at all; but that it is always unlawful to put to death a man, whom God willed to be a sacred animal."[17] Arnobius, writing about 310, implies that nonresistance was the accepted practice of Christians from the beginning, and says: "If all without exception . . . would lend an ear for a little to his [Christ's] salutary and peaceful rules . . . the whole world, having turned the use of steel into more peaceful occupations, would now be living in the most placid tranquility,

[14] Ibid., 4:666 (Origen vs. Celsus, 8:70).
[15] Ibid., 4:668 (Origen vs. Celsus, 8:73-75).
[16] Ibid., 5:277 (Epistles of Cyprian, 1:6). Cf. G. J. Heering, The Fall of Christianity (London, 1930), 51.
[17] Ibid., 7:187 (Divine Institutes, 6:20).

and would unite in blessed harmony, maintaining inviolate the sanctity of treaties."[18]

In addition to these statements by individual church leaders there have come down from the third and fourth centuries a number of documents known as church orders and canons which are definite regulations against serving as magistrates or soldiers. These regulations evidently did not have universal application, but they do show that, in certain communities and churches, service in the army was officially forbidden. One of these orders says: "He who is a soldier among the believers, and among the instructed, . . . and a magistrate with the sword or chief of praefects, . . . let him leave off or be rejected. And a catechumen or believer, if they wish to be soldier, shall be rejected, because it is far from God." Another says: "Let a catechumen or a believer of the people, if he desires to be a soldier, either cease from his intention, or if not let him be rejected. For he hath despised God by his thought, and leaving the things of the Spirit, he hath perfected himself in the flesh, and hath treated the faith with contempt."[19]

Eusebius, the church historian, tells the story of a Roman officer of high rank who became a Christian about the beginning of the fourth century and who then "by his voluntary confession and after nobly enduring bitter scourging succeeded in getting discharged from military service."[20] There were many who did likewise and also some who paid for their nonresistant faith with their lives. Perhaps the best-known case is that of Maximilian, the young Numidian who in 295 was brought before the proconsul of Africa for induction into the army. Maximilian refused induction and the military uniform, saying: "I cannot serve as a soldier; I cannot do evil; I am a Christian."[21] When told that his refusal would mean death he calmly replied: "I shall not perish, but when I shall have forsaken this world my soul shall live with Christ my Lord." He was then put to

18 *Ibid.*, 6:415 (*Arnobius vs. the Heathen*, 1:6).
19 Cadoux, *op. cit.*, 122-23.
20 Heering, *op. cit.*, 52.
21 Cadoux, *op. cit.*, 149.

death at the age of twenty-one and his father "returned home giving thanks to God that he had been able to bring such a present to the Lord."[22] Throughout the church there was much sympathy for the stand which Maximilian had taken and in course of time he was recognized as one of the heroes of the church. Cadoux says there were numerous cases like that of Maximilian near the beginning of the fourth century and that this may have helped to bring on the great persecution of A.D. 303.[23]

The Church After A.D. 313

In spite of examples like that of Maximilian, however, many Christians were in the Roman army by the beginning of the fourth century. As Cadoux says, the admission of a few soldier-converts to the church about A.D. 174, "proved to be the thin end of the wedge" which slowly, but surely, opened the church for the general admission of soldiers as members. Then in A.D. 313 a startling thing happened. Constantine, the Roman Emperor, declared himself a Christian and recognized Christianity as a legal religion. From this point on a great change came over the Christian Church. The emperor himself being a Christian soldier, it was natural that soon there would be many Christians in the army. In the course of time the church gave up its nonresistant position and Christianity became the religion of an imperial state. As Cadoux puts it: "The sign of the cross of Jesus was now an imperial military emblem, bringing good fortune and victory. The supposed nails of the cross, which the Emperor's mother found and sent to him, were made into bridle-bits and a helmet, which he used in his military expeditions."[24]

Other changes took place at a rapid pace. In 314 the Council of Arles announced a decision that "they who throw away their weapons in time of peace shall be excommunicate."[25] The statements of the church fathers now begin to sound a different note from that so familiar before 313. About 350 Athanasius

22 Heering, *op. cit.,* 53.
23 Cadoux, *op. cit.,* 150-51
24 *Ibid.,* 256.
25 Heering, *op cit.,* 57.

said: "Murder is not permitted, but to kill one's adversary in war is both lawful and praiseworthy." A little later Ambrose, Bishop of Milan, made the case even stronger: "And that courage which either protects the homeland against barbarians, in war, or defends the weak at home, or saves one's comrades from brigands, is full of righteousness."[26] Then in 416 the Empire even went so far as to forbid non-Christians to serve in the army at all.[27] And so the nonresistant Christian brotherhood founded by the suffering Christ, after three and one-half centuries was transformed into a militant imperial state church.

In attempting to explain this "astonishing and shocking" change which came over the church a number of reasons are frequently given. One is that Christians generally appreciated the law and order provided by the Roman magistrates and soldiers and so gradually began to take part in these professions themselves. Another is that the common use of military figures to describe the Christian life threw some Christians off guard in their attitude toward war. In the third century the use of such figures in Christian literature seems to have increased, as did also perhaps a reliance on the war stories of the Old Testament, which were not always properly understood.

No doubt the most important factor in bringing about the change, however, was the gradual growth of moral laxness during this period; and as time went on the rate of decline seemed to increase. James Westfall Thompson has given us a most vivid picture of what happened in the fourth century.

The triumph of the Church in the fourth century was one of the dearest bought victories in the history of humanity. With Constantine the governing classes, the rich, the worldly came into the fold in numbers, bringing with them their normal moral qualities and social standards, their normal ways of conduct. The result was a blurring of the line between the Church and the world, the subordination of religion to policy and politics, the invasion of "marginal" men and women into the Church, the lowering of ideals, the corrupting influence of sudden wealth, spiritual sclerosis. . . . The Church yielded to the world in order to gain support of and acquire the

---

[26] *Ibid.*, 58, 59.
[27] Cadoux, *op. cit.*, 257.

property of the rich and influential pagan aristocracy. The increase of its authority was paid for by a loss of spiritual vitality. The speed of this degeneration is as astonishing as the magnitude of the corruption. It was so great that before a century had passed there were not a few of those more spiritually minded who declared that the Church had more reason to deplore its prosperity than the adversity and persecution which it had suffered in the third century. . . . A study of the moral and the religious physiology of the Church in the fourth century is a study not of health but of disease; of moral lesions, corruptions, abuses.[28]

Although there have been notable exceptions in every period of its history, this state of ill health described by Thompson has characterized considerable portions of the church more or less continuously from the time of Constantine to our own. Following Constantine the church became a universal institution, made up of all kinds of persons, the great mass of whom did not meet the high standards of conduct taught in the New Testament. "Heathen hordes flocked into the Christian church, and quickly allowed themselves to become fanatics for their new faith, and the 'holy war' was speedily proclaimed."[29] The standards of the pagan world met those of the church halfway, and the kingdom of heaven was badly confused with the kingdom of this world.

The New Testament demands, however, could not be ignored entirely. Therefore many church leaders began to reinterpret the nonresistant teachings of Christ and the Scriptures in a compromising way so as to make them fit the lower moral standards which the church had adopted. Augustine, for example, the most influential of all the church fathers, who died in 430, said: "He who can think of war without feeling sore pain, must have lost all feeling for humanity."[30] Nevertheless, Augustine was able to work out a plausible theory of "just wars" which might be fought with the approval of God. He was much impressed with the law and order maintained by the Empire, and to him the imperial efforts to hold back the bar-

[28] J. W. Thompson, *An Economic and Social History of the Middle Ages* (New York, 1928), 64.
[29] The sentence is Harnack's, quoted in Heering, *op. cit.*, 55.
[30] Heering, *op. cit.*, 59.

barian tribes did not seem inconsistent with Christianity. He thought of war as a police measure against evildoers who themselves benefit by the punishment which the war inflicts. Both church and state aim at peace; hence the two are in agreement. They constitute two divine spheres, somewhat equal in importance, and to each of which the Christian has equal obligations. Therefore, if the state requires war to carry out its purposes, the Christian must take part.

With this foundation Augustine worked out an elaborate argument in favor of "just wars" waged at the command of God. Unjust wars, he says, are those which come through envy, revenge, cruelty, and lust for power. But just wars are those which God commands men to wage in punishment of these evils. When Moses waged war he did not manifest ferocity, but obedience to God. When God commanded wars He did not act in cruelty, but in righteous judgment.[31] In Augustine's time there was a group of heretics known as Donatists, who caused the church much concern. Earlier in his life Augustine had urged that these people be dealt with in kindness and love; later he approved their persecution with the sword, thus forcing them back into the church. He argued that if coaxing and kind words do not bring a lost sheep into the fold, the good shepherd must chastise it with whips. Then he quoted the words of Jesus from the parable of the great supper: "Go out into the highways and hedges, and compel them to come in."[32] Here he found divine approval of persecution and war for a good cause; the Donatists must be brought into the kingdom of heaven by force. Then he cites a series of passages from the New Testament to show that Christ approved of war:[33] John the Baptist did not tell the soldiers to quit their profession, but said they should be content with their wages.[34] Jesus said, "Give to Caesar the things that are Caesar's,"[35] and He praised the faith of the centurion.[36]

[31] *Nicene and Post-Nicene Fathers* (P. Schaff, editor. New York, 1901), 4:300, 301 (*Reply to Faustus*, 22:74).

[32] Luke 14:22, 23; J. C. Ayer, *A Source Book for Ancient Church History* (New York, 1933), 452, 453.

[33] *Nicene and Post-Nicene Fathers*, 4:301 (*Reply to Faustus*, 22:74).

[34] Luke 3:14. See appendix 2 for the author's comments on these passages.

[35] Matt. 22:21.   [36] Matt. 8:5-10.

Augustine's idea was developed still further by Thomas Aquinas, the great Catholic theologian of the thirteenth century. In Aquinas' way of thinking the church and state were united into a single body, and wars waged by the ruler in a just cause, with the approval of the church, were likewise approved of God. Aquinas lived in a Europe which had recently been stirred by the Crusades, a series of religious wars for the recovery of the Holy Land, and these served as illustrations of the religious wars which God approves.

Nevertheless, in spite of this close union between church and state, the people of the Middle Ages could not get away entirely from the standards of the New Testament. Jesus' teaching on nonresistance, and the idea of the kingdom of God which is not of the world, continued to make an impression. Those Christians who were most conscientious withdrew from the world and lived as monks in secluded monasteries where they devoted their time to prayers, and religious exercises, and living a type of life to which the ordinary Christian could not attain. Thomas Aquinas definitely approved this double standard. The ordinary Christian might engage in just wars, but the monks and the clergy must not take part in fighting because they have been set apart for a higher and better kind of life. He finds support for this idea in Christ's command to Peter to put up his sword into its place.[37] According to Catholic teaching Peter was the first pope; therefore this command to Peter was meant for the popes and the clergy, and they must not fight. But this strict requirement does not apply to the ordinary Christian. In this way the church of the medieval period developed a graduated system of morals to which the Catholic Church still adheres. By this scheme the church accepts the inferior moral performance of the more worldly Christians at the lower end of the scale; but the monks and nuns and priests who stand at the top of the scale, apart from the world, make up for this deficiency by living a righteous life vicariously for the general body of Christians who cannot attain the highest moral standards.

[37] Heering, op. cit., 72-74; P. Hartill, Into the Way of Peace (London, 1941), 50, 51.

In the Middle Ages, however, there were also certain small groups of Christians who remained apart from the Catholic Church, and who refused to accept this compromise with the world. They emphasized religious equality and brotherly love after the manner of the early church, and held up high moral standards for the entire group instead of permitting a double standard of morals as did the Catholic Church. Among these groups were the Montanists, the Donatists, the Paulicians, the Waldensians, and others.

Lutheranism[38]

The Protestant separation from the Catholic Church began with Martin Luther in 1517. All of the Protestant groups found it necessary to come to some conclusion on the question of war and the teachings of the Scriptures. Luther was much impressed with the doctrine of nonresistance as found in the New Testament and said that the Christian ought to live this kind of life. But his was also a universal state church. Everyone who lived in the territory of a Lutheran prince was required by law to be a member of the Lutheran Church, regardless of his personal convictions. Consequently there were many weak Christians in the church who found it difficult to live up to the New Testament standard. Furthermore, the Lutheran revolt was carried through with the help of the state, so that the relation between church and state under Lutheranism was much the same as under Catholicism.

In solving the problem of war for the Christian, Lutheranism also made a compromise, although in a slightly different form from that of the Catholic Church. Lutheranism does not have any order of monks nor a graduated system of morals. All the members of the Lutheran Church, including the ministers, are considered on the same moral level. But Luther said the individual is both a Christian and a citizen of the state. As a Christian he ought to obey the Sermon on the Mount; but as

---

[38] For a thorough treatment of the social and ethical views of the various Christian groups see Ernst Troeltsch, *The Social Teaching of the Christian Churches*, 2 vols. (New York, 1931).

a citizen of the state he must do whatever the state requires, even if this conflicts with the Scriptural teaching of nonresistance. Thomas Aquinas had divided the Catholic Church into two parts, giving the sword to the worldly laymen, and taking it away from the holy clergy. Luther divided the service of each individual Christian into two parts. Under the one he serves the state with the sword, and under the other he follows the steps of Christ. According to the Lutheran system, therefore, the Christian, as a citizen, must do whatever the state requires, short of renouncing his faith in Christ.

Calvinism

Although Luther's church was a state church, Lutheranism has never concerned itself very much with the affairs of state. It allows the state to manage its own affairs without interference by the church; it expects the state not to interfere with the church; and it expects the individual to serve both the church and the state. John Calvin, however, was a Protestant state-church reformer of the sixteenth century with a different emphasis. He believed that the church and its ideas should control the state. In Geneva, Switzerland, where he set up his program, the state authorities worked very closely with the ministers and enacted whatever laws the latter desired. In this way, Calvin believed that even the wicked people should be compelled to live righteously. A righteous society would be maintained on the earth by putting the church at the head and placing the power of coercion, the police and the military, under its direction. Of course, this meant that Calvinism could not be a nonresistant faith. But Calvin derived his moral and ethical principles largely from the Old Testament, instead of the New; therefore the Sermon on the Mount and related teachings did not have such an important place in his thinking.

The Mennonites, Friends, and Brethren

The Anabaptists or Mennonites were another important Protestant group of the sixteenth century, originating in Switzerland and Holland. The Friends or Quakers, a similar group, appeared in the seventeenth century in England, under the leadership of George Fox. The Church of the Brethren or Dunkers originated in western Germany in the early eighteenth century. These three groups make up what have come to be called the "historic peace churches." They have taken the Sermon on the Mount seriously, and from the beginning of their history they have taught that all warfare is wrong. While they are not nearly as large in membership as many other denominations, they have exercised an influence down through the centuries which is far out of proportion to their numbers. Since this book deals with the doctrine of nonresistance as held by the Mennonite Church, the teachings of the early Mennonite leaders and the history of the church as it relates to peace and war are presented in the following chapters. In Chapters VIII and IX some reference is made to the Friends and the Brethren, comparing their views and practices with those of the Mennonites.

The Church in Recent Times

The larger Christian denominations of today, and many of the smaller ones, have a heritage which comes down from sixteenth-century Catholicism, Lutheranism, or Calvinism. Four centuries of time have brought many modifications in their teachings and practices, to be sure. In the past one hundred and twenty-five years, for example, many of the churches have even been influenced by nonresistant or pacifist teachings of various kinds.[39] Nevertheless, in the many wars of the past four centuries the different church groups have taken their part much in the way that their teachings as described above would lead one to expect. In 1917, during the World War, William T. Russell, the Catholic bishop of South Carolina, expressed the Catholic idea of the "just war" in much the same way that Augustine and Thomas Aquinas had done in the Middle Ages:

God is the author of every just government, and is its sanction. From him all powers derive their authority .... The President and Congress rule by this divine right ... the citizen is bound to uphold

[39] Chapter IX is a discussion of modern pacifism, including the role of the churches.

the authority of the state in obeying its laws and by defending it if need be with his life against an unjust attack.[40]

About the same time the Lutheran point of view was expressed in a most vivid fashion by Frederick Naumann, a Lutheran of Germany:

> The Gospel is one of the standards of our life, but not the only standard. Not our entire morality is rooted in the Gospel, but only a part of it. Besides the Gospel there are demands of power and right without which human society cannot exist.... The state rests upon entirely different impulses and instincts from those which are cultivated by Jesus .... All constructions which attempt to explain the state from brotherly love to our neighbor are, considered historically, so much empty talk .... Not every doing of one's duty is Christian .... Hence we do not consult Jesus, when we are concerned with things which belong to the domain of the construction of the state and of Political Economy.[41]

The editor of *The Lutheran*, an American journal, expressed a similar view as follows:

> The church has the right to plead with a free people that war be avoided .... But when war is declared, it must keep silent. It must submit to the powers that be. The church is subject to the state in the temporal sphere just as every citizen must be ... it must say, "I submit to the authority of the powers that be." The church may be called upon to suffer for her convictions, but it may never be a rebel.[42]

Presbyterian and other Protestant ministers, however, were not inclined to see any conflict between the ethics of the church and those of the state. Theoretically, no doubt, they believed in the separation of church and state, this having been an accepted American idea for over a century. But in practice many of them thought of the church and the state as united for the promotion of the war, much as Calvin did in the sixteenth century. George F. Pentecost, a Presbyterian minister, put it as follows:

[40] Ray H. Abrams, *Preachers Present Arms* (New York, 1933), 73.

[41] *Ibid.*, 71, 72.

[42] *Ibid.*, 73.

We are fighting not only for our country, and for the democracy . . . of the world, . . . but for the Kingdom of God . . . . If this is God's war we should have Christian soldiers to fight it . . . . [We cannot] draw any line between Christianity and patriotism . . . . The two go together . . . . The Church of Christ itself must enter the war . . . . Every Presbyterian church should be a recruiting station.[43]

Having gone this far it was not difficult to take the next step and argue that the Sermon on the Mount itself condones war. W. Douglas Mackenzie of Hartford Seminary declared that:

. . . nowhere has the Sermon on the Mount, the embodiment of the Spirit of Christ, exercised more visible and amazing power than in the matter of war.

. . . this war, when carried by the Allies and America to the right issue, will be another proof of the divine power of the Sermon on the Mount.[44]

E. I. Bosworth, the dean of Oberlin College and a congregational minister, spoke of the love and friendship with which the soldier slays his enemy:

The Christian soldier in friendship wounds the enemy. In friendship he kills the enemy. In friendship he receives the wound of the enemy. He keeps his friendly heart while the enemy is killing him. His heart never consigns the enemy to hell. He never hates. After he has wounded the enemy he hurries to his side at the earliest possible moment with all the friendly ministration possible . . . with an invincible hope that sometime . . . he and his enemy shall find common ground . . . in some great enterprise of God.[45]

In comparing statements such as these with the simple teachings of the New Testament, and with the testimony of the church fathers and the practice of the early church, one must agree that the title which Heering used for his book[46] which describes the changed attitude of Christianity toward war, was well chosen. Certainly this great change has been nothing short of a "fall of Christianity."

It must not be forgotten, however, that through all the centuries there have always been some Christians who have re-

[43] Ibid., 72, 73. [45] Ibid., 67.

[44] Ibid., 66. [46] G. J. Heering, The Fall of Christianity (London, 1930).

fused to bow their knees to the god of war. In our day there are many Christians, from all denominations, who refuse to take part in military service. Following the first World War the American churches, for example, generally recognized that they had been too much carried away by a militaristic spirit which was foreign to the spirit of Christ. As a result, a much larger percentage of the American ministers, and of their church members, were pacifists in the second World War than in the first. Chapters V to VII tell the story of the Mennonite peace testimony. Chapter IX speaks of pacifism, especially in recent times.

SELECT BIBLIOGRAPHY

The best authority on the attitude of the Christian Church toward war from its beginnings through the time of Constantine is C. J. Cadoux, *The Early Christian Attitude to War* (London, 1919). An earlier work by Adolph Harnack, *Militia Christi* (Tuebingen, 1905), treats the subject without bringing out the opposition of the early church to war as sharply as Cadoux does. Harnack's research did not go as far as that of Cadoux, however, and Harnack himself in 1921 cited Cadoux's work as "the authoritative conclusion of the investigations made on this question." For a brief discussion of the literature on the subject see Edward Yoder, "The Early Christians and War," *Gospel Herald* (Scottdale, Pa., Oct. 21, 1937), 30:651-56. Ernst Troeltsch, *The Social Teaching of the Christian Churches*, 2 vols. (London, 1931), is an excellent work covering the entire field of church history from the early beginnings to modern times. The comparison of the views of the various denominations and sects which have developed during the history of the church is very enlightening. G. J. Heering, *The Fall of Christianity* (London, 1930), covers in a brief way the material treated by both Cadoux and Troeltsch. Also helpful is Percy Hartill (Ed.), *Into the Way of Peace* (London, 1941). Ray H. Abrams, *Preachers Present Arms* (Scottdale, Pa.: Rev. Ed., 1968), is a discussion of the attitude of the American clergy during the World War. Umphrey Lee, *The Historic Church and Modern Pacifism* (New York, 1943), also covers the entire period of church history, leaning on Harnack, whom he considers the standard authority rather than Cadoux, for the early church period. Covering the entire field from ancient to modern times is R. H. Bainton, *Christian Attitudes Toward War and Peace:* A Historical Survey and Critical Re-evaluation (Nashville, 1960).

5. The Mennonites in Europe

The Sixteenth Century

The Mennonite Church was founded in Zurich, Switzerland, in 1525, by a group of earnest Bible students, known as the Swiss Brehren. They were commonly called **Anabaptists** because of their practice of adult, as opposed to infant, baptism. As these men searched the Scriptures, they were convinced that not only the Catholic but also the Protestant churches of their day failed to meet the standards of the New Testament. In these churches children were baptized in infancy and became members of the church as a matter of course. Consequently there were, without doubt, many members of the church who had no definite experience of regeneration. The result of this policy, as pointed out in Chapter IV, was that all of the churches compromised greatly on the ethical teachings of the New Testament. This was especially true in the case of the doctrine of nonresistance.

These early Mennonite founders believed, however, that the experience of regeneration was necessary for membership in the kingdom of God. This meant that membership in the church should be restricted to regenerated believers who came into the church voluntarily, and who sought to obey the commands of the Scriptures. The early Mennonite Church, therefore, was a brotherhood of regenerated believers who accepted the Word of God as the only rule of faith and practice. Great emphasis was placed on discipleship: a literal obedience to the commands of Christ, and faithfully following His steps. They searched the Scriptures diligently, and the way of life which they found there they lived within the brotherhood, and taught in their meetings, as well as in their missionary witness.

Among the doctrines which they stressed were freedom of conscience, the separation of church and state, and nonresistance. They believed, indeed, that the state was necessary and ordained of God for the maintenance of order in the unregenerate society of this world. But they also believed that according to the Scriptures the Christian could have no part in the use of force, whether as a soldier in the army or as a magistrate in the civil government. The use of the sword, the exercise of vengeance, and the taking of human life were strictly forbidden to the disciple of Christ.

In 1524 Conrad Grebel, the first leader of the Swiss Brethren, stressed the difference between the old and the new covenants, and said:

True, believing Christians are as sheep in the midst of wolves. . . . They . . . must reach the fatherland of eternal rest, not by overcoming bodily enemies with the sword, but by overcoming spiritual foes. They use neither the worldly sword nor engage in war, since among them taking human life has ceased entirely, for we are no longer under the old covenant.[1]

Felix Manz, a close associate of Grebel, said in 1525: "No Christian smites with the sword nor resists evil."[2] The first Mennonite confession of faith adopted by the Swiss Brethren at Schleitheim in 1527 says Christians must lay down "weapons of force, such as sword, armor and the like, together with all their use, whether for the protection of friends or against personal enemies."[3] In 1532 a spokesman of the Swiss Brethren in the Canton of Berne cited Matthew 5 as evidence that "Christ forbids the believers all use of force. He says that rather than go to law they should permit others to defraud them, they should not strive with anyone and should give the cloak to him who takes away their coat."[4] The Hutterian confession of faith of 1545 says: "A Christian has no part in war nor does he wield the sword to execute vengeance."[5] Menno Simons has given a

---

[1] John Horsch, *The Principle of Nonresistance as Held by the Mennonite Church* (Scottdale, Pa., 1951), 7.
[2] *Ibid.*, 7, 8.
[3] *Ibid.*, 9.
[4] *Ibid.*, 11.
[5] *Ibid.*, 15.

splendid testimony for the doctrine of nonresistance in which he says:

The regenerated do not go to war, nor engage in strife. They are the children of peace who have beaten their swords into plowshares and their spears into pruning hooks, and know of no war . . . . Since we are to be conformed to the image of Christ, how can we then fight our enemies with the sword? . . . Spears and swords of iron we leave to those who, alas, consider human blood and swine's blood of well-nigh equal value . . . .

I am well aware that the tyrants who boast themselves Christians attempt to justify their horrible wars and shedding of blood . . . by referring us to Moses, Joshua, etc. But they do not reflect that Moses and his successors, with their iron sword, have served out their time and that Jesus Christ has now given us a new commandment and has girded our loins with another sword.[6]

The early Mennonites recognized, however, that this nonresistant way of life was possible only for Christian people. In 1532 the Swiss Brethren in Berne said: "The civil government was ordained of God to punish the evildoers and protect the good. . . . Whatever we owe to the government: interest, tithes, taxes and customs, we give willingly and obediently. We obey the government in everything that may be asked of us that is not contrary to the will of God."[7] According to this view the Christian must disobey the government when it requires something which is contrary to the command of Christ. But disobedience is never justified merely as a means of obtaining justice. This position was forcibly stated in 1528 by Hans Marquardt, a minister of the Swiss Brethren:

We confess that civil government is necessary and is a divine appointment . . . and we say with Paul, Romans 13, that every man should be subject and obedient to the higher power, not only to a mild and peaceful but also to a tyrannical government . . . . Therefore all believers, under whatever government they may live, will not complain of heavy burdens, nor will they resist the government or cause trouble or uproar on account of what they may be called upon to bear. In matters of their faith, however, the believers are responsible to God alone to whom they owe greater obedience than to man. Therefore all our brethren esteem their faith in God

[6] *Ibid.*, 18.
[7] *Ibid.*, 11.

through Christ Jesus, our Saviour, as the highest, greatest and most valuable thing, and of this we do not suffer ourselves to be robbed even if our life is at stake. But in matters which do not concern faith and conscience and do not conflict with our duty to God, we are ready to obey the civil government in anything that may be asked of us. And if the government, contrary to justice and right, confiscates our property and reduces us to poverty, we bear and suffer it, since it is impossible for us to escape such oppression without transgression and disturbance.[8]

Since the early Mennonites recognized the need of civil government for the world, but believed that Christians were required to live a life of nonresistance, it was logical that they should believe in the separation of church and state. In 1538 the Swiss Brethren at Berne said: "Christ, in teaching the principle of nonresistance, does not desire to abolish the civil government. He recognizes the rightfulness of the government, but teaches that it should be outside the Christian church."[9] A few years earlier they had said: "We believe the civil government should be separate from the church of Christ and not be established in it."[10] Hans Marquardt had said: "That the Christian should be an executive of the government, or a magistrate, we do not admit."[11] In 1589 the Swiss Brethren of the Canton of Zurich said: "To be a magistrate using the sword and to be a Christian are two things which do not agree."[12] A few years earlier they had said: "We confess that the magistracy, according to Paul's teaching (Rom. 13), is ordained of God. But that a Christian may serve in such an office to exercise vengeance by the sword, for such teaching we demand Scriptural evidence. All believers are pointed to the example of Christ. His apostles have neither engaged in war nor used the sword for punishment but have manifested love toward enemies as well as friends."[13]

These were the views of the sixteenth-century Anabaptists, or Mennonites, as set forth in their confessions of faith and in their writings. A study of the Scriptures had convinced them

8 *Ibid.*, 10.
9 *Ibid.*, 11.
10 *Ibid.*, 11.

11 *Ibid.*, 10.
12 *Ibid.*, 14.
13 *Ibid.*, 13.

that this was the way of true discipleship, and they were willing to follow it even in spite of opposition and persecution. Moreover, in their day when the state church was everywhere in control, the persecution was very great. Most of the early Anabaptist leaders died a martyr's death. In the first ten years more than 5,000 of the Swiss Brethren were put to death in Switzerland and the surrounding territories. Although the last martyr in Switzerland was executed in 1614, the Swiss Mennonites were not fully tolerated until 1815. In Transylvania and Hungary the Hutterian Brethren were still being put to death late in the eighteenth century. The Dutch government granted toleration earlier than the other states, but even in Holland executions continued until 1574. The story of these persecutions has been preserved in the Swiss and Dutch hymnbooks, such as the *Ausbund,* and in T. J. van Braght's *Martyrs' Mirror.*[14]

In spite of persecutions, however, the early Mennonites remained true to their faith to such an extent that even their enemies were impressed. One contemporary Catholic writer, Christoph Andreas Fischer, said of them in 1603:

> Among all the heresies and sects which have their origin from Luther, to the destruction of the Catholic church, not a one has a better appearance and greater external holiness than the Anabaptists. Other sects are for the most part riotous, bloodthirsty and given over to carnal lusts; not so the Anabaptists. They call each other brothers and sisters; they use no profanity nor unkind language; they use no weapons of defense. They are temperate in eating and drinking, they use no vain display of clothes . . . . They do not go to law before judicial courts, but bear everything patiently, as they say, in the Holy Spirit. Who would suppose that under this sheep's clothing only ravening wolves are hidden?[15]

In 1582 Franz Agricola, another Catholic writer, put it as follows:

> Among the existing heretical sects there is none whose adherents lead in appearance a more modest, better, or more pious

---

[14] The *Ausbund* was first published in 1564, and many subsequent editions have been printed. This hymnbook is still used in the services of the Old Order Amish churches. The first edition of the *Martyrs' Mirror* was published in Holland in 1660; the latest edition at Scottdale, Pa., in 1950.

[15] R. J. Smithson, *The Anabaptists* (London, 1935), 116, 117.

life than the Anabaptists. As concerns their outward public life they are irreproachable. No lying, deception, swearing, strife, harsh language, no intemperate eating and drinking, no outward personal display is found or is discernible among them, but only humility, patience, uprightness, meekness, honesty, temperance, and straightforwardness in such measure that one would suppose that they have the Holy Spirit of God.[16]

The Netherlands[17]

These were the qualities which characterized the early Mennonites and which continue to characterize many of them today, after four hundred years of history. As time went on, however, some of the European Mennonites began to depart from their original faith. This tendency, which first manifested itself among the churches of Holland in the late seventeenth century, continued among them to such an extent that by the end of the nineteenth century the Dutch Mennonite Church was something quite different from the Bible-reading and Bible-believing nonresistant Anabaptist brotherhood of the sixteenth century.

Apparently a combination of causes was responsible for this change. First was the influence of the liberal religious movement known as Socinianism. Although Faustus Socinus (1539-1604), the founder of this movement, opposed war, his system of thought lacked certain elements which are basic to Mennonite theology, such as the pre-existence and essential deity of Christ, as well as the orthodox view of the atonement. Some of the Mennonites came under the direct influence of Socinianism, but others did so indirectly through their association with a religious group known as the Collegiants, and by their attendance at the schools of the Remonstrants. The Dutch Mennonites had no schools of their own and many of their ministers received their education in these schools where some of them lost whatever they had once had of original Mennonitism. Among other

---

[16] *Ibid.,* 117, 118.

[17] This account of the later development in the Netherlands, Switzerland, and Germany is based largely on C. H. Smith, *The Story of the Mennonites* (Newton, Kansas).

things, their nonresistance gave way to a humanistic sort of pacifism, and then in course of time even this was lost.

In the second place, the Dutch Mennonites became wealthy, and their wealth seems to have had a devitalizing effect upon their religious life. As their wealth increased their concern for the purity of the Christian brotherhood declined. Sons of wealthy Mennonite families married into non-Mennonite families and thus became more interested in the social life of the urban aristocracy than in the solidarity of the Mennonite community. In the third place, the growth of religious toleration in the Netherlands seems to have led to a toleration of non-Mennonite ideas and practices by the Mennonites themselves. In the eighteenth century they began to compromise on the principle of nonresistance. During the Napoleonic wars a number of Mennonites served in the army; and this occurred again during the trouble with Belgium in 1830. As late as 1850, however, most of the leaders were opposed to voluntary service in the army. At that time it was still possible to secure exemption from service by hiring a substitute. But when the new military law was passed by the Dutch parliament in 1898 without any exceptions or special privileges for Mennonites, even the leaders failed to offer any objections.

As a result of these changes and compromises the Mennonite Church of Holland at the beginning of the first World War was something quite different from the nonresistant Mennonite brotherhood of the sixteenth century. In theology it was largely liberal and unitarian. Socially it was largely urban, capitalistic, and aristocratic; and ethically many of its members had compromised the high standards of the New Testament. A Mennonite has served as governor-general of the Dutch East Indies, and others have been members of the supreme court. Usually there have been a number of Mennonites in both houses of the legislature. A deacon of the Mennonite Church at The Hague was at one time minister of the navy; and during the first World War the burgomaster of Amsterdam was a Mennonite. These political Mennonites had little interest in the historic Mennonite principle of nonresistance. Many of the Mennonites seldom attended church services. The membership of the church itself had greatly declined. At the beginning of the eighteenth century it had stood at 200,000, but it steadily declined from that time until in 1820 there were only 30,000 Mennonites in Holland. Except for a slight increase in membership the above describes the status of the Dutch Mennonites up to the time of the first World War. Beginning about 1915, however, important new trends became evident, which within one generation had developed into a movement bringing significant changes in the life of the Dutch Mennonites. This newer development is discussed in Chapter VII.

Switzerland

If the Mennonites of Holland eventually suffered from too much toleration, the Mennonites of Switzerland certainly suffered from too much persecution over a long period of years. By 1815, when the Swiss government finally granted complete religious toleration, only a few Mennonites remained. They had paid a heavy price for their faith. Most of those who had not been put to death were driven out, eventually finding homes in Alsace, in the Palatinate, and many in America. Those who remained were driven up the mountains into the poorest lands. Years of persecution had developed within them a spirit of self-depreciation from which they never fully recovered. In 1968 the baptized membership of the Mennonite Church in Switzerland was 2,500. The Swiss Mennonites are poor; they had no meetinghouses until recently; and even now some hold their meetings in private homes. Their church and institutional life is meager. Through the years the Swiss Mennonites held more closely to their nonresistant faith than did their brethren in Holland. But Switzerland also adopted conscription in the nineteenth century, and the Mennonites who did not emigrate eventually accepted military service, although they had the privilege of choosing so-called noncombatant service, which for many years most of them did.

Germany

The Anabaptists or Mennonites originated in Switzerland and in the Netherlands, and from here they spread to other parts of Europe. By the middle of the sixteenth century Mennonites from Holland had migrated into certain parts of northwest Germany and also into the Vistula delta. These migrants frequently left their old homes because of persecution, and were welcomed to their new homes by the authorities because of their worth as farmers. They were especially welcome in the Vistula delta, where they rendered a great service in draining the swamplands and rendering them fit for agriculture.

It is well to remember that in the sixteenth and seventeenth centuries the Mennonites were seldom asked to perform actual military service, because in that time such service was performed by professional, hired soldiers. The persecution which the Mennonites suffered at that time was due to their religious and social views as a whole, including their nonresistance and their views on the separation of church and state, but not because they refused conscription, since there was no conscription. Toward the close of the eighteenth century, however, conscription began to be introduced in a small way; and then with the coming of Napoleon to power after 1799 it became the universal practice on the continent of Europe. As the pressure of militarism became greater in the late eighteenth century, those Mennonites who took their nonresistance most seriously removed to new homes where their faith and their way of life would be respected. In the 1780's the Mennonites in eastern Prussia were required to give financial support to a military academy. They also suffered other forms of oppression, such as restrictions in land ownership. As a result of this situation large numbers of the Mennonites from eastern Prussia moved to Russia in 1788-1820, where they were exempt from military service.

No doubt the Mennonites who migrated to Russia were those who took their nonresistance most seriously. Nevertheless, those who remained in eastern Prussia and the Vistula delta did not give up their faith without a struggle. During the

Napoleonic wars, for example, when one of the members of the Elbing congregation volunteered for service, and fought at Waterloo, he was excommunicated. Following the enactment of the Prussian universal military training law in 1814 the Mennonites appealed for exemption, which was granted, however, only on condition that they pay a heavy tax instead of the personal service. This was a special tax in addition to that paid for the support of the military academy. In the Revolution of 1848, when the Frankfort Assembly drew up a constitution for the proposed new German confederation, a non-Mennonite delegate from Danzig suggested a provision for the exemption of Mennonites from military service. Astonishing as it may seem, however, a Mennonite delegate from Crefeld, in northwestern Germany, opposed the suggestion, with the result that it was turned down. Since the proposed German confederation did not materialize, the new constitution never went into effect. But from what happened at the Assembly it is clear that the Mennonites of the lower Rhine, who were rapidly losing their nonresistance, were also helping to make it more difficult for their brethren of northeastern Germany to maintain their faith.

In the seventeenth century large numbers of persecuted Mennonites had also moved from Switzerland into the Palatinate and other parts of southern Germany. They continued to suffer many hardships here, however, both from persecution and from the wars at the end of the century. As a result, many of these South German Mennonites moved to America in the first half of the eighteenth century. As the pressure of militarism increased, and opportunities for migration opened up, the Mennonites of all parts of Germany continued to migrate to America and to Russia during the late eighteenth and the nineteenth centuries.

The end of nonresistance among the Prussian and all of the North German Mennonites came following the founding of the North German Confederation in 1867. In that year a new universal military service law was enacted, with no exemption for Mennonites. After the law was passed the Mennonites appealed to Berlin, but the only concession they received was a cabinet order, on March 3, 1868, permitting noncombatant military service for those who had scruples against regular service. After the cabinet order was issued many of those Mennonites who were genuinely nonresistant migrated to Russia and America. As a rule, those Mennonites from all parts of Germany who were true to their nonresistant faith were among those who migrated. Those who remained, at first accepted noncombatant military service. This was especially true of the North German Mennonites after the cabinet order of 1868. It soon became clear, however, that there was no difference in principle between noncombatant and regular service. As a result, the Mennonites of Germany gradually gave up all objection to war, and in the World War practically all Mennonites in the army were in the regular service. Only a few chose noncombatant service provided for by law. Thus, for more than a century, the process of compromise went on until it culminated in the almost complete abandonment of the nonresistant faith by the Mennonites of Germany. Before the opening of the second World War, in fact, the *Vereinigung der Mennonitengemeinden im Deutschen Reich,* the official conference which included the churches of northern Germany and the Palatinate, had taken official action repudiating the nonresistant position. From this experience it seems clear that, once a nonresistant people compromise their faith to the extent of accepting noncombatant military service, it will be only a matter of time until they lose their faith altogether. In 1968 the Mennonite population of Germany, including children, was about 12,000.

France

The number of Mennonites in France has never been large. The records show that a number of Anabaptists suffered persecution in Alsace in the sixteenth century. During the Thirty Years' War (1618-48), however, some Mennonites from Switzerland migrated into this region. At the beginning of the eighteenth century others moved into the principality of Montbeliard where some of their descendants are living today. When France introduced universal military training in the nineteenth century, however, many of the Mennonites emigrated. The French military service laws after 1870 made no provision whatever for conscientious objectors. In 1968 the number of Mennonites in France, including Alsace, was about 2,700.

Russia[18]

The story of the Mennonites in Russia begins in 1770 when a group of persecuted Hutterites moved from Wallachia to a new home on the river Desna in the Province of Tscherinogov in western Russia. They were followed in 1788 by Mennonites from Prussia, who also settled in South Russia at the special invitation of Catherine the Great, who needed thrifty farmers to build up the country around the Black Sea in the southern Ukraine. As a special inducement, Catherine promised these settlers religious toleration and military exemption. This was a welcome relief to the Prussian Mennonites, whose nonresistance was being severely tested at that time, and so they began to migrate at once. In the course of time about 8,000 Mennonites migrated from the Vistula delta to South Russia. By 1874 the natural increase had been such that the Mennonite population in Russia had reached the figure of 45,000.

When these people came to Russia they were guaranteed complete exemption from military service. This policy of exemption was continued according to promise until 1870. In that year, however, the Russian government issued a ukase abolishing all special privileges to non-Russian settlers in South Russia, including the Mennonite exemption from military service. The Mennonites were given ten years to adjust themselves to the new order; after 1880 they were to be included in the universal military service program of Russia.

The imperial edict caused great concern among the Mennonites, and from the beginning some of them considered the situation serious enough to warrant emigration. Numerous official delegations were sent to St. Petersburg from 1871 to 1873 in an appeal to the Russian government to withdraw its

---

[18] This account is based on the two works of C. H. Smith, *The Coming of the Russian Mennonites* (Berne, Ind., 1927), and *The Story of the Mennonites* (Newton, Kans., 1950).

order regarding military service. But as these efforts proved fruitless, an emigration to America, which began in a small way in 1873, actually assumed mass proportions in the following year. In 1873 the total population of the Mennonites in Russia was 45,000, and before the migration movement was concluded one third of this number had gone to the prairie regions of the United States and Canada.

The Russian government now became alarmed, realizing too late that it had not taken Mennonite nonresistance seriously enough. Determined to hold as many of them as possible the Tsar sent General von Totleben to the colonies in April, 1874. After acquainting himself with the faith and the convictions of the Mennonites he offered them civilian service of an entirely nonmilitary character as an alternative to military service. Services he suggested were forestry, fire fighting, and ship building. The Mennonites inquired whether ship building would have to do with warships. He replied that it would have to do only with small wooden ships used for civilian purposes. The Mennonites then informed General Totleben that if this program would be carried out the majority of the Mennonites would remain in Russia.

In 1875, therefore, an official *ukase* was published announcing the service program for the Mennonites as promised by Totleben the year before. The term of service was to be of the same length as that for the men in the army; and those in the service were to be so grouped as to enable them to maintain worship services after the manner of their faith. After the completion of their term of service the Mennonites would be placed into the reserves, liable to be called again in case of war. When the program was actually inaugurated in 1880 it was confined to forestry alone. In June of that year the ministry of the interior announced its readiness to place the Mennonite selectees into forestry work in the provinces of South Russia, providing the churches would undertake to house, clothe, and feed the men. If the churches would undertake this program the men could be placed into six groups, so that in the course of three years six camps would need to be built. In case the churches were unwilling to undertake this program it would be necessary to place the men in smaller groups, more widely scattered and in distant provinces. The Mennonites accepted this challenge and proceeded at once to organize a forestry service commission to carry out their part of the program.

It will be seen that the program here outlined was similar to the Civilian Public Service program in the United States in the second World War. In the Russian forestry service the government provided tools and paid the men twenty kopeks (about ten cents) per working day. The churches housed, clothed, and fed the men. To administer the program the Mennonites organized an official forestry service commission. The chief task of the service was to plant and cultivate forests in the steppes of South Russia. The term of service of each man was four years. The forestry work itself was under the direction of the state's technical service, while the life of the men, apart from this, was entirely under the direction of the Mennonite forestry service commission. Apart from the technical service, the tools, and the twenty kopeks per day for labor, the entire cost of the project was met by the church. As there were no abandoned CCC camps available, as in the United States in 1940, the service commission built its own camps, fed and clothed the foresters, heated and cared for the buildings, and assumed all the expenses involved. The commission appointed a superintendent and a minister for each camp, the former to be in charge of the business and administrative work, and the latter to administer the spiritual and educational needs of the campers. The money was raised by the churches by more or less voluntary contributions, although an allotment plan was worked out to distribute the burden as equitably as possible.

For some years after 1880 the average enrollment in the camps was about 400, with an annual maintenance cost of $35,000 (70,000 rubles), not counting the original cost of the buildings. Later the enrollment increased until in 1913, the year before the beginning of the World War, the men in the service numbered about 1,000, with an annual expense of $175,000. When the war began the demands for service increased, and during the course of the war some 12,000 Mennonites were engaged in government service, about 6,000 in the forestry, and another 6,000 in the hospital and sanitary service. The latter formed complete hospital units of its own who gathered soldiers from the battlefields and took them back to hospitals, on hospital trains manned by the Mennonites. The expense of all this service was met by the Mennonites themselves. During 1917 alone the Mennonites contributed over $1,500,000 for the support of their men in these two forms of service.

Following the Communist Revolution many Mennonites were driven out of Russia or "liquidated." Hence the story of conscientious objection in that country ends with the coming of the Communist regime. The Soviet government did, however, continue recognition of CO's in principle until about 1935, and granted some form of alternative state service to eligible CO's on individual application quite regularly down to 1925. Thereafter it was made increasingly difficult, but a few cases were reported as late as 1935 by Mennonite refugees reaching Germany in 1943-45. The treatment varied from one case to another. In some cases the CO's were reported to have been shot, and in others the alternative service was practically the same as the forced labor of the concentration camps. The policy of the Soviet government in the second World War of not conscripting German colonists because of their political unreliability, which enabled many Mennonites to escape military service, was something quite different. The action of some Mennonites of the Ukraine in organizing a self-defense corps (*Selbstschutz*) in 1918 with the help of officers of the German army of occupation, followed by some actual fighting between armed Mennonites and groups of Russian bandits, no doubt increased the difficulties for Mennonite CO's.

From the above brief sketch it will be seen that, until the middle of the eighteenth century, the Mennonites of Europe, on the whole, maintained their historic antiwar testimony. In some cases even then, particularly in Holland, they had departed from their original faith. Thereafter, with the growth of the universal compulsory military service systems, the Mennonites of Europe gradually receded from their historic position until by the close of the nineteenth century they had accepted military service, with few exceptions, in all the European countries save Russia. This experience of the European Mennonites is evidence of the vigilance which is required if the nonresistant faith is to be maintained in our day. The forces of nationalism and militarism had grown so strong that the nonresistant testimony was all but lost among the Mennonites of western Europe. By the opening of the twentieth century only in Russia, in the United States, and in Canada were the Mennonites exempted from all military service, although in Switzerland and in Germany they were allowed the privilege of so-called noncombatant service.

SELECT BIBLIOGRAPHY

The best brief treatise on the nonresistance of the European Mennonites is John Horsch, *The Principle of Nonresistance as Held by the Mennonite Church* (Scottdale, Pa., 1951). Horsch's larger work, *Mennonites in Europe* (Scottdale, Pa., 1942), should also be consulted. C. H. Smith, *The Story of the Mennonites* (Newton, Kans.,1950), is the standard general work on Mennonite history. C. H. Smith, *The Coming of the Russian Mennonites* (Berne, Ind., 1927), is an excellent treatment of the Russian story. The story of the beginning of the Russian forestry service is told in Jacob Sudermann, "The Origin of Mennonite State Service in Russia, 1870-1880," *Mennonite Quarterly Review* (Goshen, Ind., January, 1943), 17:23-46. J. B. Toews, *Lost Fatherland* (Scottdale, 1967) is the story of nonresistance and emigration following the Revolution to 1927. C. H. Smith, *Christian Peace: Four Hundred Years of Mennonite Peace Principles and Practice* (n.p. 1938) is a pamphlet covering the entire history of the church. R. J. Smithson, *The Anabaptists* (London, 1935) is helpful. Important books are Robert Friedmann, *Mennonite Piety Through the Centuries* (Scottdale, Pa., 1949); H. S. Bender, *Conrad Grebel, The Founder of the Swiss Brethren* (Scottdale, Pa., 1950); F. H. Littell, *The Anabaptist View of the Church* (Beacon, 1958); and Guy F. Hershberger (ed.), *The Recovery of the Anabaptist Vision* (Scottdale, Pa., 1957). The following articles are valuable: H. J. Hillerbrand, "The Anabaptist View of the State," *Mennonite Quarterly Review* (1958), 32:83-110; "Conscientious Objector," "Nonresistance," "State, Anabaptist-Mennonite Attitude Toward," and other articles in *The Mennonite Encyclopedia* (Scottdale, 1955-1959).

6. The Mennonites in America

As mentioned in the previous chapter, many of those European Mennonites who were most concerned for the preservation of the nonresistant faith migrated to America. This was especially true after the introduction of universal military service by Napoleon early in the nineteenth century. By far the largest Mennonite migration prior to the first World War was that from Russia in the 1870's, and this was brought about almost entirely by the Russian threat to the nonresistant way of life of the Mennonite people.[1] Prior to the time of Napoleon the preservation of nonresistance was perhaps not as important a cause of Mennonite migration as it was after this time, but it was always one of the causes.

The French and Indian War and the American Revolution

The first permanent Mennonite settlement was made at Germantown in Pennsylvania, in 1683, by a few families of Dutch ancestry who came from Crefeld in Germany. In 1702 a few families from Germantown settled at Skippack in what is now Montgomery County. In 1709 a few Mennonite immigrants from the Palatinate came to the same region. In 1710 a group of Swiss immigrants settled on Pequea Creek in what is now Lancaster County. These settlements were the beginning of a steady immigration from the Palatinate and Switzerland which continued until by 1776 there were from 5,000 to 7,500 Mennonites living in eastern Pennsylvania. By this time there also were Mennonite settlements in Maryland and Virginia.

The Pennsylvania Mennonites took their nonresistance seriously. As they saw the French and Indian War approaching they took steps to provide literature which would prepare their youth to meet the test successfully. In 1742 they published a

---

[1] Migrations since the first World War are discussed in Chapter VII.

new edition of the old Mennonite hymnbook, the *Ausbund*,[2] which contained many hymns telling the story of their Anabaptist forefathers who had suffered for their nonresistant faith. In 1748 they published a German translation of the Dutch *Martyrs' Mirror*,[3] which contains a full account of the Mennonites in Europe who had suffered for this faith. In a letter to their brethren in Holland they explained why they desired to publish this book. They said: "As the flames of war appear to mount higher, no man can tell whether the cross and persecution of the defenseless Christians will not soon come, and it is therefore of importance to prepare ourselves for such circumstances with patience and resignation, and to use all available means that can encourage steadfastness and strengthen faith. Our whole community have manifested a unanimous desire for a German translation of the Bloody Theatre of Thieleman Jans van Braght, especially since in this community there is a very great number of newcomers, for which we consider it to be of the greatest importance that they should become acquainted with the trustworthy witnesses who have walked in the way of truth, and sacrificed their lives for it."[4] This edition of the *Martyrs' Mirror*, containing more than 1,400 pages, was the largest book printed in the English colonies before the Revolution.

In 1754 the war actually came to Pennsylvania and continued at intervals until 1763. Although there is no record of any Mennonite using force against the Indians, many Mennonites did suffer at the hands of the Indians after the war began. In 1757 the members of the Jacob Hochstettler family in Berks County, Pennsylvania, were either killed or taken prisoner. Mennonites in Virginia suffered in a similar way, one entire family having been murdered.[5] In all of these trials, however, the Mennonites seem to have remained true to their faith and did not use force to protect themselves.

---

[2] *Ausbund* (Germantown, Pa., 1742).

[3] T. J. van Braght, *Der Blutige Schau- Platz oder Martyrer-Spiegel der Tauffs Gesinnten oder Wehrlosen-Christen* (Ephrata, Pa., 1748).

[4] S. W. Pennypacker, *Historical and Biographical Sketches* (Philadelphia, 1883), 193-94.

[5] W. J. Bender, "Pacifism Among the Mennonites, Amish Mennonites, and Schwenkfelders of Pennsylvania to 1783," *Mennonite Quarterly Review* (July, 1927), 33, 34.

In the United States the government has always maintained a reasonably liberal policy with respect to conscientious objectors, although not as liberal as that of Canada. During the American Revolution there was something approaching modern conscription in the three colonies where the Mennonites lived. Citizens were required to attend military musters and join companies of soldiers, known as associations, which were organized to fight the British. In all three colonies, however, it was possible to remain a non-associator because of religious objections or for other reasons by paying a fine or providing a substitute. In Virginia in 1777 a law was actually passed which exempted Mennonites from military service when called, but put them under obligation to provide for a substitute who was to be paid for by a levy on the membership of the entire church. The public was sometimes less tolerant of the conscientious objector than was the government. Frequently a great amount of public pressure was brought to bear upon citizens to become associators, and when nonresistant people refused to enroll considerable feeling was aroused against them. In Pennsylvania there were actual cases of mob violence so that the civil authorities had to warn the public to respect the consciences of these people.

The Pennsylvania Assembly and the Continental Congress both declared their readiness to respect the religious beliefs of the nonresistant people, but at the same time urged them to *"contribute liberally,* in this time of universal calamity, to the relief of their distressed brethren in the several colonies, and to do all other services to their oppressed country which they can, consistently with their religious principles."[6] To this appeal the Pennsylvania Mennonites responded, jointly with the Dunkers, in a petition which was read in the Pennsylvania Assembly on November 7, 1775. The petition thanked the Assembly for its good advice and for its liberality in granting freedom of conscience. It said the Mennonites and Dunkers were ready at all times to help those in need or distress, "it being our principle to feed the hungry and to give the thirsty drink; we have dedi-

---

[6] *Colonial Records* (Harrisburg, Pa., 1852), 10:293.

cated ourselves to serve all men in every thing that can be helpful to the preservation of men's lives, but we find no freedom
in giving, or doing, or assisting in any thing by which men's
lives are destroyed or hurt."[7]

As this statement says, Mennonites have always been ready
to offer their goods for the relief of suffering, and they must
have done much for this cause during the American Revolution. We know, for example, that a Mennonite preacher, John
Baer, and his wife, helped to nurse wounded men at Ephrata in
Pennsylvania. As a result they received infections and both of
them died early in 1778. Individuals and congregations did
what they could, independently, and in their various communities. One writer says: "We may be sure from what we know of
their character and customs, that many a weary straggler, in-
valided soldier or destitute refugee received aid and comfort
from the rich farms and hearths of the Pennsylvania pacifists"
in the vicinities where the fighting took place.[8]

The Pennsylvania Mennonites were united in their stand
against military service, and in favor of giving relief to the suffering. On the question of paying war taxes to the Pennsylvania
government, however, they were not entirely agreed. Some paid
the tax but others refused to do so. Then when the government
seized the property of those who refused to pay the tax, the
latter allowed them to take it without resistance. The Pennsylvania Mennonites also refused to take the oath of allegiance
to the revolutionary government, because the taking of a legal
oath is also contrary to their principles. But even if the affirmation had been permitted in place of the oath the Mennonites
would have hesitated to take it. They had earlier made a
promise of loyalty to the king, and to renounce this promise now
seemed like dishonesty to them. Furthermore, if they renounced
allegiance to the king they believed they would be taking part in
revolution and would be involved in war, which would be contrary to their nonresistant principles. Fortunately, the Penn-

---

[7] *Pennsylvania Archives, Eighth Series,* 8:7349. A copy of a contemporary broadside
containing the petition is in the Goshen College Library.

[8] W. J. Bender, *loc. cit.* (October, 1927), 25, 46.

sylvania officials generally understood the principles of the Mennonites and other nonresistant people well enough to know that they had nothing to fear from their hesitancy to take the oath. As a result they were lenient toward them and the law was not strictly enforced. In the larger Mennonite communities the Mennonites were so well understood that they were seldom molested. In some of the more isolated communities, however, where their principles were not so well understood, they were frequently mistreated by local communities, and even by mobs.

War is always a trying experience for nonresistant people. In such a time of stress there is naturally a temptation to compromise one's faith. No doubt there were some Mennonites who did not always act consistently with their faith during the American Revolution. But there are good reasons to believe that most of them endeavored to do so. At any rate, in those days the Mennonites and Dunkers made a great impression on Benjamin Rush, the famous physician of Philadelphia. In 1789 Dr. Rush made a reference to the nonresistant groups in Pennsylvania in which he said: "Perhaps those German sects of Christians among us who refuse to bear arms for the purpose of shedding human blood, may be preserved by divine providence as the center of a circle, which shall gradually embrace all nations of the earth in a perpetual treaty of friendship and peace."[9] This dream has not been realized, of course, but it should be a challenge to the Mennonite and other nonresistant people to be true to their faith at all times, whether this circle be large or small.

Mennonites in the Civil War

The first experience of the American people with actual conscription came during the Civil War. Interestingly enough, since it was a civil war, there were two nations for the time being, and two systems of national conscription. Both in the North and in the South, however, the draft was slow in getting under way and at no time was it an absolute draft, since it was always

[9] Benjamin Rush, *An Account of the Manners of the German Inhabitants of Pennsylvania* (Philadelphia, 1875), 62.

possible, at least theoretically, to secure exemption through the hiring of a substitute. Compared with the Civil War, American conscription in the second World War was a streamlined affair, indeed.

In the North the first limited draft, inaugurated in 1862, was administered by the states. In 1863 Congress placed the administration of conscription in the hands of the federal government. The law did not mention conscientious objectors, but it did provide two methods by which anyone might be exempted from the draft: (1) by furnishing an acceptable substitute, (2) by paying $300 "for the procuration of such substitute."[10] Among the conscientious objectors, however, there was considerable objection to this act, since the only way of securing exemption was to hire a substitute, either directly or indirectly. It did not seem consistent to hire another man to do that which one could not conscientiously do himself.

Due to this opposition, no doubt, the new draft act passed early in 1864 contained a section dealing specifically with conscientious objectors. It specified three alternatives to military service available to the CO: (1) assignment to duty in hospitals for the care of sick and wounded soldiers, (2) assignment to duty in the care of the freedmen, (3) payment of a commutation fee of $300 to be applied to the benefit of sick and wounded soldiers. In actual practice it seems that only the last of these three alternatives was used.

During the Civil War the official position of the Mennonite Church in America on war and military service remained true to its historic tradition. On the other hand, it is also true that at this time the church was less effective in its teaching program than it had been in the eighteenth century. The period prior to the Civil War was one of spiritual decline in the Mennonite Church. For a long time no peace literature had been produced and in many cases the young men were not prepared to meet the test of war and conscription. As a result a considerable number of them accepted military service.[11]

[10] E. N. Wright, *Conscientious Objectors in the Civil War* (Philadelphia, 1931), 51.
[11] Edward Yoder, "Teaching Nonresistance," *Gospel Herald* (Scottdale, Pa., April 18, 1940), 33:78.

This failure aroused the church to the performance of its duty, however, so that it became the occasion for the revival of teaching following war, and a cause for a great awakening in the Mennonite Church. In June, 1863, appeared two little booklets on nonresistance, "the first trickles of a stream of literature that has flowed into the church in growing volume since." One was entitled, *Warfare, Its Evils, Our Duty,* and was written by John F. Funk, the young minister who was to found the *Herald of Truth* the following year. The other, entitled *Christianity and War,* was written by John M. Brenneman, Mennonite minister of Elida, Ohio. The *Herald of Truth* which began publication in January, 1864, promoted the cause of nonresistance from the very beginning.

In an editorial in the January, 1865, issue of the *Herald,* Funk discussed various alternatives to military service and evaluated them as to their consistency. He presented a convincing case against the hiring of substitutes. "It is now generally admitted to be wrong," he says, "and there is probably scarcely a single one who professes to hold to the doctrine of nonresistance, that would be willing to send a man to do that which he himself . . . considers altogether against the gospel of Jesus Christ."[12] This editorial brings out the interesting point that townships or other local units of government sometimes formed organizations to raise sufficient substitute money to exempt the entire unit from the draft. Funk warns his readers against the inconsistency of nonresistant people joining in with this practice. The August, 1864, issue of the *Herald of Truth* has an article extracted from a pamphlet, published earlier that same year, by Daniel Musser of the Reformed Mennonite Church.[13] This extract also argues effectively against the hiring of substitutes, as does an article by a contributor from Indiana in the issue of March, 1865.[14] From this evidence it is clear that the leadership of the church during the Civil War was definitely opposed to the hiring of substitutes as a method of securing exemption from the draft.

---

[12] "A Serious Consideration," *Herald of Truth* (January, 1865), 2:6.

[13] D. Musser, *Nonresistance Asserted* (Lancaster, Pa., 1864).

[14] "Preventing the Draft," *Herald of Truth* (March, 1865), 2:21.

It is interesting to note, however, that both Funk and Musser approved the payment of the commutation fee on the ground that it was a tax. Musser argues that the money belongs to the government, and the government has a right to claim that which is its own. Furthermore, the Scriptures command the payment of taxes. Funk says: "In paying the commutation fee, we give to the government what it demands of us in the same manner as we pay our taxes, which is our Christian duty.[15] Although Funk held that the use which is made of the tax proceeds is the responsibility of the government rather than that of the taxpayer, he nevertheless stressed the idea that when the money is used for the aid of sick and wounded soldiers as provided in the draft act of 1864 it is being used for a good purpose.

Another alternative provided by the draft act was personal service in the care of sick and wounded soldiers. Funk approved this service in two of his editorials,[16] but from the available evidence it is not clear exactly what he meant by this approval. The draft law itself did not state where, or in what way, conscientious objectors might give this service. And apparently the Department of War did not do so either. In January, 1865, Funk said that so far the Secretary of War had in all cases directed the payment of the commutation fee. No one had been required to serve in hospitals. This was only a few months before the close of the war; so the problem of personal service probably never came up. The fact is, however, that sick and wounded soldiers of the Civil War were cared for by the medical bureau of the army and by the United States Sanitary Commission. The latter was an agency recognized by the Department of War and related to it in much the same way that the Red Cross is related to the army medical corps in wartime today. So at first thought it would seem that Funk was giving his approval to the equivalent of present-day service in the medical corps of the army.

On the other hand, since the problem never came up in actual practice, it is possible that Funk was simply referring to the general principle of giving relief to the sick and suffering

---

[15] *Herald of Truth* (January, 1865), 2:6, 7.
[16] *Ibid.*, (August, 1864), 1:50; (January, 1865), 2:6, 7.

without having thought through the possible relation of the individual to the military organization in this service. At any rate it has been the official position of the Mennonite Church during the two recent world wars that, in order to be consistent, the relief work of nonresistant Christians must be performed through organizations detached from the military. To perform such work as a part of the military organization is simply to be a part of an organization whose task it is to wage war. This nonresistant Christians cannot do. While Funk was far ahead of his people in his understanding of the problems of his time, his thinking on this point is nevertheless somewhat immature. This is perhaps due in part to the fact that the church did not actually have to face the problem of hospital service. It may also be a reflection of the spiritual immaturity of the church at that time.

It is interesting to note that many Quakers were dissatisfied with the draft law of 1864 and objected just as seriously to the payment of commutation fee as they did to the hiring of a substitute. Their reason, however, was one which Mennonites could hardly share. They thought of the commutation fee, or any form of alternative service, as a penalty imposed for obeying their conscience, and they did not think they should be penalized for obeying God rather than men.[17] The Mennonite attitude would be that any service which in itself is right should be performed, if the government requires it, even though it be required as an alternative to war. The Mennonites showed a weakness during the Civil War, however, in not being alert to grapple adequately, on the basis of their own principles, with the issues at hand. If they had been more alert they would have had a clearer idea of what their nonresistant faith required of them. And if they had had greater clarity of vision it seems likely that the government would have responded to their convictions.

The federal authorities took a very considerate attitude toward the problem of the conscientious objector. At the close of the war Secretary of War Stanton said he and President Lincoln had "felt that unless we recognized conscientious religious scruples, we could not expect the blessing of Heaven."[18] This

---

[17] E. N. Wright, op. cit., 83, 84.   [18] Ibid., 129.

statement is verified by the fact that in the administration of the draft Stanton went farther than Congress had gone in giving consideration to conscientious objectors. When he discovered that many Quakers were opposed to payment of the commutation fee he issued an order to army officials to parole all such objectors from the army "until called for."[19] *The Friend,* a Quaker periodical, expressed the opinion that if all Quakers had stood firmly for this position none would have been required to pay even the commutation fee.[20] It seems certain, therefore, that if the Mennonites had been sufficiently advanced in their thinking to conceive and promote a comprehensive program of civilian alternative service, in complete harmony with their nonresistant principles, it would have been granted them. As it was, the record of the Mennonite Church in the Civil War was not as satisfactory as might be desired.

The only Mennonite group of any size in the South during the Civil War was that living in the Shenandoah Valley, in Virginia, the scene of Sheridan's raid, which took place in October, 1864. They were therefore unfortunate enough to live directly in the area of battle. For this reason, and also because of the desperate straits of the Confederate government toward the close of the war, the Mennonites of Virginia suffered many more hardships than did those of the North. Furthermore, the Southern conscription laws were more stringent from the very beginning than were those of the North. When Virginia called out the militia in 1861, there was no provision for the exemption of conscientious objectors. Therefore anyone who failed to respond, either personally or by hiring a substitute, was liable to arrest. Under this test a few of the younger Mennonites weakened and joined the ranks with the volunteers. Some hid themselves in the mountains, however, and came home to visit their families from time to time at night. Others when drafted went into the army under protest, with the understanding among themselves that they would not shoot.

This no-shooting pledge was carried out by a sufficient number of Mennonites and Dunkers to cause General T. F. (Stone-

---

19 *Ibid.,* 86.   20 *Ibid.,* 87.

wall) Jackson to say: "There lives a people in the Valley of Virginia, that are not hard to bring to the army. While there they are obedient to their officers. Nor is it difficult to have them take aim, but it is impossible to get them to take correct aim. I, therefore, think it better to leave them at their homes that they may produce supplies for the army."[21] In the meantime some of these men were taken out of the front ranks and detailed "as cooks, teamsters and on the relief corps, to attend to the sick and wounded."[22]

In the spring of 1862 two groups of about ninety Mennonites and Dunkers liable for military service made an effort to leave Virginia, planning to go to West Virginia and Ohio as refugees for the duration of the war. They were captured, however, and eighteen of them were taken to Harrisonburg, while the remaining seventy were taken to the Libby prison at Richmond. Here they were examined by Sidney S. Baxter of the Confederate War Department, who found them sincere conscientious objectors with no desire to aid the enemy. Baxter reported later that some had tried to hire substitutes, that one man had sent in his money for this purpose, and that others had helped the families of volunteers. Some had furnished horses for the army and would be willing to give up their property if it were asked. Baxter said he understood a law would soon be passed exempting these people upon payment of a commutation fee. Since all were willing to pay, he recommended their release.[23] The following October the Confederate Congress did enact a new law exempting the conscientious objectors upon the hiring of a substitute or paying a tax of $500. This law led to the release not only of the men in prison, but also to the return of "such who were in the army and such as were in hiding near their homes."[24] It is also important to observe that the Virginia Mennonites came to the assistance of the imprisoned men and those in the army, helping them to raise the commuta-

---

[21] *Ibid.*, 167.

[22] L. J. Heatwole in Hartzler and Kauffman, *Mennonite Church History* (Scottdale, Pa., 1905), 208.

[23] E. N. Wright, *op. cit.*, 168-69.

[24] L. J. Heatwole, *loc. cit.*, 210, 211.

tion money and to pay the price to the authorities to secure their release.[25]

From the fall of 1862 to the spring of 1864 the Mennonites in Virginia were relatively undisturbed by the war. In the summer and fall of 1864, however, the provisions of the conscription law with respect to conscientious objectors were interpreted more and more narrowly and the administration of the law became increasingly rigid, until it looked as if all the privileges of the law of 1862 would be lost. As a result, many of the Virginia Mennonites who were liable for the draft made their escape across the mountains into the Northern territory. Others who remained in hiding to escape impressment in the army were in constant danger.[26]

The Virginia Mennonites, being located in the South and in the very heart of a battle area, found their nonresistance more severely tested than that of any other part of the church. Considering this fact, and also the period in the history of the church in which they lived, their record during this time of trial was fairly satisfactory. It is true that some of their younger men succumbed to pressure and accepted military service. But this was never condoned by the church, and Heatwole cites the case of at least one such young man who was restored to fellowship through public confession.[27] The record of the Virginia church, despite its severe trials, seems to have been better than that of many of the churches west of the Allegheny Mountains. This was no doubt due in part to the fact that it was an older and more established settlement. But more important, perhaps, was the vigorous leadership of Bishop Samuel Coffman, who stood out courageously for the Mennonite faith at the risk of his own life, in a time when weaker men might have lost heart. On the other hand, the payment of the commutation fee, the hiring of substitutes, and the acceptance of service as cooks and teamsters in the army are evidence that the Mennonite Church in the South was no more mature than the church in the North in its

[25] *Ibid.*, 211.
[26] *Ibid.*, 212.
[27] E. N. Wright, *op. cit.*, 206.

thinking on the question of alternative service. The intellectual and spiritual immaturity of the church in the Civil War period was universal; no part of the church escaped its influence.

Mennonites in the First World War

For a full half century following the Civil War the American Mennonites had no experience with war or conscription. The first World War which came at the close of this period, however, brought new problems and testings which in many ways were more severe than any experienced before in America. In this war conscription was absolute and universal; there was no escape through the employment of a substitute or the payment of a commutation fee. Each man when drafted was required to meet the test in person, and even though the United States was in the war only nineteen months, nearly 2,000 Mennonite young men were called to camp during that period.

The problems of conscription were greater in 1917 than they were in 1864, but it is also true that the church was better prepared spiritually and intellectually to meet the test than she was in the earlier period. The great awakening which began with the work of John F. Funk had accomplished a splendid work. In one other respect American Mennonitism of 1917 was different from that of the 1860's. The nineteenth century had brought many Mennonites from Europe, and particularly from Russia, to the American shores. Those who came from western Europe differed from the Russian groups in some of their customs, practices, and doctrinal emphases. All of the European groups experienced some difficulty in fitting into the existing American Mennonite pattern, due to differences in language and in practice on various points. Even those who had been in America for a longer period did not constitute a single ecclesiastical organization. As a result the Mennonites of America in 1917 were made up of seventeen groups who differed somewhat in their teaching and practice on certain points. All of them, however, adhered to the doctrine of nonresistance. It is true that they varied in the quality of their leadership, in the effectiveness of their teaching, and in the solidarity of their group life, so that in practice the nonresistant record of the church was not uniform. All of the Mennonite groups, however, had a concern for this vital element in their faith, and all of them contributed to the nearly 2,000 conscientious objectors in the army camps of the United States in 1917 and 1918.

The Selective Service Act of May 18, 1917, provided exemption for conscientious objectors. The exemption clause was qualified, however, with the further provision that "no person shall be exempted from service in any capacity that the President shall declare to be noncombatant." Since the President did not define noncombatant service until March 20, 1918, the intervening ten months were filled with confusion as to what the law actually meant. From the beginning, however, Mennonite leaders of various groups were diligent in their efforts to obtain an interpretation of the law which would be consistent with their principle of nonresistance. As a result of these efforts Secretary of War Newton D. Baker, on September 1, 1917, ruled that conscientious objectors when drafted should report to the military camps where: (1) they would be segregated, (2) they would not be required to wear the military uniform nor to engage in drill, (3) they would be offered a list of services considered noncombatant by the Department of War, but they need not accept any in violation of their conscience, (4) those who could not accept any service under the military arm of the government would be held in detention camps to await such disposition as the government should decide upon.

Apparently Secretary Baker assumed, even as late as this, that so-called nocombatant military service would be generally acceptable to conscientious objectors. Since this did not prove true, however, and since no one had a clear solution for the problem at hand, the result was months of confusion and distress for both conscripts and military officials. Then, too, the President's belated definition of noncombatant service did not help matters, because, as he defined it, it included only military service, which no real conscientious objector could accept. In March, 1918, however, Congress enacted a law which opened the way to relief. Due to a prospective shortage of farm labor this law authorized furloughs to men in the army "to engage in civil occupations and pursuits." Then in June, 1918, the Secretary of War applied this law to conscientious objectors and opened the way for their release from camp for farm labor. In the same month of June the Department of War established a civilian Board of Inquiry to visit the military camps and review all cases of conscientious objectors. Those found sincere in their position were to be granted furloughs either for farm service or to engage in relief work with the American Friends Service Committee then operating in France. This proved to be the solution for the problem. When the war came to a close in November, 1918, the Board of Inquiry had not yet completed its work. Nevertheless, it had succeeded in sifting out 1,300 sincere conscientious objectors, of various religious beliefs, who accepted either farm service or reconstruction work in France, upon recommendation of the board.

No complete analytical study has been made of the Mennonites who were conscripted in the World War. Apparently, however, the number in camp was nearly 2,000. The various Mennonite groups demonstrated varying degrees of loyalty to the principle of nonresistance; but the large majority of the conscripted Mennonites refused service of any kind under the military. They were genuine nonresistants. A substantial minority accepted noncombatant service, while a few accepted combatant service. Limited records of the Mennonite majority who declined all service under the military indicate that approximately 10 per cent were court-martialed and sent to prison, chiefly at Leavenworth; 60 per cent accepted alternative service, either farm or reconstruction work; and 30 per cent remained in the camps until the close of the war, most of these not having had an opportunity to appear before the Board of Inquiry.

Experiences in the Army Camps

The court-martials and prison sentences referred to above suggest that the experience of the men in the army camps was not always a happy one. C. Henry Smith has summarized this situation very well in the following quotation:

> These were frequently roughly handled by petty officers who had little sympathy for their scruples . . . . In all the camps they were subject to ridicule and were considered fair game for any army officer or YMCA secretary who cared to take a hand in converting them. Even some of the higher officers in some of the camps, being entirely out of sympathy with the liberal policy of the war department, permitted unnecessary abuse of the conscientious objectors, as those were called who refused to work in the camps even at noncombatant work, and usually refused to don the uniform. In Camp Funston the worst abuses prevailed, and two officers, a major and a captain, were removed for negligence in permitting rough treatment of the conscientious objectors. Some of these were brutally handled in the guardhouse; they were bayoneted, beaten and tortured by various forms of the water cure; eighteen men one night were aroused from their sleep and held under cold showers until one became hysterical. Another objector had the hose played upon his head until he became unconscious. The war department finally was forced to interfere a short time before the armistice was signed with the result noted above.
>
> In other camps similar abuse prevailed, carried on usually by under officers for the purpose of breaking down the morale of the conscientious objector, or perhaps to retaliate for his refusal to obey peremptory military orders. Men were forced to stand at attention, sometimes with outstretched arms for hours and days at a time on the sunny or cold side of their barracks, exposed to the inclemencies of the weather as well as to the jeers and taunts of their fellows until they could stand no longer; chased across the fields at top speed until they fell down exhausted, followed by their guards on motorcycles; occasionally tortured by mock trials, in which the victim was left under the impression to the very last that unless he submitted to the regulations the penalty would be death. Every conceivable device—ridicule, torture, offer of promotion, and other tempting inducements were resorted to in order to get them to give up their convictions; but with only few exceptions the religious objectors refused to compromise with their consciences.[28]

When Secretary Baker ordered the segregation of the conscientious objectors in the camps it was no doubt his intention

---

[28] C. H. Smith, *The Story of the Mennonites* (Newton, Kansas, 1950), 794-95.

that they should be treated with justice. They were to be offered noncombatant military service, but if they could not conscientiously accept such service they were to be detained until their cases could be disposed of. The appointment of the Board of Inquiry was a helpful though belated means of carrying out this program. Few if any Mennonites were court-martialed after the board reviewed their cases. But in many instances the segregated objector had to wait for weeks and months before he had an opportunity to appear before the board. It was during this period that scenes like that described above took place, and most court-martials of Mennonites came as the culmination of a series of such experiences. Army officers frequently did not understand the conscientious objector at all, and had no sympathy for the law or for the ruling of the Department of War which gave respect to his beliefs. They considered it their duty to induce him to take up arms, and when they failed in this the only treatment they could think of was that fit for one guilty of a crime next to treason itself.

Conscientious objectors were never court-martialed for conscientious objection as such, but rather for disobedience to some specific order. Once the officers had decided to get rid of a man by sending him to prison he was commanded to perform some specific act which they knew he could not conscientiously perform. If he refused, he was tried for disobeying a military order. As a rule these trials had no semblance of justice and many of them were very hurriedly conducted. One trial which ended in a twenty-five year sentence is reported to have been conducted in eighteen minutes.[29] The total number of objectors court-martialed and sentenced was 503. Of these, 360 were religious objectors; and of the latter, 138 were Mennonites. Prison sentences ranged all the way from one year or less to life. Life sentences were given to 142 men, and 17 men were even sentenced to death. Sentences from five to thirty years were very common.[30] None of these severe sentences were fully served. Within a few

---

[29] Norman Thomas, *The Conscientious Objector in America* (New York, 1923), 176.
[30] *Ibid.*, 48, 49.

months after the close of the war most of the prisoners had been given their freedom, by Presidential pardon.

The darkest chapter in the entire story of the treatment received by the conscientious objectors is that of the four Hutterian Mennonites, Joseph, Michael, and David Hofer, and Jacob Wipf. After spending two months in the guardhouse in a military camp these four men were court-martialed and sentenced to twenty years' imprisonment. They were taken to Alcatraz federal prison in California, chained in pairs, in charge of armed army officers. Upon arrival, when they again refused to wear the military uniform, they were stripped of all clothing except light underwear and placed in a dark and filthy dungeon where they had to sleep on a cold concrete floor without blankets. For four and one-half days the only food they received was one-half glass of water every twenty-four hours. For the next day and a half their arms were crossed above their heads and manacled to bars so high that their feet barely reached the floor. They were beaten with clubs until one of them became unconscious. They were then kept in solitary confinement in their cells for four months, being given only one hour for exercise on Sundays. In November, 1918, they were removed to Leavenworth, again in chains and in charge of armed guards. When they arrived they were forced to walk through the streets of the city, from the railway station to the prison, at the points of bayonets. When they arrived at the prison, wet with sweat, they were forced to remove their outer clothing and to stand outside in the cold for two hours in the middle of the night. At five o'clock in the morning they were again compelled to stand in the cold until Joseph and Michael Hofer became ill and were taken to the hospital, where they died a few days later. David Hofer and Jacob Wipf were placed on a bread and water diet and manacled to bars nine hours each day. This treatment continued for some weeks, but eventually both of these men were discharged.[31]

[31] C. H. Smith, *The Coming of the Russian Mennonites*, 277-82.

Experiences in the Home Community

Since modern warfare tends to be total in its scope and effort, it affects those conscientious objectors who remain in the home community as well as the men who are called by the draft. In the World War every Mennonite community had to face the problem of purchasing war bonds and of contributing to the war fund of such agencies as the Red Cross and the YMCA. Most Mennonites agreed that a contribution to these causes was a contribution to the war effort.

Everywhere, however, the pressure of public opinion was so great that, in actual practice, some Mennonites of all groups made contributions to causes to which they were opposed in principle, including the purchase of war bonds. In some communities Mennonites avoided the purchase of bonds by leaving a given sum of money on deposit in local banks for a specified period of time, with the understanding that it was not to be used for the purchase of bonds, although it might release other money for such purposes. In the course of the war practically all of the Mennonite communities, however, contributed large sums of money for the relief of war sufferers. Such contributions served a twofold purpose; they were in line with the historic principle of giving aid to the suffering, and they were regarded as an alternative to contributions for war purposes. Often these contributions exceeded those which their neighbors made for war purposes, but in some cases this was given little consideration by the non-Mennonite population.

In some communities Mennonites were most severely criticized, and even abused. In Kansas and Illinois and in other places a number of meetinghouses were painted yellow. In Kansas several men were tarred and feathered because of their nonresistant objection to the purchase of bonds. In Oklahoma one man was actually strung up on a telephone pole by a mob, although he was rescued by the officials. In at least two cases meetinghouses were burned to the ground. One minister in Ohio was dragged from his home at night, and his hair was clipped from his head. In South Dakota a mob, with the connivance of a local bond committee, actually robbed the Hutterian community of livestock worth $40,000. This, with other abuses, was responsible for driving the Hutterites out of the state into Canada. No doubt this is the worst example, but if there were space it would be possible to enumerate cases of mistreatment and mob violence by the score.

Clarifying the Issue of So-called Noncombatant Service

Since they had had no previous personal experience with war, many questions arose which the American Mennonites of 1917 found it difficult to answer. The church was alert, however, and able to learn by the experiences of the war itself. As a result, many specific issues which were not very clear at the beginning of the war became more so as time went on. One thing which the war did was to reveal the true nature of so-called noncombatant service. Although the statement adopted by the Mennonite General Conference in 1917 shows that the Mennonite Church took a definite stand against noncombatant service in the army, there had been little or no teaching on this specific point prior to the war, with the result that some young men wavered on the issue. But in many cases the camp experience itself settled this question for men who had been uncertain in their minds before going to camp.

A friend of the writer relates how he went to camp in 1917 or 1918 with the intention of accepting some form of noncombatant service. He had always been taught, however, that warfare and killing were wrong. During the first week of his camp life, while going through the routine of physical examinations, inoculations, and other preliminaries, and before he came to the point of putting on a uniform and engaging in drill he had an opportunity to make some observations and to compare his parental teaching, and his own innermost convictions, with what he was seeing. One day while sauntering about the camp grounds he happened upon a group of soldiers in the midst of a spirited bayonet drill. It so happened that one man in the group wielded his bayonet rather timidly as he brought it in line for a thrust into the abdomen of his dummy victim. Upon seeing this manifestation of soft-heartedness the officer in charge swore at the timid private and commanded him to step to the front and "cut out his guts," reminding him that it was a war, and not a Sunday-school picnic, that he was engaged in. After thinking over what he saw on that occasion, the young Mennonite draftee says the question of noncombatant military service was settled for him. He made up his mind that if that is what the army means he can have nothing whatever to do with it. The nonresistant Christian can have nothing to do with an organization which specializes in disemboweling his fellow men. From that moment the writer's friend was a thoroughgoing conscientious objector, and eventually climaxed his camp experience with a brief term at Leavenworth.

Another issue which the war helped to clarify in the thinking of the Mennonites was the question of alternative service. In its official statements, and in its teachings and advices, the church had always said or implied that it was willing to render the government any service which is not in conflict with its nonresistant principles. But in almost a century and a half the church had added little, if anything, by way of definition, to the general statement of the Pennsylvania Mennonites in 1775 to the effect that they had dedicated themselves "to serve all men in everything that can be helpful to the preservation of men's lives." Even the statement of the Mennonite General Conference in 1917 did not go beyond the expression of "the hope that when the powers that be fully understand our position with reference to military service, this clause referring to noncombatant service may be accordingly modified."[32] Exactly how they would like to see this clause modified, and precisely what service the church would be willing to perform, the statement does not say. Evidently the framers of the General Conference statement of 1917 did not know exactly what they wanted in the way of service. It was a point they had not thought through. But if they were not settled on this point they were at least sure

[32] *Gospel Herald* (Scottdale, Pa., Sept. 6, 1917), 10:420.

that they could not accept noncombatant service, and from this point they gradually found their way.

In its efforts to find a solution for the conscientious objector problem the Department of War in the summer of 1918 devised "a special class of noncombatant service" which it hoped would be satisfactory to conscientious objectors. This was to be service in "reconstruction hospitals," under the reconstruction branch of the medical corps, and devoted to the aid of sick and wounded soldiers who would not be returned to military service. The Department of War evidently hoped that service in the reconstruction branch of the medical corps would be acceptable, since the men treated there would not be returned to the field of battle.

This service was still under the army, however, requiring the wearing of the military uniform, and was therefore *military* service. For this reason it never received the approval of the Mennonite Church. On October 2, 1918, at a meeting of representative leaders called by the Military Committee of the Mennonite General Conference, to formulate a position on this question, it was agreed that reconstruction hospital service would be acceptable only if it could be performed under civilian direction and without the wearing of a military uniform. This meant that the Mennonite Church rejected all service in the army medical corps as military service. Aaron Loucks, the chairman of the Military Committee, evidently stated the sentiment of the meeting mentioned above, when he said: "If we are to maintain a consistent testimony 'that carnal warfare is wrong for Christians to engage in,' then any identification that associates us willingly with and as a part of that system in performance of duties directly under that system would becloud if not compromise our testimony and would be out of harmony with the Gospel teaching on that subject."[33] Evidently this decision received the approval of the men in camp who had taken a stand against noncombatant service. At least one of them, on hearing a rumor that reconstruction hospital service under the army had

[33] Aaron Loucks to S. C. Yoder, Oct. 8, 1918, *World War Papers*, Archives of the Mennonite Church, Goshen, Ind.

been approved, wrote a letter of inquiry in which he stated in an emphatic way his disapproval of such service. The secretary of the committee was able to inform him, however, that this rumor was incorrect.[34]

Finding the Way to Alternative Service

Evidently one of the War Department's reasons for proposing the reconstruction hospital service was the fact that in some communities the farm furlough plan was not entirely successful due to unsatisfactory public relations. But the Military Committee of the Mennonite Church was satisfied with nothing short of strictly civilian alternative service, and hopefully continued working on the problem at a time when some leaders considered the situation dark indeed, and felt that nothing could be done. In the letter correcting the rumor mentioned above, the secretary of the committee mentions a plan which he had recently proposed to the War Department for the assignment of conscientious objectors to an Indian reservation in Arizona where they would engage in agricultural experimentation and development, and also serve as teachers of the Indians. The War Department was favorably impressed with this idea and indicated that if the war were to continue the plan would receive further attention. Since the war did not continue, however, the proposal was carried no further.[35] If it had continued, it is not impossible that the suggestion would have been acted upon. In that case the arrangement would have been similar to that of the Civilian Public Service program of the second World War. It is clear therefore that the CPS system was conceived in part through the hard experiences of the first World War. The men who were tortured in the guardhouse and in prison cells in 1917-18 suffered there that conscripts under the Selective Training and Service Act of 1940 might render their country a useful service under humane working and living conditions, and under sympathetic civilian direction. In a similar manner, the gen-

[34] O. B. Gerig to J. S. Hartzler, Oct. 9, 1918, and reply, Oct. 11, 1918, *Ibid.*
[35] See correspondence in *World War Papers*, Archives of the Mennonite Church.

erous contributions of the Mennonites for the relief of war sufferers, while protesting against the purchase of war bonds and
similar projects, went far toward the establishment of an alternative for the financial support of war, which also came to be
definitely recognized in the second World War.

The Mennonites of Canada in the First World War[36]

The traditional policy of the Canadian government with
respect to conscientious objectors has been much more liberal
than that of the United States. A law passed in 1808 applying
to Upper and Lower Canada, exempted "Quakers, Mennonites,
and Tunkers, who from certain scruples of conscience decline
bearing arms." This exemption was contingent, however, upon
the payment of twenty shillings annually in peacetime, and
four pounds in wartime, by persons otherwise subject to draft.
This policy was continued in later legislation until a law enacted in 1855 exempted the nonresistant people uncon-
ditionally.

In 1867 the Dominion of Canada was organized. The following year a militia law was passed which provided that Quakers, Mennonites, and Tunkers, "or any inhabitant of Canada
of any religious denomination otherwise subject to military
duty but who from the doctrines of his religion is averse to bearing arms," should be exempted from military service, both in
peace and in wartime "upon such conditions and such regulations as the Governor or Council may from time to time prescribe." In 1873 an Order in Council of the Dominion government promised complete exemption from all military service
to the Mennonites who were about to migrate from Russia to
western Canada. A similar Order in Council made the same
promise in 1898 to the Dukhobors, another nonresistant group
which came from Russia at that time.

Following the enactment of the Canadian conscription law
of 1917, however, there was a certain amount of confusion regarding the status of conscientious objectors. This act exempted

---

[36] See C. H. Smith, *The Coming of the Russian Mennonites*, 294-96.

conscientious objectors from combatant service only, but specified that the Russian Mennonites in western Canada, and the
Dukhobors, who came under the provisions of the Orders in
Council of 1873 and 1898, should have complete exemption.
In some cases the Russian Mennonites were not even required
to register. In others they registered and then claimed exemption. In all cases, however, the promises made to the Russian
Mennonites and the Dukhobors in 1873 and 1898 were kept
to the letter. The status of the Ontario Mennonites, on the
other hand, was not quite so clear. Technically the Order in
Council of 1873 did not apply to them, while the conscription
act of 1917 required conscientious objectors to accept noncombatant military service, something the Mennonites could not
do. Would the government attempt to force these people into
the army, or would it give them the same standing which it gave
to the Russian Mennonites? In the beginning the government
attempted to follow the first of these two policies. A number
of Ontario Mennonites were taken to camp where they were
court-martialed for refusing to serve. Some received prison
sentences, but were later released.

Eventually, however, the Dominion government adopted
a policy which in practice placed all of the Canadian Mennonites on the same footing. Those called by the draft in Ontario
were now required to present certificates of church membership upon which the military authorities were instructed to
issue a "leave of absence" which was extended indefinitely.
This plan worked satisfactorily in most cases, although in a
few instances the leaves of absence were obtained only with
considerable difficulty. It should be noted, however, that other
conscientious objectors in Canada did not fare as well as did
the Mennonites and the Dukhobors. Since the Orders in
Council of 1873 and 1898 did not apply to them, all were required to go to the military camps and take their stand there.
Some members of the Brethren in Christ Church, or Tunkers,
were court-martialed and given prison sentences, but eventually their sentences were canceled and the men were given
leaves of absence.

In the World War the Canadian Mennonites took a definite stand against the purchase of war bonds. The Russian Mennonites of western Canada, however, contributed liberally to the Red Cross. They also endorsed the last war loan when the government promised to use the money for relief work and not for direct war purposes. Under this plan the Russian Mennonite churches raised about $500,000. In 1917 the Ontario Mennonites, in co-operation with the Tunkers, organized the Nonresistant Relief Organization which raised over $70,000 for relief during the war. This organization worked closely with the Mennonite Relief Commission for War Sufferers[37] and also distributed funds to various relief channels at the suggestions of the Canadian government.

One result of the hysteria of the wartime was the rise of considerable opposition to the Mennonites of western Canada. This opposition was directed against the government's liberal policy in dealing with them, and for a time there was a strong sentiment demanding the repeal of all special concessions to the Mennonites. After the Hutterites moved in from the United States,[38] this opposition became so strong that an Order in Council was passed in 1919 forbidding the further immigration of Mennonites to Canada. Appeals were even made to the government to prevent the settlement of the Hutterites, but this was not accomplished. This strong war feeling was responsible for legislation in certain provinces requiring the use of the English language in all schools, one result of which was the migration to Mexico of the more conservative Russian Mennonites in Manitoba. It is important to note, however, that none of the hostile legislation mentioned above survived the period of war hysteria. Eventually all of the restrictions were removed except those requiring the use of the English language in the schools. Not only were the restrictions against the immigration of Mennonites removed, but a few years later, between 1923 and 1927, the Canadian Pacific Railway, with the encouragement of the Dominion government, actually

---

[37] See below, p. 135.
[38] See S. C. Yoder *For Conscience Sake*, (Goshen, Ind., 1940), 94-96.

helped to settle about 20,000 new Mennonite immigrants from Russia in western Canada, with additional numbers coming in the years which followed. This story is told more fully in the following chapter.

The Second World War

One of the effects of the first World War was to arouse all of the peace churches to the need for an aggressive program of peace teaching and peace action. The various Mennonite groups appointed official peace committees who were responsible for the carrying on of this program. The Brethren and Friends groups did likewise. Following the war, the amount of peace literature produced by all of these groups was greater than ever before in their history. Peace Conferences sponsored by the peace groups, both individually and co-operatively, were a common thing during this period. The most important of the co-operatively sponsored meetings was that held at Newton, Kansas, in 1935, at which time the name "Historic Peace Churches" was first used. This meeting appointed an unofficial Continuation Committee whose duty it was to plan for future conferences and to guide the co-operative efforts of the Historic Peace Churches. Among these co-operative efforts was the bringing of a testimony for the Christian way of peace to the official bodies of other Christian denominations. In 1937 representatives of the Historic Peace Churches called on President Franklin D. Roosevelt. Each of the three groups (Mennonites, Friends, and Brethren) presented a letter stating its views on war and peace, and giving the reasons why those who adhere to this faith cannot conscientiously bear arms. A similar delegation visited the President again on January 10, 1940, with concrete proposals for alternative service in case of universal military training and service.

In 1939 the international situation in Europe was growing so serious that the peace churches realized the need of knowing what to do in case war should actually break out. All were aware that a single plan of action would be best if one could be agreed upon. To this end the various Mennonite groups organized a Mennonite Central Peace Committee which then drafted a proposed Plan of Action in case of war, which received official approval on September 30, 1939. The other Historic Peace Churches also gave official approval to this plan of action. As a result of these efforts the provision for conscientious objectors in the Selective Training and Service Act of 1940 was more generous and satisfactory than that of the draft law of 1917. Under the new law all persons "who, by reason of religious training and belief," were conscientiously opposed to all forms of military service, should, if conscripted for service, "be assigned to work of national importance under civilian direction." An effort was also made to obtain the complete exemption of men with objection to all forms of service, including civilian service, under conscription. It was pointed out that the English conscription laws provided for such absolutists. This effort failed, however, with the result that the Selective Training and Service Act of 1940 made no provision for the absolutists.

In the administration of conscription Selective Service placed the classification of conscientious objectors and their assignments to camp in the hands of local draft boards. In case a man was dissatisfied with his classification, provision was made for him to appeal his case to an appeal board under a plan in which the Department of Justice investigated the sincerity of his claims and made final recommendation. The Historic Peace Churches and other groups interested in the conscientious objector organized the National Service Board for Religious Objectors, (NSBRO) as an agency through which they worked in dealing with Selective Service. The latter likewise dealt with the peace churches through the NSBRO. Following conferences between Selective Service and the NSBRO a Civilian Public Service system was approved by the President on December 20, 1940.

Civilian Public Service

The CPS camps and units as originally set up were operated by the Mennonite Central Committee, the Brethren Service

Committee, and the American Friends Service Committee, under the administration of Selective Service through the NSBRO. In the case of the base camps the government provided housing, bedding, and a certain amount of equipment for the living quarters. The church agencies provided maintenance for the men, administrative personnel for the camps, fuel, light, and such equipment for living quarters as the government did not provide. From 1941 to 1947 nearly 12,000 conscientious objectors were drafted and assigned to CPS camps. Of this number, 4,665 were Mennonites. Camps administered by the Mennonite Central Committee received most of the Mennonite campers, as well as a considerable number of others. The maintenance of the CPS system, and of the men, involved an expenditure of large sums of money. The cost of maintaining a man in a base camp was estimated at $35 per month. In the case of Mennonites the funds for this were raised by contributions from the church, reckoned on a quota basis. The quota varied from time to time, depending on the number of men in camp, but for several years it stood at fifty cents per month for each member of the Mennonite Church. For others this maintenance cost had to be paid either by the man himself, by his friends, or his church.

The total of contributions received by the MCC for the operation of CPS from its beginning in 1941 to its end on March 29, 1947, was $3,032,268.75. Besides these contributions the MCC also received, during the CPS program, approximately $290,000 for the support of non-Mennonite men in camp, and for the support of Mennonites whose churches were not on the quota basis. This included contributions from non-Mennonite churches, from non-Mennonite campers, and other individuals. In addition to this the Mennonite churches raised large sums to provide small gifts, personal allowances, medical expenses, and dependency allowances for the men, besides financial aid to ex-CPS men who continued their education after discharge. The total amount of all these contributions incident to Mennonite CPS has never been calculated, but it was probably not far from $4,000,000. When it is remembered that the men in base camps received no wages from the government, and those in detached service projects, such as mental hospitals, received only a nominal wage, an uncalculated loss in earnings might well be added to this figure. The Friends and Brethren churches had a similar experience, although in each case the number of men involved was smaller, which would reduce the financial contributions accordingly.

From the beginning, CPS work projects were chosen by Selective Service, in co-operation with the National Service Board and the administrative agencies. At first Selective Service offered only forestry, soil conservation, and park service projects. One reason for limiting the service to such subjects was the fact that numerous Civilian Conservation Corps camp sites, with buildings and equipment, were available for the establishment of the new CPS camps at very little cost. Another reason was the fact that such projects were understood by the public. From the point of view of public relations, therefore, this was perhaps the easiest point at which the program could have begun. As time went on, however, other projects were added. Among them were land reclamation, agriculture, dairy herd testing, mental hospital service, and public health. In most of the latter services the men were given their board and room by the employing agency, thus relieving the MCC of the maintenance expense. These services also paid the men a wage, although only a nominal one as mentioned above. Private employers of CPS labor, such as farmers, paid the standard wage for the work performed, but the government allowed the men only $15 per month and placed the remainder in a "frozen fund." At the close of CPS this frozen fund in the hands of the federal treasury amounted to more than $1,247,000. In 1952 the fund had not been disposed of.[39]

The Mennonite Central Committee and the Peace Committees

From the above account it was observed that during 1939 and 1940 the task of preparing the various Mennonite groups

[39] For a full account of Mennonite Civilian Public Service see Melvin Gingerich, *Service for Peace* (Akron, Pa., 1949).

for the emergency of war was carried on by the Mennonite Central Peace Committee, which adopted its plan of action on September 30, 1939. When the MCPC was faced with the actual problem of operating CPS camps, however, in the fall of 1940, it assigned the task to the Mennonite Central Committee, an organization which seemed better fitted for this task in view of its twenty years of experience in foreign relief and colonization projects. Thus there were two organizations working on different aspects of the same problem. The MCPC served as a general policy-making organization in matters relating to the fundamental Mennonite position on war, peace, and military service, while the MCC was the operating organization for CPS. In practice, however, there was some overlapping of functions, resulting in a certain amount of confusion. It became clear, therefore, that it would be better to merge the two organizations, which was done in January, 1942. With this action the MCPC ceased to exist, being replaced by a peace section within the MCC.

The different Mennonite groups co-operating with the MCC, however, continued to have active peace committees for the promotion of peace teaching within the group. These committees continued to publish literature, to do publicity work through their own church papers, and to lead in the peace thinking of their particular groups. The peace section of the MCC, however, performed a similar task in cases where it seemed desirable for all Mennonite groups to present some joint statement of policy or position, as in the publication, in 1943, of Edward Yoder's booklet, *Must Christians Fight*. This booklet was designed to meet the anti-nonresistant teachings of certain religious groups and teachers encountered by all of the Mennonites.

An illustration of the relation of the different peace committees to the MCC is found in the manner in which they informed their own groups on methods of procedure in connection with registration, filling out of questionnaires, filing of appeals, and a score of other matters on which information was needed. The procedures themselves were worked out by the

MCC, or received by the MCC from Selective Service through the National Service Board. The MCC even published notes and information in the various church papers covering many of these points. But it still remained the task of the individual peace committees to see that the information available actually got to the person who needed it. If a local congregation was in need of special help for any reason; if it needed information on classification procedures; if it had some misunderstanding with its local draft board; if any of its young men subject to conscription were confused as to the kind of service which is consistent for a nonresistant Christian to engage in; or if there were other needs of a similar nature, it was the task of the peace committees to supply the need.[40]

After the conscription law was passed in 1940, the MCPC, with the co-operation of the peace committees of the various Mennonite groups, prepared literature for distribution to the membership in every Mennonite congregation, giving counsel to men subject to the draft: counsel on registration procedures and filing of questionnaires, counsel as to personal attitudes, information on the CPS program, and numerous matters. Ministers were advised as to their own privileges, opportunities, and responsibilities for assisting the young men. In many other ways the peace committees of the Mennonite groups were a real help to local congregations and to individuals. The help extended in relation to the purchase of bonds is an illustration. It is clear, of course, that nonresistant Christians cannot consistently purchase war bonds. Therefore the Mennonite Central Committee, through patient negotiation with the treasury department of the United States government, made it possible for nonresistant people to purchase civilian bonds, the proceeds of which were not to be used for war purposes. After the MCC had finished its negotiations for the sale of civilian bonds it became the task of the peace committees to inform the churches of this fact, so that individual members could purchase these bonds instead of war bonds.

---

[40] For a fuller description of the work of the peace committees see Guy F. Hershberger, *The Mennonite Church in the Second World War* (Scottdale, Pa., 1951).

In some cases members needed help so as to understand the difference in principle between the two kinds of bonds. In other cases members of the peace committees helped leaders of Mennonite congregations to explain the civilian bond program to committees of local citizens who had charge of the sale of war bonds. When these local committees learned that the civilian bonds would count on the county's quota for the purchase of bonds, they were generally satisfied. This is, no doubt, one reason why there was less friction between the nonresistant churches and the public over the bond question during the second World War than in the first. The records of the Mennonite Central Committee show that by the end of the war the sale of United States civilian bonds had reached $6,740,161.14. Of this amount, $4,911,277 had been purchased by Mennonites.

Likewise when local citizens came to understand that the Mennonites were maintaining the CPS camps without cost to the government, and when they came to understand the large relief program which was being financed by the church, they were ready to concede these contributions as a satisfactory alternative to contributions for war purposes. This helped to reduce to a minimum the conflict between the peace groups and local civilian defense units in the second World War. Every local Mennonite congregation in time of war will probably at some time have some problem in connection with which it needs help. The problem of the war program introduced into the public schools is an illustration. When students were asked to purchase bonds or stamps, or to engage in other school activities inconsistent with the nonresistant faith, the peace committees were ready to help where they could do so.

In all of these ways the peace committees of the various Mennonite groups worked directly with their congregations in order that the nonresistant principles in which they believed might be preserved. From the above description it should be clear that the Mennonites were better prepared in a practical way to meet the war situation and conscription in 1940 than they were in 1917. Issues which might cause conflict between the church and the local community were anticipated in advance, and methods devised for meeting them. An organization was built up for the execution of an effective alternative service program at every point where the war touched the individual, in a way that no one dreamed of in 1917. The effect of this was to make the role of the nonresistant people a more happy one in the second World War than it was in the first. The conscientious objector was still far from popular, but there is little doubt that he had gained in the respect of the general public.

Mennonites of Canada in the Second World War

Most of the Canadian Mennonites are affiliated with the Mennonites of the United States in their conference relationships. They have therefore been closely associated with the peace committees which serve the various conferences in the United States. A number of Canadian representatives were present and took part in the organization of the Mennonite Central Peace Committee in 1939. Furthermore, the work of the various Canadian Mennonite peace and relief organizations is closely related to that of the Mennonite Central Committee.

For purposes of peace education, especially in time of peace, it is possible for a single committee to serve both Canadian and American sections of the church. In their relations with the government, however, it is necessary that the peace groups in Canada be represented by committeemen from Canada, and the American groups by committeemen from the United States. In order that the various peace groups in Ontario might approach their government with a united program, they organized the Conference of Historic Peace Churches, on July 22, 1940.[41] It included the different Mennonite and Amish groups, the Brethren in Christ, the Old Order Dunkers, and the Friends. The conference then appointed a Committee on Military Problems, whose task it was to deal with such problems as war loans, conscription, and alternative service. Although Canada entered the war in September, 1939, conscription was not inaugurated until more than a year later; and when it was introduced it was limit-

---

[41] See *Minutes of the Conference of Historic Peace Churches.*

ed in scope, and enlistments were only for a brief period of training, four months in length. Later the term of service was extended for the duration of the war, but even to the end of the war the Canadian government did not actually conscript men for overseas service, although great pressure was used to urge them to go overseas.

Conscription of conscientious objectors under the Canadian government in the second World War operated somewhat differently from that under the American government. In Canada, when a man was called up for physical examination, if he wished to take his stand as a conscientious objector, he was required to file a written application for "postponement" of his military service. If the application was honored, the applicant was then placed under the jurisdiction of the Alternative Service Work Administration. This administration might then assign the man to essential work in private life, such as farming or industry, or it might require him to serve in an Alternative Service Camp. If he remained in private life, he was allowed board and room and a small amount of cash as personal income. What was earned above this amount was withheld and given to the Canadian Red Cross.

By the end of the war over 5,000 Canadian Mennonites had been classified as CO's and had given some form of alternative service. The farm labor situation in Canada was such, however, that by the end of 1943 most of the men were being assigned to agricultural work without being sent to camp at all. Twelve of the Canadian Alternative Service Camps were located on Vancouver Island, and five on the mainland coast of British Columbia. In all of these camps the men were engaged in forestry and fire fighting service. In addition to these seventeen camps on the west coast there were several camps in Alberta and Saskatchewan, one at Montreal River, and another at Chalk River in Ontario.

From the above account it is clear that the Canadian program with respect to conscientious objectors in the second World War was similar to that of the United States; yet there were important differences. In the United States the camps were operated by the church agencies, under the direction of Selective Service, with only the work projects under the direct supervision of government officials. In the Canadian system, on the other hand, the camps themselves were operated by the government, but the peace groups were permitted to appoint religious advisers to have charge of the spiritual welfare of the men. In the United States the government provided housing for the men, but maintenance beyond this, including the feeding of the men, was provided by the church groups, and the men received no pay. In Canada the entire cost of maintenance was provided by the government, and the men were paid fifty cents per day.

In the matter of war bonds and stamps the Canadian government also followed a policy similar to that of the United States. On December 11, 1940, the government at Ottawa announced a Dominion of Canada loan of $1,000,000 in registered non-interest-bearing certificates, the proceeds of which would be used by the government for the alleviation of distress or human suffering due to war. Here was a bond issue for relief purposes, and not for war, which nonresistant people could purchase with a clear conscience; and the government announced that the purchase of these bonds by members of the peace churches would satisfy as a suitable substitute for the purchase of war bonds. Later it was provided that conscientious objectors who desired to receive interest on their loans might purchase the regular war bond, with a special sticker attached, indicating that the loan would be used for relief purposes, the same as the non-interest-bearing certificates. In June, 1945, the Ontario Mennonite Conference reported that the total amount of non-interest-bearing certificates purchased to date by all branches of Mennonites in all of Canada was $822,660.16, and the total of interest-bearing bonds was $3,849,750.

SELECT BIBLIOGRAPHY

C. Henry Smith, *The Story of the Mennonites* (Newton, Kans., 1950) and *The Mennonites of America* (Goshen, Ind., 1909) are the standard general Mennonite histories covering the period.

Wilbur J. Bender, "Pacifism Among the Mennonites, Amish Mennonites, and Schwenkfelders of Pennsylvania to 1783," in the *Mennonite Quarterly Review* (Goshen, Ind., July and October, 1927), tells the story of the Mennonites in the American Revolution. This article has also been printed as a pamphlet, *Nonresistance in Colonial Pennsylvania* (Scottdale, Pa., 1934). Chapter XIII in J. S. Hartzler and Daniel Kauffman, *Mennonite Church History* (Scottdale, Pa., 1905), has an account by L. J. Heatwole of the experiences of the Virginia Mennonites during the Civil War. An interesting story on the same theme is P. S. Hartman, "Civil War Reminiscences," *Mennonite Quarterly Review* (Goshen, Ind., July, 1929), 3:203-19. Edward N. Wright, *Conscientious Objectors in the Civil War* (Philadelphia, 1931), treats the entire problem of conscientious objectors in the Civil War, including considerable material on the Mennonites. A helpful discussion of the status of the Mennonite Church during the Civil War time is Edward Yoder, "Teaching Nonresistance," *Gospel Herald* (Scottdale, Pa., April 18, 1940), 33:77, 78. C. Henry Smith, *The Coming of the Russian Mennonites* (Berne, Ind., 1927), has a chapter on the Mennonite experiences during the first World War. A fuller treatment is found in J. S. Hartzler, *Mennonites in the World War* (Scottdale, Pa., 1921). A sympathetic book dealing with conscientious objectors in the first World War is Norman Thomas, *The Conscientious Objector in America* (New York, 1923). Walter Guest Kellogg, *The Conscientious Objector* (New York, 1919), is inclined to be unsympathetic. E. J. Swalm, *Nonresistance Under Test* (Nappanee, Ind., 1938), is the personal story of a Canadian conscientious objector, a member of the Brethren in Christ Church, in the first World War. Two books relating the personal experiences of war objectors, with frequent reference to Mennonites, not always sympathetic, are Harold S. Gray, *Character "Bad"* (New York, 1934), and Ernest L. Meyer, *"Hey! Yellowbacks!": The War Diary of a Conscientious Objector* (New York, 1930). For a treatment of Mennonites in the second World War see Melvin Gingerich, *Service for Peace: A History of Mennonite Civilian Public Service* (Akron, Pa., 1949); Guy F. Hershberger, *The Mennonite Church in the Second World War* (Scottdale, Pa., 1951); and John A. Toews, *Alternative Service in Canada During World War II* (Winnipeg, 1959). Two recent books are J. C. Wenger, *The Mennonite Church in America* (Scottdale, Pa., 1967) and Samuel Horst, *Mennonites in the Confederacy* (Scottdale, Pa., 1967), the latter important for the Civil War. Articles in *The Mennonite Encyclopedia* are also of importance.

7. A World-wide Peace Witness

Mennonite Migrations and Relief

Ministering to the needs of suffering humanity is a manifestation of Christian love which in Mennonite history has been closely associated with the principle of nonresistance. Menno Simons, in characterizing the life of the church, and of the Christians which compose it, says:

All those who are born of God, who are gifted with the Spirit of the Lord, who are, according to the Scriptures, called into one body and love in Christ Jesus, are prepared by such love to serve their neighbors, not only with money and goods, but also after the example of their Lord and Head, Jesus Christ, in an evangelical manner, with life and blood. They show mercy and love, as much as they can. No one among them is allowed to beg. They take to heart the need of the saints. They entertain those in distress. They take the stranger into their houses. They comfort the afflicted; assist the needy; clothe the naked; feed the hungry; do not turn their face from the poor; do not despise their own flesh.[1]

In the seventeenth century, when persecution in Holland had ceased, the Dutch Mennonites began to assist their persecuted brethren in Switzerland, giving them financial aid and helping them to remove to new homes among friendlier people. When the great migration of Mennonites from Switzerland and the Palatinate to America began in the early eighteenth century, the Mennonites of Amsterdam organized a Commission for Foreign Needs to assist the emigrants, many of whom were too poor to pay for their passage.[2] During the American Revolution the Mennonites not only informed the Pennsylvania Assembly that it was according to their principles "to feed the hungry and give the thirsty drink,"[3] but they freely gave food, shelter, and other forms of assistance to many who suffered from the war.

[1] *The Complete Writings of Menno Simons* (Scottdale, Pa., 1956), 558.
[2] C. H. Smith, *The Story of the Mennonites*, 541.
[3] *Pennsylvania Archives, Eighth Series*, 8:7349.

In the 1870's when 15,000 Mennonites came from Russia to America for the preservation of their nonresistant faith, the American and Canadian Mennonites assisted them in a large way. C. Henry Smith estimates that the assistance in money and services given by the Mennonites in the United States amounted to more than $100,000. The Ontario Mennonites secured a loan of $88,000 from the Canadian government to assist in the settlement of the immigrants who came to Canada, and guaranteed the repayment of the loan. In addition, private loans and gifts in money and in services brought the aid given by the Canadian Mennonites also considerably above $100,000.[4] The loan from the Canadian government was entirely repaid in due time. During the closing years of the nineteenth century the relief interests of the American Mennonites found expression in bringing aid to the famine sufferers of India. In 1896 the Home and Foreign Relief Commission was organized at Elkhart, Indiana, to carry on this work; and in 1899 the Emergency Relief Committee was organized at Newton, Kansas.

During the first World War the Mennonite Relief Commission for War Sufferers was organized at Elkhart, Indiana, in 1917. Its officially stated purpose was "to solicit, receive, hold and dispense or distribute funds or supplies for the relief of war sufferers."[5] In 1917 the Mennonite and Brethren in Christ churches of Ontario organized the Nonresistant Relief Organization. These two organizations, besides other local committees, worked closely together. By November, 1918, when the war came to a close, their combined efforts had resulted in the raising of more than $400,000 for relief purposes.[6] From the beginning of its organization in December, 1917, the Mennonite Relief Commission regularly contributed $5,000 per month to the work of the Friends Reconstruction Service in France. Additional amounts were contributed from time to time, sometimes as much as $20,000 in one sum. In 1918 a number of Mennonite CO's in the army camps were given furloughs to serve with the Friends Reconstruction Service. Others joined the service after

[4] C. H. Smith, *The Coming of the Russian Mennonites*, 110-13.
[5] J. S. Hartzler, *Mennonites in the World War*, 179.
[6] *Ibid.*, 180.

their discharge from camp at the close of the war, and some did so after being released from the Leavenworth disciplinary barracks. Altogether more than fifty Mennonites were engaged in the reconstruction program. Another twenty-nine served under the Near East Relief.

In 1920 the American and Canadian Mennonites organized the Mennonite Central Committee to carry on relief work in the famine areas of South Russia. This organization, composed of representatives of relief committees of the various Mennonite groups, was destined to become a permanent organization. Its work began with the shipment of twenty-five tons of clothing, accompanied by three workers, Orie O. Miller, Arthur W. Slagel, and Clayton Kratz, in September, 1920. The first task of this delegation proved to be the caring for refugees who had fled from Russia to Constantinople. Here the newly organized MCC opened an orphanage, a home for women and girls, a home for Russian Mennonite refugees, and a number of centers for the distribution of clothing, soap, fuel, medicine, and other necessities. The work continued for two years, during which time more than $200,000 was expended.[7]

In October, 1921, the Russian and the Ukrainian Governments signed agreements with Alvin J. Miller, the director of the Russian work, authorizing the MCC program. Although the American Relief Administration had received permission in August, 1921, to open work in Russia, authorization to do so in the Ukraine was not granted until January, 1922, three months after the MCC agreement was signed. The MCC operated in that part of Russia where the Mennonites lived, but relief was given to the entire population regardless of race or creed. By May, 1922, the MCC was feeding 25,000 persons daily, and by August the figure had reached 40,000. Feeding operations continued through the summer of 1924. In addition, the MCC distributed food packets sent by Americans directly to their relatives and friends in Russia. Fifty or more tractors were also shipped to the Mennonite villages by the MCC, these to take the place of horses lost to the villages during the war. Alto-

[7] P. C. Hiebert and O. O. Miller, *Feeding the Hungry* (Scottdale, Pa., 1929), 90-110.

gether, the American Mennonites spent about $1,200,000 for the relief work in Russia, and this was supplemented by several hundred thousand dollars contributed by the Mennonites of Holland. The total amount contributed by the American Mennonites, and distributed through its own organizations for the relief of war sufferers in Europe and the Near East during the period of the first World War and immediately afterwards, is estimated at about $2,500,000.[8]

Every century of Mennonite history has featured migrations for religious reasons. The greatest Mennonite migrations of all time, however, have been those of the thirty-year period from 1920 to 1950. Thousands were torn from their old homes by the upheavals which accompanied and followed the first World War; and the same happened again in connection with the second World War. During this time more than 40,000 Mennonite refugees found their way from Russia to Canada, Brazil, Paraguay, and Uruguay, with a few to the United States. Following 1945 others from Russia were obliged to remain in western Germany, as were also some thousands from East and West Prussia, although some of the latter found their way to Uruguay. In most of these migrations the refugees received much aid from the Mennonite Central Committee and organizations associated with it. In South America, especially, this aid has followed migration. The MCC has assisted in the purchase of land in Paraguay, and has kept in close touch with the progress of settlements in all countries through visits by special commissioners, through direct assistance by relief workers, and in other ways.[9]

Besides assistance to Mennonite refugees, the American Mennonites carried on an extensive general relief program following the second World War. As early as 1937 the Mennonite Relief Committee operating under the Mennonite Board of Missions and Charities opened a relief work in Spain where there was much suffering incident to the Civil War. This work was never large, but by the time it was closed in 1940 the Amer-

---

[8] *Ibid.*, 323-30; Smith, *Story of the Mennonites*, 493, 94.

[9] S. C. Yoder, *For Conscience Sake* (Goshen, Ind., 1940).

ican Mennonites had contributed about $57,000 to this cause. The Dutch Mennonite Peace Group had also made some contribution to the program. Less than three months after the second World War had begun the Mennonite Central Committee sent its first commissioner to Europe to investigate the opportunities for bringing relief to war sufferers. In a short time work had been opened in Poland, France, and England. In Lyons, France, for example, a large food and milk distribution program was carried on. Refugee homes in southern France cared for sick and starving children. Others in the same region were assisted by food distribution programs. For many people this aid meant the difference between life and death. In the month of January, 1942, more than 17,000 persons received fifty grams of dried vegetables daily, while another 38,000 received some food during the same month. In England much assistance was given to refugees and to children evacuated from the cities.

In 1945 work was begun in Belgium, Holland, and Italy. In 1946 Mennonite relief workers were able to enter Germany, Denmark, Austria, and Poland. In these countries many different types of relief work were carried on, such as emergency feeding and clothing programs, building and reconstruction work. In Belgium there was a building program and also a direct relief service to families of men who were in prison for collaboration with the German occupation forces. In 1947 forty-three MCC workers in Germany distributed 4,538 tons of food, clothing, and other supplies. In the month of June alone they supplied food to 80,000 people, including children, old people, convalescents, disabled persons, refugees, and prisoners of war. During 1947 the MCC shipped 578 tons of food and clothing to Austria where five workers were in charge of distribution. In May of that year a relief program was opened in Hungary. The unique feature of the Polish work was an agricultural program, including a tractor unit of twenty-five men, the purpose of which was to increase agricultural production and to instruct native farmers in the use of modern machinery. In Italy the work consisted of food and clothing distribution, work in refugee camps, and in children's colonies maintained as centers for rest, recreation, and religious instruction. Here the MCC workers were assisted by native Waldensian workers.

In 1944 the MCC had relief workers in Egypt working among the Greek refugees of this area. The following year several of these workers were transferred to Ethiopia, where a medical and educational program was developed. As early as 1942 MCC relief workers were found in India, where the work was largely in famine-stricken areas. In 1946 a work was opened in China, where a medical and health program was carried on, as well as an agricultural rehabilitation program. By the end of 1947 forty MCC workers were in China. Other areas in the Far East served by the MCC were the Philippine Islands, Java, Sumatra, and Japan. Another important relief project undertaken during the second World War was that in Puerto Rico. The work began with the opening of a CPS unit at La Plata in June, 1943. By the end of 1944 the unit had forty members, twenty-four of whom were CPS men. Two years later the unit was exactly the same size, although due to discharges following the end of the war, the number of CPS men had been reduced to eight. A large number of the remaining thirty-two members, however, were ex-CPS men. The Puerto Rico program included educational work, recreation, health, agriculture, and homemaking.

It is obvious that the Mennonite relief program after 1937, which included many countries of the world, represented a large outlay of contributions in cash, of gifts-in-kind, and of personal services. It is also obvious that the resettlement of refugees from one hemisphere to another represented an even greater cost. Transportation for Russian Mennonites to Canada in the 1920's was provided on a credit basis by the Canadian Pacific Railway and Steamship Company. Although the credit extended amounted to about $2,000,000, the immigrants had paid off the debt by the end of the second World War. The migration of the Mennonites to South America during the 1930's had been facilitated by loans from the German government, and aid from various philanthropic organizations, including European Mennonite groups. The original expenditure of the MCC in settling the refugees in Paraguay was nearly $200,000. This sum was augmented by the continuing assistance which the MCC carried on in that country. In the later migrations, following 1945, a portion of the cost was met by the International Refugee Organization. Altogether during 1947 and 1948 the International Relief Organization (IRO) assisted in the moving of Mennonite refugees to the amount of $401,400.

During the same period, however, the cash contributions to the MCC for this purpose by the various Mennonite groups were $1,040,000. In addition to this a total of $220,000 was made available in the form of loans. Apart from the resettlement program, the total relief program of the Mennonite Central Committee and the Mennonite Relief Committee during the years 1937 through 1948 represented cash contributions amounting to $3,520,000, and gifts-in-kind amounting to $6,100,000. The year 1947 represented the high point in MCC and MRC expenditures for relief and resettlement. In this year cash contributions for both of these purposes were $1,472,000, and gifts-in-kind amounted to $2,086,000, making a total of $3,558,000. In the same year the total loans for resettlement amounted to $85,000. The bringing of this help *In the Name of Christ* to needy people represented a direct personal ministry of 572 men and women, besides occasional short-term commissioners. The usual term of service of a relief worker was two years, although many served longer than this, and also some for shorter periods. By 1948 the emergency phase of the European relief program had passed its crest, and a gradual transition to the rehabilitation type of work was under way. Similar changes in the Mennonite program had taken place in other parts of the world, resulting in a gradual reduction of the number of workers in the field. Even so, the annual meeting in March, 1950, reported a total of 156 MCC and MRC workers still on the field, distributed as follows: Latin America, twenty-one; Ethiopia, eighteen; Palestine, three; the Far East, twenty-six; and Europe, ninety-one.[10]

[10] See Guy F. Hershberger, *The Mennonite Church in the Second World War*, Ch. XV; Irvin B. Horst, *A Ministry of Goodwill* (Akron, Pa., 1950).

Relief a Phase of the Mennonite Peace Testimony[11]

Mennonites have always considered relief to war sufferers as an integral part of their peace testimony. From the beginning of the CPS program in 1941 many of the men in the camps had volunteered for foreign relief work and it had been the hope of the MCC, as well as the administrative agencies of the other peace churches, that this type of service could be offered to all men in CPS who desired it. In 1943 President Roosevelt had even authorized the sending of a unit of seventy CPS men to China. An advance unit of seven men, including one Mennonite, had actually sailed for China when Congress unexpectedly passed legislation forbidding the service of CPS men in any territory outside the United States and its territorial possessions.

The Mennonite colleges had an important part in helping CPS to develop its proposed foreign relief program. In 1942 they reached an agreement among themselves to remain clear of all connections with the war effort. On the other hand, they proposed "to set up a training program for prospective workers in relief and reconstruction service, both at home and abroad, which can be offered to conscientious objectors who are willing to volunteer for service, provided arrangements can be made with Selective Service whereby men in such training can be assigned to such service either before or after induction into Civilian Public Service."

Selective Service approved this idea and issued an order establishing a foreign relief and rehabilitation project to be known as Civilian Public Service Camp No. 101. The project was to consist of "pursuing a course of study in preparation for duty on foreign relief and rehabilitation" and the preparation of materials for such study. Under this program the "main camp" was to be located at Philadelphia, where a small group of research men were to prepare outlines, bibliographies, mimeographed materials, and other helps for the study of relief and reconstruction. The "side camps" were to be located at various Mennonite, Quaker, and Brethren colleges, where groups of

[11] Guy F. Hershberger, *The Mennonite Church in the Second World War*, 179-84.

students would engage in study. The plan was that after the completion of their training the men would engage in foreign relief work, this service to continue for at least one year after the close of the war. The program was begun in the summer of 1943 when a special nine weeks' training school under the auspices of CPS Camp No. 101 was conducted at Goshen College, with sixty-six CPS men and sixteen women volunteers enrolled. Similar training schools were conducted in Quaker and Brethren colleges.

Unfortunately, however, the legislation forbidding the use of CPS men in foreign service made it impossible to continue the CPS relief training program in colleges. It was possible, however, to continue a restricted relief training program within certain CPS camps and units, as part of the regular camp educational program. This restricted program began in September, 1943, and continued into 1946, during which time several hundred men received the relief training. After their discharge from CPS many of these men gave a term of relief service with the MCC in Europe, or in one of the other fields mentioned above.

Peace Testimony Through Voluntary Service[12]

Another type of peace testimony which emerged out of the CPS and wartime experience was that of Voluntary Service. In the summer of 1944 two voluntary service units for women were organized in the state hospitals of Ypsilanti, Michigan, and Howard, Rhode Island, and integrated with the MCC relief training units in operation there. Voluntary Service units in hospitals were continued in 1945 and 1946. In the latter year a unit was also established in connection with the CPS unit at Gulfport, Mississippi, which was engaged in public health work. The war was now over and many of the CPS men were receiving their discharges. Some of these continued their service, however, on a voluntary basis for from two to twelve months after their discharge. After the close of CPS in 1947 the Gulfport project continued on a voluntary basis exclusively. By 1948 the

---

[12] *Ibid.*, Ch. XVI.

Voluntary Service program had assumed rather large proportions. Throughout the year 336 different individuals took part in the program, 62 of them on a full-year basis, and the remainder for shorter terms. This year's program included two Voluntary Service units in Europe. From this point on the Voluntary Service program, as operated by the MCC and by the various conferences, experienced a steady growth so that by 1950 it had come to be recognized as an established part of the Mennonite Christian witness.

Plans of Action in Case of War[13]

This recognition related itself in a definite way to Mennonite plans for action in the event of future war or conscription. CPS, foreign relief, and Voluntary Service constitute a genuine Christian ministry to the needs of mankind. As such, they are a witness against war and other forms of social conflict; and from the government's point of view they can rightfully be considered as an alternative to participation in war. Moreover, the progress of the Korean War in 1950 revealed as never before a world in a continuous state of tension and warfare. That being the case, it was more important than ever that the Christian ministry of love and service be continuously kept in the foreground. Accordingly, in October, 1950, the Peace Section of the MCC urged the enlargement and strengthening of the Voluntary Service programs of the MCC and the various conference agencies, especially in areas which might be approved for alternative service in case of conscription. It was urged that more persons enter the service, for longer periods, and that the areas of service be enlarged to meet the needs of a larger number of people, both in our own country and in foreign lands.

In the meantime the MCC Peace Section, and the peace committees of the various constituent groups, gave increasing attention to possible plans of action in case the conscription of conscientious objectors should be renewed. While recognizing that the CPS program of 1941-47 was superior to any method of dealing with CO's hitherto used in the United States, it was also

[13] *Ibid.*, Ch. I; Gingerich, *Service for Peace.*

recognized that the system had certain unsatisfactory features, which should be remedied in any future program. Consequently, in line with these convictions, the following views were generally included in the public and private expressions of these agencies in 1950 and 1951.

1. In case conscientious objectors are conscripted, the program of service should be under civilian direction, entirely separated from the Department of Defense or Selective Service.

2. Work of "national importance" to which CO's might be assigned should be interpreted to include services of international significance, such as: relief and reconstruction, health services, agricultural development, scientific experimentation, technical assistance, and other fields of humanitarian endeavor.

3. The program should be flexible enough to permit projects under different types of administration. (a) Projects administered and supervised by a civilian government agency. These could be either projects designated from among regular operations of government agencies, or projects especially established for CO's. Costs, including wages for the men, should be borne by the agency concerned. The churches should be permitted to provide a spiritual ministry for these men. (b) Individual civilian employment in fields contributing to the national health and welfare. Such persons should be paid by their employers under conditions not giving them any financial advantage over drafted men in other forms of service. (c) Humanitarian projects which are a regular part of the program of a recognized church agency. This would mean that the relief and Voluntary Service projects of the MCC would be recognized as performing work of national importance under the terms of the conscription act. Persons referred or assigned to these projects would serve under the same conditions as other persons serving in the same project. (d) Civilian service projects established especially for conscientious objectors, and under church or service agency administration and supervision. By this was meant a modified CPS camp. The chief difference between this proposal and the older CPS was that men assigned to the church agency would be under the administration and supervision of the latter.

The church agency would make reports to the responsible government agency, but would not serve as an administrative agency of the government in the sense that was true of the church agencies under CPS. Under this plan administrative costs of the camps would be paid by the church agencies, but the government would pay wages to the men.

4. Persons who by religious training or belief are opposed to registration for conscription, should not be required to do so if their objections are sustained after inquiry and hearing.

These proposals were a combination of what were thought to be the best features of the British, Canadian, and American systems in operation during the second World War. As it actually worked out, when the conscription of CO's was renewed in 1951, the law omitted some of the desirable provisions proposed above, but was also in other respects more desirable than had been hoped for. Wartime conscription had come to an end in 1947. In 1948, however, a new draft law was passed, which became inactive in 1949. It was extended in July, 1950, for one year, then reactivated in August, 1950. This law provided for the deferment of all conscientious objectors. Then in June, 1951, the law was amended to provide that the CO registrant should "be ordered by his local board, subject to such regulations as the President may prescribe, to perform for a period equal to the period prescribed . . . for conscripted men in the armed forces, such civilian work contributing to the maintenance of the national health, safety, or interest as the local board may deem appropriate. . . ." It was the definite intention of this law that there should be no CPS system, but that conscripted CO's should give their service in some other manner.

The new program was inaugurated in the summer of 1952 and provided for the assignment of drafted CO's to approved government and private agencies for work which would contribute to the "national health, safety, or interest." The term of service was fixed at two years, equal to that of men drafted into the army, and the CO's were to be remunerated at the prevailing wage rate of the employing agency. Once the man was assigned to a government or private agency for alternative service he was responsible to that agency until the assignment was completed. The agency would then report the completion of the assignment to Selective Service, after which the latter would certify the man's draft obligations as having been completed. By September 26, 1952, Selective Service had approved the United States Public Health Service throughout the United States and territories as a federal agency to which CO's might be assigned. On the Selective Service list, as of the same date, were no less than 155 specific public and private agencies in 29 states which had been approved for the assignment of CO's. A high percentage of these agencies were hospitals and welfare agencies of various types. On the list of nonprofit private agencies nationally approved for the employment of CO's, were the Mennonite Central Committee, the Brethren Service Committee, and the Near East Foundation. Seventeen domestic and thirty-two foreign projects of the Mennonite Central Committee had been placed on the approved list. The foreign projects consisted of work in relief and voluntary service units in Europe, the Middle East, the Far East, and Latin America, in some cases known later as Pax service units. The domestic projects included service in Mennonite hospitals, homes, and charitable institutions, service units among Indians, migrant laborers, and similar services, including two units in Puerto Rico.

Thus in the summer of 1952 the Mennonites of the United States were entering a new era with respect to conscription. Obviously the new law was more liberal in its provisions for conscientious objectors than any previous law had been. Inasmuch as the CPS system was completely excluded, it was in that respect even more liberal than the Mennonite proposals cited above. On the other hand, it was less liberal than these proposals inasmuch as the law made no provision for the absolutist who objected to registration and any form of service under conscription. A gratifying feature was the approval of foreign relief and service as meeting the requirements of alternative service, a recognition which was not granted during the second World War. The absence of CPS camps, and the provision for remuneration for the men avoided certain administrative and financial problems for the church, although it seemed certain that the new program would also bring many new and unforeseen problems. It was confidently hoped, however, that the new program would be an improvement over all previous programs for the conscription of CO's, with greater opportunities for a consistent witness and service for peace. The alternative service program as here described continued in operation, with only slight modification, in 1969.

A World-wide Peace Witness

This story of migration, relief, voluntary service, and civilian work projects as an alternative to military service, constitutes a twentieth-century Mennonite peace testimony which is world-wide in its scope. The story of the Mennonite migrations for conscience' sake has attracted the attention of the entire world, and their relief and humanitarian service projects have touched many countries in every continent on the globe, except Australia. Their record as conscientious objectors in the United States and Canada is likewise well known. Whereas a generation or two ago mention of the name "Mennonite" raised questions as to who they were, today the name brings favorable responses of recognition everywhere. Inquiries from far and wide find their way to various Mennonite headquarters desiring more information concerning the peace testimony and the evangelical faith which undergirds the Christian service which has been observed, or which perhaps has ministered to the inquirer personally, or to his friends and acquaintances. Accompanying this ministry of action and service has gone an active peace-teaching program, through the publication of literature, the holding of conferences and institutes, the sending out of peace teams on speaking tours, and by other means. Whereas a generation earlier there was almost no Mennonite peace literature which reached beyond their own circles, by 1950 the pacifist reading public was acquainted with the nonresistant views of the Mennonites, and writers were quoting the literature in which those views were set forth. The Mennonite voice was being heard at conferences of the churches for the discussion and promotion of peace, whether in America, or Europe, or in Asia. In the mid-twentieth century the world-wide Mennonite peace testimony was being heard.

Revival of Nonresistance Among the Dutch Mennonites

The influence of this witness was being felt by Mennonites in all parts of the world, even by those who during the previous century had given up their nonresistant faith. In Chapter V reference was made to the Mennonites of Holland, among whom new trends became evident in the twentieth century—trends which within one generation had developed into a movement bringing significant changes among them. About 1820 the decline in the membership of the Dutch Mennonites was halted, and changed into a slow but gradual increase. In 1968 the baptized membership was about 40,000. Moreover, beginning about 1915, a spirit of revival was introduced among them, which by 1950 had turned the church in the direction of its original evangelical and nonresistant principles. This spirit of revival is symbolized by Jan Glijsteen, the one and only Dutch Mennonite who took his stand as a conscientious objector when called up for military service during the first World War. Glijsteen served a term in prison for taking this stand. At the same time a young minister named T. O. Hylkema, through a study of the Bible and church history, began to find his way back to the early position of the church. In this he was helped to some extent by his contacts with the English Quakers. In course of time Hylkema became an outstanding leader among the Dutch Mennonites. In 1917 he and those associated with him formed the Gemeentedag movement, the aim of which was to bring the church back to a more thoroughly Biblical faith. Included in its emphasis was nonresistance. During the 1920's and 1930's there gradually developed among the Dutch Mennonites a vigorous body of opinion opposing military service. In 1925 this led to the formation of a Dutch Mennonite Committee against Military Service, which about ten years later prepared a *Mennonite Peace Manifesto,* appealing to its members "to witness vigorously to our peace testimony in our congregations everywhere," and calling "all Mennonites throughout the world to fulfill the task entrusted to us by the history of our Mennonite forefathers, in the propagation of the Gospel of peace." This *Manifesto* was signed by representatives of Mennonites in various countries, and after the organization of an International Mennonite Peace Committee in the summer of 1936, it was widely circulated among the Mennonites of the world.

Shortly before the beginning of the second World War the Dutch government liberalized its military laws so as again to give some recognition to conscientious objectors. Following the war a program of alternative service was inaugurated, with Civilian Public Service camps for conscientious objectors similar to those in the United States. The program included service in mental hospitals and other similar assignments. In 1952 several hundred Dutch conscientious objectors were engaged in this service, about thirty of them being Mennonites. In 1952 also two Dutch Mennonites whose CO position was not recognized by the government were serving prison sentences. Following the war the organized peace work of the Dutch Mennonites also underwent some change. The earlier Committee against Military Service became the Mennonite Peace Group. This change of name symbolized a changing emphasis in the group's peace teaching and peace work. If the earlier emphasis was largely one of antimilitarism, the later emphasis was increasingly that of Biblical nonresistance, so that by 1950 the Biblical position was dominant in the Dutch Mennonite peace movement. The fact that by 1950 about one half of their ministers were members of the Peace Group is evidence enough that the Dutch Mennonites had made much progress in the recovery of their earlier faith.

Mention was made above of the organization of an International Mennonite Peace Committee. This took place following the third Mennonite World Conference in Holland in the summer of 1936. Participating in the formation of the new organization were members of the Dutch Mennonite Committee against Military Service and representatives of several peace committees from North America. Harold S. Bender of the

United States was chosen chairman of the committee, and Jacob ter Meulen of the Netherlands was chosen secretary-treasurer. The achievements of the new organization, however, were very modest. Moreover, with the coming of the second World War the connections between America and Holland were broken, so that the International Mennonite Peace Committee became dormant and inactive. In the summer of 1949, however, an international Mennonite peace conference in Holland provided the occasion for its revival. In its reorganized form Harold S. Bender again became chairman, and Carl F. Brüsewitz of Holland was chosen secretary.

Revival of Peace Interests in Europe and Beyond

The most significant feature of the 1949 conference, however, was the presence of representatives of the German, French, and Swiss Mennonites, as well as those of Holland and America. Representatives from each of these countries were also named officials of the new organization: Christian Schnebele of Germany; Pierre Widmer of France; and Hans Gerber of Switzerland. The new organization held a second international Mennonite peace conference at Heilbronn, Germany, in the summer of 1950, and a third conference in France in 1951. In 1952 it held a meeting in connection with the fifth Mennonite World Conference in Basel, Switzerland.

The participation of the German, French, and Swiss Mennonites in this movement was of great significance, indicating as it did, a growing interest in nonresistance among these people. In 1951 it was too early to know whether or not this interest would grow into a movement as significant as that of the Dutch Peace Group. The leaders of the movement in these countries were only a few, and their following was not large. And yet there were signs that the movement had genuine life. In Germany a peace conference for German Mennonites was held in 1949. In both 1949 and 1950 the question of nonresistance was discussed at official conferences of the German Mennonites. The constitution of the new West German Republic provided that no one should be compelled against his conscience to perform military service. When the question of re-militarization arose, the German parliament took steps to enact legislation to implement this constitutional provision, and the German churches were given the opportunity of stating their position on conscientious objection. In 1950 the German Mennonite conferences officially went on record as supporting the position of the conscientious objector. Then in 1956 legislation was enacted providing alternative service for German CO's. The program began operation in 1961 and by June 1962 German Mennonites were engaged in alternative service, five of them under EIRENE, a service program for European CO's similar to the American Mennonite Pax program.

In France, with no legal provision for CO's, the Mennonites had succumbed to military service almost as completely as had their German brethren. By 1950, however, influential leaders were being committed to nonresistance once again and in the summer of that year an all-day conference of French Mennonite ministers was devoted to a consideration of the ancient nonresistant testimony, an event without precedent in the memory of those present. Later an appeal was sent to Paris asking legal recognition of CO's. Other pacifists were exercising similar influence with the eventual result that a law of 1963, revised and broadened in 1966, permitted objectors to perform alternative service in a variety of civilian forms.

In Belgium after 1964 Mennonites and other CO's had the privilege of alternative service under the Ministry of the Interior in the context of the Civilian Protection Corps which operates in the event of natural disasters and other emergencies. In 1968 Switzerland had no legal provision for CO's beyond that of noncombatant service in the army medical corps. Among Mennonites, however, the recent trend toward the acceptance of combatant service was being reversed, and influences were at work looking toward eventual provision for civilian alternative service such as in neighboring France and Germany.

In all of these developments the American Mennonites were closely associated with their European brethren. With the

1949 International Mennonite Peace Conference in Holland as a beginning there followed a continuous procession of conferences, peace deputations, and consultations, first among Mennonites and eventually with church leaders among Protestants, and occasionally also with Catholics in Europe, chiefly in the West, but also in the East. Harold S. Bender, Erland Waltner, and C. J. Rempel gave the summer of 1949 to this work which was repeated by Bender and Waltner in 1951. During 1949-1950 Guy F. Hershberger gave a year to peace work in Europe, including a study of European pacifism.

Later in the decade this work was continued and enlarged by John H. Yoder, Albert Meyer, Paul Peachey, William Keeney, and others working closely with the Dutch Mennonite Peace Group, with representatives of the Friends and the Church of the Brethren and other European peace leaders. One fruit of their labors was the statement, *Peace Is the Will of God,* published in 1953 for presentation to the Evanston Assembly of the World Council of Churches in 1954. Following this beginning the Delhi Assembly in 1961 issued a mandate for an official study of the peace question by the World Council, a study which was held in May-June 1968, with two Mennonites, John H. Yoder of the United States and Heinold Fast of Germany, participating. The results of this study were then referred to the Uppsala Assembly later that year. Another significant development was the series of Puidoux conferences, the first in Puidoux, Switzerland, in 1955, for dialogue in depth on the peace question with representatives of the Historic Peace Churches and Protestant church leaders in participation.

In the meantime the Peace Section of the Mennonite Central Committee and the mission boards of the various Mennonite groups were in continuous cooperation for the promotion of the peace witness among the Mennonite churches beyond Europe and North America. During the decade up to 1968 commissioners with responsibility for this work were found in Indonesia, India, and Japan; in numerous countries of Africa; and in South America, particularly Argentina, Uruguay, and Brazil. Their work included that of occasional conferences in which representatives of the various missions and churches in a given area came together for the finding of ways and means by which to make their peace witness increasingly effective.

Mennonites and the Vietnam War

Overshadowing all else in this decade, however, was the impact of the Vietnam War upon the peace witness of Mennonites around the world. In 1954 the MCC had begun a modest relief work, and in 1957 the Eastern Mennonite Board of Missions and Charities opened mission work in South Vietnam. Then as the American military forces replaced the French in that country the gradual buildup of troops to 23,000 in March 1965 became a rapid upsurge to 545,000 by mid-1968.

As the countryside and the homes of the people were increasingly laid waste the number of refugees in South Vietnam increased from 800,000 in early 1965 to 2,500,000 or more in 1968—in a country whose total population was only 15,000,000 people. This situation which aroused opposition to American foreign policy around the world, and within the United States itself to an extent seldom seen in wartime, was the occasion for a greatly intensified Mennonite world-wide peace witness.

In 1967 Lutheran World Relief and Church World Service joined the MCC in forming a cooperative organization known as Vietnam Christian Service and administered by MCC. In 1967 VNCS had 87 Western personnel in eleven areas of the country, 45 of the 87 being MCC personnel. The total MCC personnel in Asia was 81. MCC workers were also stationed in nine African countries, 68 in the Congo alone. In 1967 the total number of MCC personnel in countries outside the United States, which included Latin America, Israel, Jordan, Greece, and even Yugoslavia, was upwards of 300. A few Dutch Mennonites were included in the MCC personnel in Africa. Besides this the European Mennonites had recently formed the International Mennonite Organization for carrying on foreign relief and other projects under their own direction.

When it is remembered that all this was in addition to the combined foreign missionary personnel of the various Mennonite groups, the potential Mennonite peace witness throughout the world was clearly evident. That this potential was realized at least in part is clear from the forthright manner in which the Mennonite churches spoke out against the Vietnam War, of which the following are but three illustrations.

1. Mennonite periodicals through the war years, particularly from 1965, were vigorously outspoken in their testimony against the war and in their plea for peace. In January 1966, for example, the *Mennonite* and the *Gospel Herald,* two leading denominational organs, each devoted an entire issue to the Vietnam question.

2. In 1967 the Mennonite General Conference addressed a letter to President Johnson, pleading "with you on behalf of those who suffer in Vietnam, both North and South, and of the deprived in our own midst: turn back from the immoral course on which the nation is now embarked in Vietnam."

3. That same year the Mennonite missionaries in Vietnam addressed a *Letter from Vietnam to American Christians,* calling on them "to become aware of the image being given to our faith" when the suffering Vietnamese "hear that our president prays God to bless 'our pilots' on their missions of destruction," thus giving "the impression that the Christians' God is behind our country's action in Vietnam." The letter closed with a plea for "a change of heart . . . a change of policy . . . a tolerant spirit . . . a fresh demonstration of our confession that in Christ there is no East or West."

Thus at the beginning of the last third of the twentieth century there was a growing conviction within the Mennonite brotherhood that the way of peace was an integral part of the Gospel of Christ, and the Mennonite peace witness was growing ever more world-wide in its scope, and more intensified in its proclamation and in its effort.

SELECT BIBLIOGRAPHY

In addition to C. Henry Smith's general works, J. S. Hartzler, *Mennonites in the World War* (Scottdale, Pa., 1921), has helpful material on the relief program of the Mennonite Church following the first World War. P. C. Hiebert and Orie O. Miller, *Feeding the Hungry: Russian Famine, 1919-1925* (Scottdale, Pa., 1929), tells the story of Mennonite relief in Russia during that period. Several books treating the Quaker relief program are Rufus M. Jones, *A Service of Love in Wartime* (New York, 1920), and Lester M. Jones, *Quakers in Action* (New York, 1929). The story of the migration from Russia to Paraguay is well told in Walter Quiring, *Deutsche erschliessen den Chaco* (Karlsruhe, Germany, 1936), and *Russland-deutsche suchen eine Heimat: Die Deutsche Einwanderung in den Paraguayischen Chaco* (Karlsruhe, Germany, 1936). Sanford C. Yoder, *For Conscience Sake* (Goshen, Ind., 1940), gives a complete survey of Mennonite migrations resulting from the first World War. Irvin B. Horst, *A Ministry of Goodwill: A Short Account of Mennonite Relief, 1939-1949* (Akron, Pa., 1950), tells the relief story during and following the second World War period. Melvin Gingerich, *Service for Peace* (Akron, Pa., 1949), and Guy F. Hershberger, *The Mennonite Church in the Second World War* (Scottdale, Pa., 1951), deal with the Mennonite peace testimony during the same period. Samuel A. Yoder, *Middle-East Sojourn* (Scottdale, Pa., 1951), is the intimate personal account of a Mennonite relief worker's experiences, 1944-45. The story of the Mennonite witness in Puerto Rico is told in Justus G. Holsinger, *Serving Rural Puerto Rico: A History of Eight Years of Service by the Mennonite Church* (Scottdale, Pa., 1952). The most recent book on the subject is John D. Unruh, *In the Name of Christ: A History of the Mennonite Central Committee and Its Services, 1920-1951* (Scottdale, Pa., 1952). *The Mennonite Encyclopedia* has articles on peace and nonresistance and on Mennonite relief and service. A pamphlet specifically designed as a witness to Christendom is *Peace Is the Will of God: A Testimony to the World Council of Churches,* a statement by the Historic Peace Churches and the Fellowship of Reconciliation (1953). A helpful recent booklet on the Christian peace ministry in Vietnam is Atlee and Winifred Beechy, *Vietnam: Who Cares?* (Scottdale, Pa., 1968).

8. Nonresistance and the State in Modern Life

The New Testament is concerned with redemption through Jesus Christ and with the manner of life which Christians should live. All other matters are incidental to this. Consequently the New Testament is not concerned with the political questions of the day. Jesus and Paul do not suggest what type of state is most desirable, nor how it should be conducted. It is not suggested that Christians should play any role in the affairs of state. The Sermon on the Mount is not a piece of legislation for a secular state in a sinful society; it is a set of principles to govern the conduct of members of the kingdom of God; and Jesus said this kingdom is not of this world, and that its members do not fight.[1]

The Christian's Relation to the State

It is impossible to escape the fact, however, that Christians must live in a world where the secular state is everywhere present. How, then, shall the nonresistant teachings of the New Testament be carried out in practice? Historically, the state has been primarily an organization for the maintenance of law and order, by means of coercion, in a sinful society; and the nonresistant Christian must have some relationship to that state. What should this relationship be? One might also raise the theoretical question as to the place of the state in a genuinely Christian society. Suppose the entire Jewish nation in the time of Christ had accepted Him. Should they have constituted a state of their own? Or if not that, what should have been their relation to the Roman state? Again, what would be the political

[1] John 18:36.

156

relations of a Christian nation in our own time? Is it possible
to think of Christians being active politically to the extent that
they control a state and operate it by the nonresistant principles
of the New Testament, thus removing the sharp distinction between the kingdom of God and the sinful society of this world?

Certain aspects of this problem are discussed in Chapter
IX. At this point it is sufficient to say that there never has been
anything like a truly Christian state on a national scale, even
though there have been national states which have professed
Christianity. At best we have states governing sinful societies
which contain individual Christians. These Christian citizens
have a wholesome influence on the society in which they live,
and upon the state itself. But as long as the entire society is
not Christian, the state will need to employ the coercive means
which it always has used. It will continue to be primarily an
organization for the maintenance of law and order, by coercive
means, in a sinful society. A truly Christian society would be
something quite different from anything which we know today.
Such a society would, of course, require some organization for
the orderly management of its affairs. But the coercive function
would necessarily be absent; and, as Marsiglio of Padua and William of Occam pointed out in the fourteenth century, with this
element removed a given society would no longer be a state.[2]
Some other name would be required to describe it.

The Anabaptist Attitude Toward the State

Our question then resolves itself to this: What is the relation of the nonresistant Christian to the state which uses force
and resistance? To ask the question is almost to answer it. It is
obvious that one cannot be nonresistant and resistant at the same
time. One cannot be the state's hangman and obey the Sermon
on the Mount. To this point the question is easily answered.
The nonresistant Christian cannot wield the sword for the state.
The history of the church as outlined in Chapter IV amply veri-

[2] Cf. W. A. Dunning, *A History of Political Theories, Ancient and Medieval* (New
York, 1919), 1:247.

fies this point. In the early period, when church and state were separate, the church was nonresistant. But in the fourth century when the church was united with the state its nonresistance came to an end.

This loss of nonresistance through the union of the church and state is one reason why the sixteenth-century Anabaptists, who later came to be called Mennonites, from the beginning of their history believed in a voluntary church, separated from the state. They believed that the Christian must be obedient to the New Testament doctrine of nonresistance. They believed that the church should be a holy brotherhood, separate from the state. Individuals who experienced conversion were welcomed into the holy society. But the Anabaptists did not attempt to control the unregenerate society of the world through their church in the manner that Calvin did. Nor did they permit the state in any way to interfere with the affairs of the church. They believed that the unregenerate world was not capable of living a nonresistant life. To have the church and the state united in any way, they believed, would mean the loss of the principle of nonresistance by the church. Therefore the Anabaptists rejected compromise and saved the principle of nonresistance by maintaining a strict separation of the church and state.

The Quaker Attitude Toward the State

In the seventeenth century in England, another interesting religious group came into existence. This was the Society of Friends, called Quakers. The Quakers, like the Mennonites, were opposed to war. Like the Mennonites, they did not believe that the state should direct the affairs of the church. But in another way they were very different from the Mennonites. They believed it possible for members of the church to play an active part in the affairs of state, and in this way induce the state to adopt the peaceful ways of the church. In 1682 William Penn, a great Quaker leader, came from England to Pennsylvania to undertake his so-called "holy experiment" in government. Pennsylvania was the most democratic of all the colonies, but Penn was interested in more than democracy. He firmly believed that the peaceful nonresistant ways of the New Testament could be carried out in government. He planned to get along without an army and a navy; and he seems to have thought that it might eventually be possible to get along without jails and policemen as well. On one occasion he advised his people: "Strive not, read the fifth of Matthew, the twelfth of Romans . . . you will see what becomes Christianity even in government."[3] In these words Penn laid his finger on the heart of our problem.

Could the teachings of Matthew five and Romans twelve be realized even in government; or would the Quakers in the government sooner or later have to decide to give up their nonresistance in favor of their offices; or would they give up their position in government to retain their religious principles? In the end, after seventy-five years of effort, it came to exactly this point. In 1756, when the pressure for participation in the French and Indian War became strong, the more religious Quakers resigned from the government to preserve their nonresistant faith, while their more political-minded brethren gave up their faith and remained in the government. All in all, the result of the holy experiment was to show that nonresistance and the coercive functions of the state can not go together. One must choose one or the other; he cannot have both.

There is no space here to discuss in detail the causes for the failure of Penn's experiment, but certainly one of the causes was the fact that Pennsylvania was a mixed society. Some of the people were Quakers, Mennonites, Dunkers, and Moravians who believed in nonresistance, and others were Scotch Presbyterians who did not believe that way. And then there were some who were not even Christians. Perhaps if all the people of Pennsylvania had been faithful Quakers or Mennonites, all of them firm believers in New Testament nonresistance, and if Pennsylvania had not been under the British government, the experiment might have succeeded. But as it was, Pennsylvania was a mixed society, approaching too nearly the sinful society which requires the coercive methods which have always belonged to

---

[3] Dreer Mss. Collection, Hist. Soc. of Pa., *Letters and Papers of William Penn*, 38.

the state; and Pennsylvania was also an integral part of the British state which demanded support of military operations. And so Penn's experiment seems to verify the proposition mentioned before, that a nonresistant Christian cannot engage in the administration of a political state, at least in a mixed society, without being in danger of losing his nonresistance. One cannot be resistant and nonresistant at the same time. One cannot be the state's hangman and obey the Sermon on the Mount. The nonresistant Christian cannot wield the sword for the state.

A General Attitude of Submission to the Government

The modern state has many secondary functions, however, besides the primary function of maintaining law and order. In recent times the state has become a great welfare organization for the promotion of health, education, transportation, communication, and a hundred other activities which once were largely in private hands, and in many of which nonresistant people have always engaged. What, now, should be the relation of the Christian to these activities when they are performed by the state? Is it possible to draw some kind of line, placing on the one side those state functions in which the nonresistant Christian can participate, and on the other those in which he cannot participate? If so, where shall the line be drawn, and how shall the various functions of government be classified? There is no attempt here to make a final analysis. But the following is what seems to the author a reasonable, workable, and Scriptural view of the nonresistant Christian's relation to the modern state.

The nonresistant Christian should have a submissive and respectful attitude toward the state and its rulers. Paul speaks in positive terms when he says: "Let every soul be in subjection to the higher powers . . . he that resisteth the power, withstandeth the ordinance of God: and they that withstand shall receive to themselves judgment."[4] Nonresistant Christians should be the most law-abiding citizens of the state. Laws are intended for

---

[4] Rom. 13:1, 2 (ASV).

the suppression of evil and for the promotion of the public welfare. The Christian cannot be on the side of evil; he must be on the side of right. There are laws against stealing and murder, laws against improper driving on the highways, laws requiring sanitary precautions in the preparation of foods for the market, laws requiring the purchase of a license and payment of a fee for the privilege of driving an automobile, laws requiring a license for teaching in the schools. All of these, and a thousand other laws intended for the public good, must be obeyed by the Christian, who should be the nation's greatest benefactor. This attitude of submission to the state and respect for its rulers has been clearly stated in article 13 of the Dortrecht Confession of Faith: "We are not permitted to despise, blaspheme, or resist the same; but are to acknowledge it as a minister of God and be subject and obedient to it, in all things that do not militate against the law, will, and commands of God; yea, to be ready to every good work; also faithfully to pay it custom, tax, and tribute; thus giving it what is its due, as Jesus Christ taught, did himself, and commanded his followers to do."[5]

Prayer for Those in Authority

It must also be remembered that, even though many of the state's functions are of the kind in which the nonresistant Christian cannot participate, there is after all a real sense in which the state is instituted by God. Thus it serves a divine purpose in the achievement of God's purpose in this world. For this reason the New Testament enjoins Christians to pray for the government and its officials. The Apostle Paul says: "I exhort therefore, that . . . supplications, prayers, intercessions, and giving of thanks, be made for all men; for kings, and for all that are in authority; that we may lead a quiet and peaceable life in all godliness and honesty."[6] Certainly the nonresistant Christian, so much of whose life is concerned with and affected by what the state does, and whose daily life is one of devotion, must not

[5] See this article printed in full in appendix 4.
[6] I Tim. 2:1, 2.

fail continually to pray for his own government, and for all governments of the world, that under the providence of God those in positions of responsibility and authority may be directed so to perform their duties that God's purposes may be accomplished. This duty of the Christian toward the state, so clearly stated in the New Testament, is prominently mentioned in the various Mennonite confessions of faith, and has always been stressed throughout the history of the church. In the twentieth century, with the tasks and duties of state officials growing ever more complex, nonresistant Christians have a solemn obligation to take seriously this responsibility of praying for those in authority.

State Functions in Which the Nonresistant Christian May Not Participate

For the maintenance of law and order, the state maintains jails, police, and a department of justice. Violators of the law are arrested by the police, brought before the judge for trial and sentence, and then fined or committed to prison, or in extreme cases even put to death. All of these operations involve methods which do not harmonize with the New Testament way of nonresistance. Most of them may be necessary for the successful operation of a state in a sinful society. But as observed before, the Christian is called to live a life on a higher level than this. Military operations, likewise, are one of the functions of state which obviously cannot be engaged in by the nonresistant Christian.

The question is sometimes raised whether a nonresistant Christian can serve in an administrative or legislative capacity, such as that of president, prime minister, member of a parliament or national legislature, or a mayor or councilman of a city. The answer should not be very difficult, however, when it is remembered that the president is commander in chief of the army and navy, and that the city police are under the direction of the mayor. Congressmen and members of parliaments have the responsibility of declaring war and appropriating funds for military purposes; American state legislatures appropriate funds for the state militia; and all types of legislative bodies fix penalties for violation of the law. It would seem difficult, therefore, for a believer in New Testament nonresistance to hold, with any degree of consistency, a major executive, legislative, or judicial position in a modern state. As a rule those Mennonites who have held important state positions have not been active in the promotion of the church's peace testimony and frequently they have not been nonresistant at all.[7]

The fact that there have been exceptions to the rule, however, should caution one against declaring it impossible to occupy an important state position and remain nonresistant. Some of the consistently nonresistant Quakers, who because of circumstances were forced to resign in 1756, afterwards, when circumstances had changed, returned to their place in the Pennsylvania legislature. Would this suggest that, under certain circumstances, certain state positions would be a possibility for the nonresistant Christian, and that under other circumstances they would not be possible? The statement above suggests the difficulty which would be encountered by a Mennonite in the state legislature, because legislators appropriate funds for the militia. Peter Jansen, a well-known member of the General Conference Mennonite Church a generation ago, served several terms in the Nebraska state legislature, but refused the nomination for the governorship which had been offered him, because as a nonresistant Christian he could not serve as commander in chief of the militia. The author is not certain what Jansen did about voting appropriations for the militia while he was in the legislature. Presumably, however, a legislator could refuse to vote for such appropriations. Another member of the General Conference Mennonite Church who served for a time in the state legislature

[7] An illustration is the case of a city official, a member of one of the Mennonite conferences in North America, who wrote a letter of congratulation to one of the city's war production factories, upon its receipt of an army-navy award for outstanding performance in "providing vital war materials," knowing that the "men in the armed forces . . . will be cheered to receive this information." During the campaign prior to the election which brought this Mennonite candidate into office, the same political advertisements which urged the public to vote for the candidate, also urged them to buy war bonds for the purchase of guns to shoot the enemy. European Mennonites who have held major offices in government have not, for the most part, been nonresistant.

was H. P. Krehbiel of Kansas. Krehbiel was a minister who was very active in his peace testimony, and took a leading part in the Newton, Kansas, meeting in 1935 which led to the formation of the Conference of Historic Peace Churches. These seem to be exceptions to the rule, however.

Theoretically it would be possible for a nonresistant Christian to serve as a congressman or a national legislator without compromising on the war question. He could refrain from casting his vote for military appropriations or military measures of any kind. He could even vote against them. There may be some states in certain periods of history where such a nonresistant national legislator could continue for years without encountering embarrassing involvements on the war issue. The same might be true of city mayors in certain countries at certain times. It is doubtful, however, whether this would be possible in a powerful country like the United States in the twentieth century. What is said here refers to involvement on the war issue only. To remain clear of involvement in the police functions of the state, however, would seem even more difficult; and from the viewpoint of New Testament nonresistance there is no essential difference in kind between the police and the military.

State Functions in Which the Nonresistant Christian May Participate

Among the functions which the state has assumed in modern times for the promotion of the general welfare there are many activities which in themselves are legitimate for the nonresistant Christian to engage in. In many cases Christians were engaged in these services before the state took them over. The fact that the state now performs them is no reason why the Christian cannot continue in them, providing participation does not involve promotion of other activities which are unlawful for the Christian. Teaching in a state school in itself would seem to be permissible. But if a situation should arise where the teacher would be required to promote an anti-Christian education, he could not consistently remain in his position. Cer-

tainly a nonresistant teacher could not be part of a school program for the promotion of war. Employment in the state's
postal service would seem to be permissible for a nonresistant
Christian, but consistency would certainly require that he draw
the line short of using a gun for the protection of the mails.

Among other state services which might be mentioned as
legitimate for the nonresistant Christian are public health service, building of roads and streets, forestry, soil conservation,
agricultural and scientific experimentation and research, forest
and other fire fighting, and other services. Many such functions
might be mentioned which are legitimate in themselves. But
in all of them the Christian needs to be alert and ever on his
guard, lest in the performance of a legitimate function he be
required along with it to perform some other function which is
inconsistent with his nonresistant testimony.

Functions Which the State May Not Legitimately Assume

When Jesus granted that to Caesar should be given what belongs to Caesar, He also added: "And [render] unto God the
things that are God's."[8] The negative of this statement would
be: Do not give to Caesar the things that are not Caesar's. The
Christian must never forget that there are some things which
do not belong to Caesar. The state may legitimately increase
its functions along certain lines for the promotion of the general
welfare. But this extension of function has a definite limit.
When the state reaches into the realm of religion, conscience,
and the home, and attempts to control these, it is demanding
what does not belong to it. Modern totalitarian states attempt
to dominate the whole of life. They regard their own authority
as the source of all authority. They do not recognize the independence of religion, culture, education, and the family.
They seek to impose on all citizens a uniform philosophy of life.
Education, up to a certain point, is a legitimate function of the
state, but totalitarian states make an illegitimate use of education when they seek to create a particular type of man with a
totalitarian world view.

[8] Luke 20:25 (ASV).

It is the duty of the church and the individual Christian to be on guard against such illegitimate encroachments of the state. If the state enters this realm and makes demands which are in conflict with the will of God, the Christian must have the courage to say: "We must obey God rather than men." The Anabaptists of the sixteenth century insisted strongly that the state must not rule in these matters, and many of their leaders died as martyrs to a faith which required a separation of church and state.

A Strong Emphasis on the Church's Own Program

The Christian must always remember that his first obligation is to God and not to the state. Perhaps the best antidote for a totalitarian state is a society of self-reliant people who know how to do things for themselves. The better a society can meet its needs, without the aid of the state, the less the danger that the state will encroach upon those areas where it ought not to operate at all. The church as well as the state has an obligation for education. If the church takes this obligation seriously, and does its share of the task well, there is a reasonable hope that it will continue to hold the respect of the state. The church has a great opportunity in medicine, health, and nursing. If it does this task well the state will have further warning that not all of life should be brought under state control. The relief and reconstruction programs of the peace churches have been a great help in proving to the state the sincerity of the nonresistant people, and have been a means of preventing an encroachment upon their religious liberty. Various forms of social security, such as old-age pensions, unemployment insurance, and government aid and loans to farmers, would seem to be legitimate functions of the state. But there is always danger that if Christians depend too much on the state they will eventually become too much obligated to the state. On the other hand, if many groups of Christians find it possible to provide their own social and economic security along these lines it will help the church greatly to maintain its life and integrity.

If the church does these things and does them well, not merely as a humanitarian program but out of a deep-seated religious conviction, it will be doing much to save its own life as well as to strengthen democracy in the state and nation. When individuals and groups are able to stand on their own feet the result is democracy; when they can no longer do this the state takes them over and then the result is a long step on the road to totalitarianism. In this connection it is fitting to quote the words of J. H. Oldham, who feels that for the sake of Christianity and democracy the church must play a much larger role in education than it now does:

It may well be that the main conflict between Christian faith and the secular interpretation of life will have to be waged in the field of public education. The church will have won little in obtaining liberty to preach and to conduct its own worship services, if the whole weight of a public system of education is directed towards inculcating in the impressionable mind of youth beliefs about the world and man and conduct which are incompatible with the Christian understanding of life.[9]

The Contribution of Nonresistance to Society

The question is sometimes raised whether such detachment from political life as has been described above is the best policy for the Christian. After all, Christians are interested in clean and good government, and is this not more likely to be had with Christians in the government than if they remain on the outside? Is this aloofness adopted for the purpose of helping society, or is it to save one's own religion? If it is the latter, is one not taking a narrow attitude? Does not the Christian owe something to his community and to the state? And if he remains aloof will he not be derelict in his duty? Is the nonresistant Christian a parasite living at the expense of organized society?

These questions are fair enough and deserve an answer. In finding the answer it will be helpful to remember that while the Christian has an obligation to his fellow men, his first obliga-

[9] J. H. Oldham, *Church, Community, and State: a World Issue* (New York, 1935), 17, 18.

tion is necessarily to God. If political activity prevents the discharge of his obligation to God it would better be sacrificed. Decisions and choices would always be wiser if they were determined by the will of God as revealed in the Scriptures, rather than by what seems socially the most useful for the time being. It is the writer's sincere belief, however, that in this case at least, that which to some may seem socially least useful is actually the contrary. It is his belief that ultimately the Christian will render society a greater service by remaining politically aloof and living a life of genuine nonresistance, than by being politically active where sooner or later he may sacrifice or compromise this principle.

Seventy-five years ago Adin Ballou, a New England preacher who believed in nonresistance, stated the case as follows: "Would not persons of the moral and religious type I have indicated [the nonresistant type] do quite as much good to a town, state, or nation, and at as little cost as an equal number who should manipulate and manage party politics . . . ?" Ballou does not mean by this that public officials are to be despised. They are to be respected; and government, he says, is right and good on its proper level. But Christian morality is vastly superior to this, and those who adopt it and live by it "are the most advanced and the wisest leaders of mankind to their divinely ordained destiny." "The high calling of" the church is to "stand morally at the front of the procession of humanity, to lead it on to a truer righteousness, to leaven it with regenerating influences, to salt it with divine principles, to a more 'excellent way' . . . ."[10]

This idea has recently been stated afresh by T. S. Eliot, an English writer. While Eliot is not a pacifist, he is a Christian who believes that the Christian can make his greatest contribution to society, even to the state, outside rather than inside the political arena. Eliot says:

The Christian and the unbeliever do not, and cannot behave very differently in the exercise of office; for it is the general ethos of the people they have to govern, not their own piety, that determines

---

[10] Adin Ballou, *Primitive Christianity and Its Corruptions* (1870), 2:180, 201-2.

the behavior of politicians . . . . It is not primarily the Christianity of the statesmen that matters, but their being confined, by the temper and traditions of the people which they rule, to a Christian framework within which to realize their ambitions and advance the prosperity and prestige of their country . . . . What the rulers believed, would be less important than the beliefs to which they would be obliged to conform. And a skeptical or indifferent statesman, working within a Christian frame, might be more effective than a devout Christian statesman obliged to conform to a secular frame. For he would be required to design his policy for the government of a Christian Society.[11]

According to this view a Christian political organization would have relatively slight influence on the general society, if that society were itself not Christian. What is more, William Penn's "holy experiment" seems to show that under such circumstances the officials of this Christian government would be in danger of losing their own Christianity, or at least their nonresistance. The mission of nonresistant Christians, therefore, is not a political one. It is rather a curative mission. It is to bring healing to human society; to prevent its further decay, and that through a consistent witness to the truth. The same Sermon on the Mount which commends the way of nonresistance to the disciples of Christ also says, "Ye are the salt of the earth,"[12] and if the earth is to be salted, the salt dare not lose its own savor through activities which destroy its essential nature.

Without doubt the present world conflict, and the ills which accompany it, have been brought upon us by the paganism of our age. The world suffered its second war in a generation, and now seems to be in a third, not primarily because its international organization has failed to function, but because its morals and its ethics do not conform to the mind of Christ. This world sadly needs the ministry of nonresistant Christians whose light, set on a hill, stands as a glowing witness to the way of truth and righteousness. A people who provide this ministry are not parasites living at the expense of organized society. In the words of Origen: "It is not for the purpose of escaping public duties

---

[11] T. S. Eliot, *The Idea of a Christian Society* (New York, 1940), 25-27.
[12] Matt. 5:13.

that Christians decline public offices, but that they may reserve themselves for a diviner and more necessary service in the Church of God—for the salvation of men." "For the Men of God are assuredly the salt of the earth; they preserve the order of the world; and society is held together as long as the salt is uncorrupted."[13]

Nonresistant Christians must remember, however, that salt cannot perform its curative work without actually making contact with that which is to be cured. Although the nonresistant Christian may not be "of the world," he is nevertheless "in the world," and is therefore responsible to testify to all men concerning the truth as he understands it. Likewise, while he cannot perform certain functions of state which would compromise his position, the nonresistant Christian is nevertheless a member of the national community. As such he has an obligation to testify to officials of state and to his fellow citizens, both by word and deed, concerning the way of love as taught by Jesus Christ.

If war is sin, Christian people have an obligation to make this truth known. When racial discrimination and other forms of social injustice abound on every hand, it is the Christian's privilege and duty to set forth the way of love which does justice to all men, regardless of station, color, race, or creed. As Edward Yoder has said: When the nation errs, in this and in other ways, the Christian citizen rightly may "feel a genuine sorrow and express a genuine repentance and confession for the sins of his national community. As did Daniel and Nehemiah and other prophets in Israel, so should Christians feel moved to confess the sins of the nation of which they are a part. To stand aloof in a self-righteous manner and assert that the sins and evils of the community are not our responsibility seems just a little like the action of the Pharisee who prayed in the Temple and proudly thanked God that he was not as bad as some other people."[14]

---

[13] *Ante-Nicene Fathers* (New York, 1925), 4:666, 668 (*Origen vs. Celsus*, 8:70, 75).
[14] Edward Yoder, "The Obligation of the Christian to the State and Community," *Mennonite Quarterly Review* (Goshen, Ind., April, 1939), 13:113.

SELECT BIBLIOGRAPHY

Ernst Troeltsch, *The Social Teaching of the Christian Churches,* 2 vols. (London, 1931), gives an excellent historical account of the attitude of the various Christian groups toward the state. Nils Ehrenström, *Christian Faith and the Modern State* (Chicago, 1937), is a summary of present-day theories of church and state, with some historical background. All of the standard works on Mennonite and Quaker history have sections or chapters on the attitude of these groups toward the state. Guy F. Hershberger, "The Pennsylvania Quaker Experiment in Politics, 1682-1756," *Mennonite Quarterly Review* (Goshen, Ind., October, 1936), and "Pacifism and the State in Colonial Pennsylvania," *Church History* (Chicago, March, 1939), are the most recent examinations of Quaker political theories under the test of actual practice in colonial Pennsylvania.

T. S. Eliot, *The Idea of a Christian Society* (New York, 1940), treats the relation of the state to the making of a Christian society. Adin Ballou is a nonresistant whose *Primitive Christianity and Its Corruptions,* published in 1870, contains a section on the relation of the nonresistant Christian to the state. Helpful articles are: H. S. Bender, "Church and State in Mennonite History," *Mennonite Quarterly Review* (April, 1939), 13:83-103; Edward Yoder, "Christianity and the State," *Mennonite Quarterly Review* (July, 1937), 11:171-95; and Edward Yoder, "The Obligation of the Christian to the State and Community," *Mennonite Quarterly Review* (April, 1939), 13:104-22.

The Mennonite Encyclopedia has various articles, and Guy F. Hershberger, *The Way of the Cross in Human Relations* and Hershberger (ed.), *The Recovery of the Anabaptist Vision* have chapters treating nonresistance and the state. Four recent books of importance on church and state are: John C. Bennett, *Christians and the State* (Scribner, 1958); Paul Peachey (ed.), *Biblical Realism Confronts the Nation* (Fellowship, 1963); Thomas G. Sanders, *Protestant Concepts of Church and State* (Holt, 1964); and John H. Yoder, *The Christian Witness to the State* (Newton, Kans., 1964).

9. Biblical Nonresistance and Modern Pacifism

Nonresistance and Pacifism

While Christendom in general has surrendered almost completely on the question of war, the Biblical doctrine of nonresistance has nevertheless continued to live through more than nineteen centuries. Certain groups like the Waldenses helped to keep it alive in the Middle Ages, and the Mennonites have had a large part in doing so in the period since the Reformation. In addition to the Mennonites, other individuals and groups have likewise had a share in this great mission. From the beginning of its history the Society of Friends has maintained a constant testimony against war. The Church of the Brethren has held to the Biblical doctrine of nonresistance from the beginning of its history in 1708, and in many other points of doctrine and practice the Brethren have resembled the Mennonites. In 1815 David Low Dodge, a Presbyterian layman, founded the New York Peace Society. He based his peace teachings entirely on the Bible and he was as thoroughly nonresistant as the Mennonites, or as the New Testament itself. Adin Ballou was another advocate of nonresistance in the early nineteenth century, although his teaching was not as Bible-centered as that of Dodge. Both of these men avoided political activity, however, because they believed this would involve them in actions inconsistent with the doctrine of nonresistance.[1]

Dodge and Ballou were active in the promotion of peace in an organized way, through the publication of literature, through addresses and sermons, and in numerous other ways. In addition to these men, many other leaders were similarly engaged.

[1] For citations on the views of Ballou see p. 168.

Their number was so large, and their activity was so great, that this movement came to be known as the "peace movement" of the early nineteenth century. Since that time the peace movement has been a permanent institution in American life. In times of war it has always declined in influence, but once the war is over it has generally become more active than before. It is important to observe, however, that not everything in the modern peace movement is Biblical nonresistance. The term commonly used to describe the view which refuses participation in warfare is pacifism. Many leaders in the peace movement, however, could not even be called pacifists, since they are merely striving for more satisfactory international relations. They would not necessarily refuse to support a war in case it should actually come.

Nonresistance and pacifism are both Scriptural terms, taken from the Sermon on the Mount. The former is taken from the words of Jesus, "Resist not him that is evil."[2] The latter comes from the words, "Blessed are the peacemakers."[3] In the Latin Bible the word for peacemakers is *pacifici,* the direct English form of which is *pacifists.* There is nothing objectionable about the term "pacifism" as far as its original meaning goes. In some ways it is preferable to nonresistance, because it is positive in its suggestion, while nonresistance seems more negative. In evaluating any term, however, its original meaning is not as important as its present use. The term "nonresistance" as commonly used today describes the faith and life of those who accept the Scriptures as the revealed will of God, and who cannot have any part in warfare because they believe the Bible forbids it, and who renounce all coercion, even nonviolent coercion. Pacifism, on the other hand, is a term which covers many types of opposition to war. Some modern pacifists are opposed to all wars, and some are not. Some who oppose all wars find their authority in the will of God, while others find it largely in human reason. There are many other differences among them. It is therefore important to attempt a classification of modern pacifists, and to compare and evaluate their philosophies.

<hr />

[2] Matt. 5:39 (ASV).   [3] Matt. 5:9.

International Peace Plans

During the past six centuries many plans have been offered for maintaining the peace of the world.[4] The authors of some of these plans were pacifists in the sense that they would take no part in war themselves, but most of them were not. They merely believed that war is undesirable, and offered plans which they hoped might prevent it. If these plans failed and their country became involved in war, however, they were ready to support it.

In the fourteenth century a French statesman named Pierre Dubois offered a plan for the federation of Europe under the leadership of France. He suggested an international court of arbitration, and proposed united military action on the part of the federated powers against any nation which would violate the peace or reject the decisions of the court. About the same time Dante and Marsiglio of Padua proposed a world state under an all-powerful emperor. In the seventeenth century Henry IV, king of France, and his minister Sully, proposed an association of states with an armed international police at its command to enforce the maintenance of peace. About the same time Hugo Grotius of the Netherlands published a learned treatise on the laws of war and peace. In 1840 William Ladd, an American, published *An Essay on a Congress of Nations*. This was an elaborate plan for a parliament of representatives from all of the national states, and for a world court for the settlement of disputes. The establishment of the Hague Court in 1899 marked the beginning of some actual achievement along this line, and after the World War many hoped that the League of Nations and the permanent World Court would be able to continue these efforts and make them so effective as to prevent another war. Following the second World War a renewed effort in the same direction was made through the organization of the new United Nations. In the period between the two world wars numerous American organizations were active in the promotion of peace plans in line with the ideals of the League of Nations

---

[4] For an excellent survey of international peace plans see S. J. Hemleben, *Plans for World Peace Through Six Centuries* (Chicago, 1934).

and the World Court. Among the organizations placing special emphasis on such efforts were the National Council for Prevention of War, the Committee on the Cause and Cure of War, the League of Nations Association, the Foreign Policy Association, and others.

Some of the leaders in these organizations were pacifists who would refuse to take part in any war, and others were not. Certainly anyone who desires a more peaceable world would welcome a political system able to bring some order out of the present state of international anarchy. This would be true of nonpacifists, pacifists, and Biblical nonresistants alike. Such an international organization would no doubt find it necessary to resort to force from time to time for the administration of justice. But, if its affairs were honestly and sincerely administered, such use of force would be much less objectionable than that now exercised in our world at war. This is simply recognizing the fact that, since the world cannot get along without the use of force, it is better to put force behind law and order than behind the criminal.

This should make it clear that an international government, such as that described here, could not operate on nonresistant principles; and therefore a nonresistant Christian could hardly have any part in its administration. Many pacifists, however, would disagree with this point of view. They think of the armed force of a league of nations as a police force rather than a military force, and they believe that the functions of the police and the military are fundamentally different. They think of the police as officials for the lawful maintenance of order in a lawful society. The army on the battlefield, however, is thought of as engaged in a kind of banditry in an anarchistic international society. From this point of view the police is a law-abiding and law-preserving force, while the military is a law-breaking and criminal force.

While it is true that the motives of an international police force sent out by a league of nations to punish an outlaw nation would be different from the motives of an army under the direction of an irresponsible conqueror, the resulting violence and bloodshed in the one case would perhaps be little different from the other. At best, both the domestic and the international police are instruments for the maintenance of order by means of physical force. This is necessary in a sinful society, but is forbidden to nonresistant Christians who seek to follow the Christ who taught men when smitten on the one cheek to turn the other also. There may be intelligent and unintelligent, or just and unjust, uses of force by both the domestic and the international police. This makes the difference between good and bad government. But from the point of view of the statesman, as well as that of the nonresistant Christian, the domestic police and the international police, or army, are fundamentally the same. To attempt a fundamental distinction between them is to attempt a distinction without a difference.

Quaker Pacifism

In that section of the modern peace movement which is concerned with international organization and politics the Quakers have had a rather prominent part. In Chapter VIII some reference was made to their active participation in the affairs of state. This interest is explained in part by their view of human nature. Many Quakers are not inclined to view the sinful nature of human society as seriously as the Mennonites do. Rufus Jones, leading world Quaker, a few years ago made this statement: "To apologize for sin as though it belonged to man's nature, to assume that he is a worm of the dust and necessarily evil are contrary to the entire idea of the Quaker."[5] From this point of view the state is hardly an organization for the maintenance of order through the use of force in a sinful society, as it has been defined in this book. Walter C. Woodward, a leading Quaker editor, has characterized the Quakers as "holding to a single standard of morality for the individual and for the political groups; they believe that the state should be and can be Christianized."[6] Henry J. Cadbury has expressed the belief

---

[5] S. B. Laughlin (Ed.), *Beyond Dilemmas: Quakers Look at Life* (New York, 1937), 40, 41.
[6] *Ibid.,* 219.

"that the kingdoms of the world may become the kingdom of the Lord and of his Christ."[7] This same optimism was expressed more than a hundred years ago by the Quaker theologian, Jonathan Dymond, in his book, *Essays on the Principles of Morality*: "There is however nothing *necessarily* incidental to the legal profession which makes it incompatible with morality"; "In political life we must exercise some of that confidence in the protection of God which we admire in individual life"; "That there are indications of an advancement of the human species toward greater purity in principle and in practice cannot, I think, be disputed."[8]

William Penn's ideas were much the same. Penn says: "They weakly err, that think there is no other use of government than correction, which is the coarsest part of it; daily experience tells us, that the care and regulation of many other affairs more soft and daily necessary, make up much the greatest part of government; and which must have followed the peopling of the world, had Adam never fell, and will continue among men on earth under the highest attainments they may arrive at, by the coming of the blessed second Adam, the Lord from Heaven."[9] This statement gives the key to Penn's plan for the government of Pennsylvania. It was to be a government like that before the fall of Adam when "there was no need of coercive or compulsive means."[9] And yet this same William Penn in 1693 proposed an international peace plan similar to the Grand Design of Henry IV, including an international army or police for the coercion of offenders. If this seems inconsistent with Penn's hatred of war it can probably be explained that he believed such an organization, under Christian leadership, would soon bring about such a happy state of affairs in the world that the power of coercion would never need to be used.

This belief is shared by many pacifists today. They believe that, if well entrenched in the government, they could direct

---

[7] H. J. Cadbury, "The Individual Christian and the State," *Friends World Conference Official Report* (Philadelphia, 1937), 35.

[8] J. Dymond, *Essays on the Principles of Morality and on the Private and Political Rights and Obligations of Mankind* (1829), 183-84, 323, 470.

[9] From the preface of the *Frame of Government for Pennsylvania*, reprinted in the *Colonial Records*, 1:29, 30.

the affairs of state into channels which would avoid the complications of war. In case the issue actually came to a head they believe they could take their stand and prevent a declaration of war. There is of course no doubt that a pacifist in government would have a more wholesome attitude on the war question than would a militarist. Christians will cherish every effort put forth by statesmen for the prevention of war. But to the present time history has not produced a single example of a pacifist state, in the mixed society of the world, which has succeeded in the permanent prevention of war, let alone operating without prisons and a domestic police. Penn's holy experiment was the nearest approach to such a success, but after seventy-five years even this failed to the extent that the genuine peaceful Quakers, who could not agree to military operations, found it necessary to resign from the legislature which was appropriating funds for military purposes. The Pennsylvania experiment also proved rather unsuccessful from another point of view. Its politics, like politics everywhere, seemed to foster a struggle for power. Political parties were formed and pitted against each other to such an extent and in such a way as to destroy the peaceful spirit among them. This was related in a very direct way to the breakdown of the experiment in 1756.

Many Quakers do not feel, however, that this failure was necessary. Isaac Sharpless urged Quakers to give more attention to politics in his day, and believed they should not have resigned from the government of Pennsylvania in 1756.[10] William I. Hull says the events of 1756 do not represent "the failure of the holy experiment and its principles, but the failure of those who failed to remain loyal to those principles. . . . Theoretically, I believe it *possible*, therefore, to base both private and public life on Matthew V and Romans XII."[11] Paul Comly French says: "I have the feeling that some group again should try the Quaker experiment of Penn to see if it isn't possible to work out. I personally think it is and believe it should be tried."[12]

---

[10] Isaac Sharpless, *Quakerism and Politics* (1905), 87, 88.

[11] Letter from William I. Hull to Walter C. Woodward, April 5, 1937.

[12] Letter from Paul C. French to Guy F. Hershberger, March 11, 1943.

Liberal Protestant Pacifism

The modern peace movement owes much to the leadership of pacifist ministers of various Protestant denominations. An outstanding example is Noah Worcester, a New England minister who founded the Massachusetts Peace Society in 1815. Worcester was not a Biblical nonresistant. He did not urge individual Christians to refuse military service. He proposed rather to conduct a program of education for peace until war itself would be abolished. He believed that if statesmen would once be educated to see that peace is better than war they would cease to wage war, and then military service would no longer be a problem to the individual. He believed that if the school and the church and the press did their duty, within a hundred years the scourge of war would be completely wiped out of human society.[13]

A similar view was held by William Ellery Channing, the Unitarian minister, a contemporary of Worcester, whose chief concern was to change the social order so that war would no longer occur. That this happy state of affairs would come about in course of time, he did not doubt: "The tendencies of civilization are decidedly towards peace." "The influences of progressive knowledge, refinement, arts, and national wealth are pacific. The old motives of war are losing power. Conquest, which once maddened nations, hardly enters now into the calculation of statesmen."[14] Channing was spokesman for a school of religious idealists who had great faith in man and his possibilities for progress. He represented a new type of Christianity which drew its strength in part from the New Testament, but perhaps more from the eighteenth-century philosophers of France and England and their idea of progress.

Channing emphasized the dignity and goodness of man to such an extent that he underestimated the power of sin; and he was too optimistic as to the possibilities for social progress through the mere application of human intelligence. In his

---

[13] Cf. Noah Worcester, *Solemn Review of the Custom of War* (1814) and his periodical, *The Friend of Peace* (1815 ff).

[14] W. E. Channing, *Discourses on War*, 45-71.

thinking, human reason is above revelation; man has a spark of the divine within himself; sin is not part of his nature. There is no sharp contrast between holiness and sin. According to this view Christ is not the redeemer of man, but rather his example. This view removes the need of personal regeneration; man through his own efforts, with a noble example to inspire him, is capable of infinite progress. Inspired by this idea, Channing looked for the early dawn of a golden age, not through regeneration as taught in the New Testament, but through intellectual and social enlightenment. In so doing he pointed the way to modern religious liberalism and the popular idealistic pacifism of the twentieth century.

Pacifism and the Social Gospel

An outstanding phase of religious liberalism in the early twentieth century was the type of thought known as the "social gospel," the leading exponent of which was Walter Rauschenbusch. According to the New Testament the kingdom of God is a brotherhood of individuals who have renounced the sinful world, and who have experienced individual salvation through faith in Christ. It is to this brotherhood of saved individuals that Jesus spoke the Sermon on the Mount and the doctrine of nonresistance. According to the social gospel, however, there is no sinful world to be renounced, in the New Testament sense. Man is inherently good; hence he is not in need of personal salvation. Sin is not a personal, but rather a social, evil. The only salvation is social salvation. This constitutes making the world better by means of education and reform. Preachers of the social gospel did not strive to bring souls to salvation in Christ. They endeavored rather to remake the community, the city, the state, and the international world. Then in such a remade world, they believed, everyone would be a Christian as a matter of course.

According to the social gospel, sin is not due to any genuine evil in man. It is due only to his unfavorable environment. The social gospel would change the environment, so that whereas "it used to be hard to be good, it will become difficult to be bad."[15] When the social gospel is adopted the church gives up its evangelistic mission for the salvation of individual souls, and becomes an agency for social reform. The emphasis is on the social order and its institutions. Advocates of the social gospel even speak of saved and unsaved institutions. An institution is saved if it is democratic, and unsaved if it is undemocratic. Monopolistic corporations are unsaved, but they can be saved through conversion into co-operatives. In the words of Rauschenbusch: "The corresponding step in the case of governments and political oligarchies, both in monarchies and in capitalistic semi-democracies, is to submit to real democracy. Therewith they step out of the Kingdom of Evil into the Kingdom of God."[16]

Twentieth-Century Pacifism

Twentieth-century pacifism has been greatly influenced by the ideas of the social gospel. In the two decades following the World War the majority of American churches passed resolutions of one kind or another expressing opposition to war. It is interesting, however, to compare some of these resolutions.

Take, for example, the Mennonite Church. In 1937 the Mennonite General Conference expressed "appreciation for the endeavors of our governments . . . to promote peace and good will among nations, and to keep from war . . . and pray that their endeavors toward peace may be crowned with success." Here it should be noted that the church appreciates and prays for the government. It also gives to the government a clear testimony as to its own convictions on war, but there is no attempt to control the government, and no demand that it follow a given course with respect to specific points of foreign policy. Its only demands are those which the New Testament directs to Christians themselves as regenerated members of the kingdom of God. "We believe that war is altogether contrary

---

[15] Quoted in John Horsch, *The Social Gospel* (Scottdale, Pa., 1920), 6.

[16] Quoted in C. H. Hopkins, *The Rise of the Social Gospel in American Protestantism* (New Haven, 1940), 232.

to the teaching and spirit of Christ and the Gospel, that therefore war is sin. . . . Therefore, if we profess the principles of
peace and nevertheless engage in warfare and strife we as
Christians become guilty of sin and fall under the condemnation of Christ, the righteous judge. . . . We can have no part in
carnal warfare or conflict between nations, nor in strife between classes, groups or individuals. . . . According to the
teaching and spirit of Christ and the Gospel we are to do good
to all men. Hence we are willing to aid in the relief of those
who are in need, distress or suffering . . . we are ready to render
such service in time of war as well as in time of peace. . . . If
our country becomes involved in war, we shall endeavor to continue to live a quiet and peaceful life. . . . We confess that our
supreme allegiance is to God, and that we cannot violate this
allegiance by any lesser loyalty, but rather must follow Christ
in all things, no matter what it cost."[17]

The above is the statement of a nonresistant church which
thinks of peace as a fruit of the individual regenerated life.
Between the lines one can read that the authors of this statement recognize that a government operating in a sinful society
may find it necessary to do some things not in accord with the
Christian ethic. Therefore this statement does not attempt to
say what the government's policy shall be, although the rulers
of state are definitely challenged to recognize the nonresistant
demands of Christ upon those who would be Christians.

Now let us note some pacifist resolutions of religious bodies
which reflect either the modern social gospel, or the older
Calvinist tradition that the church should control the state and
the general social order. In 1925 the National Council of the
Congregational churches declared it the duty of the churches
"to find a Christian way to meet international situations which
threaten war."[18] In 1929 the Presbyterian General Assembly
renounced "war as an instrument of national policy."[19] In
1925 the Episcopal General Convention declared that "the
nations of the world must adopt a peace system . . . built on

---

[17] For the complete Mennonite statement of 1937 see appendix 5.
[18] W. W. Van Kirk, *Religion Renounces War* (Chicago, 1934), 10.
[19] *Ibid.*, 10.

the conviction that war is unchristian in principle and suicidal in practice."[20] Many of the churches passed resolutions condemning tariff barriers and other economic causes making for war. In commenting on this, Walter W. Van Kirk says: "The churches are speaking their mind on the cause and cure of war. . . . They are rapidly pledging themselves to work for such changes in the social, political and economic structure of modern society as will enhance the prospects for peace among the nations."[21] The Federal Council of Churches in 1933 urged the continuation of negotiations for disarmament and the abolition of "aggressive weapons" such as the bombing plane.[22] Van Kirk suggests further that "The churches of the world are determined to combat the whole war system . . . mankind will no longer pin its faith to any religious system that is helpless to stay the hand of the militarists. . . . Either religion will put an end to war or war will put an end to religion. . . . Not until the full implication of this sovereign truth registers indelibly in the thinking process of all who lift their faces Godward will any permanent advances be made in the crusade for a warless world."[23]

In 1941 Van Kirk attributed the failure of disarmament and outlawry of war schemes to the church's failure to get at the heart of the problem. What was needed was "a frontal attack on the anarchy of nations whose political and economic policies were dictated, in the main, by consideration of power and prestige."[24] Christians generally accept Jesus' teaching in personal relations, he says, but do not seem to realize that it applies in the relations of nations to each other as well. He pleads for an international organization able to use force for the maintenance of peace and justice. Such a use of force "is not immoral provided . . . [it] is organically representative of and responsible to the world society."[25]

Clearly, this view does not think of the state merely as an

[20] Ibid., 12.
[21] Ibid., 91.
[22] Ibid., 118-19.
[23] Ibid., 253.
[24] W. W. Van Kirk, Religion and the World of Tomorrow (Chicago, 1941), 9.
[25] Ibid., 53.

organization for the maintenance of order in a sinful society. It views the state rather as an agency for the Christianization of the social order, without the use of force if possible, but with the use of force if necessary. For the time being, force is permissible for Christians if it contributes to social progress; but eventually, no doubt, it will be eliminated through the gradual Christianization of the social order. Rauschenbusch expresses this view in the following statement: "Jesus . . . lived in the hope of a great transformation of the national, social, and religious life about him. . . . The kingdom of God is . . . not a matter of saving human atoms, but of saving the social organism. It is not a matter of getting individuals to heaven, but of transforming the life on earth into the harmony of heaven."[26]

Believers in Biblical nonresistance find the social gospel and the pacifism of religious liberalism inadequate, not because they do not contain some fine ideals, but because they have a wrong conception of sin, of Christianity, and of the kingdom of God. The New Testament sees a great gulf between God and the sinful world, a gulf which will continue until the final judgment, for not until then will sin be brought to an end. The kingdom of God which the New Testament speaks of is brought into existence only through the supernatural power of God Himself. It is made up of Christians who have experienced the saving grace of God in their personal lives; who have been saved from the sinful world to a life of service to God. Such Christians are concerned for the welfare of humanity, and their influence on society may be considerable. But such changes as this influence may bring about within the sinful society of the world, however worth while they may be, do not constitute the kingdom of God. The kingdom is made up only of those who have been redeemed from, and called out of, the sinful society.

The great mistake of modern religious liberalism has been not to see this very important point. It has confused the kingdom of God with mere moral improvements within sinful society, and in so doing it has identified the kingdom of God with the sinful social order itself. It has rejected salvation by faith

[26] W. Rauschenbusch, *Christianity and the Social Crisis* (New York, 1912), 64, 65.

and substituted a shallow, optimistic social evolution. Instead of receiving the divine will from a God who speaks from His throne above, religious liberalism speaks of experiencing God and practicing the presence of God in a way that makes Him identical with human experience. But a God who is identical with human experience is not God. Having emptied God of His reality, religious liberalism no longer speaks the word of truth in condemnation of sin. The liberal church becomes a mere social agency, engaged in a variety of activities, which too often do not lead to any clear-cut and positive action. When a Christian earnestly believes that the Sermon on the Mount was spoken by the Son of God with authority from heaven, and that this same Son of God will someday sit in judgment upon this evil world, he will go into action for God. And when an entire Christian brotherhood is possessed by this same faith it has the essentials for a solidarity which makes it possible to have a peace witness that commands respect and produces results. But when Jesus is thought of merely as a religious genius, as a product of human evolution, and when human society is thought to possess within itself the powers for its own healing, then men will adjust themselves in harmony with that world. And when the Christian Church once adjusts its program in harmony with the sinful world, it has lost its own soul.[27]

Several years ago a stimulating book appeared which charged that this very thing had occurred in American Christendom.[28] The authors declared that the Christian Church confronts a worldliness, within and without, which threatens to destroy it. The paramount issue of today is not: What can the church do to save civilization? It is rather: What can the church do to save itself? The church has adjusted itself too much to the world, and must turn away from temporal to eternal relations. The root of all this difficulty is substitution of faith in man for faith in God. "There has emerged a secularism which claims to

---

[27] For a penetrating analysis of the modern idea of progress as compared with the New Testament kingdom of God see H. Emil Brunner, *The Theology of Crisis* (New York, 1929).

[28] H. R. Niebuhr, W. Pauck, and F. P. Miller, *The Church Against the World* (Chicago, 1935).

represent the same high moral ideals that Christianity does, but without dependence upon the religious beliefs which are characteristic of the church. . . . It is an atheistic movement which claims to cultivate moral ideals of the same value as those defined by the church." This man-centered religion "has made man himself the end-all and be-all of existence." And as long as man lives for himself the world will be filled "with the cults of blood and race and nation. And in so far as that doctrine continues to dominate Western thought we may expect the recurring horrors of war and revolution, because it is a doctrine whose logic deprives mankind of a common frame of reference and in the end sets every man against every other man."[29]

Nonviolent Resistance

A type of pacifism very prominent at the present time is that known as nonviolent resistance. Sometimes the term "nonviolent coercion" is used; sometimes nonviolent direct action. This type of pacifism owes much to William Lloyd Garrison (1805-79), the American abolitionist, who was a strong opponent of war. Although Garrison himself used the term "nonresistance" to describe his own faith, this term did not mean the same to him as it does to Biblical nonresistants such as the Mennonites. While his language was more Biblical than that of most modern pacifists, and while he perhaps did not carry his direct action as far as Gandhi and his followers do today, he was nevertheless pointing in their direction.

Perhaps the crucial point of difference between Biblical nonresistance and nonviolent coercion is the attitude taken toward the question of social justice. The Old Testament prophets maintained a vigorous testimony against the social injustice of their time. Amos condemned those who were "at ease in Zion" and "not grieved for the affliction of Joseph."[30] The requirements of the Lord as enumerated by Micah are "to do justly, and to love mercy, and to walk humbly with thy God."[31]

[29] *Ibid.*, 32, 33, 110-11.
[30] Amos 6:1-6.   [31] Micah 6:8.

The New Testament likewise speaks approvingly of justice and mercy. Jesus says: "Blessed are the merciful: for they shall obtain mercy,"[32] and Paul commands masters to give their servants "that which is just and equal."[33]

It should be noted here, however, that the emphasis in these Scriptures is on *doing justice* rather than on *demanding justice*. There is, of course, no reason why the Christian should not desire justice for himself at the hand of his fellow men, or even seek the same, through Christian means. When the Apostle Paul was placed under arrest by the Roman authorities he did not hesitate to state his case, or even to appeal to Caesar himself for a just decision.[34] There is no evidence, however, that Paul's quest for justice went beyond a simple statement of his case and an appeal for right. The appeal carries with it no spirit of arrogance, revenge, or threat; from his own teaching it is clear that he could not have used any pressure devices to compel the authorities to give him justice. Paul told the Corinthians that they should not use the courts to compel others to do them justice. Rather than do this they should allow themselves to be defrauded, and suffer injustice.[35] His epistle to the Romans enjoins a nonresistant submission, even to Nero's government, which was frequently unjust; and his teaching rules out all vengeance on the part of the Christian. It is therefore impossible to believe that Paul would have condoned any revolutionary movement, for his sake, on the part of his friends; or that he would have engaged in a hunger strike or similar means of forcing the government's hand. In the trial of Jesus one is impressed, even more than in the trial of Paul, by the completely nonresistant attitude of the Master. When He was accused He answered "never a word; insomuch that the governor marvelled greatly."[36]

A good illustration of the Christian attitude toward social injustice is found in Paul's epistle to Philemon. In this letter

3 2 Matt. 5:7.
3 3 Col. 4:1.
3 4 Acts 25:11.
3 5 I Cor. 6:7.
3 6 Matt. 27:14.

Paul says he is sending home the runaway slave, Onesimus, admonishing him to be faithful to his master and to serve him in the spirit of Christian love. At the same time Paul admonishes the master to deal with his slave in the same Christian spirit. The relation of Philemon and Onesimus, therefore, was no longer one of master to slave, but rather that of Christian brotherhood. Certainly human slavery is incompatible with social justice, and yet Paul does not demand the abolition of slavery. Instead, he places the whole matter on a different basis by reminding both master and slave that they are brethren and that their relations, one with the other, must be on the basis of Christian love. Certainly, where this relationship actually exists, the institution of human slavery cannot continue; and it would seem that Paul's approach in this case is the Christian solution for every form of injustice. It is not a demand for justice that the New Testament upholds, but rather an appeal to both parties to deal with each other in the spirit of love. When this condition is achieved justice follows as a matter of course. But justice achieved without love often carries the seeds of corruption within itself.

On the other hand, when one who is wronged begins to place the emphasis on a *demand* for justice, he has taken the first step on the road which leads away from Christian nonresistance. This is precisely the thing which Garrison did. While he personally opposed violence, and disapproved of the Civil War, his manner of demanding justice for the Negro was nevertheless a contributing cause of that war. He described his own method as a "state of activity, ever fighting the good fight of faith, ever struggling for 'liberty, equality, fraternity.' "[37] He conceived it his task to "disarm, in the name of God, every slaveholder and tyrant in the world."[38] He denied "the right of any man over the liberty of another . . . under no pretext has any man the right to dominate . . . over his fellows."[39] Had the United States government required Garrison to own slaves, the Scriptures would have justified a humble, nonresistant disobedi-

---

[37] F. G. Villard, *William Lloyd Garrison on Nonresistance* (New York, 1924), 30.
[38] *Ibid.*, 37.
[39] *Ibid.*, 49.

ence to the command; for the New Testament clearly says that Christians "ought to obey God rather than men."[40] But as it was, the government simply permitted Garrison's fellow citizens to own slaves if they so desired. In such a case it would not seem out of line with the spirit of nonresistance humbly to testify to one's conviction on the matter, and rest at that point. But the spirit of nonresistance certainly would not permit a pressure campaign to compel the government to change its policy. This is precisely what Garrison did, however, in a variety of ways. He tried to persuade England to boycott the Southern slave-holders of the United States, and buy its cotton from India, where labor was free. He publicly burned a copy of the fugitive slave law; he even burned the United States Constitution itself, declaring it a "covenant with death and hell"; and he took part in a state convention called to urge separation from the slave states.[41] Thus Garrison, while opposed to violence, nevertheless engaged in a program of political pressure, in defiance of established government, in a demand for justice. This is not Biblical nonresistance. It is rather nonviolent resistance, which is not Biblical.

Tolstoy

Tolstoy, the Russian novelist and pacifist of the nineteenth century, was influenced to a large extent by Garrison. He had a rationalistic type of religion which did not think of God as a person, but rather as identified with reason and the supreme good. He did not think of Jesus as the Son of God, but rather as a great man because His teachings coincide with human reason. His religion was entirely man-centered, although he called himself a Christian. He renounced violence because Jesus had given the command not to resist evil, a command which, he believed, coincides with reason. Tolstoy believed with Rousseau that man is good; therefore the Sermon on the Mount is for all men, not merely for those who have been regenerated by divine grace. In other words, he identified the kingdom of God with

---

[40] Acts 5:29.

[41] Ernest Crosby, *Garrison the Nonresistant* (Chicago, 1905), 30-42.

human society, after the manner of the social gospel. But since he believed in an absolute renunciation of violence for all men, Tolstoy was an anarchist, repudiating the state entirely. Biblical nonresistance declines to participate in the coercive functions of the state, but nevertheless regards coercion necessary for the maintenance of order in a sinful society, and is not anarchistic. Tolstoy, however, found no place for the state in human society at all; and because of his faith in the goodness of man, he believed that eventually all coercion, including the domestic police, would be done away. Despite the basic difference between Tolstoy and the Biblical nonresistants, however, he would have agreed with them in the social expression of their nonresistance, while disagreeing with a program of nonviolence such as that of Gandhi. Tolstoy represents a complete disavowal of all coercion.[42]

Gandhi

The fullest expression of the idea of nonviolent resistance is found in the teachings and practices of Gandhi, the nationalist leader of India. Gandhi was influenced to some extent by Tolstoy. The teachings of Jesus also made a great impression upon him. But the chief source of his philosophy, no doubt, was the idea of sacrificial suffering as found in the Hindu religion of his native India. The Hindu idea of sacrificial suffering is quite different from that of Christianity. Christianity teaches that Christ suffered a sacrificial death to expiate the guilt of man. It also teaches that Christians out of love for Christ should at all times be obedient to His will, at whatever cost, and be ready to suffer for that faith, if need be. The Hindu idea, however, is that men must undergo self-imposed sacrificial suffering as a means of appeasing the gods. Even the most selfish and tyrannical gods will give men what they desire when they have suffered enough. As Shridharani says: "Even the most whimsical of gods cannot resist the power of suffering. Born

---

[42] See E. A. Steiner, *Tolstoy the Man* (New York, 1904), and E. H. Crosby, *Tolstoy and His Message* (New York, 1903).

of sacrifice, suffering is the human power which produces desired ends and defeats evil."[43]

The special contribution of Gandhi was to apply this Hindu idea of victorious suffering to political relationships, and to use it as a means of appeasing human tyrants. Gandhi disliked the British rule in India; therefore he resorted to fasts and other forms of suffering in the belief that eventually, through much suffering, the British would be moved to grant independence to India. When Jesus was asked about the lawfulness of paying taxes to the foreign Caesar who ruled over Palestine He said: "Render . . . unto Caesar the things that are Caesar's."[44] And Paul said: "Ye must needs be subject, not only for wrath, but also for conscience sake. For this cause pay ye tribute also."[45] It must be remembered that both Paul and Jesus here were speaking of a foreign emperor who was not loved by the Jews any more than the British rule was loved by India, yet they say: Be subject, do not revolt, pay taxes. Of course, this does not mean submission to the point where the Christian does everything which the state demands, for in case of conflict between the demands of God and those of the state the New Testament requirement is to "obey God rather than men." It does, however, mean that when disobedience to the state becomes necessary the emphasis must be on obedience to God rather than on a demand for justice. Furthermore, such disobedience must be undertaken in the spirit of humility and love, and without the use of pressure methods to force the government's hand. This is nonresistance. Gandhi, however, took quite the opposite view. He refused to pay taxes; he sought to embarrass the British rulers; he did everything he could to throw off the British rule; he attempted to force the government's hand in every way he could, except through the use of violence. This is nonviolent resistance.

The nonresistant Christian cannot take part in a political revolution for the overthrow of the government in power. But political revolution was Gandhi's primary objective. Gandhi's program was not one of nonresistance or peace. It was a new

[43] K. Shridharani, *War Without Violence* (New York, 1939), 169.
[44] Matt. 22:21 (ASV).
[45] Rom. 13:5, 6.

form of warfare. The very title of Shridharani's book, *War Without Violence,* brings this out most vividly. Shridharani, a disciple of Gandhi and an exponent of nonviolence, himself says: "And perhaps to the surprise of my Western readers, Satyagraha[46] seems to have more in common with war than with Western pacifism."[47] He goes on to explain that there are also important differences between Satyagraha and violent warfare. Obviously, bloodshed is absent, at least as long as Satyagraha is kept under control. But this does not do away with the fact that nonviolent resistance is resistance. It is a form of coercion or compulsion. Its purpose is to compel the enemy to give up. Besides fasting and prayer, Satyagraha uses such methods as negotiation, arbitration, agitation, demonstration, the ultimatum, the general strike, picketing, the sit-down strike, economic boycott, nonpayment of taxes, emigration, non-co-operation, ostracism, civil disobedience, and setting up a new government to take the place of the old.

Most of these techniques have a strange sound to Mennonite ears. True, Mennonites believe in negotiation and arbitration, and they have often resorted to emigration. But in their case emigration has had a different purpose from that of Gandhi. Mennonites have emigrated to find new homes when they were no longer tolerated in the old. But Gandhi used emigration as a means of embarrassing the government, for if no people are present there will be no one to govern. Mennonites also have disobeyed the government, but if they were true to their faith they did so only when to obey would have been disobedience to God. They disobeyed in order to do right, and perhaps to do justice. But Gandhi disobeyed in order to get justice. This is a fundamental difference. Gandhi also resorted to non-co-operation as a means of making the state powerless, or to end the present political system. Nonresistant Christians likewise might find it impossible to co-operate with the state in certain projects which they believe contrary to the will of God, but in such cases their motive would be altogether different from that of Gandhi.

[46] This is the term used by Gandhi and his followers to describe the practice of nonviolence.

[47] Shridharani, *op cit.,* xxx.

Their object would not be to destroy the power of the state. Whatever influence they might have in that direction would be altogether incidental to their positive program of obedience to God.

In recent years Gandhi's program of nonviolence has had a rather strong influence in America, so that much of the popular pacifism of today is a mixture of religious liberalism, the social gospel, and Satyagraha. Many pacifist leaders seem to think that Gandhi's program was essentially Christian in its character. A recent newspaper editorial described a conversation with a Protestant minister who declared his belief in the teachings of Christ and his unwillingness "to forego those teachings and accept the code of the killers." Then he cited a list of nationally known ministers with similar views and said: "These men believe, as I do, in nonviolent resistance. They believe in what Gandhi preached in India."[48] In the mind of this minister the program of Gandhi follows the teachings of Christ. Harry Emerson Fosdick in a recent article, in which he declares his unwillingness to use the church for the promotion of the war because to do so would mean disloyalty to Christ, also gives approval to Gandhi and his program of Satyagraha.[49] In 1934 the Christian Youth Council of North America adopted a resolution renouncing war as an instrument of national policy. A smaller group of delegates pledged themselves "not only to refuse to participate in war, but to actively oppose it by means of the general strike, destruction of war materials, and spreading of counter propaganda."[50] This approach is similar to that of Gandhi, unless the destruction of war materials perhaps goes farther than he would go; but to the Biblical nonresistant it seems far removed from the spirit of Christ.

Perhaps one reason why Gandhi's program of nonviolence has found so much favor among some religious pacifists is a realization that the social and political changes which they so earnestly desire cannot be brought about without the use of force.

[48] The *Elkhart Truth* (Elkhart, Ind.), July 25, 1942.

[49] H. E. Fosdick, "If America is drawn into the war, can you, as a Christian, participate in it or support it?" *The Christian Century* (Chicago, Jan. 22, 1941), 58:115-18.

[50] W. W. Van Kirk, *Religion Renounces War*, 16.

Therefore they turn to the strike, the boycott, and other forms of compulsion, as less objectionable than physical violence. At any rate, Shridharani insists that they must do something of this sort if their ends are to be reached. He speaks of pacifism's

inadequate understanding of the nature of *social change* .... When their [the pacifists'] hope of peace is frustrated in the process of social change, as often happens, they are in a dilemma. The demand for social change offers them but one alternative, viz., that of upholding the violent method or of maintaining the *status quo* .... There is no other choice left them, for the pacifists fail to realize that something more than good will is required to grease the wheels of a changing order .... In other words, force is necessary to insure certain social ends, and in a state or a world state which does not recognize the people's right to decide crucial issues by plebiscite, recourse to "direct action" (which can be nonviolent as well as violent), however illegal, becomes not only necessary but incumbent on those who strive to end social injustice.

It is at this point, however, that the pacifists are confronted with the dilemma of either going to the camp of the militarist, or of joining the ranks of inactive pious-wishers who by implication become the pillars that sustain the *status quo,* however unjust. And it is also at this crucial point that Gandhi's Satyagraha offers a way out and proves its utility as a nonviolent means to social justice. The distinction between pacifism and Satyagraha on the one hand ... and war and Satyagraha on the other ... becomes at this stage at once evident and significant. Hereupon the pacifists stop too soon, and the militarists go too far .... [51]

In order to be fair it must be admitted that Shridharani is right when he says that the nonviolent coercionists do not go as far as the militarists do. Certainly the strike and boycott are lesser evils than the shedding of blood with musket, sword, and bomb. On the other hand, as Shridharani also admits, Gandhi and his followers resort to Satyagraha, not in an attempt to apply the golden rule, or the Sermon on the Mount, or the principle of love, but rather to compel the enemy to comply with their wishes against his will. This is not Christ's way. He said: If a man compels you to go a mile, go with him two miles; but He never gives Christians the right to compel others. They may

[51] Shridharani, *op. cit.,* 270-74.

appeal to the enemy, and reason with him, but they must not compel him. It is this element of compulsion, however, which gives Satyagraha its appeal, and which makes it a "substitute" for war. But it is also this element of compulsion, which makes it different from Biblical nonresistance. Richard B. Gregg, who has written an authoritative book and a number of pamphlets[52] on this subject, even advocates a discipline for nonviolence, borrowed from the military discipline, consisting of folk dancing, rhythm exercises, manual work, joint meditation, and other activities designed to develop morale, courage, and a readiness to undergo whatever suffering nonviolent coercion may require.

No one has done better than Reinhold Niebuhr in showing the sharp distinction between nonviolence and New Testament nonresistance. With clarity of analysis he shows that the doctrine of the New Testament is an absolute nonresistance which makes no compromise with the relativities of politics. He shows the futility of trying to make a militarist of Jesus by arguing that He drove the men out of the temple with whips. But, he says, many pacifists engage in an equally futile attempt to water down the nonresistance of Jesus to their own program of nonviolent resistance, which permits all kinds of compulsion so long as it does not take life. Niebuhr says:

There is not the slightest support in Scripture for this doctrine of nonviolence . . . . The *reductio ad absurdum* of this position is achieved in a book which has become something of a textbook for modern pacifists, Richard Gregg's, *The Power of Nonviolence*. In this book nonviolent resistance is commended as the best method of defeating your foe, particularly as the best method of breaking his morale. It is suggested that Christ ended his life on the Cross because he had not completely mastered the technique of nonviolence, and must for this reason be regarded as a guide who is inferior to Gandhi, but whose significance lies in initiating a movement which culminates in Gandhi.[53]

In a final evaluation of Satyagraha as a peace program it should not be forgotten that even Gandhi gave his support to

---

[52] See R. B. Gregg, *The Power of Nonviolence* (Philadelphia, 1934); *Training for Peace* (Philadelphia, 1937); *A Discipline for Nonviolence* (Pendle Hill Pamphlet, No. 11).
[53] Reinhold Niebuhr, *Christianity and Power Politics* (New York, 1940), 10, 11. The passages referred to are in Gregg, *op. cit.*, 85 and 202.

the first World War, hoping that this would serve as a short cut to home rule for India. Gandhi's own words in a letter to the Viceroy of India with reference to this action follow:

I recognize that in the hour of its danger we must give, as we have decided to give, ungrudging and unequivocal support to the Empire of which we aspire in the near future to be partners in the same sense as the Dominions overseas. But it is the simple truth that our response is due to the expectations that our goal will be reached all the more speedily. I do not bargain for its fulfillment, but you should know that disappointment of hope means disillusion.[54]

This shows again that the primary objective of nonviolence is not peace, or obedience to the divine will, but rather certain desired social changes, for personal, or class, or national advantage. New Testament nonresistance is concerned first with obedience to God and the creation of loving brotherhood. Desired advantage and social change are secondary to this, and are striven for only in so far as the methods used are not in conflict with the will of God. Nonresistance does not adopt suffering as a means of achieving justice, although it does stand ready to suffer even injustice for the sake of obedience to God, if there is no other way. Satyagraha, on the other hand, deliberately adopts suffering as a means of enforcing justice as long as this method seems to promise the best results. But, in Gandhi's case at least, when better or quicker results seemed possible by doing so, he rejected the suffering method and actually waged war for the achievement of justice, even though this might cause others to suffer, to say nothing about its conflict with the teachings of Christ.

The following paragraph from Shridharani is an excellent summary of the difference between the nonviolence of Gandhi and the nonresistance of the New Testament. Here the disciple of Gandhi says that if modern pacifism would succeed in the task which it has set out to perform it must move farther away than it now is from the peaceful way of Jesus Christ, and adopt the more warlike methods of Satyagraha:

[54] Shridharani, *op. cit.*, 122.

Gandhi's Satyagraha has more in common with war than with pacifism . . . . Contrary to general belief, the Indian movement is essentially secular. Its strength lies in the fact that it seeks political, economic, and social successes here and now.

Whatever religious and mystical elements there are in the Indian movement—and they have been greatly exaggerated by the American journalists and scholars—are there for propaganda and publicity reasons as well as for the personal satisfaction of deeply conscientious men like Gandhi and the members of the Gandhi Seva Sangha. But what has swayed the multitudes of India, on the contrary, has been the fact that the movement has been a weapon to be wielded by masses of men for earthly, tangible, and collective aims and to be discarded if it does not work.

American pacifism is essentially religious and mystical. West can be more unworldly than East, and the history of the peace movement in the United States is a good illustration of that. American pacifists, as well as the British and French, have held too closely to the New Testament dictum of "nonresistance to evil." That is why they have failed.[55]

Nonviolent Coercion and Race Relations

Gandhi's first experiment with Satyagraha took place in British South Africa where it was applied to the problem of race relations. In the nineteenth century European planters and mine owners had imported a large number of laborers from India to South Africa. As time went on these Indians began to operate farms and small business concerns of their own. The result was the development of a serious race conflict between the majority white and the minority Indian populations, similar to the conflict between Japanese and American whites on the west coast of the United States, or between whites and Negroes in the South. The Indians were discriminated against in various ways, and finally in 1906 a law was passed requiring them to be registered and finger printed. Every Indian was required to keep his registration certificate on his person at all times, and produce it upon the demand of any police officer. Those who failed to register were to be deported.

This law was very humiliating to the Indian people who felt they were being treated like criminals. At this point Mr.

[55] Shridharani, *My India, My America* (New York, 1941), 272, 276.

Gandhi, who was then a young practicing lawyer in South Africa, entered the picture and led his people in his first campaign of "civil disobedience." Many of the Indians bound themselves by oaths and pledges not to obey the law, and when they did so they were imprisoned. So many joined the movement that soon the jails were full of nonregistered Indians, with others waiting to get in. During the conflict other typical nonviolent devices, such as picketing British coal mines, were also used. This strategy had its effect, and in the end the government of South Africa modified its anti-Indian legislation.

For a long time we have had a serious race problem in our own United States. Until the time of the Civil War the Negroes in the South were slaves. Since then they have been free, but nevertheless subject to humiliating disabilities. In all of the southern states segregation prevails. So-called Jim Crow laws require Negroes to worship in separate churches, and their children to attend separate schools. Negroes may ride only on the back seats of buses, or in separate sections of railway coaches. They may not use the same waiting rooms in bus or railway stations that are used by whites. They may not eat in restaurants which feed white people. Even the North has modifications of this Jim Crow practice, and nowhere in the United States are jobs and professions open to Negroes on an equality with whites. Whites generally regard Negroes inferior to themselves, and feel that they must be kept "in their place." If a Negro eats where a white man eats or does other things which white men do, he is "out of his place," and something must be done about it. Needless to say this is a very unchristian attitude, for the New Testament teaches that in Christ "there is neither Greek nor Jew, circumcision nor uncircumcision, Barbarian, Scythian, bond nor free: but Christ is all and in all."[56] With Christ all men, regardless of race or color, are on one common level. Therefore, Christians can have no part in programs of discrimination against Negroes, Jews, or any other minority group. The attitude of the nonresistant Christian in this matter is discussed more fully in Chapter XII.

[56] Col. 3:11.

It is the writer's purpose at this point, however, to show how pacifist groups are beginning to apply the Gandhi technique, which is not Christian, to the race problem in the United States today. The coming of the second World War served to increase race tension in America. This may have been caused in part by the fact that a nation of another race attacked the United States. More important, however, is the realization on the part of the Negro that he has had a large part in the war effort. He feels that if he has done his part in the fight against Hitler and Japan he should have equal rights with white people here at home. Many pacifists, realizing the justice of the Negro's demands, have begun to champion his cause. In doing so, however, they have resorted to nonviolent coercion, which is a form of warfare. Therefore, even though their intentions may be good, these pacifists are actually engaged in a race war; and the war may turn out to be a violent and bloody one before it is over.

Late in 1942 a conference at Columbus, Ohio, sponsored by the Fellowship of Reconciliation, a leading pacifist organization, devoted one half-day session to a discussion of the use of nonviolent action to promote the rights of the Negro.[57] In February, 1943, the executive committee of the Fellowship of Reconciliation endorsed a campaign of civil disobedience which the March on Washington movement, a Negro organization, had proposed to launch for the purpose of breaking down Jim Crow practices.[58] It was proposed that Negroes refuse to use Jim Crow cars and waiting rooms, and that they go to the white eating places day after day demanding to be served. The FOR warned that such action "requires the most careful training and severe discipline, including spiritual exercise," and offered to provide training and guidance for such of its members and others who might wish to join in the movement. Later in the year the March on Washington movement officially adopted a program of nonviolent action which was to be built around local units in twenty-six leading cities where workers would be

[57] *Fellowship* (February, 1943), 9:35.
[58] *Ibid.*, 9:35.

trained in the techniques of nonviolence.[59] In the summer of 1943 a group of FOR members in Los Angeles joined with Negro pickets in picketing Wrigley Field "to protest the ban on Negro ball players."[60]

In Washington, D.C., a Negro group calling itself the Institute of Race Relations has organized itself to fight discrimination in eating places through the use of nonviolent action. Their method is for groups to enter eating places and seat themselves, requesting service. When they are refused service they remain seated until the restaurant closes. In this way they keep other customers from being served, thereby decreasing the profits of the proprietor. By this method they hope eventually to force the proprietor to serve Negroes on an equal basis with whites.[61] In the summer of 1943 in Denver a workshop of nonviolent action, sponsored by members of the Fellowship of Reconciliation, engaged in a campaign to picket certain theaters to force them to stop the practice of racial segregation. Among the demonstrators was the secretary of the Rocky Mountain section of the FOR.[62] In September, 1943, the Fellowship of Reconciliation established within its organization an official department of race relations which presumably will encourage and promote the use of the Gandhi technique for the accomplishment of its purposes.[63] Needless to say, nonresistant Christians will agree that the injustices which these organizations are protesting against are very real. Nevertheless, the methods used in opposing them are in reality a form of warfare. They are pressure methods designed to compel the opposition to submit. They are not the way of love and nonresistance as taught in the New Testament.

The Political Objector to War

In addition to the different types of pacifism discussed above, passing mention should also be made of the political objector to war who is not a pacifist at all, although sometimes

---

[59] *The Conscientious Objector* (August, 1943), 2.
[60] *Fellowship* (July, 1943), 9:131.
[61] *The Conscientious Objector* (October, 1943), 5.
[62] *Fellowship* (October, 1943), 9:180.
[63] *Ibid.*, (November, 1943), 9:195.

thought of as such. This type is illustrated by Carl Haessler who in 1918 served a term in prison for refusing to bear arms in the first World War. In his own statement to the military court which sentenced him Haessler frankly says:

I am not a pacifist . . . but regard myself as a patriotic political objector, acting largely from public and social grounds.

. . .

[I believe] that America's participation in the World War was unnecessary, of doubtful benefit (if any) to the country and to humanity, and accomplished largely, though not exclusively, through the pressure of the Allied and American commercial imperialists . . . . I further believe that I shall be rendering the country a service by helping to set an example for other citizens to follow in the matter of fearlessly acting on unpopular convictions instead of forgetting them in time of stress. The crumbling of American radicalism under pressure in 1917 has only been equalled by that of the majority of German socialist leaders in August, 1914.[64]

The reference to American radicalism and German socialism brings to the writer's mind the memory of hearing Haessler say in the summer of 1925 that he had no objection to war as such. It was rather his objection to the imperialistic World War in particular which caused him to take the stand which he did in 1917-18. He stated frankly that he could not participate in a war for the promotion of capitalism and imperialism, but intimated that, in case of a war for the establishment of a more just social order to replace the capitalist system, his position might be quite different. While not all political objectors would take this position, perhaps most of them would agree with Haessler in reserving the right to decide which war should be supported and which not. The political objector does not object to war as such. Religious convictions do not necessarily enter into consideration at all. He simply objects to particular wars which to his mind are unwise, or unjust, or otherwise unjustifiable.

Difficulties of Classification

The classification outlined in this chapter is a broad general classification of the various types of nonresistance and pacifism

---

[64] Norman Thomas, *The Conscientious Objector in America* (New York, 1923), 24, 25.

found in America today. It should not be assumed, however, that every objector to war can be made to fit perfectly into one of the categories here set forth. Perhaps this can be done in the majority of cases, but certainly not in all. Furthermore, the types here outlined overlap to some extent, so that a particular pacifist may be found in several of these categories at the same time. The Biblical nonresistant is the easiest to identify and classify. He renounces war because it is contrary to the teachings of the Scriptures, and he holds aloof from such activities of the state as are associated with methods of compulsion. During the second World War Mennonites constituted about 40 per cent of the conscientious objectors in Civilian Public Service in the United States and, except for the few among them who have been influenced by religious liberalism, they must all be classified as Biblical nonresistants. In addition, there are a considerable number of Biblical nonresistants who are not Mennonites.

Among other pacifists, classification is more difficult. As previously stated in this chapter, many Quakers are active in the promotion of peace plans. Some are closely associated with the social gospel of modern Protestantism, and others are advocates of Gandhi's program of nonviolence. Many perhaps belong in all of these categories at the same time, while other Quakers are not interested in pacifism at all. From its early beginnings Quakerism was characterized by nonviolent coercionism rather than nonresistance. Nonviolent coercion was practiced to some extent by the Quakers in the colonial government of Pennsylvania, and definitely advocated by Jonathan Dymond in the early nineteenth century.[65] Richard B. Gregg, a leading American advocate of nonviolent compulsion, is a Quaker. As pointed out above, much of modern pacifism, even apart from Quakerism, is a combination of religious liberalism, the social gospel, and nonviolent resistance. Political objectors also may resort to nonviolent compulsion; such political objectors may or may not claim to be religious. Some of the modernist-pacifists may vary from a definite faith in God to a humanism which rejects the

---

[65] Jonathan Dymond, *Principles of Morality* (1829), 332 ff.

idea of a personal God altogether. Among the Quakers there is perhaps even more variation, ranging from Christian orthodoxy, on the one hand, to extreme humanism on the other.

Nonresistance and Pacifism in Civilian Public Service

In "normal" times, before the second World War, Biblical nonresistants and modern pacifists generally went their separate ways, without much co-operation, and often indeed without becoming very well acquainted with each other. The crucible of the second World War, however, brought all types of American conscientious objectors into a new relationship. The Mennonite, Brethren, and Quaker service organizations each had a share in the operation of the CPS camps. Other church organizations, as well as the pacifist Fellowship of Reconciliation, joined with them in supporting the National Service Board for Religious Objectors as a liaison between the peace groups and Selective Service. Most important of all, the 12,000 conscientious objectors assigned to CPS camps by Selective Service were a heterogeneous group of many types, ranging all the way from Biblical nonresistants to political objectors and absolutists who objected to conscription, for whatever purpose, as much as to military service itself.

Perhaps one of the best statements of the nonresistant attitude toward CPS is found in an editorial in the camp paper of a Mennonite CPS camp. This editorial says:

. . . to the average man in CPS, serving without pay has made it possible to experience the realization that money, after all, is not the thing life is made of, and that the really enduring values which have now had a chance to come to the fore, mean far more than "filthy lucre" ever could.

Since less of our time is taken up with seeking the elusive satisfaction of "laying up for ourselves treasures on earth," we have become more acutely aware of the needs of others, and are now interested in finding some kind of solution for those needs. More than ever before have we had our eyes opened to the great need of "going into all the world and preaching the gospel to every creature." Our part in this great program of the church is taking on new meaning and the tremendous possibilities are seen more clearly every day. For these things a growing number of us thank CPS.[66]

This statement expresses an attitude of willingness to serve one's country and one's fellow men, even at a sacrifice, and under terms which might be considered unjust. It is an expression of readiness to do that which is considered right and just, without too much concern as to whether one receives that which is just to himself. It should be noted, however, that this is one of the best Mennonite statements which can be cited. Not all Mennonites reached this high level of attitude and spirit. First of all it must be admitted that 40 per cent of the Mennonite men called by the draft accepted service in the armed forces, and failed to remain true to the nonresistant position of their church. Furthermore, not all of the 60 per cent in CPS succeeded in grasping the true meaning of nonresistance as fully as they should have. Consequently the spirit of CPS camp life was not always on the high level which is reflected in the above editorial. This was especially true during the last year of CPS, when many men were in their fourth year of service without pay, and were anxiously looking forward to the time when they would be released from camp. The strain under which they lived and worked in those days was often such as to take away the spirit of sacrificial service which should have characterized CPS life and work. Consequently Mennonite CPS in the later period was not always what it should have been. On the whole, however, it would be correct to say that the editorial quoted above does reflect the spirit of Mennonite CPS to a reasonable degree of accuracy.

As one would expect, conscientious objectors of a more extreme type, whether religious or secular in their philosophy, who objected to every kind of service under conscription, took an attitude, and manifested a spirit, quite different from that of the Mennonite CPS editorial. One assignee in a Quaker camp wrote as follows in his camp paper:

Now I find myself in a CPS camp, playing nursemaid to pine

[66] *The Jasper-Pulaski Peace Sentinel* (CPS Camp No. 28, Medaryville, Ind.), Feb. 12, 1943.

trees. It is called "work of national importance" and so it may be in the minds of the foresters, but I am not a forester and haven't the slightest desire of being molded into one . . . . We have accepted the role of conscripted labor; but should we accept, as social-minded American citizens, these out-of-the-way jobs that have been given to us? Are we prisoners in a camp or men striving for a faraway goal?[67]

In this same camp, when Selective Service lengthened the working week from forty to forty-eight hours, in March, 1942, five of the men went on a strike. In a letter explaining their action to men in other CPS camps, the strikers said:[68]

We see in this move the beginning of a trend toward complete usurpation of our basic civil rights and privileges . . . we must object to the type of official reasoning which keeps some two thousand Americans isolated in remote camps at a time when our country suffers from many crying human needs which we might help to alleviate.

A leading article in another paper objects to the work of "material" construction in which the men are engaged. The writer insists that unless Selective Service and the NSBRO provide work of a "spiritual" nature very shortly "it will be necessary for some of us to make a demonstration. . . . Those CO's who are conscientiously opposed to internment at this strategic time for pacifist action should make a *carefully* planned and publicized demonstration of civil disobedience."[69]

In several Quaker camps certain men who shared this point of view actually carried their protest to the point where they engaged in slowdowns, in hunger strikes, and in other non-violent techniques of the Gandhian variety. A number walked out of camp, for which offense they were later arrested and sentenced to prison. Some of these men objected to service in a church-administered camp. For this and other reasons Selective Service opened a government-operated CPS camp in 1943, followed by two others later on. To these camps Selective Service assigned those men who preferred service in a government camp,

[67] *Cooperstown* (CPS Camp No. 12, Cooperstown, N.Y.), Feb. 21, 1942.
[68] *Ibid.,* March 21, 1942.
[69] *Calumet* (CPS Camp No. 19, Marion, N.C.), April 25, 1942.

and men who were a source of trouble in the church camps. Since 40 per cent of all CPS men were Mennonites, the majority of men in the MCC camps were Mennonites. MCC camps therefore had fewer problems of the type described above, than did the others, although a few non-Mennonites of the absolutist type had also been assigned to them. Most of these men later transferred to government camps, however, and in 1943 the MCC also adopted the policy of admitting to its own camps only such men as willingly subscribed to its policy and program.

While the Mennonite type of conscientious objection is quite different from that described above, it is nevertheless recognizd that this latter type must also be respected and dealt with. The British government granted complete exemption to those men who had conscientious objections to conscription, as such. There is no good reason why the United States should not have done likewise. As long as such exemption is not granted, however, the only alternative for this more extreme type of objector is prison. That this is a genuine problem in the United States can be seen from the fact that in addition to the 12,000 men in the CPS camps, there were several thousand conscientious objectors of one type or another who served prison terms. A more enlightened policy on the part of the government should make many of these imprisonments unnecessary.

SELECT BIBLIOGRAPHY

The best summary of international peace plans is S. J. Hemleben, *Plans for World Peace Through Six Centuries* (Chicago, 1943). For an understanding of the Quaker view on war and peace see S. B. Laughlin (Ed.), *Beyond Dilemmas: Quakers Look at Life* (New York, 1937); H. J. Cadbury, "The Individual Christian and the State," *Friends World Conference Report* (Philadelphia, 1937); Jonathan Dymond, *Essays on the Principles of Morality and on the Private and Political Rights and Obligations of Mankind* (London, 1829); Isaac Sharpless, *Quakerism and Politics* (Philadelphia, 1905); Margaret E. Hirst, *The Quakers in Peace and War* (New York,

1923). Guy F. Hershberger, "Some Religious Pacifists of the Nineteenth Century," *Mennonite Quarterly Review* (Goshen, Ind., January 1936), is an analysis of the views of five outstanding pacifists of the first half of the ninteenth century. Walter W. Van Kirk, *Religion Renounces War* (Chicago, 1934), and *Religion and the World of Tomorrow* (Chicago, 1941), offer a good picture of liberal Protestant pacifism today. Merle Curti, *Peace or War: The American Struggle, 1636-1936* (New York, 1936), is an excellent historical account of the American peace movement.

Fanny G. Villard, *William Lloyd Garrison on Nonresistance* (New York, 1924), and Ernest Crosby, *Garrison the Nonresistant* (Chicago, 1905), give brief pictures of this forerunner of the modern school of nonviolence. Three excellent books for an understanding of Gandhi and nonviolence are K. Shridharani, *War Without Violence* (New York, 1939), K. Shridharani, *My India, My America* (New York, 1941), and Richard B. Gregg, *The Power of Nonviolence* (Philadelphia, 1934). Pamphlets by R. B. Gregg are, *Training for Peace* (Philadelphia, 1937), and *A Discipline for Nonviolence* (Pendle Hill Pamphlet No. 11). Valuable for its comparison of nonresistance and nonviolence is Clarence Marsh Case, *Nonviolent Coercion: A Study in Methods of Social Pressure* (New York and London, 1923). An excellent analysis bringing out clearly the distinction between New Testament nonresistance and the nonviolent techniques of modern pacifism is found in Reinhold Niebuhr, *Moral Man and Immoral Society: A Study in Ethics and Politics* (New York, 1932), and *Christianity and Power Politics* (New York, 1940). A recent book describing the race problem in America is Charles S. Johnson, *Into the Main Stream* (Chapel Hill, N.C., 1947).

Rufus D. Bowman, *The Church of the Brethren and War,* 1708-1941 (Elgin, Ill., 1944), gives the record of this historic peace church. The role of this church in CPS is told in Leslie Eisan, *Pathways of Peace* (Elgin, Ill., 1948). The story of the Mennonite role in CPS is told by Melvin Gingerich, *Service for Peace* (Akron, Pa., 1949). Edward Yoder and Don. E. Smucker, *The Christian and Conscription* (Akron, Pa., 1945), set forth the Mennonite attitude toward conscription. Guy F. Hershberger, *The Mennonite Church in the Second World War* (Scottdale, Pa., 1951), describes the impact of that war upon the Mennonites. Denis Hayes, *Conscription Conflict* (London, 1949), tells the story of British pacifism since 1900. *Challenge of Conscience* (London, 1949), by the same author, is the story of British conscientious objectors, 1939 to 1949. Another recent British work is Leyton Richards, *Christian Pacifism After Two World Wars* (London, 1948). Two recent American books of importance dealing with the conscientious objector and the state are *Conscientious Objection*, 2 vols. (Selective Service System, Washington, D.C., 1950); and M. Q. Sibley and P. E. Jacob, *Conscription and Conscience: The American State and the Conscientious Objector, 1940-1947* (Ithaca, N.Y., 1952).

Two recent books by nonpacifists are John C. Bennett (ed.), *Nuclear Weapons and the Conflict of Conscience* (Scribner, 1962) and Paul Ramsey, *War and the Christian Conscience* (Duke, 1961), the latter a studied effort to place nuclear war within the pale of the "just war." Three pamphlets by John H. Yoder are: *Peace Without Eschatology?* (Scottdale, Pa., 1954); *Karl Barth and Christian Pacifism* (Church Peace Mission, n.d.); and *Reinhold Niebuhr and Christian Pacifism* (Scottdale, Pa., n.d.). The most recent history of American pacifism is Peter Brock, *Pacifism in the United States: From the Colonial Era to the First World War* (Princeton, 1968).

10. The Social Implications of Biblical Nonresistance

From the beginning of their history the Mennonite people have given much thought to the Biblical doctrine of nonresistance as applied to the personal life of the individual, to ordinary litigation, to the relation of the Christian to the state, and to international warfare. In recent years, however, the American Mennonites, especially, have become increasingly aware that the social implications of nonresistance are much more far-reaching than this. To be sure, it has always been recognized that the principle of nonresistance must be applied in every area of life. As early as 1545 Peter Riedemann said that, "since Christians should not use or exercise vengeance, they must not make the weapons by which such vengeance and destruction may be exercised.... Therefore we make neither swords, spears, guns nor other similar weapons. But whatever is made in the interest and for the daily use of men . . . we may consistently make and do make."[1] Here Riedemann lays down the principle that economic life, the manner and method by which the Christian makes his living, must be consistent with his refusal to participate in war. Other statements from the sixteenth-century fathers indicate that they were concerned with the application of the Christian ethic to other areas of life as well.

The social and economic life of the twentieth century is so complex, however, and its specific problems and issues are so numerous and varied, that it would have been impossible for the sixteenth-century fathers to anticipate all of them in their present form. For this reason it will profit Christians little to glorify

[1] Quoted in John Horsch, *The Principle of Nonresistance as Held by the Mennonite Church* (Scottdale, Pa., 1927), 24.

the principles of the fathers if they fail to exercise the thought and heart processes necessary for making clear the manifold social implications of these principles today. Furthermore, since it is the rank and file of the brotherhood which is in closest contact with these problems and issues, it is essential that each individual Christian assume personal responsibility for understanding the principle of nonresistance as it applies to his own concrete social and economic situation. Ministers and leaders are responsible to teach principles and to clarify issues, but unless the rank and file understands the issues and carries them out in practice, the teaching of principles will be of little avail.

Nonresistance and Industrial Conflict

An important illustration of the point in question is that of modern industrial relations. Until two generations ago industrial conflict as we know it today was virtually nonexistent in America, and only within the present generation has it affected the American Mennonites directly in any important way. For more than two centuries American life was largely rural and agricultural. Land was abundant. The newly arrived immigrant might work in the employ of another for a time; but sooner or later, he was likely to move to the western edge of settlement and take up land for himself. In this way even the poorest indentured servant might become an owner of land, free to chart his own career. Such eighteenth-century observers as Hector St. John de Crevecoeur and Thomas Jefferson believed that the health and prosperity of American civilization depended upon the continuation of this simple, agricultural life. "Those who labor in the earth," says Jefferson, "are the chosen people of God. . . . While we have land to labor then, let us never wish to see our citizens occupied at a workbench, or twirling a distaff . . . for the general operations of manufacture, let our workshops remain in Europe. . . . The mobs of great cities add just so much to the support of pure government, as sores do to the strength of the human body."[2]

___

[2] Quoted in V. L. Parrington, *The Colonial Mind, 1620-1800 (Main Currents in American Thought,* Vol. I, New York, 1927), 347.

Needless to say it is a far cry from the simple agrarian society of Crevecoeur and Jefferson to the industrialized economic order of New York or Detroit today. When Jefferson became president of the United States in 1801, he was responsible for the political welfare of approximately 5,000,000 people, the great majority of whom lived on the farm as did he himself. At that time the population of New York was less than 70,000, but in 1950 it was much larger than that of the entire country in 1801. The total population of the country in 1950 stood at 150,000,000. Accompanying this growth of the nation's population was the steady industrialization of the country. In 1950 only 15.8 per cent of the American population was engaged in agriculture, and even as early as 1890 the United States stood in first place among the industrial nations of the world. This process included the centralization and consolidation of numerous small industries into great industrial corporations, which constituted what now came to be known as "big business." The Standard Oil Company, for example, accomplished the merger of numerous small companies until by 1890 it controlled 90 per cent of the nation's petroleum business. Andrew Carnegie and Charles M. Schwab brought together a host of small steel mills to form one United States Steel Corporation, producing one half of the nation's steel, and employing by 1901 something like 168,000 men.

While the organization of industry on this large scale had certain advantages, it also had certain disadvantages. It gave industrialists like Schwab a virtual monopoly of the steel business, with power to make unfair profits at the expense of a helpless consumer public. It also gave them power to control the destiny of hundreds of thousands of workingmen and their families. Such mass control of the workingman was bound to bring evil results. In an earlier day when industries were small it was possible for the laborer to know his employer personally, and often to work side by side with him. If he was not satisfied with wages or working conditions he was relatively free to bargain with his employer on a basis of equality, and if he was unable to make the bargain he desired he could change his employment,

or take up land and cultivate a farm for himself. By 1890, however, a great change had taken place. The industrial laborer
was no longer a free man. The American frontier was closed;
the best land was occupied, and he was not free to turn to the
farm as his father might have done. When he turned to his employer, he found that he could no longer bargain on a basis of
equality; for his employer was a great soulless corporation which
stated the terms and he must either accept or starve.

Of course, conditions in the United States never became
as serious as they had one time been in England. There it was
necessary to enact a law in 1842 forbidding the labor of boys
under ten years, and of all women and girls, in coal mines, where
women had been creeping along on hands and knees drawing
little cars of coal behind them. A law of 1833 had also limited
to nine hours the working day for children from nine to thirteen
years of age. But we realize that conditions were bad enough,
even in the United States, when we recall that in the 1830's
20,000 women in our eastern cities were employed in factories
at wages of $1.25 per week or less. Wages in shoe factories
ranged from ten cents to fifty cents per day. In 1870 there were
115,000 children, ten to fifteen years of age, working in factories whose owners declined to employ adult men in their place
because it would cost them more money. Even as late as 1932 a
popular American magazine carried the story of a worker in the
Yale Dress Shop, one of Connecticut's notorious needle trade
sweat shops, who received a check of less than two dollars for
two weeks of hard work.

Under these circumstances what was the laboring man to
do? In all of the industrial nations, in Europe and America, the
answer was the same: organization to restore the balance of bargaining power. In America the organizations took the form of
trade unions, many of which were brought together under a
federation in 1881 which later came to be known as the American Federation of Labor. This was followed in the 1930's by the
formation of the Congress of Industrial Organizations which attempted to merge all the workers of a given industry into one
great union of laborers who would be class conscious, waging a

triumphant fight against their industrial overlords. This movement seemed determined to continue its fight until the entire working class would be organized solidly for the achievement of its ends. Since many Mennonite people were now in the cities, this turn of events meant that they were facing the challenge of industrial conflict in a serious way for the first time. Those who were industrial laborers would sooner or later be caught in the dragnet of unionization and class struggle. Then what should they and the church do? Are the principles and the methods of the labor unions in harmony with the nonresistant teachings of the Scriptures, or are they not?

The ultimate objective of organized labor is economic and social justice for the workingman. Labor also believes that under the present industrial system, with its mass employment of thousands of workers by impersonal, soulless corporations, it is virtually impossible for the workers to obtain the concessions which they believe essential for their welfare, without organized power with which to coerce their powerful overlords. Certainly there is no reason why the Christian should not desire social justice at the hands of his employer. It should be remembered, however, as has been stated before, that the Bible places its great emphasis on the *doing of justice* rather than on the *demand for justice*. When the individual sets the receiving of justice for himself as his primary goal, and pursues it relentlessly, he is in danger of violating the Scriptural principle of love and nonresistance. In fact, the relentless pursuit of justice as the highest good, when human obstacles stand in the way, cannot do otherwise than violate the way of love and nonresistance. The Christian way, however, is to accept love and nonresistance as the primary goal, with willingness to suffer even injustice if need be, in order that this goal may be reached. Here is where the principle of nonresistance and the methods of organized labor frequently come into conflict with each other.

It is freely granted that in many cases the methods of organized labor are peaceful enough. Certainly the labor movement is much more mature than it was even a generation ago, and its procedures have been greatly refined. Some unions have been successful in continuing their program for years without the use of violence or the strike. The author is not aware, however, of any union that has renounced its right to the use of violence or the strike, as a last resort, when other methods have failed. Between the doing of justice and the practice of nonresistance as taught in the Scriptures there can be no conflict, since both are based on the principle of love. The *pursuit of justice,* however, may or may not be based on the principle of love; and when it is not so based it is bound to come into conflict with the principle of nonresistance. When the pursuit of justice cannot be carried through to its goal without violating the principle of love, the nonresistant Christian will stop short of that goal and suffer even injustice, if need be. If the achievement of justice is set as the primary goal, however, and if the pursuit of this goal is not based on love, when it is seen that the goal cannot be reached without violating the principle of love, the latter will be sacrificed for the sake of the primary goal.

For this reason numerous nonresistant people employed in industries where the union is in control are confronted with a serious practical problem. Shall they join the union, with the possibility that they may become involved in methods which sacrifice their nonresistant principles? Or shall they stand by their principles and sacrifice their jobs if need be? Or can they find some way of working with the union without sacrificing the principle of nonresistance? Or ought they search for some other solution to the problem? An investigation would probably show that all of these alternatives are in actual practice among the Mennonites of America today. It must be admitted that some have become involved with the union to the extent of sacrificing their nonresistant principles. It is also true that Mennonites as a whole have not taken the problem of industrial conflict as seriously as they have that of military service. While all of the official Mennonite bodies have adopted statements of position against war and military service, not all have done so in the case of industrial conflict and affiliation with labor unions. This is understandable, inasmuch as the degree of violence involved in industrial conflict is small as compared with that involved in military service. The majority of American Mennonites do have a definite testimony against union membership and industrial conflict, however, the Mennonite General Conference having adopted an official statement of position on industrial relations as recently as 1941. In line with this testimony some members of the church changed occupations in recent years when it became difficult to retain their old positions without union membership; and there have been cases where Mennonites were literally forced out of their jobs because they declined to sign up as union members.

In 1939 the Mennonite General Conference appointed a Committee on Industrial Relations, which has followed a policy established earlier, in negotiating agreements with unions. The form of agreement has become somewhat standardized, following the general pattern of a proposed "Basis of Understanding" which was approved by the international officials of both the AF of L and the CIO. In these agreements it is provided that, in the factory or establishment under consideration, the Mennonite employee will: (1) Contribute to a specified cause, usually some charitable or benevolent cause, a sum of money equivalent to the amount of dues paid by union members. (2) Refrain from interference with or resistance to union activities. (3) In case of conflict, resulting in a strike or similar action between the union and the employer, maintain an attitude of sincere neutrality. (4) Abide by the regulations of the shop and union with regard to wages, hours, and working conditions. The agreements provide that the union, on the other hand, will excuse the nonresistant employee from membership in the union, payment of union fees and dues, attendance at meetings, and other union activities. Since 1939 a large number of these agreements have been signed. In this program the Committee on Industrial Relations has worked closely with a similar committee of the Brethren in Christ Church.

Industrial Conflict and Materialism

It was suggested in Chapter I that our present civilization is sensate and materialistic, and that modern warfare is one of the fruits of materialism and secularism. It is important to re-member that industrial conflict is also a fruit of this same materialism. Organized labor and big business appeared in the nineteenth century when the interests of the American people were absorbed in mechanical inventions and devices which would contribute to their physical comfort. There is, of course, no virtue in discomfort. Nevertheless, when the dominant in-terest of any people is ease and physical comfort it is clear that they have lost their grip on the higher values of life. It has been said that whereas the minister was once the most influential person in the typical American community, this place has come to be taken by the medical doctor. Irving Babbitt says the obvious reason for this is that "Men once lived in the fear of God, whereas now they live in the fear of microbes." Norman Foerster comments that this change in interest is reflected even in the meaning of the word *comfort* itself, which once had refer-ence only to spiritual consolation, but now refers primarily to physical ease. Even "the word *comforter,* once applied to the Holy Spirit, is now used as the name of a bed cover."[3]

In the nineteenth century, while the general population concerned itself with the more superficial aspects of material-ism, scholars and philosophers probed deeper until they ad-vanced an interpretation of man and society which was material-istic to its very roots. In 1867 Karl Marx published his famous work, *Das Kapital,* in which he argued that the basic urge in the breast of every human being is an economic urge; that the entire course of history has been determined by economic forces; and that history is primarily the story of a continuous struggle be-tween the poor and the rich. Marx believed the time had arrived when the oppressed classes everywhere must unite to overthrow their exploiters. The higher religious and moral values as found in the Christian faith must be ignored. The satisfaction of economic desires is the supreme end of man. In 1859 Charles Darwin published his *Origin of Species* in which he argued that man is the product of biological evolution, characterized by a struggle for existence which continually results in the death of

---

[3] Norman Foerster, *The American State University* (Chapel Hill, N.C., 1937), 40.

the weaklings and the survival of the fittest. In the sixteenth century the Italian Machiavelli had argued that the world is the playground of human lions and foxes; that it is the ruler's business to conquer and rule in the spirit of these beasts; and that he cannot be bound by any moral considerations. Darwin's work now brought a biological argument to the support of Machiavelli's doctrine. Men who were acting like lions and foxes justified their acts by the "laws of nature" as set forth by Darwin. War was regarded a necessary struggle for life. Values were stated in terms of brute force. It was argued that might makes right. The crowning work of materialism was wrought by Friedrich Wilhelm Nietzsche (1844-1900), who emphasized the dominance of the strong over the weak as the most fundamental fact in human society.

It is not surprising, therefore, that the past seventy-five years were a period of intense political and international rivalry, of racial conflict, and industrial struggle. The nations of the western world were struggling for positions of dominance. They built up vast industries for which they required raw materials and markets. This led to a struggle for colonies which necessitated the formation of secret alliances, and the building of vast armaments for warfare on the land, on the sea, and in the air. The nations were engaged in a great struggle in which the fittest would survive. This is not to suggest that the majority of the people in the nineteenth and twentieth centuries were conscious followers of Marx, or Darwin, or Nietzche. Even some who were active in the struggle for political or economic power would have repudiated the ideas of these writers. Furthermore, some who did accept Darwin's main thesis believed that mutual aid was a more important factor in evolution than was struggle. Writers of the latter school developed an evolutionary view of human society which envisioned the gradual development of the world to the point where warfare and strife would be outgrown. It was an optimistic and idealistic view of life, which nevertheless had a materialistic basis, and which ignored the reality of human sin.

So great was the impact of materialism on western society

that no one escaped its influence. The struggle for power, wealth, and prestige was everywhere present. Nations dealt with each other in the spirit of lions and foxes, and so did individuals and corporations in the business world. In 1871 Charles Francis Adams, son and grandson of two American presidents, remarked that the short period since the Civil War had

witnessed some of the most remarkable examples of organized law-lessness, under the forms of law, which mankind has yet had an op-portunity to study . . . certain . . . men at the head of vast combina-tions of private wealth . . . have declared war, negotiated peace, re-duced courts, legislatures, and sovereign states to an unqualified obedience to their will . . . . Single men have controlled hundreds of miles of railway, thousands of men, tens of millions of revenue, and hundreds of millions of capital. The strength implied in all this they wielded in practical independence of the control both of governments and of individuals; much as petty German despots might have governed their principalities a century or two ago.[4]

Andrew Carnegie (1837-1919), leader in the American steel industry, argued effectively for the virtue of individualism, private property, competition, and the accumulation of wealth. The law of competition, he said, "is here; we cannot evade it; no substitutes for it have been found; and while the law may sometimes be hard on the individual, it is best for the race, be-cause it ensures the survival of the fittest in every department."[5]

Nonresistance and Economic Relations

Even though the program of organized labor may frequent-ly violate the principle of love and nonresistance, the above dis-cussion should make it clear that the employer class, organized capital, and big business are equally capable of such violation. If their methods are sometimes more refined than those of labor, they are also more subtle and fully as vicious, if not more so. Employers' unions, organized as manufacturers' associations, or in some other form, have frequently used methods of force similar to those of the workingmen's strike. The lockout, the

---

[4] R. H. Gabriel, *The Course of American Democratic Thought* (New York, 1940), 144.
[5] *Ibid.*, 150.

black list, the use of labor spies, and finally actual violence, have often been used. During the 1930's, when the automobile industry was being organized, a senate investigating committee revealed that the General Motors Corporation had invested over $1,000,000 in espionage and munitions. Another automobile manufacturing company spent over $275,000 for the same kind of service, which was euphemistically called "protective engineering." It is obvious, of course, that the nonresistant Christian cannot share in such a program as this.

So complex is modern economic life, however, and so subtle are its ways, that the individual may become involved in its unchristian practices before he is aware of what is happening. It is commonly taken for granted that it is proper for the Christian to save his money and to invest it where and when it will earn adequate returns. Is not this good stewardship? But, what if the corporation in which he invests his money engages in unchristian practices which violate the principle of nonresistance? Can the nonresistant Christian invest a thousand dollars in the stocks and bonds of an automobile corporation which in turn invests a million dollars in forms of protective engineering such as those mentioned above? Some years ago some members of Trinity Church in New York City became concerned about living conditions in a certain slum section of the city. As a first step toward remedial action they made inquiry as to the ownership of these slum dwellings and learned to their amazement that they were owned by Trinity Church, the trustees having placed the church's endowment funds in these dwellings years before as an investment which would produce a satisfactory income. Evidently the trustees had failed, however, to ask the more important question as to whether this income was being produced by methods consistent with the principles of love and brotherhood.

Earlier in this chapter reference was made to Peter Riedemann's testimony against the manufacture of weapons of war. This is a much more serious problem today than it was in the sixteenth century, both as to the quantity of such material being produced, and as to the multiplicity of ways in which it is possible to become involved in the problem. When a great armament program is under way the industrial might of the nation is marshalled to support that program. A major portion of every great industry is converted from peacetime industry to war production, with the result that those responsible for the management of the industry and those whose capital is invested therein, are directly and vitally engaged in the war business. Workingmen employed in such industries are also engaged in the same business unless perhaps they are located in some division of the plant devoted to civilian production. Even in wartime certain divisions of some large industries are so devoted, and there are always some smaller industries which even in wartime continue with civilian work. Obviously, the only consistent course for a nonresistant laborer in wartime is to find employment in an industry given wholly to civilian work, or at least in a civilian division of an industry which in its other divisions may not be so engaged. If this is not possible, the only remaining alternative is to transfer to agriculture or some other civilian employment which is free from support of the war effort.

Nonresistance and Agriculture

This is not to suggest, however, that modern agriculture is free from organizations, methods, and procedures which frequently violate the way of love and nonresistance. It is true that Jefferson had declared farmers to be "the chosen people of God . . . whose breasts he has made his peculiar deposit for substantial and genuine virtue. . . . Corruption of morals in the mass of cultivators," he said, "is a phenomenon of which no age nor nation has furnished an example."[6] Agricultural life is not as simple today as it was in Jefferson's time, however, and whatever the morals of farmers in his day may have been, it is certain that in the mid-twentieth century they are subject to manifold temptations to engage in practices which are out of line with the Christian ethic. Just as industry and labor have found it to their advantage to organize for the furtherance of their interests,

[6] Quoted in Parrington, *op. cit.*, 347.

so has agriculture. This movement began as early as 1867 when the Patrons of Husbandry was organized. This organization, later known as the Grange, was a secret society aiming at the social, intellectual, moral, and economic improvement of the rural classes. It engaged in co-operative buying, selling, and manufacturing. It also engaged in political action aimed at removing unfair practices and abuses in the area of railway transportation, tariffs, interest rates, monopolies, and other abuses. Other farmers' organizations emerged in the following decades and culminated in the formation of the Populist party, in the 1890's. Since then various specialized agricultural interests have come into being, such as the Farmers' Union, dairy unions, fruit growers', poultrymen's, and potato growers' associations, and others. Attempts have been made to form a general federation of these various specialized farm organizations. An organization of a somewhat different type is the Farm Bureau which among other things works with the agricultural colleges and county agents for the carrying on of agricultural extension work. An important part of this picture is the recent growth of co-operatives for the purchase, sale, and distribution of agricultural products, such as wheat, fruit, dairy, and other farm products.

As in the case of employers' and labor organizations in the field of industry, these farmers' organizations have many good features and serve many useful purposes. There is a helpful exchange of information, the quality of agricultural products is raised, and marketing facilities are improved through the services offered by these organizations. In many cases the methods employed by them are honorable, but as in the case of labor and industrial organizations engaged in the pursuit of justice for themselves, some of these farmers' organizations are pressure groups, operating for selfish ends, and using methods as vicious as those of any other pressure groups. Organized dairymen who pressure their congressmen to place a tax on oleomargarine, or to enact some other form of discriminatory legislation against it, are using tactics no different in kind from those used by organized industry and labor against each other. Farmers also have been known to withhold meat from the market in protest against government price policies, and during the depression of the 1930's certain radical farmers' organizations even took the law into their own hands and exercised violence in an effort to prevent the foreclosure of mortgages, or the execution of bankruptcy sales. The latter type of violent action is so clearly outside the range of Christian ethics that it may be assumed that no Mennonites took part in it. Some of the other unethical practices of farm organizations are more subtle, and here one can speak with less certainty. As to membership in farm organizations, and participation in them, there is a considerable amount of variation among the American Mennonites. Some dissociate themselves completely from organized agriculture. Others are active participants in certain of the farm organizations. Some of the latter would contend that their participation is for information and improvement purposes only and that it does not violate the Christian ethic of love and nonresistance. In some cases this contention is perhaps a valid one, although there is no doubt that a considerable number of Mennonite farmers are involved in farm organizations employing questionable methods of the more subtle type.

This emphasizes the fact that the Mennonite social conscience needs to grow sharper, more sensitive, and more discriminating. In an earlier period of organized labor when violent methods were taken for granted, and when the whole field of labor lay somewhat beyond the range of the Mennonite agricultural economy, it was relatively easy for the church to reach the conclusion that it could have nothing to do with organized labor. As agriculture became more scientific and complex in its character, however, Mennonites in many sections became participants in the more innocent of the farm organizations, and in course of time some may have become involved in organizations and movements which are actually less innocent in character and method than some labor organizations. The need for a sharper and more discerning social conscience is illustrated by the story of a Mennonite farmer who lost his temper and swore when the dairy rejected the milk from his farm because it was not clean. The high regard of the church for reverence to God and purity of speech is seen in that this brother was disciplined for taking the Lord's name in vain; but the dullness of its social conscience is also seen in the fact that there was no disciplinary action for unsanitary methods which would endanger the health of people using dairy products.[7] Whether this story is true in all of its details the author is unable to say. Be that as it may, however, it points up the need for a social conscience able to discern the varied ramifications of the doctrine of nonresistance in a complex social and economic world. A person who dies of a tuberculosis germ obtained from a glass of milk is as dead as a man who dies from a bullet wound. The nonresistant Christian who would not be part of a military organization which takes human life must be doubly certain that in his ordinary civilian occupation he be not unwittingly trapped into doing the very thing to which he has so just an aversion.

An incident which occurred several years ago serves to illustrate how easy it is for well-meaning people who are fairly well acquainted with the Bible to overlook some very important things. A class of middle-aged Mennonites was asked what the Bible has to say about economics and business. They promptly quoted, "not slothful in business,"[8] and "go to the ant, thou sluggard; consider her ways, and be wise."[9] They might also have added, "the hand of the diligent maketh rich."[10] Not until they were reminded of it, however, did any remember about the man whose soul was required one night because he had been diligent in business to the exclusion of more important matters;[11] or the words of Isaiah pronouncing "woe unto them that join house to house, that lay field to field, till there be no place, that they may be placed alone in the midst of the earth!"[12] It is strange that these good people should remember those Scrip-

---

[7] W. Rauschenbusch, *A Theology for the Social Gospel* (New York, 1917), 135.

[8] Rom. 12:11. In the original Greek this passage admonishes diligence and devotion to the things of the Spirit rather than attention to business as the English King James Version suggests.

[9] Prov. 6:6.

[10] Prov. 10:4.

[11] Luke 12:16-20.

[12] Isa. 5:8.

tures which, if taken alone, would encourage one to follow the
course which leads to war, while forgetting those which give the
necessary warning antidote to this erroneous course.

The Economics of the Mennonite Rural Community

It is obvious that the industrialization of America has
brought to every Christian community its share of problems.
The author believes, however, that it is possible to plan the life
of the community in such a way as to bring it more nearly in
line with the way of Christian nonresistance than it now is in
many cases. In its report to the Mennonite General Conference
in 1941 the Committee on Industrial Relations included the
following statement:

While our present labors with industrial organizations are nec·
essary and worth while, it would be better if the social and economic
situation of the Mennonite Church were such as to make them unnecessary. So long as the brethren work in factories where industrial
unionism threatens the principles of the church, the church must do
what it can to protect its members and its principles. But a more
worth-while task would be for the church to get nearer the roots of its
problem and do what it can to provide a social and economic situation where its members would not be troubled with unionism at
all. If this could be done, the Mennonite testimony to the world
would be greatly strengthened. A few nonunion workers in a factory
can and do give a testimony, but a Mennonite community, co-
operatively directing its entire economic and social life in such a way
as to exemplify the economic and social ethics of the New Testament, would be a stronger and a better testimony . . . . Your committee believes that if the Mennonite and Christian way in economic
relations is to prevail among our people the church will need to examine more closely the roots of its problem and take steps to develop
a forward-looking program of community building, so challenging
as to keep the thought and the energies of all the members focused
upon it. Your committee believes that the church does not yet
realize as it should the possibilities for fostering the Mennonite, and
we believe the Christian, way of life through such means as effective
organization for mutual aid, hospitalization, medical care, the co-
operative purchasing of land to assist young farmers in need of help,
and the co-operative operation of community industries where New
Testament business and social ethics and means of security prevail.[13]

[13] *Minutes of the Twenty-second Mennonite General Conference* (Scottdale, Pa., 1941),
46, 47.

This statement is in line with the author's view that the economic life of the community should be planned so as to bring it more nearly in line with the nonresistant principles of the Mennonites. While this suggestion may be pointing to a way which seems new to some Mennonites, the author is inclined to believe that it is full of possibilities; and certainly it is in line with the Mennonite tradition of brotherhood and mutual aid. Among the Mennonites of America today there are a number of industrial employers. These Mennonite employers of labor have an excellent opportunity, and a responsibility, to give a clear witness to the nonresistant faith. Sociologists, and experts in the United States Department of Agriculture, today are citing Mennonite agricultural communities as models of agricultural stability and community solidarity. These writers recognize that there is something about the Mennonite faith and the Mennonite way of life which helps to make these agricultural communities what they are. If this view is correct, then it would seem that the Mennonite way of life should have something to contribute in the field of industry as well. It should, for example, keep Mennonite factories from growing so large that they become impersonal, soulless corporations. These should remain small enough for the maintenance of wholesome personal relations between employer and employee. Mennonite employers dare not delay the introduction of progressive measures for the improvement of working and living conditions, and for the development of wholesome employer-employee relationships, until compelled by some outside force to do so.

Mennonite factories should be the happiest, the most contented industrial units in America, where employer and employees labor together in conscious co-operation, and where the class struggle has no opportunity of taking root because employer and employee belong to one and the same class, and will have it no other way. In the course of their history Mennonite farmers of Europe and America have frequently been visited by agricultural experts interested in studying their methods. It is just as reasonable that sociologists, economists, and experts in the field of industrial relations should visit Mennonite industrial plants today to learn the secret of their success in maintaining wholesome relations without a struggle for power. The exact pattern of the ideal nonresistant industrial situation may not yet be entirely clear, but several points might be suggested. The writer would expect to hear of a yearly wage, providing some security against seasonal and periodic layoffs; he would expect to hear of a division of profits that is outstanding for its fairness to both labor and capital; and he would expect to hear of other devices for the maintenance of cordial relations. But above all, he would expect the visiting expert in the Mennonite factory to learn of the Christian faith and the nonresistant way of life which prevails there, and which causes the employer to seek the highest welfare of his employees for the employees' sake, while it at the same time causes the employees to seek the welfare of their employer for the employer's sake.

It is the writer's opinion, however, that such industries can best be maintained if they are closely integrated with the life of the Mennonite rural community. Certainly no environment is more favorable for the perpetuation of the nonresistant faith than is the rural community; and for this reason the Mennonite churches will do well to keep themselves established in such communities, with a high percentage of their members directly engaged in agriculture. On the other hand, it is too much to expect all of the Mennonite people to engage in actual farming. Today only 15.8 per cent of the American population is engaged in agriculture; and authorities of the United States Department of Agriculture estimate that, in the future, improved methods in agriculture will cause even this figure to be lowered considerably.

This does not mean, however, that it is necessary for those Mennonites who do not engage in actual farming, continually to flow from their communities to the larger cities, there to lose their touch with the brotherhood. What we need is a new picture of rural life. If we get this vision, we can think of the rural community as more than a group of farmers. The Mennonite community of the future should be, and can be, a community characterized by a balanced integration of agriculture and industry. A large percentage of the families in the Mennonite community perhaps should live on family-size farms and operate them. But in the village, at the center of the community, there should also be a number of small industries, many of them devoted to first-stage processing of farm products. Poultry packing, dehydration of foods, preparation of mixed feeds, and many other processes closely related to agriculture, can be carried on as effectively and as economically in the rural community as in the city. The same could be said of other industries not so closely related to agriculture.

To build a successfully functioning community of this type will require careful, co-operative planning. There must be a counseling service to assist members of the community in finding their individual occupations, and a credit service to help some of them in getting started. Some worthy young people who wish to engage in farming lack the funds to make a beginning. If the community has a credit service, providing funds at a low rate of interest, these people can get the help they need. The community counseling service should be alert to see the need of a new industry whenever it arises. Steps should then be taken to establish the industry, which would provide a livelihood for members of the community not engaged in actual farming. In such a community one could expect to find a number of families who do part-time farming. They might live on little farms, five or ten acres in size, which would produce a considerable portion of their food, while their cash income would be earned through employment in one of the community industries.

In such a planned Mennonite rural community one would expect to find a strong spirit of Christian brotherhood. There should be a well-organized system of mutual aid. The community should have its own social security program, well organized and carefully financed. In case of sickness or death in any family this system should function so as to prevent any destitution. Members of the community should think in terms of the community welfare, in terms of the brotherhood, and not in terms of their personal interest. Brethren with money to spare, instead of investing it in industrial stocks and bonds, where it might be used in the industrial conflict, should place it in the custody of the community credit service, which would use it to assist those in financial need.

This brotherhood spirit should permeate the entire community, and affect all of its members. Young people who attend college should have a desire to give a life of service to the Mennonite community. If they are farmers, this service can be given as farmers. But this community also needs ministers, teachers, doctors, and nurses, as well as workers and leaders in the community industries. College graduates interested in these fields of service should plan to give that service in the Mennonite rural community. In some cases small community hospitals might well be erected, these together with the entire medical service of the community, managed and financed on a cooperative basis, giving equal medical services to all. But most important of all, this ideal community must be permeated with the spirit of Christ. The nonresistant way of life must direct its every work and motive. The spirit of Christian brotherhood must govern all of its relationships. In such a community there should be no opportunity for the seeds of industrial conflict even to take root. And in such a community, so conceived and so dedicated and so managed, there ought to be happiness, contentment, and security, such as will prevent any appreciable drift of the Mennonite rural population to the larger urban centers of industrial conflict.

The Christian Attitude Toward Other Races and Peoples

The community here envisioned is not one which exists for its own sake, or whose chief end is economic values. It is the true Christian community where men dwell together as brethren, exemplifying the way of love and peace as set forth in the New Testament, using economic values merely as a means to a greater end. This greater end is the bringing of the way of love and brotherhood to all men. The truly Christian community is a missionary community which, like those of the early church, sends out its emissaries to found new Christian communities everywhere. The sixteenth-century Anabaptists were community-minded, but there was no isolation in their conception of community. Their communities were the springboard from which their emissaries were sent forth into every part of Europe to establish new Christian communities, and thus extend the borders of the kingdom. "No words of the Master," says Littell, "were given more serious attention by His Anabaptist followers than His final command: Go ye therefore, and make disciples of all the nations."[14] Nowhere can one find a better illustration of the relation of community and missions than in the writings of Menno Simons himself. In one place he says: "This love, charity, and *community* we teach and practice."[15] In another place he says: "we seek and desire with yearning and ardent hearts, yea at the cost of our life and blood that the holy Gospel of Jesus Christ and his apostles may be preached throughout the world."[16]

Such a true missionary spirit can exist only where the spirit of Christian love and brotherhood goes out from the Christian community to all men everywhere, regardless of race, or color, or social or economic station. When this spirit is at work among men it makes for peace. So-called Christians who have not this spirit, however much they may profess to believe in nonresistance, are not making a contribution to peace, but to war. Note the following words from Arthur E. Morgan:

We think of wars as being imposed upon essentially peaceful people by governments or by big business.. Such thinking is unrealistic. While small wars may be bankers' wars or tyrants' wars, great wars are people's wars. They form out of the deeply rooted attitudes of the rank and file of men. An example is the race issue, which may be the cause of the next world war. Race discrimination imbedded in the feelings and attitudes of Americans deeply wounds the dignity and self-respect of those discriminated against. The attitude of superiority arouses hate, and leads to a determination to

[14] F. H. Littell, "The Anabaptist Theology of Missions," *Mennonite Quarterly Review* (January, 1947), 21:12.

[15] H. S. Bender and John Horsch, *Menno Simons' Life and Writings* (Scottdale, Pa., 1936), 76.

[16] *Ibid.*, 88.

prove equality by force at the first opportunity. In short, such discrimination is a cause of war. More than a thousand million men of color may unite on that issue as soon as they have mastered technology and large-scale administration. At present very many Americans who call themselves peace-loving probably would choose another world war, with all its cost of lives and treasure, and with all its cost to democratic institutions, before they would give up the attitude of racial superiority.[17]

As this statement says, one good test of the quality of our brotherhood is the attitude which we take toward the colored peoples, both at home and abroad. In our time our attitude toward the oriental peoples is of special importance. Why has the Chinese nation fallen under the control of the Communists? Is it not because those people who make up the Chinese Communist party for some reason became convinced that Communism has more to offer them than does the way of life of the supposedly Christian west? In 1951, because the government of India was urging moderation in America's Far Eastern policy, American feeling toward India was not too kind, with the result that shipments of much-needed supplies of grain to that ever famine-stricken country were being continually delayed. In the meantime as the Indian people continued to hunger, there were rumors that Russia and China were about to send them grain. In fact a little Russian grain did reach India. Although the amount received from the United States was eventually much greater, this incident will explain why some misguided Indians might conclude that Communism has more to offer them than does so-called Christian America. Recently Donald Soper of London, referring to the ricksha coolies of Ceylon, said: "For long enough Christians in Ceylon had talked about the fatherhood of God and brotherhood of man, but when the Communists came they said to the coolie, 'vote for us and when we get in there won't be a ricksha left in Colombo.' No wonder every coolie has become a Communist."[18]

When one half of the people of the world go hungry all their lives, need one be surprised that they fall for Communist

---

[17] Arthur E. Morgan, "The Small Community as the Birthplace of Enduring Peace" (Typewritten manuscript), 1.

[18] *Peace News* (London, Nov. 17, 1950).

propaganda which promises to give them what they so much need? It is true that the Communist propaganda consists mostly of untruths, and the people who accept it will ultimately be accepting slavery. But, if the western way of life has more to offer them than communism does, why have the Oriental peoples not been thoroughly convinced of this fact? Is it perhaps because the West, even the Christian people of the West, have lacked the social conscience and the driving force of love necessary for reaching the hearts of these people? The attitude of the West toward the East has been too condescending in spirit. There has been too much of a proud, complacent attitude of superiority. The American people have too commonly assumed that the United States is rich and the East is poor because of the thrifty industrious ways of the West, and the indolence of the East. They forget that China proper has a population density of more than 300 persons per square mile while that of the United States is only about 50 persons per square mile. They forget that Honan province in China, which is about the size of Kansas, has 18,000,000 farmers while Kansas has 600,000; that the amount of crop land per family is two acres while that of Kansas is 150 acres; and that the net income per family in Honan is $120 per year while that of Kansas is $3,000 per year. The people of the Orient, on the other hand, cannot understand why the United States which has only 6 per cent of the world's population should have 70 per cent of the world's automobiles, 50 per cent of the telephones, 51 per cent of the rubber, and 62 per cent of the world's oil under its control. Those Orientals who ascribe this difference to the greed and materialism of the West may not be altogether fair; but what shall be the attitude of western Christians? Shall they take pride in their high standard of living? Shall they have an inward sense of satisfaction because their national policy keeps up the bars of immigration lest the coming of more foreigners lower the American standard of living? Shall they make disparaging remarks about the inability of European and oriental countries to keep on top financially without the help of the Marshall Plan or other forms of American aid?

Whatever others do, certainly the nonresistant Christian who desires to cast his lot on the side of peace will have a deep sense of responsibility for the underfed portion of the world. He will be keenly conscious of the fact that the fortunate economic situation in which he finds himself is undeserved; and that he has no moral right to a higher standard of living than that of other peoples of the world. The least he can do is to have such a feeling of love and sympathy for the underprivileged portion of the peoples of the world that he will not only breathe a sincere prayer of gratitude every time he seats himself at a table filled with food, but just as earnestly beg the forgiveness of his heavenly Father for any desire he may have for such luxuries of life as he and his fellow Americans might obtain at the expense of their brothers in other lands.

An Awakened Social Conscience

Finally, it cannot be stressed too strongly that in this twentieth century the nonresistant Christian, and the nonresistant church, must have a keen social conscience, a thorough understanding of the social implications of the Gospel, and a strong program for the furtherance of the Gospel with its social implications. The church need not be disturbed by such critics as John C. Bennett who describe the refusal of nonresistant Christians to participate in war, or in other forms of political or social action which are inconsistent with the nonresistant position, as a "strategy of withdrawal" which fails to "assume full responsibility for the political order."[19] It should be clear enough that a true disciple of Christ cannot assume *full* responsibility for the entire political order as found in a sub-Christian society. Neither is it necessary to regard the declining of full responsibility for this sub-Christian social order as a strategy of withdrawal. It would be better to say that pursuing a consistent course of Christian discipleship is the most fruitful challenge and contribution which can be made to the political and social order. Having said this, however, the author would has-

---

[19] See John C. Bennett, *Christian Ethics and Social Policy* (New York, 1946), 41-46.

ten to add that the nonresistant Christian must assume full responsibility to achieve and maintain a fully enlightened social conscience, testifying to the world, including governments; and carrying forward an aggressive program of love and action through evangelism, relief, and various forms of Christian social service, which will command the respect of men everywhere and set a standard for Christendom and for the state.

While it is certain that the present generation of Mennonites has made an impact on the society and the state of its day, it is also certain that the goal suggested here has not yet been reached. Before it is reached, there are a number of things which they must do, among which the following should be mentioned:

1. Nonresistant people, and the Mennonite Church in particular, must acquire a better understanding of the principle of social justice as contained in the Gospel of Christ.

2. They must ever bear in mind that the Christian ethic places its emphasis on the doing of justice rather than on seeking or demanding justice for one's self. When the emphasis is placed on the demand for justice, the principle of love and nonresistance is in danger of being sacrificed.

3. They must apply the principle of doing justice consistently in every area of life.

4. They must bring together groups of brethren and help them to think through the ethics of their business, or trade, or profession, and assist them in formulating policies and procedures which will enable them to maintain a consistent witness of doing justice in line with the Christian ethic.

5. The church must find a way of lifting up her voice in protest against social injustice wherever it is found, while maintaining the proper emphasis on the doing of justice. She must raise up men and women who will become prophets of social righteousness without descending to the level of the agitator engaged in a class struggle. Here is a task requiring genuine vision and Christian statesmanship.

6. Worthy of special mention is a much-needed program of Christian race relations, both in teaching and in practical dem-

onstration. So far the Mennonite Church has hardly begun to work at this problem in any realistic way. While she conducts missions to Negroes at home and abroad, the fact remains that in 1952 she had not yet succeeded in admitting Negroes to certain homes for the aged administered by the church. When such conditions exist the goal has not yet been reached.

7. The church must continually explore new areas of evangelization and Christian social service. Voluntary Service units of every sort must be extended at home and abroad.

8. The relief program of the church must be kept up wherever opportunities can be found to serve in this way.

9. The church must rethink her responsibility for bringing the witness of peace to the governments of the nations, and take steps to promote a more aggressive witness in line with that responsibility.

SELECT BIBLIOGRAPHY

John R. Commons, *et al., History of Labor in the United States,* 2 vols. (New York, 1921), is a standard history of the American labor movement. Herbert Harris, *American Labor* (New Haven, 1938), is a briefer, more recent treatment. The struggle for power in labor's organization drive after 1930 is sharply outlined in G. E. Sokolsky, *Labor's Fight for Power* (Garden City, N.Y., 1934). Leo Huberman, *Labor Spy Racket* (New York, 1937), is based on the reports of the La Follette Committee on Civil Liberties, and describes methods used by capital in fighting the labor organizations. Two books describing the operation of organized labor under federal regulations are R. R. R. Brooks, *Unions of Their Own Choosing* (New Haven, 1939), and H. A. Mills, *et al., How Collective Bargaining Works* (New York, 1942). James Myers, *Do You Know Labor?* (New York, 1943), is a picture of organized labor by the Industrial Secretary of the Federal Council of the Churches of Christ in America. Mr. Myers is a pacifist who thinks of the labor movement as an agency for the creation of a Christian world order. Two titles worth reading by persons interested in the social and economic life of the Mennonite rural community are A. E. Morgan, *The Small Community* (New York, 1942), and A. E. Morgan, *Small Community Economics* (Yellow Springs, Ohio, 1943). Two valuable books on the social implications of the Christian Gospel are John C. Bennett, *Christian Ethics and Social Policy* (New York, 1946), and Carl F. H.

Henry, *The Uneasy Conscience of Modern Fundamentalism* (Grand Rapids, Mich., 1947). The former, by a liberal theologian, is critical of the nonresistant position, but raises many questions which should stimulate nonresistant Christians to examine with care the social implications of that position. The latter is by a conservative theologian who, while not accepting the nonresistant position, nevertheless does much to prick the Christian conscience on many social issues. Charles S. Johnson, *Into the Main Stream* (Chapel Hill, 1947), is a presentation of some of the better aspects of race relations in the American South and contains many illustrations and suggestions which should be of help to nonresistant people desiring to make their principles most effective in the area of race relations. A penetrating study of Christian ethics by a nonpacifist is Emil Brunner, *Justice and the Social Order* (New York, 1945).

Beginning in 1958 Martin Luther King published numerous works on Christian love and the race question, of which some of the more important are: *Stride Toward Freedom* (Harper, 1958); *Strength to Love* (Harper, 1963); *Letter from Birmingham City Jail* (American Friends Service Committee 1963); and *Why We Can't Wait* (Harper, 1964). A helpful pamphlet is C. Norman Kraus, *Integration: Who's Prejudiced?* (Scottdale, Pa., 1958). Guy F. Hershberger, *The Way of the Cross in Human Relations* (Scottdale, Pa., 1958) treats nonresistance in its broader social implications, including one chapter on race relations.

11. The Service of Nonresistance to Society

The Task of the Nonresistant Christian

Since the nonresistant Christian is a disciple of Christ, his supreme task is to obey the words of his Master when He said: "Go ye therefore, and make disciples of all the nations, baptizing them in the name of the Father and of the Son and of the Holy Spirit: teaching them to observe all things whatsoever I commanded you."[1] Baptism in the name of the Father and the Son and the Holy Spirit implies the need of a theological and doctrinal foundation for discipleship. He who has nothing more than the ethical teachings of Jesus is not a disciple of His. No man can enter the kingdom of God by merely imitating the outward life of Christ. Discipleship means first an experience of regeneration through the atoning work of Christ; and the ethical life of the Christian must proceed from this experience. Therefore the first task of the nonresistant Christian is to maintain an unwavering testimony for the evangelical Christian faith, and to be on guard against any kind of pacifism or social service which has its roots in human philosophy, no matter how well it may be adorned by a veneer of Christian idealism.

For regenerated Christians the observance of "all things" means a full acceptance of the whole-Gospel ethic. It means that the way of life set forth in the Sermon on the Mount and the writings of the apostles must be lived completely. True discipleship does not admit of a partial Christian ethic, limited by the omission of some teachings or by the watering down of others to the point where they mean something quite different from that which Jesus intended. Therefore, the second task of non-

[1] Matt. 28:19, 20 (ASV).

236

resistant Christians is to maintain the entire Christian ethic, which includes the practice of nonresistance toward "him that is evil." They must be on guard against any system of partial interpretation which applies the way of peace to the affairs of nations, but omits it in the relations of capital and labor, or in the common affairs of daily life. Likewise they must maintain a true nonresistance and guard against any so-called pacifism which is a mere improvement in international relations, or perhaps merely a substitution of nonviolent compulsion for compulsion by means of physical force. Finally, nonresistant Christians must guard against a one-sided emphasis which makes pacifism a religion in itself, or the driving force of their lives to which all else is subordinate. Christian nonresistance is a fruit, not a root. It is an integral part of the Gospel message; but it is not the Gospel of itself.

The Challenge of Pacifism

In taking the position outlined in the above section, however, the nonresistant Christian will find himself challenged by various forms of modern pacifism. The pacifist says that the nonresistant is too intent on obeying the Scriptures; that the doctrine of peace is too incidental to his entire world view; that his approach to the question of peace is too negative; and that he is not sufficiently concerned with the problem of social justice in a changing world order; in short that nonresistant thinking is directed too much toward the hope of heaven and not sufficiently toward the needs of the world. For these reasons, pacifism says, leadership in the peace movement will not come from the ranks of the nonresistant churches. To this challenge the nonresistant Christian would reply that the only hope for this world is a way of life which has its source in heaven. No man-centered religion can bring any permanent help to the needs of a sinful world. Nonresistant Christians are intent on obeying the Scriptures because they are the revelation of God; and since the Scriptures give the doctrine of peace a place within a larger body of teaching, they must do likewise. Again it must be said,

Christian peace is a fruit, not a root. It is one of the teachings of the Gospel; it is not the Gospel of itself.

As to the challenge that nonresistant Christians are not sufficiently concerned with the social problems of the day, it can be said in reply that they are interested in these problems, but that they work at them with a different technique, namely, through regeneration and discipleship, rather than through education and reformation. The New Testament breathes a spirit of love which has always moved Christians to engage in works of mercy for the relief and help of those who are in need. Furthermore, the teaching and practice of the Mennonite Church from its first beginnings to the present day, as reviewed in Chapters V to VII, are evidence that this spirit has remained alive among this body of nonresistant Christians. It must be admitted, however, that too often in its history the Mennonite Church has suffered from spiritual decline and lack of vision, so that it has not always been as alert to the needs of the day as it should have been. On the other hand, the growing Mennonite program of foreign relief is one indication that in our own time the church is very mcuh alive to the needs of the day.

An extensive organized relief program reaching into Puerto Rico, Paraguay, England, France, Poland, the Near East, and China is no mean showing for a brotherhood of 156,000 members whose financial support is drawn from its own resources and not from the public; and to perform this task has required genuine leadership. The pacifist critics are correct, however, when they say they cannot look to the nonresistant groups for leadership in a movement which resorts to political pressure and nonviolent resistance, for the simple reason that Mennonites and other nonresistant Christians believe that this type of pacifism has the wrong approach; that it is based on an erroneous conception of the kingdom of God and the manner of its building. It is the task of the Mennonites and other nonresistant Christians to provide leadership, not for popular pacifism, but for the building of that discipleship which produces a society of regenerate Christians, a Christian brotherhood which belongs to the true kingdom of God.

The Challenge of the Nonpacifists

The nonresistant Christian must also meet the challenge of the nonpacifists. One type of nonpacifist believes that God commands Christian people to wage war. This argument is answered elsewhere in this book.[2] Another nonpacifist challenge is that presented recently by Charles Clayton Morrison, who claims to be neither a pacifist nor a militarist. God commands men neither to fight nor not to fight, says Morrison. War is not sin: it is hell; it is God's judgment upon sin. Since the war is here, none can escape; all are helping to fight it. It is useless to call it wrong. Hell is not wrong; it is that which takes men to hell that is wrong. So when we did wrong, and as a result now find ourselves in the war, it is absurd to call the war wrong. Let us therefore make the best of the war, and out of it perhaps can come something good. If we fight, realizing that we are doing so as punishment for our previous sin, we will come out purged, and perhaps we will be able to help save the civilization of the future. "What the world needs most is not conscientious objectors to war, but conscientious objectors to injustice," which is the cause of war. So runs the argument.[3]

Unquestionably Morrison speaks the truth when he ascribes the war to the sins of men. But does it follow, then, that all men are responsible? Did all men approve the materialism, and the imperialism, and the militarism out of which the war was born? Were there none who by word and deed lived the life of Christian discipleship which makes for peace and brotherhood? Even in Israel there were seven thousand who had not bowed their knees to Baal. Surely there are a few Christians in our world of today who have loved mercy, and have done justly, and have walked humbly before their God. Surely there are some whose hands are clean and who do not deserve this hell which is war. And if so, then on Morrison's own premise, these at lease were conscientious objectors to injustice and so ought also to be conscientious objectors to war. But something more than Morri-

---

[2] Chapters II and III; appendix 2.

[3] C.C. Morrison, *The Christian and the War* (Chicago, 1942). For a critique of Morrison's argument see Edward Yoder, *Compromise with War* (Akron, Pa., 1944).

son's premise is required to satisfy the moral requirements of nonresistant Christianity. When one man wrongs another, who retaliates in turn, the first man receives what he deserves. But this does not justify the act of the second. Both the wrongdoer and the avenger have sinned in the process. "Avenge not yourselves . . . Vengeance is mine; I will repay, saith the Lord." In sinful human society men will mete out vengeance, but they always sin when they do so. War is sin, and he who would be a true disciple of Jesus Christ must abstain from it.

Is the Nonresistant Christian a Parasite

No doubt the most challenging antipacifist Christian writer today is Reinhold Niebuhr. He denies popular pacifism and the doctrine of nonviolent resistance a place in the New Testament ethic, and here he is on solid ground. He asserts that the New Testament ethic is one of uncompromising nonresistance and warns the pacifist to "leave the world of politics alone entirely and seek simply to live by the love commandment. . . . Let him, in other words, be a pure pacifist [i.e., a Biblical nonresistant] and remind the rest of us, who fool with politics, that we are playing a dangerous game."[4] Mennonites admire Niebuhr's sound evaluation of the Christian ethic, but they are disappointed to see him cast aside this pearl of great price in order that he might himself pursue "the dangerous game of fooling with politics." Niebuhr believes, however, that in the present evil world this is the most practical thing for the Christian to do. As the world now stands the use of force is necessary. In a sub-Christian or an evil social order the nonresistant way of life cannot be realized on a national scale. When the forces of totalitarianism threaten to overrun the world, the Christian must lay aside the pure Christian ethic and play his part in the struggle for the overthrow of the forces of evil.

If nonresistant Christians feel inclined to smile with satisfaction at Niebuhr's complimentary remarks in the above quota-

---

[4] Reinhold Niebuhr, "A Communication: The will of God and the Van Zeeland Report." *The Christian Century* (Dec. 14, 1938), 55:1550.

tion they may, however, feel more like wincing at the stinging
challenge of the following one:

> Let such pacifism [New Testament nonresistance] realize that
> it is a form of asceticism and that as such it is a parasite on the sins
> of the rest of us, who maintain government and relative social peace
> and relative social justice. This recognition of parasitism will pre-
> vent pacifism from being corrupted by pharisaism. It can therefore
> testify against us without tempting us to resist sinful pharisaism with
> sinful arrogance.[5]

What shall nonresistant Christians do with this challenge?
Must they admit that they are parasites? The charge is not a
new one, of course. Jeremiah, the prophet, faced it in his day.
So did the early Christians in the Roman Empire. Likewise did
the Mennonites in the sixteenth century. Today's militarists,
like those of old, freely assert that the nation would be ruined
if everyone took the stand which nonresistant Christians take.
Niebuhr has too sympathetic an understanding and too keen
an insight, however, to put it as flatly as that. No doubt he
would admit that if everyone took this Christian position there
would be no wars. But since the great majority of mankind does
not take this position, and since in our present world, warfare
and strife must be taken for granted, the nonresistant Christian,
he says, is a parasite who lives on those who do the dirty work
required to bring a semblance of order out of our ever-present
chaos.

The first answer to this challenge must be that it is the
primary duty of the Christian to be a true disciple of Christ.
Once the premise is accepted that Christ speaks with authority
from heaven, only one thing remains, and that is to obey His
command. There may be times when some other course seems
more practical, more reasonable, or socially more useful. It
often happens, however, that the way which from a human point
of view seems best, in the end proves to have been wrong. The
Book of Proverbs says: "There is a way which seemeth right unto
a man, but the end thereof are the ways of death."[6] The true

---

[5] R. Niebuhr, "Japan and the Christian Conscience," *The Christian Century* (Nov. 10,
1937), 54:1391.
[6] Prov. 14:12.

disciple believes this truth so firmly that he follows Christ even though the entire world seems to be against him. Knowing that human reason has often gone astray, he hitches his wagon to the star of divine revelation, and leaves the results in the hands of God. Such obedience is not a blind obedience. Christian faith is not a blind faith. It is belief based on evidence. And to the nonresistant Christian the evidence seems clear enough that the way of life prescribed by Christ is also the way which is best for human society. He is convinced that if he is true to his nonresistant profession he is not a parasite.

Christian Nonresistance a Genuine Service to Society

While Niebuhr and the militarists are correct in holding that the use of force is unavoidable in a sub-Christian social order, it does not follow that the use of force is the highest service a man can render to society, nor that the nonresistant Christian does not make an important contribution. In Chapter IV reference was made to the testimony of Origen, who characterized the Christians of the third century as the greatest benefactors of the Roman Empire, "an army of piety" for the promotion of godliness, performing a service to society of greater value than that performed by the magistracy. In Origen's own day this no doubt seemed a presumptuous statement to make. The Roman Empire reigned supreme; its very genius was law and order based on military prowess and political administration. An office in the state was the highest goal to which a Roman could aspire. To perform the duties commonly ascribed to the citizen was the noblest work of man, and to spurn these civil obligations in order to assume the role of a humble Christian seemed a deliberate dissipation of human talent.

Nevertheless, here is perhaps an almost perfect illustration of the fact that that which seems socially least important at the time is frequently of greatest significance. Today the Roman Empire is only a memory while the Christian Church lives on. We know now that in Origen's own time the Empire was already in process of decay. The causes for this distintegration were many and may never be adequately explained, but Professor A. E. Holt, looking back through the pages of history, makes this significant remark: "The more one thinks about the early Christian communities and the Roman Empire, the more one is convinced that the only piece of permanent social building was that carried on by the Christian community in the face of the Roman Empire."[7]

In Chapter VIII reference was made to Adin Ballou and T. S. Eliot, whose testimonies are similar to that of Origen. Ballou was quoted as saying that it is the high calling of the nonresistant Christian "to stand morally at the front of the procession of humanity, to lead it on to a truer righteousness." And Eliot says: "It is not primarily the Christianity of the statesman that matters. . . . A skeptical or indifferent statesman, working within a Christian frame, might be more effective than a devout Christian statesman obliged to conform to a secular frame." This is the point. The mission of nonresistant Christians is not a political one. It is rather a curative mission. It is to bring healing to human society; to prevent its further decay through a consistent witness to the truth. This world needs the ministry of nonresistant Christians whose light, set on a hill, stands as a glowing witness to the way of truth and righteousness. A people who provide this witness are not parasites living at the expense of organized society. They are its greatest benefactors. Let those who aspire to nothing higher perform the task of the magistracy, the police, and the military. There will always be more than enough people ready to fill these positions; but candidates for the higher place, which the nonresistant Christian alone can fill, are altogether too few. Let none forsake this cause for something of lesser importance.

This point of view will not satisfy those pacifists who hold a view of the kingdom of God which anticipates the complete Christianization of the social order. The Anabaptists and the Mennonites, however, have never anticipated such a complete Christianization of the social order. Therefore, since they as Christians could not compromise with evil, it followed that they

[7] A. E. Holt, *Christian Roots of Democracy in America* (New York, 1941), 129.

could not participate in the conduct of the general social order in any way that is contrary to the teaching of Christ and the New Testament. They placed their emphasis on the Christian social order within the fellowship of the church brotherhood. This brotherhood way of life, they believed, would constitute a standing witness to truth and righteousness, continually challenging the sub-Christian world to that which is higher and better. In this way, they believed, they were fulfilling a higher mission and a nobler service to society than if they compromised their own high ethical principles to engage in the relativities of statecraft and political action.[8]

The Nonresistant Mennonites and Religious Freedom

Perhaps nothing in our American life is more highly prized than the cherished tradition of religious liberty. The constitution of Virginia, adopted in 1776, says that "religion . . . can be directed only by reason, and conviction, not by force or violence; and therefore, all men are equally entitled to the free exercise of religion according to the dictates of conscience." Ten years later the Virginia legislature disestablished the Anglican church by a law which says that "no man shall be compelled to frequent or support any religious worship . . . but . . . all men shall be free to profess, and by argument to maintain, their opinions in matters of religion." Legalized freedom and equality of religion, now an accomplished fact in Virginia, soon spread throughout the nation. In 1791 the first amendment was added to the Constitution of the United States, making religious liberty a part of the fundamental law of the land. This amendment says: "Congress shall make no law respecting an establishment of religion, or prohibiting the free exercise thereof."

Too often these words are read without realizing the long sequence of events which lies behind them. Too many people do not know the tremendous price which was paid with the blood of many Christian martyrs before it was possible to write

[8] For a discussion of the Anabaptist view of the social order see H. S. Bender, "The Anabaptist Vision," *Church History* (March, 1944), 13:3-24, and *Mennonite Quarterly Review* (April, 1944), 18:67-88.

words like these into the laws of our land. It is true, Thomas Jefferson had much to do with the adoption of the provisions cited above. He promoted the inclusion of the provision in the Virginia constitution; he wrote the statute which was adopted in 1786; and he had much to do with the first amendment to the Constitution of the United States. So important did he consider this contribution that he requested that the following epitaph be inscribed upon his gravestone: "Thomas Jefferson, Author of the Declaration of Independence, of the Statute of Virginia for Religious Freedom, and Father of the University of Virginia." These facts are commonly known, but the following quotation from Professor W. W. Sweet, referring in particular to the statute of Virginia, brings out a still more important fact, of which most Americans are altogether too ignorant. Sweet says: "But justice compels the admission that Jefferson's part in this accomplishment was not so great as was that of James Madison, *nor were the contributions of either or both as important as was that of the humble people called Baptists.*"[9]

The tradition of the "humble people called Baptists" goes directly back to the Anabaptists of the sixteenth century. By implication, therefore, Sweet is saying that these nonresistant forefathers of the modern Baptists and Mennonites are an important source for the idea of religious liberty which we in America cherish so highly today. In fact the story of religious freedom is largely the story of an idea which was first given to the modern world by the Anabaptists, and which has grown until now it is generally accepted. The idea of the right of the Christian to worship according to the dictates of conscience was an integral part of their nonresistant faith. The Anabaptist church had its beginning in Zurich in 1525 when Conrad Grebel and Felix Manz and their associates refused to co-operate with Zwingli in the establishment of a state church. They believed that no one could be a true disciple of Christ unless he of his own free will chose to be a disciple. To compel a man to join the church was therefore useless. But it was more than that; it

---

[9] W. W. Sweet, *The Story of Religions in America* (New York, 1930), 279. Italics are by the author.

was wrong. Christians must never use force for the coercion of their fellow men for any purpose, and least of all for bringing them into the kingdom of God. Therefore the Anabaptist church was a brotherhood of nonresistant disciples who voluntarily joined themselves together for mutual edification and worship. According to Heinrich Bullinger, the successor of Zwingli and the great opponent of the Anabaptists, these people taught that:

> One cannot and should not use force to compel anyone to accept the faith, for faith is a free gift of God. It is wrong to compel anyone by force or coercion to embrace the faith, or to put to death anyone for the sake of his erring faith. It is an error that in the church any sword other than that of the divine word should be used. The secular kingdom should be separated from the church, and no secular ruler should exercise authority in the church. The Lord has commanded simply to preach the Gospel, not to compel anyone by force to accept it. The true church of Christ has the characteristic that it suffers and endures persecution but does not inflict persecution upon anyone.[10]

It is important to remember that in the sixteenth century freedom of conscience was a dangerous idea. Since the fourth century church and state had been united, and any other arrangement seemed utterly unthinkable. Authorities in church and state alike believed that a voluntary church, free from state control, could mean only lawlessness and disorder. The safety of the nation depended upon religious uniformity. This was believed by Catholic and Protestant authorities alike. Therefore the ideas of the Anabaptists were feared like communism or other dangerous political doctrines are feared today. When these nonresistant people began to organize their church, and to baptize men and women upon confession of faith alone, they were persecuted with untold cruelty. In 1529 the Diet of Spires ordered that "every Anabaptist and rebaptized person of either sex shall be put to death by fire, sword, or some other way."[11]

Most of the early Anabaptist leaders died a martyr's death. In the first ten years more than 5,000 of the Swiss Brethren were

---

[10] Quoted in John Horsch, *Mennonites in Europe* (Scottdale, Pa., 1942), 325.

[11] Horsch, *Mennonites in Europe*, 302.

put to death in Switzerland and the surrounding territories. Although the last martyr in Switzerland was executed in 1614, the Swiss Mennonites were not fully tolerated until 1815. In Transylvania and Hungary the Hutterian Brethren were being put to death in the eighteenth century. The Dutch government granted toleration earlier than the other states, but even in Holland executions continued until 1574. This is the price which the first modern advocates of religious freedom paid for their faith. But to the everlasting credit of these nonresistant people it can be said that few of them recanted. Because of their perseverance in the way of truth as they saw it, the day finally arrived when, first in the Netherlands and later in other countries, they were granted toleration. And when this occurred the day of religious freedom had dawned in the western world.

Professor Sweet says that in colonial America there were two groups of religious minorities. One group advocated religious freedom on the basis of policy; the other from principle. The group advocating it from principle was made up of the Quakers, the Baptists, the Dunkers, and the Mennonites.[12] It is important to remember that all of these groups were influenced by the sixteenth-century Anabaptists. The Mennonites of today are the direct descendants of the Anabaptists, continuing not only their idea of religious liberty, but that of nonresistance as well. They even continue many of the family names of the sixteenth-century Anabaptists. The Baptists are the product of Anabaptist ideas which found their way to England and there resulted in the founding of a new church which was not nonresistant, but which nevertheless preserved the idea of religious liberty and brought it to America, where the Baptists played a leading role in bringing about the recognition which religious freedom eventually received. The Quakers originated in the seventeenth century and the Dunkers in the eighteenth. Both groups have made unique contributions of their own; but both of them also owe a great debt to the Anabaptists and to the Mennonites from whom they received many of their ideas, and from whom in their early history they also recruited many members.

[12] W. W. Sweet, *Religion in Colonial America* (New York, 1942), 323.

Thirty-five years ago Rufus M. Jones stated the contribution of the Anabaptists as follows:

> Judged by the reception it met at the hands of those in power, both in Church and State, equally in Roman Catholic and in Protestant countries, the Anabaptist movement was one of the most tragic in the history of Christianity; but, judged by the principles which were put into play by the men who bore this reproachful nickname, it must be pronounced one of the most momentous and significant undertakings in man's eventful religious struggle after the truth. It gathered up the gains of earlier movements, and it is the spiritual soil out of which all nonconformist sects have sprung, and it is the first plain announcement in modern history of a programme for a new type of Christian society which the modern world, especially in America and England, has been slowly realizing—an absolutely free and independent religious society, and a State in which every man counts as a man, and has his share in shaping both Church and State.[13]

The modern idea of religious freedom, then, begins with the nonresistant Anabaptists of the sixteenth century. From here it was carried to America by the Mennonites and other minority groups. Not all of these groups remained nonresistant, and some of them used methods of political pressure for the legalization of religious liberty which their nonresistant forefathers would not have approved. But through the contribution of all these various groups the way was eventually prepared so that in the eighteenth century Thomas Jefferson and his associates with their French rationalist background, could write the principle of religious freedom into the laws of the land. And so the nonresistant Anabaptists of the sixteenth century were the pioneers who showed the way, and paid for it with the blood of their own martyrs, in order that the people of America today might enjoy the blessings of religious freedom. With such a record behind them, who would have the courage to say that nonresistant Christians are parasites living at the expense of society, and contributing nothing to it?

Let it be remembered that the modern idea of religious freedom was born and nurtured in the cradle of nonresistance.

---

[13] R. M. Jones, *Studies in Mystical Religion* (London, 1909), 369.

And if in the future the principle of nonresistance, and the willingness to die for this faith, should be lost to Christendom, it is not impossible that this would mean the end of religious liberty as well. This fact alone was sufficient justification for the CPS camps. Even if the men in these camps had not been permitted to do a single piece of useful work, the very existence of the camps, as a testimony to the principle of nonresistance, was a contribution to religious freedom and democracy. This is one more illustration of the fact that sometimes that which to some people seems least useful is, in the long run, the most useful service which can be rendered to society.

Nonresistance and Christian Brotherhood

There is yet another contribution of the highest order which nonresistant groups like the Mennonites have had a large part in giving to the world. This is the idea of Christian brotherhood. That quality of love which has its fruition in the nonresistant way of life leads at the same time to a unique type of Christian community whose members constitute a brotherhood, rather than a church in the traditional sense. Historically the Mennonite Church has always been such a brotherhood, deeply concerned with the entire life of its membership: spiritual, intellectual, social, and economic. One expression of this brotherhood spirit has been the work of relief and reconstruction which the Mennonites have carried on throughout their history, and particularly the work of the Mennonite Central Committee as described in Chapter VII.

One sixteenth-century writer speaking of the Anabaptist brotherhood says: "They brake bread with one another as a sign of oneness and love, helped one another truly with precept, lending, borrowing, giving, taught that all things should be in common, and called each other 'Brother.' "[14] In describing the Hutterian community another writer says: "The Christian community of goods is for the purpose of providing the needy believers who may be old, sick, crippled and unable to support themselves.

[14] R. J. Smithson, *The Anabaptists* (London, 1935), 115

so that they be furnished with the necessaries of life the same as the others."[15] According to a Protestant visitor at an Anabaptist baptismal service in Strassburg in 1557, the applicants for baptism were asked: "Whether they, if necessity required it, would devote all their possessions to the service of the brotherhood, and would not fail any member that is in need, if they were able to render aid."[16]

According to the Mennonite way of thinking, the church is a large family where God is the father and where the children think of each other as brothers and sisters. The weekly service in a typical Mennonite church is more than a worship service, and conferences are more than meetings for transacting the business of the church. These gatherings are also reunions which help to preserve the intimate personal relationships which characterize the entire life of the brotherhood. Mennonite communities are noted for their solidarity, for their efficient systems of mutual aid, and for the way in which their entire life centers around the church.

The significant thing about all this is that many thinkers of today believe that the health of our entire civilization depends upon the health, the vigor, and the solidarity of the small community. Arthur E. Morgan has stated the case as follows:

> The foundations of civilization are self-control, good will, neighborliness, mutual respect, open-mindedness and co-operativeness. Where these qualities are strong a great civilization will grow. Where they become weak, no matter how great the wealth may be, nor how many cities and factories and universities there are, a civilization will break down.
>
> Now, these qualities of neighborliness, good will, and mutual regard grow best in families and small communities where people know and trust each other, and are not afraid of acting in a civilized way. In big crowds and among strangers people tend to act in self-defense, and these finer traits do not have a good chance to develop....
>
> What can we do about it? First we must realize the importance of the community, that it is in fact the foundation of our national life. Young people who want to have some part in the making of

---

[15] John Horsch, *The Hutterian Brethren* (Goshen, Ind., 1931), 131.

[16] H. S. Bender, "The Anabaptist Vision," *Church History* (March, 1944), 13:20.

history would do well to forget for a time the great organizations of the cities, where life is consumed. They need to see that there is more genuine adventure in the small communities where life and national character are being created.[17]

In this statement Dr. Morgan is not discussing nonresistance, nor the Mennonite Church. He is simply stating the importance of the small community for the preservation or our civilization today. But if what he says is true, then it should not be hard to see that the Mennonite brotherhood is playing a very important role in the life of the American nation. If the remedy for the ills of the larger society is to be found in the small, closely knit Christian community, the Mennonites are making a most significant contribution; for their communities possess these qualities to a much higher degree than most communities do.

Other writers are warning us against the dangers to society of shifting our interest from the simple life of the small community to the complexity and the industrialism of the city. T. S. Eliot says: "The more highly industrialized the country, the more easily a materialistic philosophy will flourish in it, and the more deadly that philosophy will be. . . . The tendency of un-limited industrialism is to create bodies of men and women—of all classes—detached from tradition, alienated from religion, and susceptible to mass suggestion: in other words, a mob."[18] O. E. Baker, American agricultural economist, speaks of our con-temporary culture as "urban, . . . powerful, pervasive, permeat-ing now into the remotest rural districts, materialistic with a philosophy tending toward paganism."[19]

P. A. Sorokin, Harvard sociologist, says the present world crisis is so serious as to demand a complete transformation of our western mentality. And this, he says, can come about only by *"replacing the present compulsory and contractual relation-ships with purer and more godly familistic relationships. . . .* Not only are they the noblest of all relationships, but under the cir-cumstances there is no way out of the present triumph of bar-

[17] A. E. Morgan, *The Des Moines Register* (Aug. 26, 1941), 8.
[18] T. S. Eliot, *The Idea of a Christian Society*, 19.
[19] O. E. Baker, "The Rural Family and Its Significance to Organized Religion," *The Christian Rural Fellowship Bulletin.* No. 43. (June, 1939), 3

barian force but through the realm of familistic relationships."
This will mean *"a fundamental transformation of our system
of values, and the profoundest modification of our conduct toward other men, cultural values, and the world at large."*[20] Reinhold Niebuhr tells us that religion will always be "more fruitful in purifying individual life, and adding wholesomeness to
the more intimate social relations, such as the family."[21] Arthur E. Holt, who stresses the values of democracy, also says that
these values have their "natural roo' ʻge in the simpler and more
intimate relations of life—the home, the neighborhood and the
world of simple labor."[22] The importance of Holt's idea cited
above,[23] regarding the permanent social building work of the
early Christian communities, is recognized by C. H. Cooley,
who believes one of the causes of the fall of the Roman Empire
to have been the general decline of vigorous community life
throughout the Empire as a whole.[24] Cooley, one of the great
sociologists of the past generation, emphasized the fact that society must depend, for the refinement of the selfish, lustful desires of human beings, upon primary groups such as the family,
the neighborhood, and the brotherhood type of religious group.

Perhaps if the Roman people had directed their energies
more to the quiet and unassuming task of building the local
communities where life and national character are created, and
less to those spectacular enterprises which are life consuming,
the final story of the Empire might have been different. Therefore, the Christian youth of today who would make a permanent
contribution to American life is wise if he understands that the
most constructive work which can be done is not to be found in
those glamorous and spectacular enterprises associated with urban industry, military service, and the affairs of state, but rather
in the quiet and more fundamental task of building the small
Christian community. The Mennonite youth, in particular, if
he is wise, will understand that nonresistant groups like his own,

20 P. A. Sorokin, *The Crisis of Our Age* (New York, 1941), 320, 321.
21 R. Niebuhr, *Moral Man and Immoral Society* (New York, 1932), 63.
22 A. E. Holt, *op. cit.*, 128.
23 Pp. 240-241.
24 C. H. Cooley, R. C. Angell, and L. J. Carr, *Introductory Sociology*, (New York, 1933), 205-6.

living the Christian brotherhood type of life which has characterized them for centuries, are a veritable salt of the earth. No, the nonresistant people with their historic emphasis on religious freedom and community brotherhood are not parasites; they are making a contribution of first-rate importance to modern society.

Conclusion

This chapter has been intended as a word of encouragement to any nonresistant people who might be tempted to think that, since their cause is not a popular one, they are not performing an important service to society. Such encouragement is always in order in the case of every good cause, but especially so when the cause is unpopular. On the other hand, a word of warning is also in order to any nonresistant people who might be tempted to take a condescending or pharisaical attitude toward those who do not share their faith. It must be remembered that the society of this world at best is sub-Christian, and that such a society cannot get along without the use of force. Therefore, those who do not aspire to anything higher than this also make a contribution to society, although a lesser contribution than that of the nonresistant people, when they are actively engaged in the promotion of the state's coercive functions.

The nonviolent coercionists and many of the followers of popular pacifism also have a goal which is below the standard of the New Testament. We should not forget, however, that these people, in their own way, are doing what they can for the improvement of the social order. The writer sincerely believes that they could do more good if they followed the nonresistant way. And yet, their continuous challenge to militarism does serve a useful purpose. After all, Gandhi's nonviolent form of compulsion, though mistakenly equated with the Christian ethic, is less objectionable than the violence of the militarist. And who would not prefer a lesser evil to a greater one? The nonresistant Christian should be glad when those who cannot accept his own position, nevertheless aspire to the highest possible goal within the sub-Christian realm. For himself, however,

he cannot be satisfied with anything less than the high and absolute standard of the New Testament itself; for he believes that
in this way alone can he act in obedience to his God and make
the highest contribution to human society.

SELECT BIBLIOGRAPHY

No systematic treatise setting forth the service of nonresistance
to society is in print at the present time. Much of the literature of
popular pacifism seems to assume that Biblical nonresistance is too
negative to be of the greatest service. Charles Clayton Morrison, *The
Christian and the War* (Chicago, 1942), and Reinhold Niebuhr,
Christianity and Power Politics (New York, 1940), are two recent
books by nonpacifist authors challenging the entire antiwar position
as not in the interest of social welfare, although Niebuhr recognizes
in Biblical nonresistance a value which he does not grant to other
varieties of pacifism. Morrison's work is a reprint of a series of editorials in the *Christian Century,* beginning in December, 1941. For
a penetrating criticism of Morrison's argument see Edward Yoder,
Compromise with War (Akron, Pa., 1944), a reprint of an article
in the *Gospel Herald* (Scottdale, Pa., December, 1943), 36:829-32.
Arthur E. Holt, *Christian Roots of Democracy in America* (New
York, 1941), recognizes the contribution to society of Christian
brotherhood groups like the Mennonites. C. H. Cooley, *Social Organization* (New York, 1909), P. A. Sorokin, *The Crisis of Our Age*
(New York, 1941), and Arthur E. Morgan, *The Small Community*
(New York, 1942), stress the importance to society of primary groups
and small communities, of which the Historic Peace Church groups
are an illustration. Two authors of an earlier generation who saw
the Anabaptist movement, including its nonresistant convictions, as
contributing much of what is best in the modern world, were Rufus
M. Jones, *Studies in Mystical Religion* (London, 1909), and Walter
Rauschenbusch, *A Theology for the Social Gospel* (Macmillan, 1917).
André Trocmé, *The Politics of Repentance* (Fellowship, 1953) likewise sees the peace of the Gospel as that which ultimately is best for
human society. Chapters in Guy F. Hershberger (ed.), *The Recovery
of the Anabaptist Vision,* and in Hershberger, *The Way of the Cross
in Human Relations,* have a similar emphasis, particularly the final
chapter in the latter which sees the strenuous ethic of Christian discipleship in combination with a New Testament eschatology as the
best hope for the world.

12. Keeping the Faith

If nonresistance is a way of life conforming to the will of God and contributing to the highest welfare of human society, as set forth in this book, it is fitting that the closing chapter should be concerned with the perpetuation of this faith. How did the Mennonites, for example, come to include nonresistance in their body of belief in the first place? What have been the means by which this faith has been kept through the years? And what is required for its continuation today?

A Vital Christian Faith and Life

The literature of the sixteenth-century Anabaptists offers convincing proof that these fathers of the modern Mennonites were men with a vital Christian experience. They were men to whom God had spoken in a very real way through the Holy Spirit and the written Word. They understood the sinfulness of sin, and they knew by personal experience what it meant to be saved therefrom. In the nineteenth century, Dr. Max Goebel, a theologian of the Reformed Church, declared the distinguishing feature of Anabaptism to consist in "its great emphasis upon the actual personal conversion of every Christian through the Holy Spirit."[1] Pilgram Marpeck, an outstanding Anabaptist leader, said: "We believe that one is made a child of God and free from the law and the bondage of sin only through such a faith by which the Spirit, as the power of God, lives in the heart and does His work."[2]

This experience of regeneration gave the early Anabaptists the actual power to live an outward life of true and genuine

[1] John Horsch, *Mennonites in Europe*, 298.
[2] *Ibid.*, 375.

Christianity. They constantly referred to Christians as those who walk in *newness of life* through the regenerating work of Christ and the Holy Spirit. Regeneration and the new life were inseparable in their thinking. In the words of Menno Simons:

> This can never fail; where there is true Christian faith, there is also dying to sin, a new creature, true repentance, a sincere, regenerated, unblamable Christian. One does no longer live according to the lusts of sin but according to the will of Him who purchased us with His blood, drew us by His Spirit and regenerated us by His Word, namely, Jesus Christ.

> True faith which avails before God, is a living and saving power which is, through the preaching of the holy Word, bestowed of God on the heart; moving, changing and regenerating it to newness of mind. It destroys all ungodliness, all pride, unholy ambition and selfishness . . . . Behold, such is the faith which the Scriptures teach us, and not a vain, dead, and unfruitful illusion, as the world dreams.[3]

To the Anabaptists, regeneration meant a life of obedience to Christ. Pilgram Marpeck recognized as "true Christian faith only such a faith through which the Holy Spirit and the love of God come into the heart, . . . active, powerful, and operative *in all outward obedience and commanded works.*"[4] Menno Simons says regenerated Christians "walk in newness of life, as *willing and obedient children.*" He describes such renewed and obedient children as "poor in spirit, meek, merciful, compassionate, peaceable, patient, hungry and thirsty after righteousness."[5]

This desire for obedience, and this thirst for righteousness, led the early Mennonites to search the Scriptures for light and guidance. Their church was founded in the first place because a group of men had found new spiritual truth through regular meetings in private homes for Bible study and prayer. Pilgram Marpeck "sincerely admonished" his people "to be on the alert and personally study the Scriptures."[6] Menno Simons said he

---

[3] *Ibid.*, 374.

[4] *Ibid.*, 375. Italics are those of the author.

[5] H. S. Bender and John Horsch, *Menno Simons' Life and Writings* (Scottdale, Pa., 1936), 69. Italics by the author.

[6] John Horsch, *Mennonites in Europe*, 351.

"would rather die than to believe and teach . . . a single word" which is contrary to the Scriptures.[7] He admonished his people not to depend upon the doctrines of men, not even upon his own teachings, without first searching the Scriptures for themselves.[8]

It was inevitable that a people who took the Scriptures as seriously as these people did would come to believe in the doctrine of nonresistance. They made no attempt to rationalize the teachings of Christ; they engaged in no philosophical discussions about their meaning; they asked no questions as to their practicability. They simply took the words of Scripture as they found them and proceeded to live by them. They took for granted that Christ meant what He said, and they saw no reason why they should not obey without question. To Menno Simons it was perfectly reasonable to ask: "How can a Christian, according to the Scriptures, consistently retaliate, rebel, war, murder, slay, torture, steal, rob and burn cities and conquer countries?"[9] Since the Scriptures had forbidden such conduct, the Christian could not engage in it. It was just as simple as that.

A Need for Spiritual Strengthening

That the faith and life of the sixteenth-century Anabaptists were characterized by great strength and vitality there can be no doubt. It is clear, however, that this cannot be said with the same degree of certainty of their Mennonite descendants in all periods of their history. The mid-nineteenth century was a period of spiritual decline among the Mennonites of America, so that the church was not as well prepared to meet the crisis of the Civil War as might have been desired. Due to the great awakening which took place in the latter part of the century, however, the Mennonites were much better prepared spiritually to meet the test of war in 1917 and 1918 than they had been in the 1860's. Following 1918 the organized peace work of the church was carried on in a very effective manner, so that in the second

[7] *Ibid.,* 353.

[8] Bender and Horsch, *op. cit.,* 56.

[9] Bender and Horsch, *Menno Simons,* 91.

World War there was a much better practical preparation to meet the test than was the case in either the Civil War or the first World War. It is a question, however, whether the second World War revealed any marked improvement in the spiritual strength of the Mennonite people over that of the first World War. With all the preparation and provision for alternative service which the church had made, at great expense of money and labor, the fact remains that less than 60 per cent of the Mennonites called by the draft in the second World War enrolled in Civilian Public Service, while the remainder accepted service in the army. This percentage may be as high as the percentage of those who declined all army service in the first World War. But in consideration of the efforts which the church had made, it is too low.

Furthermore, not all of the men in CPS succeeded in capturing the true meaning of nonresistance. Some registered as conscientious objectors merely because it is traditional that a Mennonite should do so, or because it was the wish of their parents that they register that way. Men of this type did not have the conviction which they should have had, and lacked those spiritual qualities so necessary for the perpetuation of the nonresistant faith. While these men did not represent the rank and file of the church, the situation was serious enough to be a matter of genuine concern to the brotherhood. It seems to indicate that the great task of the Mennonites in the immediate future is an intellectual and spiritual awakening to the end that the coming generation may be more firmly established in the faith of the fathers, and in the teachings of the Scriptures; that, in every way, the church may be a true brotherhood of regenerated believers; and that the nonresistant way of life may come as a natural fruit of the inner Christian experience of every member of the church.

Teaching the Bible

The doctrine of nonresistance came to be a part of the Mennonite heritage because the fathers of the church were men with a deep and vital Christian experience, who searched the

Scriptures and believed that they should obey its teachings. This explains the origin of nonresistance within the Mennonite body of faith, and it also explains the primary means by which that faith must be preserved today. Men must have an experience of salvation, they must read the Bible, and they must obey its teaching. It is important, therefore, that the nonresistant churches place great emphasis on Bible reading and Bible study today.

The sixth chapter of Deuteronomy is a classic statement of the importance of knowing the Word of God. It is essential, says the writer, that men should fear God and keep His commandments. If this is to be accomplished they must be taught diligently from their childhood: "And these words, which I command thee this day, shall be upon thy heart; and thou shalt teach them diligently unto thy children, and shalt talk of them when thou sittest in thy house, and when thou walkest by the way, and when thou liest down, and when thou risest up."[10]

Periods of great spiritual revival among God's people have always been accompanied by a revival of interest in Bible study. In the days of Nehemiah it was the rediscovery of the law which caused men to bow their heads and worship God;[11] and it was the effective teaching of the Word under the leadership of Ezra which restored something of the spiritual vitality which had been lost in the days before the captivity. In the Middle Ages the monks who diligently studied the Word of God were the chief source of vitality in the church of that era. The great Protestant Reformation was preceded and accompanied by a renewed interest in the study of the Bible. John Wycliffe, the "morning star of the Reformation," aimed to place the Scriptures into the hands of the common people, and to this end he translated the Bible into the English language as early as 1382. This was followed by Tyndale's translation in the sixteenth century. In Germany Luther translated the Bible into the language of the common people, and the influence of this work had much to do with growth of the Protestant movement. It was

[10] Deut. 6:6, 7 (ASV).
[11] Neh. 8:5, 6.

the reading of the Scriptures which led Menno Simons and the other Anabaptist leaders to take the position which they did in the sixteenth century. In a later day, the great awakening among the Mennonites of the nineteenth century was accompanied by, and in a large measure caused by, a renewed interest in Bible study, especially through the Sunday school. Among the Mennonites of the twentieth century, likewise, the nonresistant faith has been preserved to the extent that the brotherhood has been grounded in the Word of God and its teachings. It is important, therefore, that the nonresistant churches maintain a thorough program of Bible teaching which is continuously effective within the entire brotherhood, among the children, the youth, and the adults.

Home Life and Teaching

While much of the task of Biblical teaching must be performed through the organized activities of the church, the foundations of the Christian and the nonresistant life must be laid in the home. In the plan of God it is Christian parents who have the first responsibility for bringing up their children "in the nurture and admonition of the Lord."[12] The Hebrew father and mother were required to instruct their children in the law, and to explain to them the meaning of the forms and the ceremonies of Israel's religious worship.[13] It was Hannah the mother who dedicated her young son Samuel to the Lord, and placed him under the charge of the priest in the temple.[14] In the case of Timothy it was the mother and grandmother who first acquainted the young man with the Scriptures.[15] Saint Augustine ascribes his conversion and salvation from a life of sin in a large measure to the influence of his saintly mother.[16] Certainly the Christian home needs the help of the school and of the church with its various teaching agencies; but it is as true in our

[12] Eph. 6:4.
[13] Ex. 12:26, 27; Deut. 6:20; Josh. 4:21, 22.
[14] I Sam. 1, 2.
[15] II Tim. 1:5.
[16] See Augustine, *Confessions.*

own day as it was at any time in the past that, unless the Christian home lays a firm foundation, the effort of the church and the school to build Christian life and character will be largely in vain.

An Understanding of Mennonitism

In addition to the primary requirement of Christian faith and life it is also necessary that Mennonites have a genuine understanding of Mennonitism. They cannot hope to perpetuate the faith of their fathers unless they know what that faith is. Therefore, they must have a ministry with a strong faith in the mission of the Mennonite Church, and a knowledge of the history of the church. Only a few need to be specialists in the study of history, but all should have an acquaintance with the general history of the church, its ideals, and its traditions. Writers on Christian faith and life should be familiar with the doctrinal writings of Menno Simons and Pilgram Marpeck, and the preachers' sermons should be replete with illustrations and quotations from Mennonite writers. Catholic writers find it necessary to draw on Thomas Aquinas, and Calvinist writers on Calvin. It is not likely, therefore, that Mennonite preachers and writers will do much for the perpetuation of their own faith if they depend too much on non-Mennonite sources for help, and not enough on the work of their own writers and leaders. It will be very difficult for a Mennonite minister to build a true Mennonite congregation if the dominant spiritual forces influencing his life are non-Mennonite in character, and antagonistic to Biblical standards, whether they are "orthodox" or "modernist." If he relies on the typical so-called "fundamentalists" of our day, with their Bible institutes, Bible conferences, and publications, he will find himself under constant pressure to surrender his emphasis on nonresistance. On the other hand, if he drinks at the fountain of modernistic liberalism he will have the very foundations of his faith taken from him. A true Mennonite Church cannot be perpetuated without a ministry which is true to the New Testament, and which understands and espouses the heritage of the church.

An Effective Program of Peace Teaching

The desired results will not be accomplished, moreover, without continuous effort. The doctrine of peace and nonresistance must be an integral part of the entire teaching program of the church. Ministers must be alert to give nonresistance its right proportion of emphasis in the Sunday sermons. Sunday-school officers and teachers must be just as diligent to see that this important theme finds its proper place in the teaching of the Sunday-school. And those in charge of the Sunday evening meetings must do the same for that part of the church's teaching program. Even the summer Bible school must not be overlooked. The agencies responsible for planning the educational curriculum of the church, must see that nonresistance is given its due emphasis in this curriculum; and the publishing agencies must co-operate with them in the production of whatever literature is needed for the carrying out of the task. Above all, every Christian home must understand its responsibility for bringing up children in the nurture and admonition of the Lord. If that Christian home is a true Mennonite home it will recognize nonresistance as an integral part of the Christian life; and it will strive with diligence, by precept and example, to instruct its children in the nonresistant way. Finally, the church colleges, the conferences, and the peace committees should contribute their share to the leadership and the stimulation necessary to keep the entire church alive to the issue of nonresistance, and moving forward in the nonresistant way. As to its content, the nonresistant teaching of the Mennonite Church must be complete and well balanced. It must have a true Biblical foundation; it must be permeated with the historic Mennonite tradition; it must provide a Biblical conception of the Christian's relation to the state and the community; it must give the brotherhood a vision of the service of nonresistance to society; and it must be practical, so as to help the youth of the church to choose wisely as it meets the many practical problems which constantly arise.

Perhaps the most serious threat to the nonresistant faith of the Mennonites today is the impact of a secular, non-Mennonite, and non-Christian education upon the youth of the church.

J. H. Oldham has warned us that the chief struggle of the Christian Church today is not so much against the state as it is against the paganizing process of our secular education. "It may well be," he says, "that the main conflict between Christian faith and the secular interpretation of life will have to be waged in the field of public education. The church will have won little in obtaining liberty to preach and to conduct its own worship and services, if the whole weight of a public system of education is directed towards inculcating in the impressionable mind of youth beliefs about the world and man and conduct which are incompatible with the Christian understanding of life."[17]

If this is a true statement of the influence of public education upon the Christian faith, it is doubly true of the influence of public education in wartime upon the nonresistant Christian faith. It is true, of course, that the child must not be so sheltered in his education as to make him ignorant of the realities of life. Sooner or later he must learn the great difference between the faith and life of the nonresistant Christian and that of a world at war. If he can learn this from actual experience in a public school, while under the guidance of strong home and church influences, the outcome may not be disastrous. It can, in fact, be a means of educating the youth in effective ways and means of counteracting militaristic influences. But, if this is to be the outcome, the church and home influences must be very strong, and the toxin of militarism which is received in school must not be too great. At its best, however, this procedure is fraught with dangers, and there are likely to be many casualties. It is therefore necessary that the church give serious attention to this task of effective teaching of the youth for the keeping of the nonresistant faith.

A True Mennonite Community Brotherhood

Since Mennonite nonresistance and the Mennonite brotherhood spring from the same root, and since nonresistance flourishes best in the brotherhood type of environment, the cultivation of the brotherhood life is perhaps as important as a positive

---

[17] J. H. Oldham, *Church, Community, and State* (New York and London, 1935), 17, 18.

program for the teaching of nonresistance. This is especially important today because of the great changes which have taken place in our American life during the past seventy-five years. These changes in industry, in agriculture, and in transportation have caused an increasing number of Mennonites to establish business and social connections outside the Mennonite community. This in turn has caused some of them to resort to commercial life insurance and similar non-Mennonite methods of aid and security. The security sought through these devices is legitimate enough; but the objection to them is that they are provided by companies organized on a commercial basis, having the profit motive uppermost, and employing methods out of harmony with the Christian way of "bearing one another's burdens." And while these agencies are offering their aid to Christian people, they also tend to break down the life of the brotherhood. The security sought is legitimate enough, but according to the New Testament way this security should be sought through the mutual helpfulness of the Christian brotherhood. It is essential, therefore, that every Mennonite community have an effective program of mutual aid, which does all that commercial life insurance and similar means of security can do.

It is also when members have numerous business connections which keep them out of touch with the brotherhood that their money is likely to be invested in the stocks and bonds of enterprises which make no contribution to the life of the church. At the same time young married couples in the community may be in need of financial help to get started on land and in homes of their own, and if they cannot get the help they need they may move to the city and find employment there, away from the community. On the other hand, if brethren with means use their money for the help of needy young people, the home community will be enriched; the young people will be started on the way to the ownership of their own land and homes; and both the young people and the investors will be able to live their lives with their families in the community, where their personalities, their influence, their money, and their land will do much to strengthen them and their way of life.

We must remember that the most effective testimony of the Mennonites in times past has been given through the group, and not merely as individuals. It has not been a matter only of a few individuals here and there preaching their message; but rather of the entire brotherhood maintaining a faith and living a life, collectively, which has been a testimony to the entire world. In the World War it was not merely the conscientious objector in the military camp who testified to the principle of nonresistance. It was rather the entire church standing together that gave this testimony to the world. In the second World War, with the Civilian Public Service program supported by the entire brotherhood, the church had a greater opportunity than ever to give a collective testimony to the principle of nonresistance.

A Consistent Policy of Nonmilitary Service

The keeping of the nonresistant faith requires more, however, than the maintenance of an integrated community life. Ultimately this is an individual matter. Each individual member of the community must be led to settle the fundamental moral question of war and peace in his own mind and heart. Is war right or wrong? Can a follower of Christ have any part in a military organization, whose business it is to kill human beings, or can he not? If the Christian finds the right answer to this question, he will be in a position to answer other questions in the right way also. To find the right answer it is necessary to do more than to sing the hymn, "Faith of Our Fathers." A member of another denomination once said to the writer: "My church has a lot of people who praise the fathers with their mouth and then do the very opposite of what their fathers did. They have gone so far astray that the fathers wouldn't recognize them." Of course, no good Mennonite desires a statement like this to be true of his church. But each one should know that it requires eternal vigilance to keep it from becoming true. Are Mennonites actually true to the faith of the fathers? Or are they in danger of departing from their ways?

We know that the Mennonites of western Europe lost their nonresistance during the past century, yielding to the various governments that adopted universal military service. Therefore, the question is sometimes asked whether the American Mennonites may have the same experience, since military service has come to be more generally required. The correct answer to this question probably is that the European Mennonites lost their nonresistance not so much because their circumstances were harder than those of their fathers, but because their faith was weaker. The perpetuation of the principle of nonresistance is ultimately a matter of personal faith and conviction. It is true, of course, that the military systems of Europe are vigorously opposed to nonresistance, and that consequently it is hard to live the nonresistant life there. But it is probably no harder now to do so, even in Europe, than it was to remain true to the faith in the sixteenth century. A firm stand for nonresistance in many countries today would mean imprisonment, of course, and in many cases death. But four hundred years ago thousands of Mennonites were imprisoned and put to death, *and through this very experience, the faith was preserved for us today.* So the important question is not: How great are our difficulties today? It is rather: How great is our faith today, and will it enable us to remain true in spite of difficulties?

Perhaps the greatest danger today does not come from the violent opponents of nonresistance; but rather from the subtle temptation to compromise, which follows a toleration of the nonresistant faith. When the government recognizes the conscience of the objector to war it offers so-called noncombatant military service as an alternative to civilian public service. Some persons not sufficiently established in the faith have accepted such service because it seems to offer the easiest way out. They defend their action by saying there is nothing wrong in performing the work of a cook, or a nurse, or a doctor in the army, because the task of these persons is not to kill, but to feed and to heal. But what would the fathers have said about this? They would have said: The purpose of the army is to kill. If we are members of the army we are engaged in the task of killing.

However innocent an assignment may seem, therefore, if it is a military assignment, we cannot accept it.

In fact, there is ultimately no such thing as noncombatant military service. Every man in the army is essential for the operation of the machine of destruction. Therefore, every man in the army is for practical purposes, a combatant. To attempt a distinction between combatant and noncombatant military service is to attempt a distinction without a difference. In some countries the army has now officially dropped the technical term "noncombatant," substituting for it the term "service units."

When a man professing nonresistance accepts so-called noncombatant army service he may do so for several reasons. He may do so because he does not fully understand the issues at stake. On the other hand, he may accept such service because of plain cowardice. If he goes into the army he wears the uniform and passes as a soldier. Thus he escapes the criticism which the public directs against the conscientious objector. But, once in the army, he may be assigned some military task comparatively free from personal danger. To put it bluntly, he is more or less safe, both from the bullets of the enemy and from the jeers of the public.

During the second World War some Mennonites accepted so-called noncombatant service because in so doing they received the pay of a soldier, whereas men in CPS camps were serving without pay. In such cases it was money which decided whether a man was a conscientious objector or not. Needless to say, any man who decides a great moral question on the basis of what men will say, or on the basis of the amount of money involved, is not a true disciple of Christ. Either war is wrong, or it is not wrong. If it is wrong, a disciple of Christ must stay out of the army. If it is not wrong let him go into the army as a regular soldier, without troubling himself about the fiction of so-called noncombatant service.

There is no question, therefore, but that if a nonresistant people desires to keep its faith, it must follow a consistent policy of strictly nonmilitary service. Members of the brotherhood who are engaged in military service in any form will inevitably tend to break down the nonresistant testimony of the brother-hood. They cannot build it up. The European Mennonites first started down the road toward militarism by compromising on noncombatant service; and should the Mennonites of America make a similar compromise the outcome would no doubt be the same. There is nothing wrong in serving the government so long as that service in itself is not wrong; but military service is always wrong for the nonresistant Christian. Therefore, the nonresistant Christian and the nonresistant church must draw a sharp line of distinction between military and civilian service.

Furthermore, if the nonresistant faith is to be kept and per-petuated, the brotherhood must be alert to draw the same line of discrimination against various activities and services which support the military. The official statement of the Mennonite General Conference says that in wartime we cannot support civilian organizations as the Red Cross or the YMCA, if they are temporarily controlled by the military or allied with it in the prosecution of the war. This statement also says we cannot take part in the financing of war operations through the pur-chase of war bonds, or through voluntary contributions to or-ganizations which promote the war. It says further that we can-not participate in the manufacture of munitions or weapons of war; and that we should not seek to make a profit out of war and wartime inflation, "which would mean profiting from the shedding of the blood of our fellow men." In other words, the nonresistant Christian must keep himself strictly clear from the voluntary support of any activity which supports the war.

Since the nonresistant Christian is not an obstructionist, however, he should always be ready to render some form of alter-native service which is right in itself. When the young man of draft age is called, he submits to conscription for civilian, but not for military service. Therefore, he who remains at home should not give his money to organizations which support the war. Instead, he should contribute to the support of voluntary service, to the relief of war sufferers, and to other projects of a similar nature. In so doing he is giving his money to a cause which benefits human society, and which is also consistent with his nonresistant faith. During the second World War the Mennonites in many communities contributed to the Red Cross, specifying that the contributions be used for the civilian work of that organization, such as disaster relief and the relief of civilian war sufferers.

In the second World War the government even recognized this principle to the extent that it offered civilian bonds, which nonresistant Christians might purchase in place of war bonds. The question has been raised whether it is worth while making a distinction between a civilian bond and a war bond. Will not the government use all the money it needs for financing the war anyway, regardless of the kind of bond which nonresistant people buy? There are two answers to this question. The first is that in addition to its war operations the government needs much money for the financing of civilian operations of various kinds. During the war the annual cost of operating the work projects of the CPS camps alone was almost as great as the amount of money subscribed by nonresistant people for civilian bonds. It would therefore seem correct to say that in purchasing civilian bonds nonresistant people were simply helping the government to finance its side of the CPS program. Under the Canadian plan the proceeds of civilian bonds were used for the relief of war sufferers. The second answer to this question is that, in making a voluntary bond purchase, the Christian gives a clear testimony to his faith, if for conscience' sake, he buys a civilian bond instead of a war bond. As long as nonresistant people are careful to discriminate clearly between that which is civilian and that which is military; as long as they support that which does not promote the war, and withhold their support from that which does promote it; as long as they take pains to follow a clear and consistent course, so that the public will know where they stand, they will keep the faith. But as soon as they begin to compromise, and to blur the line of distinction between the civilian and the military; as soon as they begin to follow a course in which the public cannot tell where they stand, they will have started down the road which ends in the loss of their faith.

A Positive Program of Christian Ministry to the Needy

Keeping the nonresistant faith means more, however, than maintaining a distinction between military and nonmilitary forms of service. Refusal to perform military service is, after all, a negative expression of the Christian doctrine of love. A ministry of comfort and healing to those who are in need, on the other hand, is a positive expression of the same doctrine. This ministry is definitely taught in the New Testament. When a certain lawyer asked Jesus what it means to love one's neighbor, our Lord simply told the story of the good Samaritan who brought relief to the man who had been waylaid by thieves on the road to Jericho.[18] James says that faith without works is dead, and then explains that pure religion is "to visit the fatherless and widows in their affliction, and to keep himself unspotted from the world."[19] Then he says: "If a brother or sister be naked, and destitute of daily food, and one of you say unto them, Depart in peace, be ye warmed and filled; notwithstanding ye give them not those things which are needful to the body; what doth it profit?"[20] Jesus never met a case of physical need without pausing to minister unto it. Therefore, we as His disciples today have an obligation to go and do likewise.

Because of the extreme emphasis on the social gospel by modern religious liberalism, which substitutes social reform for personal regeneration, some Mennonites have hesitated to endorse, for church administration, an extended program of relief, lest it become mere "social service." These people are right in objecting to such service apart from the message of the Gospel. There is no question, however, that Jesus Himself was constantly giving physical aid to the needy, incidentally to His spiritual message. And this is precisely what the early Mennonites also did. In Chapter VII the words of Menno Simons were cited in which he says:

All those who are born of God . . . show mercy and love, as much as they can. No one among them is allowed to beg. They take to

18 Luke 10:25-37.
19 Jas. 1:27.
20 Jas. 2:15, 16.

heart the need of the saints. They entertain those in distress. They take the stranger into their houses. They comfort the afflicted; assist the needy; clothe the naked; feed the hungry; do not turn their face from the poor; do not despise their own flesh. . . . The Scripture plainly teaches and says, "Whoso hath this world's good, and seeth his brother have need, and shutteth up his bowels of compassion for him, how dwelleth the love of God in him?"[21]

It was this conviction which enabled the early Mennonites to live a life of true Christian brotherhood. As pointed out in Chapter V it was this spirit of love and helpfulness which caused Catholic writers to wish that they might have communities like those of the Anabaptists within their own church. It was this nonresistant faith which inspired the Mennonites of the sixteenth and seventeenth centuries to carry on their program of Christian service in helping their persecuted brethren to find new homes where they might be free to worship God according to the dictates of their conscience. As pointed out in Chapter VI this faith was alive among the Mennonites of Pennsylvania who in 1775 were moved to inform the provincial legislature that they desired to be helpful in the preservation of men's lives, while having no freedom to assist in their destruction. It was the same spirit which produced the Mennonite program for relief in the time of the India famine in the 1890's. Again, in the days of the first World War, the Mennonite Church which could not support that war gave of its men and its money for the relief of war sufferers in Europe, and for the reconstruction of devastated lands. This same spirit of Christian service moved the church to assist thousands of persecuted refugees in finding new homes in North and South America since 1920.

When the second World War brought untold human suffering, this spirit of love and helpfulness moved the Mennonites to extend their program of relief and service to many parts of the world. By the spring of 1944 Mennonite relief workers were found in Puerto Rico, Paraguay, Egypt, England, India, and China. Work in Poland and France had been temporarily abandoned because of necessity. But the prospect was that dur-

[21] *Complete Writings*, 558-9.

ing the next five years the relief program of the church would be carried forward on an unprecedented scale. The proposal for service units, to be sponsored by the Mennonite Board of Missions and Charities for service in needy communities at home, is another expression of the same spirit. This is as it should be. This is the ministry of comfort and healing so clearly taught in the New Testament and exemplified by our Lord and Saviour Himself. The true nonresistant Christian does not engage in this service in order to purchase immunity from military service. He performs this service because the love of Christ constrains him to a mission of helpfulness to those who are in need. The same love which forbids him to slay his fellow men also commands him to feed the hungry and clothe the naked, and to render a ministry of healing wherever there is need. And so long as this love remains alive and warm among nonresistant people they may be expected to keep the faith.

Christian Business Relationships

One of the chief causes of warfare is the economic cause. The New Testament says that "the love of money is a root of all kinds of evil: which some reaching after have been led astray from the faith."[22] These words appear in Paul's first Epistle to Timothy, in a section devoted to the proper relationship of "masters and servants." Paul goes on to say that they who would be rich fall into temptation; therefore if Christians have their needs supplied they ought therewith to be content. "Godliness with contentment is great gain," he says, but where men become ambitious for more than they need of this world's goods the result is "envy, strife, railings, evil surmisings, perverse disputings."[23] In other words, wrong attitudes in economics and wrong methods in business, are real causes of war. This is a truth which nonresistant people must ever keep in mind.

It is easy enough to see that industrial strife which culminates in strikes and violence is contrary to the spirit of nonresist-

---

[22] I Tim. 6:10 (ASV).
[23] I Tim. 6:4-6.

ance. Too often, however, nonresistant people are inclined to place all the blame for such strife on labor. They seem to forget that it takes two sides to fight an industrial war, just as much as it does to wage an international conflict. As pointed out in Chapter X, modern industry and the capitalistic system, as they commonly operate, are involved in so much evil that they are largely to blame for the class struggle in America. And it should be added here that capital and industry must carry much of the blame for modern international war as well. American or European capital invested in foreign enterprises has often led to the seizure and conquest of foreign territory. Competition between the business interests of two nations has often led these nations to war with each other. Furthermore, certain industries exist primarily for the manufacture of instruments of war; and in time of war many of the ordinary peacetime industries are converted for the manufacture of war materials.

It is important, therefore, that nonresistant Christians keep themselves free from business connections and practices which would compromise their faith. If it is wrong for a Christian to take up arms for the destruction of an enemy, it is also wrong for him to engage in the manufacture of war materials. Therefore he cannot work in a war production plant; neither can he operate such a plant, nor invest his money in such a business. If it is wrong for a Christian to take part in international wars, it is also wrong for him to be associated with any business which is conducted in such a way as to be a cause of international wars. If it is wrong for a Christian to take part in industrial conflict, it is also wrong for him to operate a business, or to invest his money in a business, which employs unjust methods and unfair practices with respect to labor, or to competitors, or to the public. Such unfair and unjust practices are a major cause of industrial, as well as international conflict; and they are a most serious violation of the Christian spirit of love.

It is doubtful, however, whether the Mennonite people today are as awake to these issues as they ought to be. Although the church takes a definite position against employment in war production plants, it is nevertheless true that this principle was violated in a number of cases during the second World War. Until recently practically all Mennonites were a rural people engaged in agriculture. During the past generation, however, there has been a gradual shift toward urban life, and employment in industry. In too many cases this shift seems to have been made without sufficient consideration of the moral and ethical principles involved. Too many Mennonites seem to be satisfied with a business so long as it pays in dollars and cents. Too frequently they fail to inquire whether the business itself, or the methods which it employs, are consistent with the Christian way of life. A nonresistant people such as the Mennonites must ever strive to maintain a tender and enlightened conscience on the entire question of economic attitudes and business practices. In an age of materialism it is essential that in this area they put forth special effort to do justly, and to love mercy, and to walk humbly with their God. Failure on this point might easily result in the loss of the nonresistant faith itself.

Christian Race Relations

Another area where special effort is required, if nonresistant people are to be consistent in doing justice and mercy, is the area of race relations. This is true because race prejudice is a very subtle sin, and leads most easily to unjust practices, and often to actual hatred and to open war and violence. It seems to be a natural thing to assume that people of another race are inferior to one's own. In Christ's time many Jews believed themselves better than other people, and considered Gentiles unfit for membership in the kingdom of God. But Paul says that in Christ "there is neither Greek nor Jew, circumcision nor uncircumcision, Barbarian, Scythian, bond nor free: but Christ is all, and in all."[24]

The New Testament makes it clear that no one becomes a child of God because he is a Jew, or because he has a white skin, or because his ancestors were Mennonites, or for any similar reason. All men have sinned and come short of the glory of

[24] Col. 3:11.

God. Therefore all must receive salvation in the same way, through the atoning work of Christ. Since God is the creator of all men, and desirous that all should be saved, Christ sought all men, regardless of race or ancestry, or station, and invited them into the kingdom of God. In His sight, the despised woman of Samaria was as worthy of salvation as was Nicodemus, the ruler in Israel. And the black man from Ethiopia was as worthy to be baptized and received into the church as was Saul of Tarsus, a Hebrew of the Hebrews. If Christians bear these facts in mind it should help them to exercise justice and mercy to peoples of other races in our own day.

Race prejudice in America today frequently takes the form of hatred toward the Negro and the Jew. At various times Protestants have maintained a strong feeling against Catholics. On the Pacific coast there has long been a prejudice against the people of the yellow race, especially against the Japanese. This feeling became nation-wide after December 7, 1941, and was greatly intensified. The great majority of these Americans of Japanese ancestry were as loyal to the United States as is any white citizen, and yet they were unjustly held in concentration camps, the father often being separated from the remainder of the family. In many communities the feeling against these American citizens who happened to have a yellow skin was so bitter that it was unsafe for them to attempt to live there. Race prejudice insists that the Negro is inferior, unworthy to shake hands with a white man. The Negro may not eat at a white man's table; he is not taken into the white man's church; he is not given a white man's job on an equal basis with him; many occupations and professions are closed against him simply because he is black and not white. This is altogether foreign to the spirit of the New Testament, and a nonresistant people who claim to be disciples of Christ can have no part in it.

It is also true that nonresistants cannot take part in pressure campaigns, in strikes, in picketing, or in devices designed to compel others to do justice to the Negro, or to the Japanese. This is the method used by some of Gandhi's followers, and as explained in Chapter IX, it is really a form of class warfare. On

19

the other hand, nonresistant Christians must at all times have a feeling of true Christian love toward Negroes, Japanese, Jews, Catholics, or any other people who may be hated by others because they are in some way different from them. Furthermore, this feeling of love must express itself in some way wherever nonresistant Christians and the despised people come in contact with each other. If a Christian employer of labor would do justice and love mercy, he must be ready and willing to extend the same opportunities, without prejudice, to members of the black race that he extends to members of any other race. White Christians must be ready and willing to receive Negro Christians into their churches. And the love of Christ will make them ready and willing to feed Negroes at their own tables. A white Christian must be as ready to shake hands with a black brother as with one of his own race.

In theory, no doubt, the Mennonite people have always adhered to the principle of love toward all men, regardless of race. In actual practice, however, this principle has been violated too frequently among them. There have been cases where they have hesitated to receive into the brotherhood converts who did not happen to have a Mennonite ancestry; and there have been cases where such converts lost out in their faith, after coming into the church, because the brotherhood did not have the same friendly feeling toward them as it did toward those who were the children of Mennonite families.[25] In certain Mennonite communities there have been cases of anti-Jewish sentiment; and in other cases some Mennonites seem to share the common prejudices against the Negro. The nonresistant Christian certainly must remain free from these prejudices and attitudes in his own heart. He must do what he can to correct injustice, not by unchristian means, but by spiritual means, through prayer, and example, and by word of testimony. If the nonresistant Christian cannot follow the methods of the nonviolent coercionists in demanding justice for the Japanese, the

---

[25] Cf. John Umble, "Race Prejudice an Obstacle to Evangelism in the Mennonite Church," *Goshen College Record Review Supplement* (Goshen, Ind., September, 1926), 29-32.

Negro, and the Jew, neither can he share the common prejudices and attitudes toward these people. His own attitude and his own relations must be thoroughly Christian, ready to receive a black, yellow, or a Jewish brother as one of his own race.

Nonresistance and Nonconformity

Nonresistance in its negative aspect is simply one application of the general principle of nonconformity to the evil of this world. Disciples of Christ are definitely commanded to "be not fashioned according to this world" but to be "transformed" with a renewed mind.[26] This transformation applies to every aspect of life and conduct. The very speech and habits of a Christian are different from those of the ordinary man of the world. If the Christian really follows Christ, his social standards and his business relationships will be on a different level from those of the non-Christian. In his amusements, in the manner of his dress, and in a score of other matters, the true disciple of Christ is a nonconformist. A Christian who would be a nonconformist on the question of war, but a conformist to the world in other aspects of life, is very inconsistent to say the least. But more than that, he is following a course which is likely to end in failure. One cannot preserve the Christian way of life on one point while disregarding a number of others. Christian discipleship constitutes an integrated whole, and he who disregards one or more portions may sooner or later lose the remainder as well.

Teaching the Entire Gospel

During the two world wars the record of the American Mennonites with respect to the principle of nonresistance was a fairly consistent one. Among all of the Mennonite groups, however, it is obvious that this record was far from perfect. More than one third of the men called in the draft did not take the position of the conscientious objector. The testimony of some individuals in CPS camps was not what one would expect

[26] Rom. 12:2 (ASV).

from men with a vital Christian faith. The same can be said of some members of the church in the home communities. Some of these compromised with war on one point or another, while others failed to demonstrate the way of Christian love in their relations with their fellow men. A few Mennonites were confused in their thinking on the peace question, having substituted some form of modern pacifism for Biblical nonresistance. The nonresistance of some appeared to be largely a formal one, lacking the roots required to give it fruitful vitality.

Inasmuch as the weaknesses of the Mennonite people with respect to their nonresistant faith and life are varied, it is obvious that there is no one remedy for these ills. There is no one method for the keeping of the faith. A study[27] of influences affecting the decision of Mennonite men of draft age, during the second World War, emphasizes the importance of diligent efforts along various lines for the achievement of this end. This study shows that the environment of the individual, in the church, the home, the community, and the school, has a tremendous influence in determining whether the Mennonite youth in wartime will remain true to the nonresistant faith or not. On the basis of statistical evidence the author concludes that there is a real correlation between the amount of emphasis given to Mennonite principles, in the teaching and preaching program of the Mennonite churches, and the percentage of conscientious objectors among their men of draft age. Congregations whose ministers have a thorough understanding and appreciation of Mennonitism are likely to have a high percentage of conscientious objectors. If the minister has a sound evangelical faith, if he places a strong emphasis on the historic Mennonite principles, if he preaches peace sermons, and is alert to assist the young men during the crucial period of registration, answering of questionnaires, and receiving of classification, his men of draft age are likely to be conscientious objectors. But if the minister lacks an appreciation of Mennonitism, if he never preaches peace sermons, and if he is inclined to imitate modern Prot-

[27] Robert Kreider, "Environmental Influences Affecting the Decisions of Mennonite Boys of Draft Age," *Mennonite Quarterly Review* (October, 1942), 16:247-59; 275.

estantism in his preaching, in his methods of church work, and in his theology, the result is likely to be the opposite.

Likewise, where family, community, and educational influences are favorable, the young men are more likely to remain true to the nonresistant faith than where these influences are unfavorable. When the life of a young man is well integrated with the life of a strong Mennonite community, he is likely to be a conscientious objector. But, if he lives his life on the outer edges of the community, the result is more likely to be the opposite. If his educational contacts, his friendships, and his associates are of the nonresistant type, he is likely to be a nonresistant also. But if they are of the opposite type, he is more likely to go into the army. Another study analyzing in some detail the record of Mennonite men of draft age, 1941 to 1947, shows that factory workers had a lower percentage of CO's than any other occupational group, and that the young men of high-school age, or those only recently completing high school, had a lower percentage of CO's than any other group classified according to education.[28] It is obvious, therefore, that the keeping of the nonresistant faith requires a deep and vital Christian faith, diligent teaching, a favorable home and community environment, and eternal vigilance on the part of all.

Nonresistance alone does not constitute the Gospel, but it is an integral part of the Gospel. For the perpetuation of their faith, therefore, it is essential that nonresistant people give due attention to the teachings of the entire Gospel as found in the Word of God. Wherever this Word takes root in the hearts of men, and grows to the full maturity of a redeemed and enlightened conscience, it will bear the precious fruit of the Spirit: love, joy, peace, long-suffering, gentleness, goodness, faith, meekness, temperance.[29]

The Outreach of Christian Nonresistance

An essential requirement for the perpetuation of any faith is its active propagation. A church without a missionary zeal is

[28] For a fuller discussion of this subject see Guy F. Hershberger, *The Mennonite Church in the Second World War* (Scottdale, Pa., 1951), Ch. IV.
[29] Gal. 5:22, 23.

a dead church. A faith without a missionary zeal is a dead faith. This is especially true of the Christian Gospel, which has no meaning except as it is proclaimed to all men for their salvation everywhere. The doctrine of love and nonresistance is an integral part of the Christian Gospel, and no form of pacifism is valid except as it is based upon this redemptive Gospel of Jesus Christ. As pointed out in Chapter IX, there are many forms of modern pacifism which lack this essential foundation. For this reason the believer in Biblical nonresistance has the great responsibility of bringing to the pacifist world the challenge of the Christian Gospel. Moreover, there are indications that many leaders of this pacifist world are aware of the shortcomings of their own program. Several years ago the Fellowship of Reconciliation published a challenging book by Rachel King, entitled *God's Boycott of Sin*.[30] This book frankly says that the older liberal pacifism on which the author was brought up is much too superficial in its approach to the problem of war; that it is based upon a shallow optimism which cannot withstand the test of our time. It emphasizes the need of recognizing the wrath of God, as well as the love of God, as a part of the Christian Gospel of peace; and it appeals to pacifists to build their structure upon more sure theological foundations. When the Conference on the Church and War was held in Detroit in 1950, with Christian pacifists of every type represented, the position of Biblical nonresistance was given a welcome hearing, and the literature of Biblical nonresistance was given a conspicuous place on the official conference reading list.

Another hopeful indication of our time is found in signs of an awakening interest in the peace question within evangelical and fundamentalist circles. It is a well-known fact that many Christians with a conservative theology are unsympathetic, or even hostile, to the nonresistant position. There are various reasons for this. One reason may be an unbalanced emphasis on the Old Testament, and a failure to understand that many of the ceremonial and ethical teachings of the Old Testament have been superseded by those of the New Testament. Another rea-

---

[30] Rachel King, *God's Boycott of Sin* (New York, 1946).

son may be the fact that much of modern pacifism has been
based upon some form of religious liberalism. In their desire to
repudiate liberalism these theological conservatives have been
inclined to reject every idea, including pacifism, which liberalism has favored. As this book has shown, particularly in Chapters II, III, V, and IX, Biblical nonresistance is based, not on
liberal theology, but on the Gospel of Christ. The doctrine of
nonresistance and the atoning, redemptive work of Christ are
inextricably intertwined, making them integral parts of the
same Gospel. Thus evangelical Christianity has a solid foundation, which liberalism does not have, on which to base its peace
teaching. For this reason evangelical Christians ought to be the
most vigorous champions of the Gospel of peace. This has always been the view of the Mennonite Church, and it is her responsibility to present this view with clarity and conviction to
the Christendom of our time. As said above there are signs of
an awakening interest on this question in evangelical circles.
Several years ago James D. Bales published a book entitled *The
Christian Conscientious Objector*,[31] written definitely from the
evangelical point of view. Another booklet, *Strangers and Pilgrims*, by James R. Graham,[32] is a most challenging presentation
of nonresistant Christianity by an evangelical Christian and
missionary. A more recent work is Culbert G. Rutenber's, *The
Dagger and the Cross*,[33] published in 1950. Because of the
author's position as a professor in the Eastern Baptist Theological Seminary, and the publication of the book by the Fellowship of Reconciliation, this work is of special significance. Several years ago Carl F. H. Henry of the Fuller Theological Seminary published a significant book, *The Uneasy Conscience of
Modern Fundamentalism*,[34] in which he stresses the need for a
greater concern on the part of evangelical Christians for the
social teachings and applications of the Christian Gospel. While
Henry has not espoused the nonresistant teachings of the New

[31] James D. Bales, *The Christian Conscientious Objector* (Berkeley, Calif.).
[32] James R. Graham, *Strangers and Pilgrims* (Scottdale, Pa., 1951).
[33] C. G. Rutenber, *The Dagger and the Cross: An Examination of Christian Pacifism* (New York, 1950).
[34] Carl F. H. Henry, *The Uneasy Conscience of Modern Fundamentalism* (Grand Rapids, Mich., 1947).

Testament, his concern for the social teachings of the Gospel is nevertheless significant. These new trends in evangelical Christianity are a most hopeful sign, reflecting a new development and giving the Mennonites and other nonresistant Christians an opportunity for presenting their case to Christendom at large, such as they have not had for a long time. This opportunity must not be neglected.

In the mid-twentieth century the Mennonites of the world are called upon as they never were before to recover the Anabaptist vision of the sixteenth century, which has no other foundation than that which is laid in Jesus Christ. When they have recovered this vision in all its fullness the Mennonites may well again be, as they were four hundred years ago, a foremost missionary church of their time. As Franklin H. Littell says, "the Anabaptists were sending their missioners wherever they could get a hearing, for (said they), 'The earth is the Lord's and the fullness thereof.' "[35] We find no better illustration of this than in the words of Menno Simons who says:

> We desire with ardent hearts even at the cost of life and blood that the holy Gospel of Jesus Christ and His apostles . . . may be taught and preached through all the world.[36]
>
> Therefore, we preach, as much as is possible, both by day and by night, in houses and in fields, in forests and wastes, hither and yon, at home or abroad, in prisons and in dungeons, in water and in fire, on the scaffold and on the wheel, before lords and princes, through mouth and pen, with possessions and blood, with life and death.[37]
>
> This is my only joy and heart's desire: to extend the kingdom of God, reveal the truth, reprove sin, teach righteousness, feed hungry souls with the Word of the Lord, lead the straying sheep into the right path, and gain many souls to the Lord through His Spirit, power, and grace.[38]

This is the Menno Simons who says:

> These regenerated . . . are the children of peace who have beaten

---

[35] F. H. Littell, "The Anabaptist Theology of Missions," *Mennonite Quarterly Review* (January 1947) 21:10.
[36] *Complete Writings of Menno Simons*, 303
[37] *Ibid.*, 633.
[38] *Ibid.*, 189.

their swords into plowshares and their spears into pruning hooks, and know war no more. . . .[39] They show mercy and love, as much as they can. No one among them is allowed to beg. They take to heart the need of the saints. They entertain those in distress. They take the stranger into their houses. They comfort the afflicted; assist the needy; clothe the naked; feed the hungry; do not turn their face from the poor; do not despise their own flesh.[40]

Here is the integration of nonresistance with the Gospel which puts it on a sound and sure foundation. Here is a social conscience with sharpness and clarity, and breadth and depth. Here is a burning zeal set aflame by the Spirit of God Himself. Here is the combination of factors which will enable the Mennonite Church of our day to go onward showing forth the way of true Christian discipleship in the home and family, in the neighborhood and community, in economic and business relationships, in relationships between races and classes, between employers and employees, between nations and states. Here is true Christian nonresistance with a sure and sound foundation and with an outreach which has no end.

[39] *Ibid.,* 94.
[40] *Ibid.,* 558.

Appendix

THE SCRIPTURES SPEAK

War is Sin

But God said unto me, Thou shalt not build an house for my name, because thou hast been a man of war, and hast shed blood.— I Chron. 28:3.

From whence come wars and fightings among you? come they not hence, even of your lusts that war in your members? Ye lust, and have not; ye kill, and desire to have, and cannot obtain: ye fight and war, yet ye have not, because ye ask not.—Jas. 4:1, 2.

Now the works of the flesh are manifest, which are these; Adultery, fornication, uncleanness, lasciviousness, idolatry, witchcraft, hatred, variance, emulations, wrath, strife, seditions, heresies, envyings, murders, drunkenness, revellings, and such like: of the which I tell you before, as I have also told you in time past, that they which do such things shall not inherit the kingdom of God.—Gal. 5:19-21.

Whosoever hateth his brother is a murderer: and ye know that no murderer hath eternal life abiding in him.—I John 3:1.

The Law of Love

Jesus said unto him, Thou shalt love the Lord thy God with all thy heart, and with all thy soul, and with all thy mind. This is the first and great commandment. And the second is like unto it, Thou shalt love thy neighbour as thyself. On these two commandments hang all the law and the prophets.—Matt. 22:37-40.

For God so loved the world, that he gave his only begotten Son, that whosoever believeth in him should not perish, but have everlasting life.—John 3:16.

Love worketh no ill to his neighbour . . . . Owe no man any thing, but to love one another.—Rom. 13:10, 8.

A new commandment I give unto you, That ye love one another; as I have loved you, that ye also love one another.—John 13:34.

Beloved, let us love one another: for love is of God; and every one that loveth is born of God, and knoweth God. He that loveth not knoweth not God; for God is love.—I John 4:7, 8.

He that loveth his brother abideth in the light, and there is none occasion of stumbling in him. But he that hateth his brother is in darkness, and walketh in darkness, and knoweth not whither he goeth, because that darkness hath blinded his eyes.—I John 2:10, 11.

We know that we have passed from death unto life, because we love the brethren. He that loveth not his brother abideth in death. Whosoever hateth his brother is a murderer: and ye know that no murderer hath eternal life abiding in him.—I John 3:14, 15.

And this is his commandment, That we should believe on the name of his Son Jesus Christ, and love one another, as he gave us commandment.—I John 3:23.

If I speak with the tongues of men and of angels, but have not love, I am become sounding brass, or a clanging cymbal. . . . Love never faileth: but whether there be prophecies, they shall be done away; whether there be tongues, they shall cease; whether there be knowledge, it shall be done away. . . . But now abideth faith, hope, love, these three; and the greatest of these is love.—I Cor. 13:1, 8, 13, R.V.

Nonresistance in the Old Testament

Thou shalt not kill.—Ex. 20:13.

Say not thou, I will recompense evil; but wait on the Lord, and he shall save thee.—Prov. 20:22.

If thine enemy be hungry, give him bread to eat; and if he be thirsty, give him water to drink.—Prov. 25:21.

If thou meet thine enemy's ox or his ass going astray, thou shalt surely bring it back to him again. If thou see the ass of him that hateth thee lying under his burden, and wouldest forbear to help him, thou shalt surely help with him.—Ex. 23:4, 5.

And Abram said unto Lot, Let there be no strife, I pray thee, between me and thee, and between my herdmen and thy herdmen; for we be brethren. Is not the whole land before thee? separate thyself, I pray thee, from me: if thou wilt take the left hand, then I will go to the right; or if thou depart to the right hand, then I will go to the left.—Gen. 13:8, 9.

And the herdmen of Gerar did strive with Isaac's herdmen, saying, The water is ours: and he called the name of the well Esek; because they strove with him. And they digged another well, and strove for that also: and he called the name of it Sitnah. And he removed from thence, and digged another well; and for that they strove not: and he called the name of it Rehoboth; and he said, For now the

Lord hath made room for us, and we shall be fruitful in the land.—
Gen. 26:20-22.

Then there passed by Midianites merchantmen; and they drew
and lifted up Joseph out of the pit, and sold Joseph to the Ishmeelites
for twenty pieces of silver: and they brought Joseph into Egypt. . . .
And Joseph said unto his brethren, Come near to me, I pray you.
And they came near. And he said, I am Joseph your brother, whom
ye sold into Egypt. Now therefore be not grieved, nor angry with
yourselves, that ye sold me hither: for God did send me before you
to preserve life.—Gen. 37:28; 45:4, 5.

The Words of the Prophets

Wash you, make you clean; put away the evil of your doings
from before mine eyes; cease to do evil; learn to do well; seek judgment, relieve the oppressed, judge the fatherless, plead for the
widow. Come now, and let us reason together, saith the Lord:
though your sins be as scarlet, they shall be as white as snow; though
they be red like crimson, they shall be as wool.—Isa. 1:16-18.

For every battle of the warrior is with confused noise, and garments rolled in blood; but this shall be with burning and fuel of fire.
For unto us a child is born, unto us a son is given: and the government shall be upon his shoulder: and his name shall be called Wonderful, Counsellor, The mighty God, The everlasting Father, The
Prince of Peace.—Isa. 9:5, 6.

And he shall judge among the nations, and shall rebuke many
people: and they shall beat their swords into plowshares, and their
spears into pruninghooks: nation shall not lift up sword against
nation, neither shall they learn war any more.—Isa. 2:4.

Woe to them that go down to Egypt for help; and stay on horses,
and trust in chariots, because they are many; and in horsemen, because they are very strong; but they look not unto the Holy One of
Israel, neither seek the Lord! . . . Now the Egyptians are men, and
not God; and their horses flesh, and not spirit. When the Lord shall
stretch out his hand, both he that helpeth shall fall, and he that is
holpen shall fall down, and they all shall fail together.—Isa. 31:1, 3.

The Kingdom of God

Repent ye: for the kingdom of heaven is at hand.—Matt. 3:2.

Jesus answered and said unto him, Verily, verily, I say unto thee,
Except a man be born again, he cannot see the kingdom of God.—
John 3:3.

Verily I say unto you, Except ye be converted, and become as little children, ye shall not enter into the kingdom of heaven.—Matt. 18:3.

But Jesus said, Suffer little children, and forbid them not, to come unto me: for of such is the kingdom of heaven.—Matt. 19:14.

Thy kingdom come. Thy will be done in earth, as it is in heaven. —Matt. 6:10.

But seek ye first the kingdom of God, and his righteousness; and all these things shall be added unto you.—Matt. 6:33.

The Way of Life for Members of the Kingdom

There is therefore now no condemnation to them which are in Christ Jesus, who walk not after the flesh, but after the Spirit.— Rom. 8:1.

Therefore we are buried with him by baptism into death: that like as Christ was raised up from the dead by the glory of the Father, even so we also should walk in newness of life.—Rom. 6:4.

Therefore if any man be in Christ, he is a new creature: old things are passed away; behold, all things are become new.—II Cor. 5:17.

If ye then be risen with Christ, seek those things which are above, where Christ sitteth on the right hand of God. . . . Put on therefore, as the elect of God, holy and beloved, bowels of mercies, kindness, humbleness of mind, meekness, longsuffering; forbearing one another, and forgiving one another, if any man have a quarrel against any: even as Christ forgave you, so also do ye. And above all these things put on charity, which is the bond of perfectness. And let the peace of God rule in your hearts, to the which also ye are called in one body; and be ye thankful.—Col. 3:1, 12-15.

I beseech you therefore, brethren, by the mercies of God, that ye present your bodies a living sacrifice, holy, acceptable unto God, which is your reasonable service. And be not conformed to this world: but be ye transformed by the renewing of your mind, that ye may prove what is that good, and acceptable, and perfect, will of God.—Rom. 12:1, 2.

If we say that we have fellowship with him, and walk in darkness, we lie, and do not the truth: but if we walk in the light, as he is in the light, we have fellowship one with another, and the blood of Jesus Christ his Son cleanseth us from all sin.—I John 1:6, 7.

My little children, let us not love in word, neither in tongue; but in deed and in truth.—I John 3:18.

But the fruit of the Spirit is love, joy, peace, longsuffering, gentleness, goodness, faith, meekness, temperance: against such there is no law.—Gal. 5:22, 23.

Blessed are the poor in spirit: for theirs is the kingdom of heaven. Blessed are they that mourn: for they shall be comforted. Blessed are the meek: for they shall inherit the earth. Blessed are they which do hunger and thirst after righteousness: for they shall be filled. Blessed are the merciful: for they shall obtain mercy. Blessed are the pure in heart: for they shall see God. Blessed are the peacemakers: for they shall be called the children of God. Blessed are they which are persecuted for righteousness' sake: for theirs is the kingdom of heaven. Blessed are ye, when men shall revile you, and persecute you, and shall say all manner of evil against you falsely, for my sake. Rejoice, and be exceeding glad: for great is your reward in heaven: for so persecuted they the prophets which were before you.—Matt. 5:3-12.

And whosoever will be chief among you, let him be your servant: even as the Son of man came not to be ministered unto, but to minister, and to give his life a ransom for many.—Matt. 20:27, 28.

And whosoever shall exalt himself shall be abased; and he that shall humble himself be exalted.—Matt. 23:12.

Likewise, ye younger, submit yourselves unto the elder. Yea, all of you be subject one to another, and be clothed with humility: for God resisteth the proud, and giveth grace to the humble.—I Pet. 5:5.

The Kingdom Not of This World

Again, the devil taketh him up into an exceeding high mountain, and sheweth him all the kingdoms of the world, and the glory of them; and saith unto him, All these things will I give thee, if thou wilt fall down and worship me. Then saith Jesus unto him, Get thee hence, Satan: for it is written, Thou shalt worship the Lord thy God, and him only shalt thou serve.—Matt. 4:8-10.

When Jesus therefore perceived that they would come and take him by force, to make him a king, he departed again into a mountain himself alone.—John 6:15.

Jesus answered, My Kingdom is not of this world: if my kingdom were of this world, then would my servants fight, that I should not be delivered to the Jews: but now is my kingdom not from hence.—John 18:36.

For though we walk in the flesh, we do not war after the flesh: (for the weapons of our warfare are not carnal, but mighty through God to the pulling down of strong holds;) casting down imaginations, and every high thing that exalteth itself against the knowledge of God, and bringing into captivity every thought to the obedience of Christ.—II Cor. 10:3-5.

Finally, my brethren, be strong in the Lord, and in the power of his might. Put on the whole armour of God, that ye may be able to stand against the wiles of the devil. For we wrestle not against flesh and blood, but against principalities, against powers, against the rulers of the darkness of this world, against spiritual wickedness, in high places. Wherefore take unto you the whole armour of God, that ye may be able to withstand in the evil day, and having done all, to stand. Stand therefore, having your loins girt about with truth, and having on the breastplate of righteousness; and your feet shod with the preparation of the gospel of peace; above all, taking the shield of faith, wherewith ye shall be able to quench all the fiery darts of the wicked. And take the helmet of salvation, and the sword of the Spirit, which is the word of God: praying always with all prayer and supplication in the Spirit, and watching thereunto with all perseverance and supplication for all saints.—Eph. 6:10-18.

Thou therefore endure hardness, as a good soldier of Jesus Christ.—II Tim. 2:3.

I have fought a good fight, I have finished my course, I have kept the faith: henceforth there is laid up for me a crown of righteousness, which the Lord, the righteous judge, shall give me at that day: and not to me only, but unto all them also that love his appearing.—II Tim. 4:7, 8.

The Kingdom Invites All Races and Peoples

And they shall come from the east, and from the west, and from the north, and from the south, and shall sit down in the kingdom of God.—Luke 13:29.

For as many of you as have been baptized into Christ have put on Christ. There is neither Jew nor Greek, there is neither bond nor free, there is neither male nor female: for ye are all one in Christ Jesus.—Gal. 3: 27, 28.

For this cause I bow my knees unto the Father of our Lord Jesus Christ, of whom the whole family in heaven and earth is named.—Eph. 3:14, 15.

For by one Spirit are we all baptized into one body, whether we be Jews or Gentiles, whether we be bond or free; and have been all made to drink into one Spirit.— I Cor. 12:13.

For there is no difference between the Jew and the Greek: for the same Lord over all is rich unto all that call upon him. For whosoever shall call upon the name of the Lord shall be saved.—Rom. 10:12, 13.

There is neither Greek nor Jew, circumcision nor uncircumcision, Barbarian, Scythian, bond nor free: but Christ is all, and in all.—Col. 3:11.

Nonresistance in the New Testament

Ye have heard that it hath been said, An eye for an eye, and a tooth for a tooth: but I say unto you, That ye resist not evil: but whosoever shall smite thee on thy right cheek, turn to him the other also. And if any man will sue thee at the law, and take away thy coat, let him have thy cloak also.—Matt. 5:38-40.

Ye have heard that it hath been said, Thou shalt love thy neighbour, and hate thine enemy. But I say unto you, Love your enemies, bless them that curse you, do good to them that hate you, and pray for them which despitefully use you, and persecute you; that ye may be the children of our Father which is in heaven: for he maketh his sun to rise on the evil and on the good, and sendeth rain on the just and on the unjust. For if ye love them which love you, what reward have ye? do not even the publicans the same? And if ye salute your brethren only, what do ye more than others? do not even the publicans so? Be ye therefore perfect, even as your Father which is in heaven is perfect.—Matt. 5:43-48.

Then said Jesus unto him, Put up again thy sword into his place: for all they that take the sword shall perish with the sword. —Matt. 26:52.

Recompense no man evil for evil. Provide things honest in the sight of all men. It it be possible, as much as lieth in you, live peaceably with all men. Dearly beloved, avenge not yourselves, but rather give place unto wrath: for it is written, Vengeance is mine; I will repay, saith the Lord. Therefore if thine enemy hunger, feed him; if he thirst, give him drink: for in so doing thou shalt heap coals of fire on his head. Be not overcome of evil, but overcome evil with good.—Rom. 12:17-21.

Now therefore there is utterly a fault among you, because ye go to law one with another. Why do ye not rather take wrong? why do ye not rather suffer yourselves to be defrauded?—I Cor. 6:7.

Finally, be ye all of one mind, having compassion one of another, love as brethren, be pitiful, be courteous: not rendering evil for evil, or railing for railing: but contrariwise blessing; knowing that ye are thereunto called, that ye should inherit a blessing.—I Pet. 3:8, 9.

See that none render evil for evil unto any man; but ever follow that which is good, both among yourselves, and to all men.—I Thes. 5:15.

And the servant of the Lord must not strive; but be gentle unto all men, apt to teach, patient.—II Tim. 2:24.

The Example of Christ

He was oppressed, and he was afflicted, yet he opened not his mouth: he is brought as a lamb to the slaughter, and as a sheep before her shearers is dumb, so he openeth not his mouth.—Isa. 53:7.

Then said Jesus, Father, forgive them; for they know not what they do.—Luke 23:34.

And when his disciples James and John saw this, they said, Lord wilt thou that we command fire to come down from heaven, and consume them, even as Elias did? But he turned, and rebuked them, and said, Ye know not what manner of spirit ye are of. For the Son of man is not come to destroy men's lives, but to save them.—Luke 9:54-56.

Take my yoke upon you, and learn of me; for I am meek and lowly in heart: and ye shall find rest unto your souls.—Matt. 11:29.

Then said Jesus unto his disciples, If any man will come after me, let him deny himself, and take up his cross, and follow me. For whosoever will save his life shall lose it: and whosoever will lose his life for my sake shall find it.—Matt. 16:24, 25.

For this is thankworthy, if a man for conscience toward God endure grief, suffering wrongfully. For what glory is it, if, when ye be buffeted for your faults, ye shall take it patiently? but if, when ye do well, and suffer for it, ye take it patiently, this is acceptable with God. For even hereunto were ye called: because Christ also suffered for us, leaving us an example, that ye should follow his steps: who did no sin, neither was guile found in his mouth: who, when he was reviled, reviled not again; when he suffered, he threatened not; but committed himself to him that judgeth righteously: who his own self bare our sins in his own body on the tree, that we, being dead to sins, should live unto righteousness: by whose stripes ye were healed. —I Pet. 2:19-24.

Let this mind be in you, which was also in Christ Jesus: who, being in the form of God, thought it not robbery to be equal with God: but made himself of no reputation, and took upon him the form of a servant, and was made in the likeness of men: and being found in fashion as a man, he humbled himself, and became obedient unto death, even the death of the cross.—Phil. 2:5-8.

I am crucified with Christ: nevertheless I live; yet not I, but Christ liveth in me: and the life which I now live in the flesh I live by the faith of the Son of God, who loved me, and gave himself for me. —Gal. 2:20.

Be ye followers of me, even as I also am of Christ.—I Cor. 11:1.

The Spirit of Forgiveness

Moreover if thy brother shall trespass against thee, go and tell him his faults between thee and him alone: if he shall hear thee, thou hast gained thy brother.—Matt. 18:15.

Then came Peter to him, and said, Lord, how oft shall my brother sin against me, and I forgive him? till seven times? Jesus saith unto him, I say not unto thee, Until seven times: but, Until seventy times seven.—Matt. 18:21, 22.

And when ye stand praying, forgive, if ye have ought against any: that your Father also which is in heaven may forgive you your trespasses.—Mark 11:25.

And be ye kind one to another, tenderhearted, forgiving one another, even as God for Christ's sake hath forgiven you.—Eph. 4:32.

And they stoned Stephen, calling upon God, and saying, Lord Jesus, receive my spirit. And he kneeled down, and cried with a loud voice, Lord, lay not this sin to their charge. And when he had said this, he fell asleep.—Acts 7:59, 60.

A Suffering Church

Blessed are they which are persecuted for righteousness' sake: for theirs is the kingdom of heaven. Blessed are ye, when men shall revile you, and persecute you, and shall say all manner of evil against you falsely, for my sake. Rejoice, and be exceeding glad: for great is your reward in heaven: for so persecuted they the prophets which were before you.—Matt. 5:10-12.

Behold, I send you forth as sheep in the midst of wolves: be ye therefore wise as serpents, and harmless as doves. . . . And ye shall be hated of all men for my name's sake: but he that endureth to the end shall be saved. But when they persecute you in this city, flee ye into another: for verily I say unto you, Ye shall not have gone over the cities of Israel, till the Son of Man be come. . . . And fear not them which kill the body, but are not able to kill the soul: but rather fear him which is able to destroy both soul and body in hell.—Matt. 10:16, 22, 23, 28.

And who is he that will harm you, if ye be followers of that which is good? But and if ye suffer for righteousness' sake, happy are ye: and be not afraid of their terror, neither be troubled; but sanctify the Lord God in your hearts: and be ready always to give an answer to every man that asketh you a reason of the hope that is in you with meekness and fear: having a good conscience; that, whereas they speak evil of you, as of evildoers, they may be ashamed that falsely accuse your good conversation in Christ. For it is better, if the will of God be so, that ye suffer for well doing, than for evil doing. For Christ also hath once suffered for sins, the just for the unjust, that he might bring us to God, being put to death in the flesh, but quickened by the Spirit.—I Pet. 3:13-18.

Doing, Not Demanding, Justice

He hath shewed thee, O man, what is good; and what doth the Lord require of thee, but to do justly, and to love mercy, and to walk humbly with thy God?—Mic. 6:8.

Blessed are the merciful: for they shall obtain mercy.—Matt. 5:7.

Masters give unto your servants that which is just and equal; knowing that ye also have a Master in heaven.—Col. 4:1.

Now therefore there is utterly a fault among you, because ye go to law one with another. Why do ye not rather take wrong? why do ye not rather suffer yourselves to be defrauded?—I Cor. 6:7.

Servants, be obedient to them that are your masters according to the flesh, with fear and trembling, in singleness of your heart, as unto Christ; not with eyeservice, as menpleasers; but as the servants of Christ, doing the will of God from the heart; with good will doing service, as to the Lord, and not to men: knowing that whatsoever good thing any man doeth, the same shall he receive of the Lord, whether he be bond or free. And, ye masters, do the same things unto them, forbearing threatening: knowing that your Master also is in heaven; neither is there respect of persons with him.—Eph. 6:5-9.

I beseech thee for my son Onesimus, whom I have begotten in my bonds . . . not now as a servant, but above a servant, a brother beloved, specially to me, but how much more unto thee, both in the flesh, and in the Lord? If thou count me therefore a partner, receive him as myself.—Philem. 10, 16, 17.

Christians the Salt of the Earth

Ye are the salt of the earth: but if the salt have lost his savour, wherewith shall it be salted? It is thenceforth good for nothing, but to be cast out, and to be trodden under foot of men. Ye are the light of the world. A city that is set on a hill cannot be hid. Neither do men light a candle, and put it under a bushel, but on a candlestick; and it giveth light unto all that are in the house. Let your light so shine before men, that they may see your good works, and glorify your Father which is in heaven.—Matt. 5:13-16.

Do all things without murmurings and disputings: that ye may be blameless and harmless, the sons of God, without rebuke, in the midst of a crooked and perverse nation, among whom ye shine as lights in the world.—Phil. 2:14. 15.

The Christian Attitude Toward Rulers

Then saith he unto them, Render therefore unto Caesar the things which are Caesar's; and unto God the things that are God's—Matt. 22:21.

Let every soul be subject unto the higher powers. For there is no power but of God: the powers that be are ordained of God. Whosoever therefore resisteth the power, resisteth the ordinance of God: and they that resist shall receive to themselves damnation. . . . Wherefore ye must needs be subject, not only for wrath, but also for conscience sake. For this cause pay ye tribute also: for they are God's ministers, attending continually upon this very thing. Render therefore to all their dues: tribute to whom tribute is due; custom to whom custom; fear to whom fear; honour to whom honour.—Rom. 13:1, 2, 5-7.

Submit yourselves to every ordinance of man for the Lord's sake: whether it be to the king, as supreme; or unto governors, as unto them that are sent by him for the punishment of evil doers, and for the praise of them that do well. For so is the will of God, that with well doing ye may put to silence the ignorance of foolish men: as free, and not using your liberty for a cloke of maliciousness, but as the servants of God.—I Pet. 2:13-16.

I exhort therefore, that, first of all, supplications, prayers, intercessions, and giving of thanks, be made for all men; for kings, and for all that are in authority; that we may lead a quiet and peaceable life in all godliness and honesty.—I Tim. 2:1, 2.

But Peter and John answered and said unto them, Whether it be right in the sight of God to hearken unto you more than unto God, judge ye. For we cannot but speak the things which we have seen and heard.—Acts 4:19, 20.

Then Peter and the other apostles answered and said, We ought to obey God rather than men.—Acts 5:29.

The Way of Peace

Glory to God in the highest, and on earth peace, good will toward men.—Luke 2:14.

Blessed are the peacemakers: for they shall be called the children of God.—Matt. 5:9.

Depart from evil, and do good; seek peace, and pursue it.—Ps. 34:14.

Peace I leave with you, my peace I give unto you: not as the world giveth, give I unto you. Let not your heart be troubled, neither let it be afraid.—John 14: 27.

And the fruit of righteousness is sown in peace of them that make peace.—Jas. 3:18.

How beautiful are the feet of them that preach the gospel of peace, and bring glad tidings of good things!—Rom. 10:15.

Stand therefore, having your loins girt about with truth, and having on the breastplate of righteousness; and your feet shod with the preparation of the gospel of peace.—Eph. 6:14, 15.

I therefore, the prisoner of the Lord, beseech you that ye walk worthy of the vocation wherewith ye are called, and with all lowliness and meekness, with longsuffering, forbearing one another in love; endeavoring to keep the unity of the Spirit in the bond of peace.—Eph. 4:1-3.

Let us therefore follow after the things which make for peace, and things wherewith one may edify another.—Rom. 14:19.

Follow peace with all men, and holiness, without which no man shall see the Lord.—Heb. 12:14.

And the God of peace shall bruise Satan under your feet shortly. The grace of our Lord Jesus Christ be with you. Amen.—Rom. 16:20.

Finally, brethren, farewell. Be perfect, be of good comfort, be of one mind, live in peace; and the God of love and peace shall be with you.—II Cor. 13:11.

And the peace of God, which passeth all understanding, shall keep your hearts and minds through Christ Jesus.—Phil. 4:7.

Now the God of peace be with you all. Amen.—Rom. 15:33.

SOME DIFFICULT SCRIPTURES

It is a sound procedure in Biblical interpretation first to discover the norm which the Bible itself sets up, and then to interpret all Scriptures in the light of that norm. It is an easy task to compile a list of Scriptures from the Old Testament which seem to indicate a divine approval of war. There are even a few New Testament passages which, superficially considered, would lend themselves to this view. If these Scriptures are adopted as the norm, and the remainder of the Bible interpreted in the light of that norm, the conclusion will be a convincing case for war. If, on the other hand, the Ten Commandments are recognized as God's fundamental moral law; if the life and teachings of Jesus are taken as the authoritative interpretation and fulfillment of that law; and if these together are taken as the norm for the interpretation of all Scripture on the question of war, peace, and nonresistance, the conclusions reached will be quite different. It is the writer's belief that this is the norm which the Bible itself sets up, and it is this line of interpretation which he has followed.

In Chapters II and III the writer did not base his case for nonresistance on a few isolated passages of Scripture. He began with the premise that the command of love, and the words, "Thou shalt not kill," are part and parcel of God's fundamental moral law; and that the life and teachings of Christ are an authoritative endorsement, interpretation, and fulfillment of that command. He has assumed that the lower standards of the Mosaic civil code represent a temporary concession on the part of God to the lowered moral state and to the spiritual immaturity of the people of that time, a concession which ended with the full revelation of the truth and power of God in Christ. He has also assumed that all Scripture texts to which there is no satisfactory answer must be judged by the New Testament as a whole, and by the norm suggested above, and not vice versa. In Chapters II and III it was not possible to include comments on every difficult passage bearing on the subject of war, peace, and nonresistance; particularly not passages which would have involved a discussion of matters irrelevant to the purpose of those chapters. For this reason certain difficult Scriptures are presented here with comments. Even this is not a complete list, but an effort has been made to include those Scriptures most frequently quoted in support of war.

GOD IS THE AUTHOR OF GOVERNMENT AND REQUIRES OBEDIENCE TO IT. *Thou, O king, art a king of kings: for the God of heaven hath given thee a kingdom, power, and strength, and glory.*[1] *Let every soul be subject unto the higher powers. For there is no power but of God; the powers that be are ordained of God.*[2] *Submit yourselves to every ordinance of man for the Lord's sake: whether it be to the king, as supreme; or unto governors, as unto them that are sent by him for the punishment of evildoers, and for the praise of them that do well.*[3] Advocates of war frequently cite Scriptures such as these as evidence that rulers of state are appointed of God to carry out His program. Warfare is part of this program, they say, hence Christians should support it. One writer quotes Romans 13:5, "Ye must needs be subject, not only for wrath, but also for conscience sake," and then says, "There goes your conscientious objection." On the very same page, however, this writer admits that there are times when the Christian must disobey human governments. "There may come times when there will be a clash between state and church. When such a clash comes, in the words of the apostles, 'we *must* obey God rather than men.' "[4]

Writers from this point of view, therefore, do not mean to say that the government must be obeyed in all things. They recognize that there is a higher power, and that when the two are in conflict it is God that must be obeyed, and not the state. Their mistake consists in believing that warfare and the use of force are a part of God's program for Christian people. They forget, as pointed out in Chapter III, that rulers are ministers of God only in the sense that God's law of cause and effect requires evil men to suffer the consequence of their own evil. The state, under the direction of God, is merely an instrument of sinful society for the checking of its own evil. And frequently it uses one evil to check another. This is only natural because the society itself is evil. But the Christian can have no part in any of the evils of the evil society. Paul says, "Avenge not yourselves, beloved, . . . Vengeance belongeth unto me; I will recompense, saith the Lord."[5]

CHRISTIANS ARE COMMANDED TO GIVE TO CAESAR THAT WHICH BELONGS TO HIM. *And Jesus said unto them, Render unto Caesar the things that are Caesar's, and unto God the things that are God's.*[6] *He that resisteth the power, withstandeth the ordinance of God.*[7] *Render to all their dues: tribute to whom tribute is due; custom to whom custom; fear to whom fear; honor to whom honor.*[8] It dare not be assumed that whatever the state demands belongs to it. The

---

[1] Dan. 2:37.
[2] Rom. 13:1.
[3] I Pet. 2:13, 14.
[4] R. L. Moyer, *The Christian and War* (St. Paul, 1942), 17.
[5] Rom. 12:19 (ASV).
[6] Mark 12:17 (ASV).
[7] Rom. 13:2 (ASV).
[8] Rom. 13:7 (ASV).

important part of Jesus' statement in Mark 12:17 is that we should render to God what belongs to Him. To discover what this is we must go to the Word of God, not to the law books of the state. And God's Word clearly teaches that Christians can have no part in warfare and the taking of vengeance. It should also be remembered that the commands to pay tribute to Caesar, and not to resist him, are commands to be nonresistant. Jesus and Paul lived in a time when Palestine was under the rule of a foreign Caesar. Many of the Jews were anxious to rebel against this foreign ruler, and would have been ready to stop paying taxes to him at once. No doubt some of the Christians also were tempted to oppose the foreign rule. But Jesus and Paul say: Be in subjection to Caesar. Do not take part in a rebellion. To do so would be a violation of the principle of nonresistance. The nonresistant Christian must submit to the authority of the state so long as it does not require him to disobey God. And even when the Christian must disobey he must do so in humility, and not in the spirit of rebellion. Nonresistance and political revolution do not go together.

BEATING PLOWSHARES INTO SWORDS. *Proclaim ye this among the nations; prepare war; stir up the mighty men; let all the men of war draw near, let them come up. Beat your plowshares into swords, and your pruning-hooks into spears.*[9] These words were spoken to the wicked heathen nations of Joel's time and not to God's people. As pointed out in Chapter II, in the days of the prophets God's people are no longer commanded to go to war. For Israel this was a time of purification and cleansing, of repentance from sin. Israel was commanded not to form military alliances, not to trust in horses and chariots. True, Israel's oppressor nations would be destroyed, but not by the sword of God's people. God in His own way would perform it.[10] Israel was commanded to beat her swords into plowshares, not her plowshares into swords.

The words of Joel quoted above, however, are spoken to the wicked heathen nations whom God was about to judge. Since the nations had been mocking God, He seems to challenge them to come now and do their worst. A summary of the passage from Joel 3:9-13 might be put in words something like this: Come, you wicked nations who would fight against me and destroy my people; melt down your plowshares to make weapons and come out into the field of battle against me if you dare; let all the forces of evil join in a confederation against me, and I will judge them. The idea is similar to that in Isaiah where God dares the wicked nations to take counsel against Him, for they will not succeed. "Gird yourselves, and be

[9] Joel 3:9, 10 (ASV).
[10] Isa. 30 and 31.

broken in pieces. Take counsel together, and it shall be brought to nought; speak the word, and it shall not stand."[11]

SOLDIERS IN THE NEW TESTAMENT. *And the soldiers likewise demanded of him, saying, And what shall we do? And he said unto them, Do violence to no man, neither accuse any falsely; and be content with your wages.*[12] *And . . . there came unto him a centurion, beseeching him. . . . When Jesus heard it, he marvelled, and said to them that followed, Verily I say unto you, I have not found so great faith, no, not in Israel.*[13] The first reference occurs in connection with the preaching of John the Baptist. Among those who were moved by his stirring messages were some soldiers who wanted to know what was required of them. Since John said nothing against the soldiers' profession, simply telling them to do no violence and to be satisfied with their wages, it is held by some that he approved of military service for his followers. Likewise, since Jesus marveled at the faith of the centurion it is assumed by some that He endorsed the soldiers' profession. In addition to these two accounts we have the story of the converstion of Cornelius, also a centurion, in Acts 10, and of the Philippian jailer in Acts 16. All of these instances, it is held, constitute an endorsement of the military profession.

In answer to this argument it can be said that Cornelius and the Philippian jailer are the only two cases of soldiers in the New Testament who were actually baptized; and the New Testament says nothing about the subsequent career of these men. Did they continue as soldiers after their conversion? The Bible does not say. We do know, however, that the early church for several centuries was nonresistant. See the discussion on this point in Chapter IV.

In the case of the centurion who came to Jesus for the healing of his servant we are only told that Jesus marveled at the man's faith. There was no occasion for Jesus to say anything about the man's military profession. Jesus seems to be comparing the centurion's faith with that of the Jews, some of whom refused to believe, "I have not found so great faith, no, not in Israel." What the subsequent history of this man was, we do not know; the account does not even say that he became a disciple. The statement of John the Baptist seems to give least help of all to the militarist. When he told the soldiers to "do violence to no man" he would seem to have made it impossible for them to continue as soldiers. How can a soldier engage in his business of war without doing violence? Violence and the military profession definitely belong together. It might be added here, by way of illustration, that when Paul wrote to Philemon con-

11 Isa. 8:9, 10 (ASV).
12 Luke 3:14.
13 Matt. 8:5-10.

cerning Onesimus he did not forbid Philemon, in so many words, to own a slave. But if the brotherly relations commended by Paul were carried out, one cannot see how Philemon could long have kept his slave in subjection. In somewhat the same manner, it seems, John the Baptist spoke words to the soldiers which should soon have brought an end to their profession.

DOES JESUS APPROVE THE USE OF THE SWORD? *Think not that I am come to send peace on earth: I came not to send peace, but a sword.*[14] This Scripture has been cited as evidence that Jesus approved the use of the sword. The context of the passage, however, shows clearly that here Jesus was not outlining principles or commanding a course of action for His disciples. He was rather warning them of trials and tribulations which they would suffer because of their faith. They would be persecuted. In some cases Christians would even find members of their own families turning againt them. In such cases His coming would mean not peace in the family, but the opposite. Here Jesus is not speaking of the purpose of His coming, but of its immediate effect in some cases. His purpoe is to bring peace to the hearts of men, but the very effect of this is sometimes to intensify opposition and persecution by the enemies of Christ. Christians who are true to their Master may sometimes suffer from the sword of persecution.

But now . . . he that hath no sword, let him sell his garment, and buy one. . . . And they said, Lord, behold, here are two swords. And he said unto them, it is enough.[15] *Then saith Jesus unto him, Put up again thy sword into its place: for all they that take the sword shall perish with the sword.*[16] Scholars seem to agree that the first of these two Scriptures is one of the most difficult passages to understand with reference to the subject at hand. Writers who oppose the nonresistant view would say that Jesus definitely commanded His disciples to equip themselves with swords in preparation for the work which was now ahead of them. Even the second of these passages has been interpreted as condoning the sword. Some writers say that when Jesus instructed Peter to put his sword into its place He was simply saying that the time for using the sword was not now. That is, Jesus was not forbidding the use of the sword, but rather its abuse. It has also been suggested that the words, "they that take the sword shall perish with the sword," were directed not at the disciples, but at their enemies. That is, if the enemies of Christ use the sword they shall be made to perish by the sword of the disciples. These interpretations seem so much out of harmony with the message of

14 Matt. 10:34.
15 Luke 22:36-38.
16 Matt. 26:52 (ASV).

Jesus, however, and with His entire manner of life, as to make them quite unsatisfactory. The interpretation suggested for the second passage, moreover, seems to do violence to the text itself, for it seems clear that here Jesus was speaking to Peter and the disciples, and not to their enemies.

In order to understand these passages it is important to remember that both of them were spoken by Jesus the night before His trial and crucifixion. The first was spoken after the institution of the Lord's Supper, while Jesus was on the way to Gethsemane. The second was spoken immediately after Christ's agony in the garden, as the multitude with swords and staves, led by Judas the traitor, came to arrest Him. It was at that moment that Peter drew a sword to defend his Lord and struck off the ear of the high priest's servant. This act brought forth the words of Jesus to Peter, "Put up again thy sword into its place; for all they that take the sword shall perish with the sword." Both of these sword incidents seem to relate themselves to the failure of the disciples to understand the mission of Jesus, even at this late hour. For some time He had been telling them of His coming suffering and death, but it seemed very difficult for them to comprehend what He was saying. Not only were the disciples thinking in terms of an earthly kingdom, but they were even contending among themselves as to the place in this kingdom which each should occupy. Then when it was rumored that Christ's enemies were plotting to kill Him, they remembered what He had told them about His death. It was natural that they should desire to protect Him, and in that crucial hour they seem to have forgotten the nonresistant teaching which He had given them. So Peter at least, and perhaps another disciple, equipped themselves with hidden swords. At least there were two swords, and Peter had one of them.

No doubt Jesus knew all about this, and perhaps it is one thing He had in mind when He told Peter that Satan was about to sift him as wheat. To this warning Peter replied that he was ready "to go both to prison and to death" with the Lord. But from what happened later it seems that Peter was at least planning to use some other methods first before going to prison or death. The words of Jesus about buying a sword follow immediately after this incident, and seem to be a rebuke to Peter's lack of faith. On a former occasion Jesus had sent the disciples on a missionary tour and they had fared very well, even though going without purse, wallet, or shoes. So Jesus asks: "When I sent you forth without purse, and wallet, and shoes, lacked ye anything?" The disciples had to admit that they had lacked nothing even when going without this elementary equipment; so Jesus seems to speak ironically as if to say: Well then, since you know by experience that you can get along without these things be sure to equip yourselves with purse, wallet, *and a sword!* This may have been Jesus' way of telling Peter that He knew about his hidden sword. Then when the disciples admitted that there were two swords in the company Jesus said: "It is enough." This seems to be an expression of despair. Perhaps the meaning is something like this: If you have no more faith than this, what more can I say? At any rate, from Jesus' life and teaching it is impossible to believe that He approved the carrying of swords, or that He meant to say that two swords were enough to save Him from the crowd that was coming to arrest Him. When the crowd did come, and Peter used the sword, Jesus promptly healed the ear of the high priest's servant and commanded Peter to put up the sword into its place. The most reasonable explanation of this saying is that Jesus disapproved the use of the sword, and desired Peter to put it away. If he continued to use the sword Peter himself would perish by the sword. Weapons of defense do not belong in the hands of the disciple of Christ.

JESUS PREDICTS FUTURE WARS. *And ye shall hear of wars and rumors of wars; see that ye be not troubled: for these things must needs come to pass; but the end is not yet. For nation shall rise against nation, and kingdom against kingdom; and there shall be famines and earthquakes in divers places.*[17] This passage is sometimes cited to show the futility of the nonresistant position. If Jesus Himself predicted future wars, why should Christian people refuse to take part in them? This argument is hardly important enough, however, to require a lengthy answer. Here Jesus was simply giving a picture of future events, and He surely did not expect His disciples to take part in everything which would occur in the future. In the same passage Jesus predicts future famines, and no one would argue from this that Christians should assist in the promotion of famine. At one place Paul also predicts that "evil men and seducers shall wax worse and worse,"[18] but no one would argue from this that Christians should be party to the evil and the seduction which is to come.

JESUS CLEANSING THE TEMPLE. *And he made a scourge of cords, and cast out of the temple, both the sheep and the oxen; and he poured out the changers' money, and overthrew their tables; and to them that sold the doves he said, Take these things hence; make not my Father's house a house of merchandise.*[19] John is the only one of the Gospel writers who mentions the scourge in this scene, and he does not say that Jesus actually used it. Even if it is granted that He did use it, a careful reading of the text makes it clear that He used it

[17] Matt. 24:6, 7 (ASV).
[18] II Tim. 3:13.
[19] John 2:15, 16 (ASV).

only on the sheep and oxen and not on the men. The American Standard Version quoted above is a more faithful translation of the original Greek than is the authorized version. It says, "And he made a scourge of cords and cast all out of the temple, both the sheep and the oxen." Then John adds that Jesus "poured out the changers' money, and overthrew their tables." Then after this Jesus spoke to the men and said to them, "Take these things hence."

It is impossible to believe that Jesus made physical use of a whip to drive the money-changers out of the temple. In the first place, such action would have been entirely out of harmony with His manner of life. In the second place, He could not have used force on these men without provoking retaliation. The large number of money-changers could have put an immediate stop to the physical efforts of one opponent, and if they had not done so the temple police would have arrested the disturber of the peace. The most satisfactory explanation of this account is that the authority of Jesus' words, and of His looks, were such as to make the offenders wilt in His presence. It was said of Jesus that "never man spake like this man." This must have been one of those occasions. When He walked into the temple and saw what was taking place, His righteous indignation rose within Him, and the manner of His look and the sound of His voice were such that the profaners of the temple could do nothing but fold up and walk out. At most, the physical whip was used only on the animals. Perhaps a better explanation would be that Jesus used the whip simply as an outward symbol of His authority.

JESUS AS A JUDGE. *But whoso shall offend one of these little ones which believe in me, it were better for him that a millstone were hanged about his neck, and that he were drowned in the depth of the sea.*[20] *But those mine enemies, which would not that I should reign over them, bring hither, and slay them before me.*[21] *And out of his mouth goeth a sharp sword, that with it he should smite the nations: and he shall rule them with a rod of iron: and he treadeth the winepress of the fierceness and wrath of Almighty God.*[22] These and other passages of a similar nature are sometimes cited as evidence that Jesus is not nonresistant, either in His teaching or in His practice. A careful reading of these passages, however, shows that all of them refer to God's judgment upon sin; and as shown in Chapters II and III there is no conflict between the doctrine of nonresistance and the judgment of God. While Jesus was on earth He hanged no millstones about the necks of sinners, He slew no enemies, He used

[20] Matt. 18:6.
[21] Luke 19:27.
[22] Rev. 19:15.

no sword; and He likewise forbade His followers to use any of these methods. While on earth it was Christ's mission to seek and to save the lost, and to demonstrate the manner of life which His disciples must live. In the judgment, however, He will act as judge and mete out punishment where it is due. But this vengeance belongs to God alone and Christian people do not share in it. "Avenge not yourselves, beloved, . . . Vengeance belongeth unto me; I will recompense, saith the Lord."[23]

PARABOLIC SAYINGS WITH MILITARY ILLUSTRATIONS. *When a strong man armed keepeth his palace, his goods are in peace.*[24] *Or what king, going to make war against another king, sitteth not down first, and consulteth whether he be able with ten thousand to meet him that cometh against him with twenty thousand?*[25] A parable is a story or illustration intended to bring out some point which the speaker wishes to make. The only safe rule for interpreting the parables of Jesus is to discover the point He wishes to make, and to remember that the details of the story have value only as they illustrate this point. In the first saying above Jesus is explaining by what power He cast a demon out of a man. His critics said He did it by the power of Satan. But Jesus explains that it was Satan who formerly had possession of the man. Satan is strong; he rules in his palace, the world; and he had peaceful possession of this poor man, his goods. The following verse then says: "When a stronger than he shall come upon him, and overcome him, he taketh from him all his armour wherein he trusted, and divideth his spoils." By this verse Jesus means to say that He by the power of God is stronger than Satan, and that He has taken Satan's goods, the sick man, away from him. The use of military figures here is wholly for the purpose of illustration, and the passage has nothing to say at all about war, or peace, or nonresistance. Moreover, if it did have such reference, the passage would not argue very strongly for military preparedness, since the armed man kept his goods only until a stronger man came and took them away. In the second passage quoted above Jesus is teaching the need of counting the cost involved in becoming a disciple. A wise man before beginning to build a house counts his money to see if there is enough to build. And a man going to war counts his soldiers to see if there are enough to meet the enemy. Again, reference to an army is purely for the purpose of illustration, and has nothing to do with the question of war, peace, and nonresistance. If it did, one could argue just as logically that Paul con-

---

23 Rom. 12:19 (ASV).
24 Luke 11:21.
25 Luke 14:31.

dones stealing because he says, "The day of the Lord so cometh as a thief in the night."[26]

MILITARY SYMBOLISM IN THE SCRIPTURES. *Put on the whole armour of God.*[27] *This charge I commit unto thee . . . that thou . . . mightest war a good warfare.*[28] *Thou therefore endure hardness, as a good soldier of Jesus Christ.*[29] From passages such as these it is argued that Paul approves of warfare. If not, why does he make so much use of military language? One writer says: "The pacifists would need to perform a major operation on both the Old and the New Testament in order to delete such passages. . . . It is hardly conceivable that the Scripture should present the Christian life under a symbolism having to do so distinctly with soldiering and warfare and at the same time repudiate the reality for which it stands as always and everywhere wrong."[30]

It may be that some types of pacifists would be interested in deleting these passages from the Scripture, but if this writer means to ascribe such views to the Biblical nonresistants he misunderstands them completely. Nonresistant Christians are quite ready to accept the symbolical language of Scripture with the interpretation which the Bible itself gives it. The symbolism is justifiable because in the Christian life there is a warfare between good and evil, just as in the evil society there is warfare among evil forces. But the nature of the Christian warfare and the methods it uses are altogether different from the warfare of this world. In the Christian warfare, disciples of Christ *overcome evil with good.* When Paul admonishes Christians to "put on the whole armour of God," in the verse quoted above, he follows it immediately with the statement: *For we wrestle not against flesh and blood, but against principalities, against powers, against the rulers of the darkness of this world, against spiritual wickedness in high places.*[31] Paul speaks of a holy warfare, a spiritual warfare, which has nothing in common with the warfare waged by the nations of the world. In another place he says, We do not war after the *flesh . . . the weapons of our warfare are not carnal.*[32] He also mentions specific spiritual weapons, as *the helmet of salvation, and the sword of the spirit.*[33] Elsewhere he says the fruit of the Spirit includes love, peace, kindness, and meekness, whereas the works of the flesh include enmities, strife, wraths, and factions. The Christian

---

[26] I Thess. 5:2.
[27] Eph. 6:11.
[28] I Tim. 1:18.
[29] II Tim. 2:3.
[30] L. Boettner, *The Christian Attitude Toward War* (Grand Rapids, Mich., 1940), 45.
[31] Eph. 6:12.
[32] II Cor. 10:3, 4.
[33] Eph. 6:17.

warfare as described in the New Testament is of such a nature that one cannot use it as an argument for the military warfare of nations without doing great violence to the Scriptures. As suggested before, it would be just as logical to argue that the Bible approves burglary, because it says the Son of Man will come as a thief in the night.

OPPOSING EVIL. *Resist the devil, and he will flee from you.*[34] This passage, and others like it, carry a meaning similiar to that of the spiritual warfare described above. The devil is an evil spirit and Christians are to resist his influence and his temptations with spiritual weapons. This is the only way the devil can be resisted. He cannot be resisted with physical weapons because he is not a physical being. At the same time, however, that Christians are commanded to resist the devil they are also commanded *not to resist "him that is evil."*[35] Here Jesus is speaking of evil men in this world, and with them Christians are to deal by nonresistant methods altogether.

WAR A SACRIFICIAL SERVICE. *Greater love hath no man than this, that a man lay down his life for his friends.*[36] Writers who oppose nonresistance cite the above Scripture and say that the soldier who sacrifices his life on the field of battle is manifesting the greatest possible love. During the World War army chaplains even went so far as to tell the soldiers that if they died in battle they would be making a sacrifice similar to that of Christ on the cross. This is blasphemy. Furthermore, to justify warfare by the above Scripture is to violate its meaning completely. Jesus commends laying down one's life for his friends but He does not approve killing one's enemies while he is doing so. The soldier's first aim is to kill the enemy, not to lay down his own life. The nonresistant Christian is ready to lay down his life for his friends, *and for his enemies,* but he can never take the life of another.

[34] Jas. 4:7.
[35] Matt. 5:39 (ASV).
[36] John 15:13.

APPENDIX 3

SOME PRACTICAL QUESTIONS

1. *What Would You Do If a Villain Attacked Your Wife and Children? Would Christian Duty Require One to Be Nonresistant in Such a Situation?*

Questions such as these are supposed to destroy the foundations of the nonresistant position. Nonresistant Christians are frequently confronted with them, and army officers made constant use of them in testing conscientious objectors in the army camps during the first World War. That it would be inhuman and unchristian not to defend an innocent victim of murder or rape, especially a member of one's own family, is supposedly an unanswerable argument.

One weakness of such questions is that they are usually hypothetical in character, the questioner having no actual case in mind as an illustration. It is also generally assumed that nonresistance means doing nothing, which is not at all the case. The Scriptures do not command the Christian to do nothing about evil, but rather to "overcome evil with good"; and the critic has seldom thought through the possibilities of meeting, *with good,* situations such as that described above. The *Atlantic Monthly* for May, 1923, has an article entitled "The Test of Faith," written by Edward Richards, a Christian who put the hypothetical situation described above to an actual test while engaged in relief work in 1918 among the Turks and Kurds in West Persia. Mr. Richards recognized that he could not guarantee his nonresistant way of life to prevent anyone from meeting death. But he was convinced that if he acted in the spirit of love he would "be using the most effective means to prevent the killing assault from taking place." He was convinced that if he actually followed the way of love as taught by Christ he could "count on the real Divine Power of God Almighty to direct the thoughts, wills, and acts of the Kurds as He desired." Mr. Richards continues: "Also, I could safely leave the situation in His hands. If we were killed or assaulted, in spite of any refusal to fight, I could then count on it thus being God's will for us all to die or to be assaulted, and that our death or injury would be more effective in bringing about the Kingdom of God on earth than any other thing we could possibly do."

Mr. Richards' faith was put to an actual test one day when an army surrounded his town, and a band of Kurds armed with guns entered a house occupied by Richards, a group of women, and a sick man. The Kurds demanded money. Instead of resisting, which would have been useless under any circumstances, Richards invited

308

them in and helped them search the house. When they found a locked money chest, whose owner was away from home with the key, the bandits threatened to shoot Richards unless he produced the key. But his sincere behavior convinced them that he did not have it, and eventually they went away without injuring anyone in the house. On another occasion Mr. Richards met a drunken man running amuck with a gun in hand. The lives of a number of people were in danger and Richards could have taken a gun and shot him. Instead of doing so, however, he approached the drunken man unarmed, and extended the hand of friendship. As a result, the drunk saluted and handed over his gun; and the day following, after sobering up, he returned and apologized for his conduct.

In these two situations as described by Mr. Richards no lives were lost, and in the one case at least, a friend was won. In either case, if Mr. Richards had resisted with force it is certain that someone would have been killed, perhaps Richards himself. No one can guarantee, of course, that in all similar situations the result would be the same as it was in the case of Mr. Richards. But there is no doubt that the method which he used will, in the long run, save the largest number of lives. It can be granted that in some cases a person in Mr. Richards' situation would sacrifice his own life, and that of his friends or his family. But in such a case they could die in peace, knowing that they had acted in accordance with the will of God. The nonresistant Christian must be nonresistant at all times. He cannot take a gun and shoot a criminal. A family of true nonresistant Christians would do what they could to win the criminal by love. But if this method failed to win him they would gladly lay down their own lives together, rather than ask any member of the group to take the life of another.

2. *Is Nonresistance Practical for a Nation? Could We Expect England Not to Resist Hitler's Air Attacks in 1940, or the United States Not to Resist the Attack on Pearl Harbor in 1941?*

Nonresistance is as practical for a Christian nation as it is for the Christian individual. When Israel was obedient to the will of God, He saved them from the enemy without warfare on numerous occasions. It was when Israel departed from the ways of God that they became involved in war. It is just as reasonable to believe that if a nation of Christians sincerely followed the way of nonresistance today God would reward its obedience by saving it from invasion and destruction, as He saved the life of Edward Richards from the hands of the Kurds. But, if such a nation should not be spared, the Christian attitude would be to accept the sacrifice as according to the will of God. Such a sacrifice might, indeed, be the greatest service which a nation could give to the world. For who can doubt that a nation of Christians laying down its national life in martyrdom to the cause of nonresistance would release "a flood of spiritual life"[1] which would have a tremendous influence for good.

The thing to remember about all this, however, is that there is no such thing as a Christian nation. There are only nations with individual Christians in them. Every national society today is sub-Christian, and the foreign policy of none of the nations is Christian. Under such circumstances it is useless to expect England to respond to Hitler's threat of invasion with loving nonresistance, or the United States to "turn the other cheek" when Japan bombs Pearl Harbor. For many years England and the United States have followed unchristian foreign policies which have helped to bring about the present world situation. Their policies may not have been as bad as are those of Germany and Japan, but that is beside the point. The point is they have followed a course which is unchristian, and which relies on war and force to gain its ends. The fruit of such a policy is always war, and to a nation which follows such a course nonresistance is not "practical." Nonresistance can be practical only to Christians who follow the example of Christ.

3. *Should Totalitarian States with Their Anti-Christian Philosophies Be Allowed to Dominate the World? Can Such Domination Be Prevented Without War?*

There is no question that modern totalitarian states constitute a real danger to Christianity and the church. This was true of ancient despotisms as well. However, it has never been God's will that His people should fight even totalitarianism with force. The Hebrew prophets warned Israel against such action, and gave assurance that God in His own way would judge the evil nations and spare the people of God. Today we know that this promise has been fulfilled, for the ancient empires have long since crumbled to dust, while the Christian Church lives on. Christianity was founded in an era of dictators, and the early church was persecuted by Roman Caesars who attempted to destroy it completely. But the church was triumphant in the face of persecution, while the military empire has long since passed away. The nonresistant Anabaptists of the sixteenth century also flourished in spite of untold persecution, and in this way bequeathed their heritage of religious liberty to the modern world. The nonresistant faith has had many enemies in times past, and it has them again today in the form of dictator nations. But Christians can be confident that in the end the enemies of God will be brought to nought. It appears that, as has often occurred in the past, this will be accomplished through the warfare of other nations. But if Great

[1] The expression is that of G. H. C. Macgregor, *The New Testament Basis of Pacifism*, 104.

Britain and the United States are used of God to humble certain dictators by means of force, it is only because Britain and America have also sinned; for, as we have seen in Chapter II, God in His providence has often used one sinful nation to check another. But if nations like Great Britain and the United States were truly Christian, there is no doubt that the church would be saved from the wrath of the dictators by other means. God has commanded His people to follow the way of peace, and if they obey His will they need not fear the outcome.

4. *Is it Not Foolish to Advocate Disarmament as a Policy for the Nations?*

In question 2 it was stated that nonresistance would be practical for a truly Christian nation. The nations of the world are not Christian, however, and as long as they continue to follow unchristian methods we can expect wars to continue. When nations engage in military, political, or economic aggression, they can expect retaliation through similiar methods. For a nation which deliberately lives and moves on this plane, therefore, disarmament is foolish, because its policy and armaments go together. But if a nation should renounce this way of life and adopt the principles of Jesus Christ, disarmament would constitute the highest wisdom. For disarmament and the principles of Christ go hand in hand, even as do armaments and the principles of evil. It is even reasonable to believe that a nation which is only relatively Christian, but which followed a non-aggressive foreign policy, would be safer from invasion in an aggressive world than would an aggressive well-armed nation, unless perhaps the latter were more powerful than any possible combination of powers which might be allied against it.

5. *Are Not the Police and the Military Essentially the Same? If It Is Recognized That the Police Power Is Necessary for Domestic Peace, Does It Not Follow That Armies and Navies Are Necessary for International Peace?*

There is a difference in degree between the police and the military, but as pointed out in Chapters VIII and IX, the two are the same in kind. An army, at least if under a recognized international organization, may be regarded as an international police; and both the domestic and the international police are means for the maintenance of order, through force, in a sub-Christian society. It is for this very reason, however, that the nonresistant Christian cannot consistently serve as a policeman any more than he can serve as a soldier. If a state were genuinely Christian it would not require a domestic police force any more than it would require an international police. But, as pointed out in Chapter VIII, such a state would be so different in character from any state which we know today that it should have another name to describe it. The similarity of the police and the military constitutes an argument for the nonparticipation of the Christian in the police function, not for his participation in the military function.

6. *Granting That War Is Evil, Is It Not Better to Destroy a Greater Evil, Such as a Totalitarian Dictatorship, with War, Than to Allow Totalitarianism to Triumph?*

This argument will hold only for an evil society. It is true that some evils are greater than others. And for a people who move on a sub-Christian plane it is perhaps reasonable that a lesser evil be preferred to a greater one. But the Christian is required to live entirely above this level. For him the end never justifies the means. He must be obedient to Christ in all things, and if he does this, the outcome for himself and for society will be infinitely better than if he compromises with evil in any form.

7. *Does Not Nonresistance Encourage Evil? Is It Not Better to Oppose Sin Than to Do Nothing About It?*

To be nonresistant is not to encourage evil. Nonresistance overcomes evil with good. The drunken man described under question 1 above was overcome with good so that he apologized for his conduct. His soul was touched. Had those whom he opposed resisted him with force they might have put him to death, making it impossible to minister to his soul. The way of love and nonresistance does more for the overcoming of sin than force can ever do. Jesus always used the way of love and nonresistance. In fact, evil begets evil, force begets force, hate begets hate. Evil always encourages and stimulates more evil.

8. *Is Nonresistance Not a Sign of Weakness?*

No. The course followed by Mr. Richards as described in question 1 above required more strength and courage than would have been required to shoot the enemy. It requires more courage to take one's stand as a conscientious objector, against the opposition of the crowd, than it does to follow the crowd and enter military service. It was in the moment of His greatest strength that Christ manifested His most thoroughgoing nonresistance. It was when He laid down His life in loving sacrifice that He fully overcame the world. It is the Christ who meekly submitted to the crucifixion of men who is now the Lord and Judge of all men.

9. *Are All Wars Wrong, or Is the Present One Different?*

It is a common thing for people to condemn wars in general, while approving the one in which they happen to be engaged at the time, on the ground that "this war is different." It is important to observe, however, that from this point of view all wars have been different. In the eleventh and twelfth centuries the Catholic Church frowned upon wars in Europe, but approved those against the Turk in Palestine because they were different. In 1776 the Americans hated the British and fought against them, but in 1917, and again in 1941, they were fighting on the side of England because the situation was different. After the War of 1812 many Americans renounced war altogether, but when the Civil War came in 1861 many of these same people supported it because they thought this would free the slaves, making it a war that was different. In 1917 many people supported the World War because it was "a war to end all wars," and therefore different. As time went on some of these same people decided that the United States had made a mistake by getting into the first World War, but later they supported the second World War with enthusiasm because certain dictators had now appeared on the scene, which made it different. Dictators of the twentieth century, however, are no different in any important way from Nero in the time of the Apostle Paul, or from dictators of other ages. And yet Paul said, in effect: Do not make war against the Roman dictator. For the Christian, all wars are a violation of the will of God.

10. *People Who Do Not Participate in War Are Called Conscientious Objectors. Is Conscience a Safe Guide?*

No, conscience alone is not a safe guide. The content of one's conscience depends greatly on the moral and religious teaching which he has received. The Bible speaks of a good conscience and of a bad conscience. It also speaks of weak, evil, and seared consciences. For this reason it is necessary that the Christian's conscience be guided by the revelation of God as found in the Scriptures. The Christian who follows this guide will not go astray. To follow conscience without this guide may lead him to some forms of pacifism, but not to Biblical nonresistance.

11. *The Soldier Frequently Sacrifices His Life on the Battlefield. Is This Not an Illustration of What Jesus Meant When He Said: "Greater Love Hath No Man Than This, That a Man Lay Down His Life for His Friends"?*

Soldiers frequently do lay down their lives with the motive of serving their fellow men; but it must be remembered that the soldier is primarily engaged in the task of taking the lives of other men, not of laying down his own. Jesus laid down His own life for all mankind, but not while taking the life of others. The true nonresistant Christian is always ready to lay down his own life, if by so doing he can best serve God and men, but he is never willing to take life.

12. *Is It Not True That the Soldier Makes a Much Greater Sacrifice Than the Conscientious Objector Who Goes to a Comparatively Safe Place in a Civilian Public Service Camp? For This Reason Is the Conscientious Objector Not a Slacker?*

It is true that the soldier on the battlefield is in greater danger of losing his life than is the man in a CPS camp. On the other hand, the man on the battlefield is taking the lives of others, which is a sin in the eyes of God. To be a slacker is simply to fail in performing one's duty; and the failure of him who takes the life of another is a failure in man's highest duty toward man. For this reason the term "slacker" does not apply to the nonresistant Christian. Furthermore, true nonresistant Christians are always ready to serve their fellow men in the most dangerous places, in a ministry of love, of healing, and of relief. Finally, it must be remembered that the man who goes to a Civilian Public Service camp is doing his duty under the law.

13. *Are Not Soldiers in Need of the Gospel? Therefore Does Not Army Service, Especially Service as an Army Chaplain, Provide a Fine Opportunity to Testify for Christ?*

It is true that the soldier needs the Gospel as much as any other man, and that the nonresistant Christian should not hesitate to bring it to him if he can do so without himself being part of the military organization. But to be a member of an organization whose task it is to kill would certainly disqualify one to preach the Gospel of love and nonresistance. Saloonkeepers and gamblers need the Gospel, but no one would contend that Christians should therefore become saloonkeepers and gamblers in order to testify for Christ to such men.

14. *Has Not Much Good Come Out of Wars in the Past? Have Not Many of Our Liberties Been Won Through Warfare? Did Not the Defeat of the Mohammedans in Battle in 732 Save Western Europe for Christianity? Does Not Service in Battle at Times Bring Out Qualities of Courage and High Moral Purpose in the Lives of Soldiers?*

There is perhaps nothing in this world so bad that no good thing can be found in it; and no doubt elements of truth are implied in all of the above questions. We can be sure, however, that every evil act can only result in more evil than good, and to this general principle war is no exception. War has helped to win certain liberties; but it has just as often destroyed freedom and set up vicious tyrannies. Furthermore, it should be remembered, as pointed out in Chapter XI, that the modern idea of religious liberty was born in the cradle of nonresistance, and purchased with the blood of non-resistant Christian martyrs; it was not created by warriors and military men. It is true that the Mohammedan advance in western Europe ceased after the battle of Tours; but who can say whether a policy of nonresistance on the part of the Christians would not, in the long run, have been better for western Christendom than the course which was followed. And while the trial of battle may, on occasion, bring out the qualities of courage and moral purpose in the lives of soldiers, it is admitted by all that times of war are always times of great moral decline, so that the few moral gains of warfare are more than offset by the losses.

15. *Is It Not True That Some Conscientious Objectors Are Not Christian; That Some Are Mere Political Objectors Without Genuine Religious Scruples; and That Others Are Religious Liberals or Radicals Who Question the Authority of God's Word and of the Church? In That Case Would It Not Be Better for Christians to Have Nothing to Do with Objection to War?*

Such a policy would be little help to the Christian, because if he went to the army he would certainly find many more non-Christians, and certainly a much lower general level of morality, than among the conscientious objectors. Contrary to the statements of some writers, moreover, the majority of conscientious objectors are evangelical Christians who believe war is wrong because it is contrary to the will of God. The Mennonites alone made up 40 per cent of the men in CPS camps, and many others were Christians of similar beliefs. It is true, however, that conscientious objectors of the Biblical nonresistant faith need to take great care not to compromise this faith with other forms of pacifism, as was stressed in Chapters IX, X and XII.

16. *If an Individual Feels That He Cannot Personally Take a Human Life Ought He Not Accept Noncombatant Service in the Army? Are There Not Many Kinds of Necessary Work in the Army Which Do Not Involve Personal Killing?*

It is true that many assignments in the army do not involve personal killing. But it is also true that actually there is no such thing as noncombatant army service. "Combatant" means fighting, and "noncombatant" means not fighting. An army has only one purpose, and that is to fight. *Therefore everyone in the army is a fighter.* If it is wrong to fight, it is wrong to belong to a fighting organization. If it is wrong to kill, it is wrong to belong to a killing organization. *No one who really believes that war is wrong can be true to his faith and accept so-called noncombatant army service.* It has been argued that service in the medical corps of the army is consistent for a conscientious objector, because this service is designed to save life. This is very poor reasoning, however. If a member of a band of bank robbers were assigned the job of carrying the first-aid kit, while others did the shooting and lifting, the first-aid man would be considered guilty before the law with the entire band. It is membership in the organization that counts, not so much the particular task to which one is assigned. The medical corps of the army is part of a killing organization as much as is the infantry or any other part of the army. It might be added that the higher officers in the army are also noncombatant in the sense that they seldom do any personal killing, yet one would not excuse them of responsibility for the killing under their command.

17. *In Time of War Citizens Are Called upon to Make Contributions in Money or in Services, to the Red Cross and to Other Organizations Closely Allied to the War Effort. What Should Be the Attitude of the Nonresistant Christian Toward These Services and Contributions?*

The following question will serve as a test: Is the service rendered, or the money contributed, intended as an instrument of war? If it is, the nonresistant Christian can have nothing to do with it. In wartime perhaps 80 per cent of the money contributed to the Red Cross goes for war purposes. If the contributor is sure his own contribution will be used for some purpose other than the war effort, he can conscientiously contribute; otherwise he cannot do so. The Mennonite General Conference statement on "Peace, War, and Military Service," includes the following sentence: "Consistency requires that we do not serve during wartime under civil organizations temporarily allied with the military in the prosecution of the war, such as the YMCA, the Red Cross, and similiar organizations which, under military orders, become a part of the war system in effect, if not in method and spirit, however beneficial their peacetime activities may be."

18. *What Program Does the Mennonite Church Have with Respect to Various Services in Wartime?*

The Mennonite Church has a well-organized plan whereby all members of the church can contribute to the welfare of the nation in a way that is consistent with their nonresistant testimony. During World War II CO's performed civilian service under the CPS system. Since the war civilian service is carried on without CPS. The Mennonite Central Committee and the Mennonite Relief Committee are carrying on an extensive voluntary service and foreign relief program. Members of the church can contribute to funds for the support of this program instead of funds of organizations allied with the war effort. Drafted men wishing to do hospital service can find opportunities for such service in non-military hospitals. This was true during the war, and again with the renewal of the draft following the war. The Mennonite program is now so well known that in most communities its services are recognized by non-Mennonites as satisfactory alternatives to the various war activities. This also includes the purchase of civilian bonds instead of war bonds.

19. *If It Is Wrong to Buy War Bonds Is It Right to Pay Taxes, Many of Which Are Used for War Purposes?*

There is a real difference here, because the purchase of bonds is a voluntary loan, specifically for war purposes. Taxes, on the other hand, are an involuntary requirement of the government, and necessary for the performance of the functions of the government, civil as well as military, and including numerous welfare services. The New Testament approves the payment of taxes as a proper recognition of the government in authority. To refuse to pay taxes would be equivalent to revolution, something a nonresistant Christian could not take part in. But war loans are a direct, voluntary contribution to the war program of the nation, a program in which the nonresistant Christian cannot participate.

20. *Obviously It Is Inconsistent for a Nonresistant Christian to Work in a War Production Plant, Making War Materials. But Where Should He Draw the Line in These Matters? Can He Consistently Engage in Farming for the Production of Food in Wartime, Since We Are Also Told That Food Helps to Win the War?*

The safest course is to produce nothing which is war material, or which is designed specifically to contribute to the war effort. Obviously a conscientious objector cannot work in a bomber factory. Neither could one work in a rubber factory, making self-sealing gasoline tanks for army bombers. However, if this factory had a department making rubber footwear for civilian use there would be nothing inconsistent in working in this department. As to food, it should be remembered that the army in wartime uses only a small percentage of the food produced in the United States. Furthermore, the army is fed first and the civilian population gets its share next. Therefore, if nonresistant farmers should refuse to continue the production of food they would actually contribute to a civilian food shortage. Furthermore, food is not war material; its only purpose is to sustain human life. Therefore, if a portion of the food grown by a nonresistant farmer later is used by persons who engage in warfare, the responsibility is with them and not with the farmer. There is therefore no reason why a nonresistant Christian should not grow food in wartime.

21. *What Should Be the Christian's Attitude Toward High Prices and Profits in Wartime?*

The Mennonite General Conference statement of 1937 says: "We ought not to seek a profit out of war and wartime inflation, which would mean profiting from the shedding of blood of our fellow men. If, however, during wartime, excess profits do come into our hands, such profits should be conscientiously devoted to charitable purposes such as the bringing of relief to the needy, or the spreading of the Gospel of peace and love, and should not be applied to our own material benefit."

22. *What Should Be the General Attitude of the Nonresistant Christian in Wartime?*

On this point the Mennonite General Conference statement says: "If our country becomes involved in war, we shall endeavor to continue to live a quiet and peaceable life in all godliness and honesty; avoid joining in the wartime hysteria of hatred, revenge, and retaliation; manifest a meek and submissive spirit, being obedient unto the laws and regulations of the government in all things, except in such cases where obedience to the government would cause us to violate the teachings of the Scriptures so that we could not maintain a clear conscience before God. Acts 5:29."

NONRESISTANCE IN THE DORTRECHT CONFESSION

ADOPTED BY THE MENNONITES AT DORTRECHT, HOLLAND, IN *1632*

ARTICLE XIII

The Office of Civil Government

We also believe and confess, that God has instituted civil government, for the punishment of the wicked and the protection of the pious; and also further, for the purpose of governing the world—governing countries and cities; and also to preserve its subjects in good order and under good regulations. Wherefore we are not permitted to despise, blaspheme, or resist the same; but are to acknowledge it as a minister of God and be subject and obedient to it, in all things that do not militate against the law, will, and commandments of God; yea, "to be ready to every good work"; also faithfully to pay it custom, tax, and tribute; thus giving it what is its due; as Jesus Christ taught, did himself, and commanded his followers to do. That we are also to pray to the Lord earnestly for the government and its welfare, and in behalf of our country, so that we may live under its protection, maintain ourselves and "lead a quiet and peaceable life in all godliness and honesty." And further, that the Lord would recompense them (our rulers), here and in eternity, for all the benefits, liberties, and favors which we enjoy under their laudable administration. Rom. 13:1-7; Titus 3:1, 2; I Pet. 2:17; Matt. 17:27; 22:21; I Tim. 2:1, 2.

ARTICLE XIV

Defense by Force

Regarding revenge, whereby we resist our enemies with the sword, we believe and confess that the Lord Jesus has forbidden his disciples and followers all revenge and resistance, and has thereby commanded them not to "return evil for evil, nor railing for railing"; but to "put up the sword into the sheath," or, as the prophets foretold, "beat them into ploughshares." Matt. 5:39, 44; Rom. 12:14; I Pet. 3:9; Isa. 2:4; Mic. 4:3.

From this we see, that, according to the example, life, and doctrine of Christ, we are not to do wrong, or cause offense or vexation to any one; but to seek the welfare and salvation of all men; also, if necessity should require it, to flee, for the Lord's sake, from one city or country to another, and suffer the "spoiling of our goods," rather than give occasion of offense to any one; and if we are struck on our "right cheek, rather to turn the other also," than revenge ourselves, or return the blow. Matt. 5:39; 10:23; Rom. 12:19.

And that we are, besides this, also to pray for our enemies, comfort and feed them, when they are hungry or thirsty, and thus by well doing convince them and overcome the evil with good. Rom. 12: 20, 21.

Finally, that we are to do good in all respects, "commending ourselves to every man's conscience in the sight of God," and according to the law of Christ, do nothing to others that we would not wish them to do unto us. II Cor. 4:2; Matt. 7:12; Luke 6:31.

PEACE, WAR, AND MILITARY SERVICE

A STATEMENT OF POSITION ADOPTED BY THE MENNONITE
GENERAL CONFERENCE IN 1937

Introduction

In view of the present troubled state of world affairs, with wars and rumors of wars threatening the peace of the world, we, the representatives of the Mennonite Church, assembled in General Conference near Turner, Oregon, on August 25 and 26, 1937, and representing sixteen conferences in the United States and Canada, one in India, and one in Argentina, S.A., do desire to set forth in the following statement our faith and convictions in the matter of peace and nonresistance as opposed to participation in war and military service, earnestly admonishing our membership to order their lives as becometh Christians in accord with these principles.

In doing so we do not establish a new doctrine among us, but rather give fresh expression to the age-old faith of the church which has been held precious by our forefathers from the time that the church was founded in Reformation times in Switzerland (1525) and in Holland (1533), at times even at the cost of despoiling of goods and exile from native land, and in some cases torture and death. On a number of former occasions since our settlement in America we have set forth our nonresistant, peaceful faith in memorials to officers of state, such as the petition of 1775 to the colonial assembly of Pennsylvania, and in addresses to the President of the United States and to the Governor-General of Canada during and after the World War in 1915, 1917, and 1919, and at other times, thus testifying to our rulers and to our fellow citizens of our convictions. Since our position has been fully and authoritatively expressed in our confession of faith, known as "The Eighteen Articles," adopted in Dortrecht, Holland, in 1632 and confirmed at the first Mennonite Conference held in America in Germantown in 1725, reaffirmed in the declaration of the 1917 General Conference at Goshen, Indiana, and in the statement of faith adopted by the General Conference at Garden City, Missouri, in 1921, we do not consider it necessary at this time to set forth our position in detail, but rather merely to affirm in clear and unmistakable terms the main tenets of our peaceful and nonresistant faith as they apply to present conditions.

Our Position on Peace and War

1. Our peace principles are rooted in Christ and His Word, and in His strength alone do we hope to live a life of peace and love toward all men.

2. As followers of Christ the Prince of Peace, we believe His Gospel to be a Gospel of Peace, requiring us as His disciples to be at peace with all men, to live a life of love and good will, even toward our enemies, and to renounce the use of force and violence in all forms as contrary to the spirit of our Master. These principles we derive from such Scripture teachings as: "Love your enemies"; "Do good to them that hate you"; "Resist not evil"; "My kingdom is not of this world: if my kingdom were of this world, then would my servants fight"; "Put up . . . thy sword into its place: for all they that take the sword shall perish with the sword"; "Dearly beloved, avenge not yourselves"; "If thine enemy hunger, feed him; if he thirst, give him drink: for in so doing thou shalt heap coals of fire on his head"; "Be not overcome of evil, but overcome evil with good"; "The servant of the Lord must not strive; but be gentle unto all men"; "The weapons of our warfare are not carnal"; "Christ also suffered for us, leaving us an example, that ye should follow his steps: who did no sin, neither was guile found in his mouth: who, when he was reviled, reviled not again; when he suffered, he threatened not"; "Not rendering evil for evil, or railing for railing: but contrariwise blessing"; "If a man say, I love God, and hateth his brother, he is a liar . . . and this commandment have we from him, That he who loveth God love his brother also"; and other similar passages, as well as from the whole tenor of the Gospel.

3. Peace within the heart as well as toward others is a fruit of the Gospel. Therefore he who professes peace must at all times and in all relations with his fellow men live a life that is in harmony with the Gospel.

4. We believe that war is altogether contrary to the teaching and spirit of Christ and the Gospel, that therefore war is sin, as is all manner of carnal strife; that it is wrong in spirit and method as well as in purpose, and destructive in its results. Therefore, if we profess the principles of peace and nevertheless engage in warfare and strife we as Christians become guilty of sin and fall under the condemnation of Christ, the righteous Judge.

Our Position on Military Service

In the light of the above principles of Scripture we are constrained as followers of Christ to abstain from all forms of military service and all means of support of war, and must consider members who violate these principles as transgressors and out of fellowship with the church. Specifically our position entails the following commitments:

1. We can have no part in carnal warfare or conflict between nations, nor in strife between classes, groups, or individuals. We believe that this means that we cannot bear arms personally nor aid in any way those who do so, and that as a consequence we cannot accept service under the military arm of the government, whether direct or indirect, combatant or noncombatant, which ultimately involves participation in any operation aiding or abetting war and thus causes us to be responsible for the destruction of the life, health, and property of our fellow men.

2. On the same grounds consistency requires that we do not serve during wartime under civil organizations temporarily allied with the military in the prosecution of the war, such as the YMCA, the Red Cross, and similar organizations which under military orders, become a part of the war system in effect, if not in method and spirit, however beneficial their peacetime activities may be.

3. We can have no part in the financing of war operations through the purchase of war bonds in any form or through voluntary contributions to any of the organizations or activities falling under the category described immediately above, unless such contributions are used for civilian relief or similar purposes.

4. We cannot knowingly participate in the manufacture of munitions and weapons of war either in peacetime or in wartime.

5. We can have no part in military training in schools and colleges, or in any other form of peacetime preparation for service as part of the war system.

6. We ought carefully to abstain from any agitation, propaganda, or activity that tends to promote ill will or hatred among nations which leads to war, but rather endeavor to foster good will and respect for all nations, peoples, and races, being careful to observe a spirit of sincere neutrality when cases of war and conflict arise.

7. We ought not to seek to make a profit out of war and wartime inflation, which would mean profiting from the shedding of the blood of our fellow men. If, however, during wartime, excess profits do come into our hands, such profits should be conscientiously devoted to charitable purposes, such as the bringing of relief to the needy, or the spreading of the Gospel of peace and love, and should not be applied to our own material benefit.

Our Willingness to Relieve Distress

According to the teaching and spirit of Christ and the Gospel we are to do good to all men. Hence we are willing at all times to aid in the relief of those who are in need, distress, or suffering, regardless of the danger in which we may be placed in bringing such relief, or of the cost which may be involved in the same. We are ready to render such service in time of war as well as in time of peace.

Our Attitude During Wartime

If our country becomes involved in war, we shall endeavor to continue to live a quiet and peaceable life in all godliness and honesty; avoid joining in the wartime hysteria of hatred, revenge, and retaliation; manifest a meek and submissive spirit, being obedient unto the laws and regulations of the government in all things, except in such cases where obedience to the government would cause us to violate the teachings of the Scriptures so that we could not maintain a clear conscience before God. Acts 5:29. We confess that our supreme allegiance is to God, and that we cannot violate this allegiance by any lesser loyalty, but rather must follow Christ in all things, no matter what it cost. We love and honor our country and desire to work constructively for its highest welfare as loyal and obedient citizens; at the same time we are constrained by the love of Christ to love the people of all lands and races and to do them good as opportunity affords rather than evil, and we believe that this duty is not abrogated by war. We realize that to take this position may mean misunderstanding and even contempt from our fellow men, as well as possible suffering, but we hope by the grace of God that we may be able to assume, as our forefathers did, the sacrifices and suffering which may attend the sincere practice of this way of life, without malice or ill will toward those who may differ with us.

If once again conscription should be established, we venture to express the hope that if service be required of us it may not be under the military arm of the government, and may be such that we can perform it without violating our conscience, and that we may thus be permitted to continue to enjoy that full liberty of religious faith and conscience which has been our privilege hitherto.

Resolution of Appreciation

We desire to express our appreciation for the endeavors of our governments, both in the United States and Canada, to promote peace and good will among nations, and to keep from war. In particular, do we desire to endorse the policy of neutrality and nonparticipation in disputes between other nations. We invoke the blessings of God upon the President of the United States and the Prime Minister of Canada as well as upon the heads of state in the various lands in which our missionaries are serving, in their difficult and arduous duties as chief executives, and pray that their endeavors toward peace may be crowned with success.

We cherish our native lands, the United States of America, and the Dominion of Canada, as homelands to which our forefathers fled for refuge in times of persecution in Europe, and we are deeply grateful for the full freedom of conscience and liberty of worship which has been our happy privilege ever since the days of William Penn and which is vouchsafed to us as well as to all our fellow citizens by the national constitutions and the constitutions of the several states and provinces. We pray that the blessings and guidance of a beneficent God may continue to rest upon our nations, their institutions, and their peoples.

Adopting Resolution

We hereby adopt the above statement as representing our position on peace, war, and military service, and we instruct the Peace Problems Committee to bring this statement to the attention of the proper governmental authorities of the United States and Canada and other lands in which our missionaries are laboring. We would likewise suggest to each of our district conferences that they endorse this statement of position and bring it to the attention of every congregation and of all the members individually, in order that our people may be fully informed of our position and may be strengthened in conviction, that we may all continue in the simple, peaceful, nonresistant faith of the Scripture as handed down to us by our forefathers of former times.

As a matter of practical application, we request our Peace Problems Committee, as representing the church in these problems, to carefully and prayerfully consider the problems which may arise in case our members become involved in conscription, giving particular attention to the proposed legislation on this matter which is now before congress or its committees.

A DECLARATION OF CHRISTIAN FAITH AND COMMITMENT

Adopted at a study conference sponsored by the Peace Section of the Mennonite Central Committee, Winona Lake, Indiana, November 9-12, 1950.

I

At this mid-point of the twentieth century, at a critical time in a generation marked by widespread and disastrous wars and shadowed by the threat of still more ruinous warfare, this conference of delegated representatives from the Mennonite and Brethren in Christ churches of the United States and Canada unites in a renewed declaration of faith in Jesus Christ, the Prince of Peace, in His Gospel, and in His power to redeem and transform in life and in human society all those who receive Him as Saviour and Lord and are thus born anew by the Spirit of God. It also unites in a deeper commitment to follow Christ in full discipleship in the way of peace and love, the way of nonresistance and peacemaking. In this conference we have seen anew the high calling of the sons of God, having been confronted with the absolute claims which Christ makes upon us. We acknowledge these claims in full, and have sought to trace the meaning of His Lordship and the consequences of our commitment in earnest and informed conversation together and in urgent prayer to God for grace and light, seeking to know His will for us in this day.

In our common consideration we have come to certain united convictions expressed in the following declarations which we now humbly send as our message to all our churches both in America and throughout the world as well as to all others who own Christ as Lord. To our brethren we say, this is the day for us to take a clear and unwavering stand on the great essentials of the Gospel and Christian discipleship. It is a day in which to demonstrate and proclaim courageously and unflinchingly this redemptive Gospel and this life of love and service in its fullness and its glory. Let us do so in united purpose with one heart and voice, trusting in the power of God and the companionship of our Lord who has promised to be with us alway.

II

1. *It is our faith* that one is our Master, even Christ, to whom alone supreme loyalty and obedience is due, who is our only Saviour and Lord.

2. *It is our faith* that by the renewing grace of God which makes us new creatures in Christ, and alone thereby, we can through the power of the indwelling Spirit live the life of holy obedience and discipleship to which all the sons of God are called, for His grace does forgive and heal the penitent sinner and brings us to a new life of fellowship with Him and with one another.

3. *It is our faith* that redeeming love is at the heart of the Gospel, coming from God and into us to constrain us to love Him and our neighbor, and that such love must henceforth be at the center of every thought and act.

4. *It is our faith* that Christ has established in His church a universal community and brotherhood within which the fullness of Christ's reign must be practiced, into which the redeemed must be brought, and from which must go out into all human society the saving and healing ministry of the Gospel.

5. *It is our faith* that the life of love and peace is God's plan for the individual and the race, and that therefore discipleship means the abandonment of hatred, strife, and violence in all human relations, both individual and social.

III

These declarations of faith give no blueprint for peace nor do they asume that human endeavor alone can bring about a warless world within history, for only when men come under the Lordship of Christ can they make peace and fulfill the prayer of our Lord, "Thy kingdom come. Thy will be done in earth, as it is in heaven." They do, however, require certain attitudes, duties, and ministries of us, to which we do here by God's grace declare our adherence and our determination to undertake in His name.

1. Our love and ministry must go out to all men regardless of race or condition, within or without the brotherhood, whether friend or foe, and must seek to bring the Gospel and all its benefits to every one. Race or class prejudice must never be found among us.

2. We do recognize fully that God has set the state in its place of power and ministry. But, recognizing the relative and conditional validity of any particular form of government and of concrete legislative, executive, and judicial acts, we hold that we must judge all things in the light of God's Word and see that our responses to the relativities of the state and its workings are always conformed to the absolutes of Christian discipleship and love. We acknowledge our obligation to witness to the powers that be of the righteousness which God requires of all men, even in government, and beyond this to continue in earnest intercession to God on their behalf.

3. We do have the responsibility to bring to the total social order of which we are a part, and from which we receive so much, the utmost of which we are capable in Christian love and service. Seeking for all men first the kingdom of God and His righteousness, we must hold together in one united ministry the evangelism which brings men to Christ and the creative application of the Gospel to cultural, social, and material needs; for we find that the true and ultimate goal of evangelism is the Christianization of the whole of life and the creation of the fully Christian community within the fellowship of faith. For this reason the social order, including our own segment of it, must be constantly brought under the judgment of Christ.

4. We cannot be satisfied to retain for ourselves and our communities alone, in any kind of self-centered and isolated enjoyment, the great spiritual and material goods which God has bestowed upon us, but are bound in loving outreach to all to bear witness and to serve, summoning men everywhere to the life of full discipleship and to the pursuit of peace and love without limit. Separately and together we must use every feasible way and facility for this ministry: the spoken and written word; the demonstration of holiness and love in family, church, and community; relief work and social service; and all other ways. We must enlist many more of our people in such witness and service, both as a major purpose of their life and for specific projects and terms. Especially now must Christian love and redemptive action find expression in our ministry of service, when men are turning more and more to the use of force and war in futile attempts to solve the urgent problems of our world. In this service our youth can play a great part. They should give themselves to it in large numbers, both for shorter terms and in lifetime dedication.

5. Parallel with this we must practice an increasingly sharper Christian control of our economic, social, and cultural practices among ourselves and toward others, to make certain that love truly operates to work no ill to our neighbor, either short-range or long-range. Knowing how much the selfishness, pride, and greed of individuals, groups, and nations, which economic systems often encourage, help to cause carnal strife and warfare, we must see to it that we do not contribute thereto, whether for the goals of direct military operations or to anything which destroys property or causes hurt or loss of human life.

6. While rejecting any social system or ideology such as atheistic communism, which opposes the Gospel and would destroy the true Christian faith and way of life, we cannot take any attitude or commit any act contrary to Christian love against those who hold

or promote such views or practices, but must seek to overcome their evil and win them through the Gospel.

7. We cannot compromise with war in any form. In case of renewed compulsion by the state in any form of conscription of service or labor, money or goods, including industrial plants, we must find ways to serve our countries and the needs of men elsewhere, in ways which will give significant and necessary benefits, which will keep our Christian testimony uncompromised, particularly with respect to war, and which will make possible a faithful representation of Christ and His love. We cannot therefore participate in military service in any form. We cannot have any part in financing war operations or preparations through war bonds. We cannot knowingly participate in the manufacture of munitions, weapons, and instruments of war or destruction. We cannot take part in scientific, educational, or cultural programs designed to contribute to war, or in any propaganda or activity that tends to promote ill will or hatred among men or nations. We must rather foster good will, understanding, and mutual regard and help among all nations, races, and classes. And we cannot as churches lend ourselves to the direct administration of conscription or state compulsion, seeking rather to find voluntary patterns of service through which the demands of the state may be both satisfied and transcended, and going with our men in whatever civilian service they give.

8. If war does come with its possible serious devastation from bombings or other forms of destruction, such as atomic blasts, germ warfare, poison gas, etc., we will willingly render every help which conscience permits, sacrificially and without thought of personal safety, so long as we thereby help to preserve and restore life and not to destroy it.

IV

While we are deeply grateful to God for the precious heritage of faith including the principle of love and nonresistance* which our Swiss, Dutch, and German Anabaptist-Mennonite forefathers purchased for us by their faith, obedience, and sacrifice, and which we believe is again expressed in the above declarations and commitments, we are convinced that this faith must be repossessed personally by each one out of his own reading and obeying of God's Word, and must ever be spelled out in life practice anew. Hence, we summon our brotherhood to a deeper mastery of the Scriptures as the infallible revelation of God's will for us, and to a finding afresh

---

* A faith universally held by the Mennonites of all lands for the first three centuries of our history and continuously confessed by all groups in North America until this day.

under Holy Spirit guidance of its total message regarding Christ's way and its application in our present world.

We humbly confess our inadequacies and failures both in understanding and in following this way, knowing well that we have come short both in demonstration and proclamation of Christian love. As we renew our commitment of discipleship and ambassadorship for Christ, we know how much we need God's grace and each other's help in the fellowship of His body in learning and obeying. Let us therefore stand together and go on together in His name and for His cause.

A DECLARATION OF CHRISTIAN FAITH AND COMMITMENT WITH RESPECT TO PEACE, WAR, AND NONRESISTANCE

The Position of the Mennonite Church as adopted by the Mennonite General Conference at Goshen, Indiana, August 23, 1951

Introduction

In August, 1937, the Mennonite Church through its General Conference assembled at Turner, Oregon, in the face of approaching war, adopted *A Statement of Position—Peace, War, and Military Service,* in which it set forth its faith and committed itself clearly on the issues of the time. Since then we have passed through a grievous world conflict, and after a few years of uneasy peace find ourselves again in a limited war and in dread of a third world war, with constantly growing world armaments and tensions. The United States government has repeatedly extended the military service law of 1940 and now plans to establish a permanent military training system. Other nations are committed to enlarged military programs. In the face of these conditions, a renewed statement of position is desirable, setting forth more completely the full meaning of our nonresistant faith, both for the strengthening of the faith and life of our membership and for a more adequate testimony to others. Therefore, we, the representatives of the Mennonite Church, assembled in General Conference at Goshen, Indiana, August 21-24, 1951, do adopt the following *Declaration of Christian Faith and Commitment with Respect to Peace, War, and Nonresistance.*

Basic Central Truths

The peace principles of the Mennonite Church, including its historic four-century-old witness against all war, are an integral part of the Gospel of Jesus Christ and of the discipleship which we believe the lordship of Christ requires of all of His followers. They derive directly from a Christian faith which holds as central truths:

(1) That one is our Master, even Christ, who is our only Saviour and Lord, and to whom alone supreme loyalty and obedience is due. He is the basis for our faith and commitment to the nonresistant way of life, and in His strength alone do we hope to live in peace and love toward all men. "For other foundation can no man lay than that is laid, which is Jesus Christ."

(2) That by the atoning and renewing grace of God which makes us new creatures in Christ, and through the power of the in-

dwelling Spirit, we *can* live the life of holy obedience and discipleship to which all the children of God are called.

(3) That redeeming love is at the heart of the Gospel, and that
the life of love and peace is God's plan for the individual and the
race.

(4) That Christ has established in the church, which is His
body, a universal community and brotherhood of the redeemed,
within which the fullness of His lordship must be practiced and from
which must go out into all human society the saving and healing
ministry of the Gospel.

(5) That war is altogether contrary to the teaching and spirit
of Christ and the Gospel, and to God's will as revealed in His Word;
that therefore war is sin, as is all manner of carnal strife; that it is
wrong in spirit and method as well as in purpose, and destructive in
its results; and that if we profess the principles of peace and nevertheless engage in warfare and strife we become guilty of sin and fall
under the just condemnation of God.

Scriptural Basis: the Old Testament

While we believe that the Old Testament Scriptures are divine
in origin and authoritative in character, we nevertheless hold that
these Scriptures are but a part of the progressive revelation of the
nature and will of God leading to the full and final revelation found
in the New Testament under the new covenant. Therefore Old
Testament Scriptures which are sometimes cited in support of Christian participation in war may not be used to contradict clear New
Testament teaching, but must be interpreted in the light of the
teaching of Christ and the apostles, for in Christ we find the norm
for the whole of Scripture. The national history of Israel as recorded
in the Old Testament cannot be an example for us, for under the
new covenant the people of God, the church, are of every nation,
and are separate from the world and its institutions; church and
state are separate. But even in the Old Testament it is clear that it
was God's original will that there should be no killing and warfare;
and that man, made in God's image should be governed by love.

Scriptural Basis: the New Testament

Among the many New Testament passages which clearly show
the sinfulness of all war and strife, and the requirement of creative
Christian love, we point to the following: "Blessed are the peacemakers"; "Love your enemies . . . do good to them that hate you
. . . that ye may be the children of your Father which is in heaven";
"Resist not him that is evil"; "Whatsoever ye would that men should
do to you, do ye even so to them"; "If any man will come after me,

let him deny himself, and take up his cross daily, and follow me";
"My kingdom is not of this world: if my kingdom were of this world,
then would my servants fight"; "Put up . . . thy sword into its place:
for all they that take the sword shall perish with the sword"; "Dearly
beloved, avenge not yourselves"; "If thine enemy hunger, feed him;
if he thirst, give him drink: for in so doing thou shalt heap coals
of fire on his head"; "Be not overcome of evil, but overcome evil
with good"; "The servant of the Lord must not strive; but be
gentle unto all men"; "The weapons of our warfare are not carnal";
"Christ also suffered for us, leaving us an example, that ye should
follow his steps: who did no sin, neither was guile found in his
mouth: who, when he was reviled, reviled not again; when he suffered, he threatened not"; "Not rendering evil for evil, or railing
for railing: but contrariwise blessing"; "From whence come wars and
fightings among you? come they not hence, even of your lusts";
"Hereby perceive we the love of God, because he laid down his life
for us: and we ought to lay down our lives for the brethren"; "If
a man say, I love God, and hateth his brother, he is a liar . . . . And
this commandment have we from him, That he who loveth God
love his brother also"; "But the greatest of these is charity [love]"
(Matt. 5:9; 5:44, 45; 5:39; 7:12; Luke 9:23; John 18:36; Matt. 26:52;
Rom. 12:20, 21; II Tim. 2:24; II Cor. 10:4; I Pet. 2:21-23; 3:9; Jas.
4:1; I John 3:16; 4:20, 21; I Cor. 13:13).

Christ, the Example of Suffering Love

All these words Christ brought to living expression in Himself.
In the life and work of Him, who in His incarnation became one
with man, is given the full revelation of God's will, reaching its
supreme meaning at Calvary. Integral to this divine-human life of
our Lord was His innocent and nonresistant endurance of the evil
inflicted upon Him, His identification of Himself in His suffering
with all sinners, thus bearing man's sin in His own body on the cross,
and His triumphant victory over sin by the very means of His death.
What He taught in the Sermon on the Mount He fulfilled in His
life and practice, including the cross. As those who believe in this
Christ are united with Him in death and resurrection experience,
they also will become identified with Him in His way of nonresistant suffering and triumphant overcoming. In this "way" of Christ,
war and its related evils can have no place.

The Way of the Cross

But beyond the specific New Testament words and even the
example of Christ, we hold that the whole tenor of the Gospel, being
redemptive, forbids the destructiveness of war and calls for love.

The very cross of Christ itself, the means by which God's love operates redemptively in a world of sinful men, speaks against war; for it
stands for the acceptance of unlimited suffering, the utter denial of
self, and the complete dedication of life to the ministry of redemption for others. This way of self-sacrifice is the cross which Christ
lays upon us when He calls us to take up our cross daily and follow
Him in the discipleship of self-denial, nonresistance, and suffering
love.

The Way of Discipleship

We believe further that the Christian, having been laid hold of
by God through Christ, must follow his Lord in all things regardless
of consequences. He must pay the price of complete discipleship,
for to him the commands of Christ and the principles of the Gospel
are not mere counsels to be accepted or rejected as may seem good
at the moment, but rather imperatives which must be followed to
the end. Once the premise is accepted that Christ speaks with authority from heaven, only one thing remains, that is, to obey His
command. And this the new man in Christ will desire from his
heart to do.

But this way of discipleship is not only a command to be
obeyed; it is the way of victory and peace for the individual and
society, to be practiced in the here and now and not to be postponed
to some future kingdom. With a joyful belief in the reality of God's
reign, we therefore forthrightly establish our lives on the power of
Christ. We are convinced that the teachings of Jesus and the power
of the Gospel are the solution to the problems of sin in man and
society: and that the reason society is still in its broken state is either
because men reject Christ and His Gospel or because those who have
taken the name of Christ will not live that Gospel and take up the
cross of utter discipleship laid upon them by their Lord. The true
Christian must move out into the world of sin and need and there
apply the Gospel to its fullest extent, uncompromisingly, and in
and through his own life. This calls for an action program requiring
the full unfolding of divine grace and power through man, but it is
the only hope of the world.

The Problem of the Use of Force in an Evil World

We recognize that in a world where the evil and the good exist
side by side, there is a necessary place, authorized by God Himself,
for the use of force by the state in the restraint of evil and the protection of the good, though always under restrictions deriving from
the higher laws of God. But we hold that the Christian cannot be
the executor of this force, his call being to operate on the basis of

love. If he abandons this way, he effectually destroys the only hope for the world, since force can never create righteousness or a Christian society; it can at best only restrain the evil in varying degrees.

Our Commitment to Total Discipleship

These declarations of faith and conviction give no blueprint for permanent peace nor do they assume that human endeavor alone can bring about a warless and sinless world within history, for only when men come under the lordship of Christ can they make peace and fulfill the prayer of our Lord, "Thy kingdom come. Thy will be done in earth, as it is in heaven." They do, however, require certain positive attitudes, duties, and ministries by Christian disciples toward all men which have far larger scope than only a testimony against war, and which call for consistent demonstration of sacrificial Christian love in all relationships. We believe, however, that the tremendous demands of this way of total love and total discipleship can by God's help be met, and we do here by God's grace declare our renewed acceptance of these demands and our determination to undertake their fulfillment in His name. Specifically, we understand this commitment to mean:

A. IN OUR OWN SPIRIT

(1) that we have peace with God.

(2) that the peace of God shall keep our hearts and minds through Christ Jesus.

(3) that the love of Christ shall reign in our natures and be the controlling motive in all our relations with our fellow men, in the family, in the church, in the community, in society, in all of our daily life.

B. IN OUR SERVICE AND WITNESS

(4) that we are bound in loving outreach to all to bear witness to Christ and to serve in His name, bringing the Gospel and all its benefits to everyone, and summoning men everywhere to the life of full discipleship and to the pursuit of peace and love without limit. For this ministry we mean to use every feasible way and facility: the spoken and written word; the demonstration of holiness and love in family, church, and community; relief work and Christian social service; and all other ways. In this service our youth can play a great part; they should give themselves to it in large numbers both in shorter or longer terms of special service, and in lifetime dedication.

(5) that we have the responsibility to bring to the total social order in which we live, and from which we receive so much, the ut-

most of which we are capable in Christian love and service. Seeking
for all men first the kingdom of God and His righteousness, we
should hold together in one united ministry the evangelism which
brings men to Christ and the creative application of the Gospel to
cultural, social, and material needs. This ministry will go to all
alike regardless of race, class, or condition.

C. IN OUR SOCIAL, ECONOMIC, AND POLITICAL RELATIONS

(6) that we practice a sharper Christian control of our economic, social, and cultural practices, to make certain that love truly
operates to work no ill to our neighbor, either short-range or long-
range. Knowing how much the selfishness, pride, and greed of individuals, groups, and nations, which economic systems often encourage, help to cause carnal strife and warfare, we propose not to
contribute thereto or to anything which destroys property or causes
hurt or loss of human life.

(7) that Christian love must hold primacy in all our economic
and labor relations, that we cannot participate in activities, organizations, investments, or systems which use the methods of force and
violence, compromise Christian ethics, or do not permit the full exercise of Christian love and brotherhood, and that we seek in our
own practices to work out this love and brotherhood in concrete applications.

(8) that though we recognize fully that God has set the state in
its place of power and ministry, we cannot take part in those of its
functions or respond to any of its demands which involve us in the
use of force or frustrate Christian love; but we acknowledge our
obligation to witness to the powers that be of the righteousness
which God requires of all men, even in government, and beyond
this to continue in earnest intercession to God on their behalf.

(9) that while rejecting any social system or ideology which opposes the Gospel and would destroy the true Christian faith and way
of life, we cannot take attitudes or commit acts contrary to Christian
love against those who promote such views or practices, but must
seek to overcome their evil and win them through the Gospel.

D. IN WAR AND MILITARY SERVICE

(10) that we can have no part in carnal warfare or conflict between nations, nor in strife between classes, groups, or individuals,
and that we can therefore not accept military service, either combatant or noncombatant or preparation or training therefor in any
form.

(11) that we cannot apply our labor, money, business, factories,

nor resources in any form to war or military ends, either in war finance or war industry, even under compulsion.

(12) that we cannot take part in scientific, educational, or cultural programs designed to contribute to war, nor in any propaganda or activity that tends to promote ill will or hatred among men or nations.

(13) that while we witness against conscription in any form and cannot lend ourselves to be a channel for its compulsions, we shall seek to find ways to serve in wartime as well as peacetime, through which the demands of the state may be both satisfied and transcended. We both expect and desire that this service be sacrificial on the part of our young men and that the church go with them all the way in their service and witness sharing in the sacrifice.

(14) that if war does come, with its possible serious devastation from bombings or other forms of destruction, such as atomic blasts, germ warfare, poison gas, etc., we will willingly render such civilian help as conscience permits, sacrificially and without thought of personal safety, so long as we thereby help to preserve and restore life and not to destroy it.

(15) that in wartime, as well as in peacetime, we shall endeavor to continue to live a quiet and peaceable life in all godliness and honesty; avoid joining in the wartime hysteria of hatred, revenge, and retaliation; and manifest a meek and submissive spirit, being obedient to the laws and regulations of the government in all things, including the usual taxes, except when obedience would cause us to violate the teachings of the Scripture and our conscience before God.

Conclusion

While we are deeply grateful to God for the precious heritage of faith, including the principle of love and nonresistance, which our Swiss, Dutch, and German Anabaptist-Mennonite forefathers purchased for us by their faith, obedience, and sacrifice, and which we believe is again expressed in the above declarations and commitments, we are convinced that this faith must be repossessed personally by each one out of his own reading and obeying of God's Word, and must ever be wrought out in practice anew. Hence we summon our brotherhood to a deeper mastery of the Scriptures as the infallible revelation of God's will for us, and to find afresh under Holy Spirit guidance its total message regarding Christ's way and its application in our present world.

We humbly confess our inadequacies and failures both in understanding and in following this way of love, peace, and nonresistance, knowing well that we have come short in demonstration and proclamation of Christian love. As we renew our commitment of discipleship and ambassadorship for Christ, we entreat God for the grace we so much need, and pledge each other our mutual help in learning and obedience.

We also appeal to all Christians to re-examine the full meaning of the Gospel of the cross and Christian discipleship to proclaim this Gospel in its fullness for the saving of men and the healing of the nations, and to exercise the entire ministry of reconciliation of man to God and man to man which is entrusted to all the followers of Jesus Christ.

A STATEMENT OF CONCERNS

Adopted at a study conference on Christian community relations, sponsored by the Committee on Industrial Relations of the Mennonite Church, Laurelville Mennonite Camp, July 24-27, 1951.

Doctrine and Practice

I. We recognize a tendency in current Christianity to make social betterment a chief concern, on the assumption that natural human goodness will assert itself if the machinery of environment is adjusted. We recognize also another tendency to emphasize exclusively the vertical relationship of man to God, on the assumption that if a man gets right with God his horizontal relationships with his fellows will automatically adjust themselves. We believe that the "social gospel" is basically in error; but we also believe that the non-social gospel is inadequate. We believe the statement of James that faith and works must go together. We therefore wish to express our deep concern that as a church we should not depart from the basic assumption that good social behavior must be secured as the outworking of a regenerated heart, that only the Spirit of God can produce the fruit of the Spirit. We would warn our people against any program of social or economic improvement which is divorced from the evangelizing purpose to bring men to Christ as both Saviour from sin and the Lord of their conduct.

We are further concerned that the church should acquire a better understanding of the principles of social justice contained in the Gospel of Christ, and urge our preachers and teachers to study and to set forth the social obligations expressed and implied in the teachings of the Old Testament prophets, of our Lord, and of all the apostles. We are deeply concerned that the social conscience of all our people may be aroused and sharpened, so that we may sense more and more the implications of Christian love and brotherhood in the complex details of modern life. We believe that our Christian testimony to the world about us can be effective only as we confess unsocial conduct to be sin and cleanse our lives of its defilement.

Nonresistance in Daily Life

II. In view of the fact that nonresistance is seen, not only in one's attitude toward war, but still more in the total spirit of the life in times of peace and war; and in view of the fact that the considerable failure of our members to take a consistent peace stand during the wars of the past decades argues a general failure in the more inclusive nonresistant life, this study conference expresses its concern:

1. That the principle of nonresistance become deeply imbedded in the thinking of our people as a result of regeneration and a continued program of teaching.

2. That our young men be encouraged and helped to such a daily behavior as will give them no embarrassment when they are asked in Form SSS-150 to describe actions and behavior which demonstrate their nonresistant conviction.

3. That our people carefully avoid every manifestation of covetousness, greed, and oppression; all willful neglect of duty by employer or employed; any relationship with agricultural, mercantile, industrial, or labor associations involving a compromise of principle; or any pressure methods designed at bettering themselves at the expense of others.

4. That we be more concerned about acting justly than about being treated justly, looking for every opportunity to witness for our Master as we overcome evil with good.

5. That we give a better demonstration of our unwillingness to profit through products of our labor or capital which contribute directly to military operations or to the destruction of property or life, or to participate in any program which tends to promote ill will or hatred among men or nations.

Christian Ethics in Business and Professions

III. In view of the extent to which the organization of modern life has been carried in the areas of business, industry, and the professions; and in view of the policies, methods, and procedures frequently used by these business and professional organizations, we are concerned with the necessity of examining with care, in the light of Christian ethics, the policies and methods of every such organization with which they have to do, to the end that all organization relationships be such as will not violate the Christian ethic. In this area we wish to state the following concerns in particular.

1. That a careful study be made of the various business, agricultural, and professional organizations affecting our brotherhood to the end that we be better informed as to their objectives, policies, and methods, enabling us to evaluate them in the light of our Christian ethic.

2. That business connections be avoided among us which would involve responsibility for unethical practices over which the individual has no control.

3. That great care be exercised in the investment of capital in large corporations and that this be done only when it is certain that business practices of the corporation, its policies with respect to competitors, and its labor policies are such as can be approved by the Christian conscience.

4. That our farmers and business and professional men exercise great care that no relations be maintained with agricultural, business, and professional organizations which will make them party to

unchristian pressure tactics, unfair competition, unfair labor policies, or other unchristian methods and procedures.

5. That we seek to promote a diversification of small industries and businesses in our various communities to the end that as many as possible of our people engaged in business and industry may be so engaged in small community industries in preference to the large-scale corporations in our larger industrial centers.

6. That our brethren in the operation of their own business organizations seek to enlighten their consciences as to the best type of internal organization and administration for the maintenance of Christian labor relations, and that they continually seek to improve these relations.

7. That as a brotherhood we continually seek to discover ways and means of bringing the economic life of our brethren more completely into the way of Christian stewardship and Christian discipleship.

Organized Labor

IV. The rise of the labor movement, accompanied by an industrial trend among our own people, has created problems arising out of our relations with organized labor. While recognizing the benefits which the workers have realized from the efforts of the labor unions, we recognize also that some of the methods employed are not in harmony with Scriptural principles, and therefore cannot be endorsed, and should not be participated in, by the Christian.

In relation to the problem thus existing and in our effort to adjust ourselves to it, we feel that we should have a concern in the following areas:

1. That our present "Statement of Position on Industrial Relations" should be re-examined with a view to its improvement as a piece of literature which will serve our purposes well in our contacts with labor leaders or the general public.

2. That a study should be made as to indoctrination literature which is needed for the instruction and guidance of our people.

3. That consideration should also be given as to effective ways and means whereby a conscience and personal convictions on this question can be developed, which we recognize as being a basic requisite in the solution of the problem.

4. That further clarification should be made as to what kinds of working arrangements can be accepted without compromise of Scriptural principles.

5. Since the lack of uniformity in attitude and practice throughout the church presents an inconsistent testimony, and since the acceptance of unqualified union membership by members of the church may well have serious implications in weakening the position of the church on the entire question of nonresistance and the recognition we seek to obtain for that position, we feel it should be our sincere concern that the position and practice of the church as a

whole may become more fully unified in harmony with Scriptural principles which should guide our relations in this area.

Race and Minority Group Relations

V. In view of the clear Scriptural teachings that God is no respecter of persons, and that there is no Jew nor Greek but that all are one in Christ Jesus; in view of the widespread prevalence of race animosity in the world of today and especially in our own country; and in view of the impact which race animosities have produced in our own brotherhood, it is the concern of those here assembled:

1. That we study means of bringing the Gospel of Christ to racial and minority groups, such as Negroes, Jews, and Japanese-Americans, and that the Gospel message be accompanied where necessary with service activities designed to raise their standard of living.

2. That we study means of better informing our brotherhood, (a) of the disabilities suffered by racial and minority groups, (b) of the lack of scientific basis for making differences between races, and (c) of the Scriptural teachings on race and minority group relationships.

3. That we witness against racial segregation or discrimination at every opportunity, and that we seek to abolish it wherever it may exist in our own brotherhood.

4. That we study means of providing opportunities for fellowship between Christians of different races and minority groups, to enable them to learn to know each other better as fellow saints.

Other Related Concerns

VI. In view of the striking increase in material prosperity in the United States and Canada and the enormous disparity in the standard of living between these areas and many other areas of the world which have urgent needs not only for the message of the Gospel of Jesus Christ but for material necessities requisite for the maintenance of life on a plane of health and decency, it is the concern of those here assembled:

1. That continued study of disparities in standards of living be made so that we may be aware of the true circumstances of other peoples.

2. That we teach without ceasing the true principles and practice of Christian stewardship of the possessions which have been entrusted to us.

3. That we recognize the great material prosperity of our countries to be the result primarily of the abundance of our natural resources provided by our benevolent heavenly Father rather than the accumulated work of our own minds or bodies or of our righteous living.

4. That we practice sharing our technical abilities and our accumulated possessions with those who are less fortunate in such a

way as to enable them to exert their own efforts to raise their standards of living.

5. That we refrain from assenting to policies of selfish nationalism embodied in such devices as the protective tariff and other restrictions on the free flow of international trade, the imperialistic exploitation of colonial peoples, and the discriminatory restriction of immigration of peoples from underprivileged countries to our own.

VII. In view of the tendency of modern governments in the United States and Canada to assume an increasingly paternalistic attitude toward their subjects, especially as related to the care of dependent aged, children, widows, and to the provision of insurances against contingencies of storm, flood, unemployment, disease, and accidents; and in view of the resulting tendency among the masses of people and even among many members of our own communion to look to the government rather than to the church for help in time of need, it is the concern of those here assembled:

1. That a study be made of the extent to which members of our own brotherhood are availing themselves of the benefits of governmental assistance.

2. That we look with favor upon the present mutual assistance activities of our local congregations, our district conferences, and other church organizations; that we urge these groups and others to study ways and means of making their present work more effective and to extend their scope of activities to other needed areas.

3. That we seek to decrease rather than increase disparity of wealth in our brotherhood, recognizing the responsibility of each member for the welfare of the household of faith.

VIII. In view of the Scriptural Mennonite emphasis upon simplicity of life, it is the concern of those here assembled that Mennonite productive resources of land, labor, and capital be engaged in the production of those goods and services which contribute more directly to the promotion of the Gospel of Jesus Christ in the world and to the supplying of the necessities for sustaining and enriching life rather than to the production of those things which weaken the mind or the body or which supply the trivial, superficial, or peripheral wants of man.

IX. In view of the rapidly changing standards of the world about us relative to rights, privileges, and obligations of women and children in the community and in the family; and in view of the lofty standards of the Scriptures with respect to the status of all human personality regardless of age or sex, it is the concern of those here assembled:

1. That there be a continued study of ways of strengthening family relationships.

2. That we maintain a consistent witness to the world of the effectiveness of the power of devotion to the kingdom of God, of the power of love and respect among all the members of the family group

in building homes which will endure and will show forth the regenerated life.

X. In view of the gross immorality manifest in our country through such sins as the liquor and narcotic traffic, gambling, and white slavery; and in view of dangers which these evils present to the welfare of our country, it is the concern of those here assembled:

1. That we maintain a continued strict and absolutist position against these evils as they appear in our brotherhood.

2. That we witness against these evils in the communities, states, and nations where we live.

THE WAY OF CHRISTIAN
LOVE IN RACE RELATIONS

A Statement Adopted by Mennonite General Conference, August 24, 1955.

Among the forces of evil challenging the advance of Christianity is a prejudice which many Christians feel towards those who are of a color or of a national origin different from their own. This prejudice, usually growing out of a feeling of superiority, often leads church members, as well as others, to practice various forms of discrimination contrary to the teachings and spirit of the Gospel. The victims of this kind of unjust treatment often become bitter towards their oppressors. Not only has this tension led to social antagonism and international ill will, but it has created conditions that have made the advance of the Gospel difficult and it has dimmed the Christian witness. Furthermore, those who have been guilty of attitudes of prejudice and superiority have been unable to experience the fullness of the Christian life.

As a fellowship of Christians which throughout its four hundred years of history has placed great emphasis in all human relations upon Christian brotherhood and the way of love, we must periodically re-examine our application of the faith which we profess in order to maintain and promulgate a vital witness in our time. This is the faith in our Lord and Master who is the true revelation of God; in the Holy Scriptures which are the written revelation of Jesus Christ; and in the way of the cross as given in His teachings, in His life, and in His death.

The Teaching of the Bible

A. The Unity of Man in the Order of Creation

The Scriptures teach that God "made of one blood all nations of men" (Acts 17:26). The Bible throughout clearly teaches this fact which is corroborated by scientific observation: that all people are one people though they may have superficial differences. Such differences, whether due to variations in the physical features of the body or the cultural differences due to social environments, have no bearing upon the worth of a person before God, for each person bears the image of the Creator.

Therefore, the Christian must regard every man as his brother in the flesh, whom he must love and seek to win to the kingdom of God even as Christ loved and sought those among whom He walked.

B. The Unity of Man in the Order of Grace

1. The Bible teaches that all men "have sinned and come short of the glory of God." This fact is corroborated by the observation: that every section of the human race is guilty of evil, and that in every man the original image of God is marred.

2. The Bible also teaches that "God so loved the world, that he gave his only begotten Son, that whosoever believeth in him should not perish, but have everlasting life" (John 3:16). Against the dark background of man's sin shines the glory of God's grace. As Paul says, "No distinction is made, for all alike have sinned, and consciously fall short of the glory of God, but are acquitted freely by His grace through the ransom given in Christ Jesus" (Rom. 3:22-24, Weymouth).

C. The Unity of the One Fellowship

The Bible teaches that it is the purpose of the Good Shepherd to bring all of His sheep as one flock into His fold. Jesus said, "And I have other sheep, that are not of this fold; I must bring them also, and they will heed my voice. So there shall be one flock, one shepherd" (John 10:16, RSV). This one flock is the church, His "one body" (Eph. 4:4), a new society of men recreated in the image of God. This new society transcends all human differences: "Here there cannot be Greek and Jew, circumcised and uncircumcised, barbarian, Scythian, slave, free man, but Christ is all, and in all" (Col. 3:11, RSV). This transcendence is not a mere matter of theory, but it is a reality among men in whom Christ dwells and is therefore to be worked out in an actual realized fellowship on a local and intercommunity level.

D. The Way of the Cross in Race Relations

1. The Bible teaches that the church must take the way of the cross in all race and group relations. This means that we must reach aggressively across all barriers with the call of the Gospel, to include all who repent in the fellowship of the church. This call includes the expression of Christ's love in both word and deed.

2. Those who follow the way of the cross in proclaiming the Gospel of love to all men, and in exemplifying Christian brotherhood, may suffer persecution and injustice which they must be ready to accept with joy. Matt. 5:9-11.

3. The way of the cross is the way of Christian nonresistance, where the egotisms of nation or race give way to Christian love and human solidarity. To refuse participation in warfare demands that Christians likewise rise above the practices of discrimination and coercion in other areas, such as race relations.

The Witness of Church History

1. During His ministry Jesus said that "men will come from east and west, and from north and south, and sit at table in the kingdom of God" (Luke 13:29, RSV).

2. While Jewish Christians sometimes had difficulty in understanding this great truth, the manifestation of God's grace in the conversion of Cornelius taught them that "God is no respecter of persons"; that "in every nation he that feareth him, and worketh righteousness, is accepted with him" (Acts 10:34, 35); that God gave the Holy Spirit to the Gentiles as much as to the Jews; that "he made no distinction between us and them, but cleansed their hearts by faith" (Acts 15:8, 9, RSV).

3. There is ample evidence that from the time of the Jerusalem Conference through the time of the Reformation the church accepted into its fellowship people of different cultural, national, and racial backgrounds. Nowhere in the New Testament are distinctions made on the basis of race or color. The baptism of the Ethiopian took place without any hesitancy, nor did it raise any question within the brotherhood. Neither in the early centuries nor in the long period of the Middle Ages and the Reformation does the literature reveal any sign of a racial basis of admission to the Christian congregation or of discrimination and segregation based on race or color.

The Sin of Segregation and Discrimination

A. Racial Discrimination a Recent Phenomenon

1. Racial tension as expressed in the denial of privileges and the segregation of peoples of different colors in public transportation, in schools, and even in churches is a relatively recent historical development.

2. In the United States colonialism produced the institution of slavery. This was followed by the struggle for its abolition, culminating in a civil war and a reconstruction period marked by bitterness and hatred, creating a situation in which the Negro members of our society were the unfortunate victims, and which affected to a greater or lesser degree all peoples of non-Anglo-Saxon stock among us.

3. Out of this situation has grown a vast mythology to the effect that people of color constitute a race which has a different ancestry from that of the Caucasian, and which in every way is inferior to it. Unfortunately, some Christian people have even deepened the confusion by claiming to find Biblical sanction and support for this myth. Thus many Christians find themselves in a position where they deny the basic principles of the Gospel, both in theory and in practice, in a manner never found before in the history of the church.

B. Racial Prejudice and Discrimination Is a Sin

We believe that racial prejudice and discrimination, as illustrated in the American pattern of segregation, or wherever it may be found, is a sin. Among the many reasons why we believe this to be true we note the following:

1. It is a denial of our professed faith that all those who are in Christ are one. Jesus prayed to the Father: "Keep through thine own name those whom thou hast given me, that they may be one, as we are" (John 17:11).

2. It is the perpetuation of a myth long proved false both by Christian faith and modern science.

3. It brands and discredits those discriminated against as undesirable and inferior.

4. It is a violation of the human personality as created by God; a denial of the opportunities and privileges which in the providence of God are meant for all peoples to enjoy.

5. It is a violation of the basic moral law which requires a redemptive attitude of love and reconciliation toward all men, and which forbids all falsehood, all feelings of hostility, and all attitudes which lead to strife and ill will among men. Matt. 5:21-48.

C. The Consequences of the Sin

The sin of prejudice and discrimination has a harmful effect not only upon those directly involved, but upon the church and upon society as a whole.

1. It humiliates and frustrates the victim so that it becomes difficult for him to behave as a normal member of society.

2. It scars the soul of the one who practices the sin.

3. It contributes to social tension, to hatred and strife.

4. It is a major cause of present-day international conflict and war.

5. It strengthens the hand of atheistic communism which claims to do away with the very sin which many Christians still defend.

6. It violates the central Christian message of redemption and love and thus discredits before the whole world the Christian church and the Gospel which it proclaims, and weakens its mission program.

The Response of the Church

A. Our Confession

In the light of the above, we are conscious of the contrast between the message of the Gospel and the conduct of men in their relations with their fellow men. As Christians we therefore humbly confess our sins. We confess that we have been blind when we should have seen the light; that we have failed to see that mere nonparticipation in violence and bloodshed is not an adequate expression of the doctrine of love to all men; that we have professed a belief in the urgency of the Great Commission without bringing into Christian fellowship our neighbors of "every kindred, and tongue, and people," and that we have failed to see that acceptance of the social patterns of segregation and discrimination is a violation of the command to be "not conformed to this world." Often we have been silent when others showed race prejudice and practiced discrimination. Too often our behavior has been determined by our selfish considerations of public and social approval more than by our desire to accept the way of the cross. Some of us have accepted the false propaganda of racism and anti-Semitism which has come into our homes in the guise of Christian literature. Too often we have equated our own culture with Christianity without sensing which elements were genuinely Christian and which were merely cultural accretions from a secular society. Many times we have made it difficult for Christians of national origin different from our own to find fellowship among us because our own cultural pride and attitudes of exclusiveness served as obstacles. For these and our many other sins we repent before our fellow men and our God.

B. Our Hope

Nonetheless we do not despair. The Gospel is not mere idealism, for within and around us we see manifestations of the grace of God working redemptively among men. There is reason for gratitude that in our brotherhood there are genuine expressions of Christian relations; and for the progress evident in many communities, we thank God. We appeal to fellow Christians everywhere with us to submit their hearts and lives to the scrutiny of the Scriptures and the Spirit. We know that in repentance and confession we experience the renewing grace of God, and that through this experience our relations with our fellow men can be healed.

C. Our Duty

Repentance means that we turn from the sins which estrange us from God and amend our ways. We therefore urge:

1. That, as Christians, we cultivate a sense of belonging together on the basis of unity in Christ and discipleship.

2. That we recognize that any acceptance of the prevailing customs of discrimination is a violation of the Scriptural principle of nonconformity to the evil of this world.

3. That our congregations and mission stations follow the policy of inviting and receiving into their fellowship all who receive Christ and follow Him in true discipleship regardless of race or color; that in

communities where there are now adjacent segregated congregations, sincere efforts toward intercongregational fellowship be cultivated.

4. That institutions and agencies of the church (as schools and colleges, hospitals, and homes for children and the aged, and the various church boards) if they have not yet done so, announce and carry out a policy of admission and service without discrimination on the basis of race, color, or nationality.

5. That in work with children, as in the case of summer Bible schools and summer camps, for example, an effort be made to conduct it on an interracial basis wherever there is a natural occasion to do so.

6. That we cultivate personal contacts among persons of various racial and other social groups.

7. That in our day-by-day social and business activities we become more sensitive to inequalities in practice.

8. That we express gratitude for the many manifestations of an awakened social conscience with respect to this question and for the many steps now being taken, especially by our government, to correct the evils of racial intolerance within our society; that in our communities we support efforts to that end which are consistent with Christian principles; and that we give our witness against the evils of prejudice and discrimination wherever they may be found.

9. That in all differences of experience, insight, and conviction on this question within the brotherhood, we exercise Christian forbearance, and seek for positive Christian solutions.

D. Our Program of Teaching and Preaching

Realizing that proper understanding is a necessary condition for the improvement of human relations on any level, we commend the following specific tasks and goals for our teaching and preaching program on race relations.

1. That we seek to present more clearly the teachings of the Bible, striving particularly to correct misunderstandings as to a supposed Biblical basis for discrimination.

2. That we help people to understand that science provides no basis for supposed qualitative differences among races.

3. That we deal with the psychological and sociological factors in race or other prejudice, helping our people to understand what this sin does to men's thought processes and social attitudes.

4. That we learn to think of all persons as persons, to meet them as such, and to be natural and at ease in their presence.

5. That we teach the necessity of uprooting from our conversation all words, expressions, and stories which lend support to racial prejudice.

6. That we call attention to the free interracial association in

such countries as Brazil and localities in our own country where good
relations have been achieved.

7. That on the question of interracial marriage we help our people to understand that the only Scriptural requirement for marriage is that it be "in the Lord"; that there is no valid biological objection to interracial marriage; and that, as in all marriages, the social implications of any proposed union should receive careful consideration.

The Conclusion

In summary, the Gospel of Christ is a Gospel of redemption, of reconciliation. God has made of peoples of diverse "races," colors, and nations a new fellowship, a new people, in Jesus Christ. He has called this new people to the ministry of reconciliation. If we have been incorporated into this fellowship, which is the body of Christ, our whole life is dedicated to the great process of redemption. This is the essence of our missionary task, and only as we rise above the differences of race and class are we truly engaged in the Christian witness.

COMMUNISM AND ANTI-COMMUNISM

A Statement of Position Adopted by the Mennonite General Conference, Johnstown, Pennsylvania, August 24, 1961

In view of the advance of communism in the world at large, the current strong anticommunist agitation which the cold-war climate has brought into our nation, and the challenge presented to our non-resistant position by these developments, we the representatives of the Mennonite Church, assembled in General Conference at Johnstown, Pennsylvania, August 23, 1961, reaffirm our commitment to our Biblical and historic nonresistant faith, calling special attention to the following points of emphasis in our General Conference pronouncements of 1937 and 1951.

1. Our love and ministry must go out to all, whether friend or foe.

2. While rejecting any ideology which opposes the Gospel or seeks to destroy the Christian faith, we cannot take any attitude or commit any act contrary to Christian love against those who hold or promote such views, but must seek to overcome their evil and win them through the Gospel.

3. If our country becomes involved in war, we shall endeavor to continue to live a quiet and peaceable life in all godliness and honesty and avoid joining in any wartime hysteria of hatred, revenge, and retaliation.

For the present situation specifically, we take this to mean, positively:

1. That we inform ourselves thoroughly and intelligently on the evils of all atheistic ideologies and practices and all materialistic philosophies, of whatever character.

2. That we must be faithful and effective in our witness against these ideologies and philosophies: (a) through the truth of the Gospel and (b) through works of mercy which demonstrate the way of love which the Gospel proclaims, even the feeding of our reputed enemies.

3. That we accept our obligation and privilege to bring in love the saving Gospel to communists everywhere, as well as to all men and to win them for Christ.

4. That our hand of love, encouragement, and help, and our prayers, must go out to Christians in all lands, especially to those who suffer for Christ behind the Iron Curtain.

5. That we must courageously proclaim all the implications of the Gospel in human life even at the risk, if need be, of being misunderstood and falsely accused.

6. That we urge upon governments such a positive course of action as may help to remove the conditions which contribute to the rise of communism and which tend to make people vulnerable to communist influence.

Negatively, we understand our commitment to mean:

1. That we recognize the incompatibility of Christianity and atheistic communism and the challenge to the cause of Christ which the latter represents.

2. That we recognize that atheistic communism can ultimately be overcome only by the witness of Christian truth in idea and life and not by force or violence.

3. That the nonresistant Christian witness in this matter must be clearly and unequivocally divorced from any and all advocacy of force and violence, either physical or intellectual.

4. That we cannot equate Christianity with any particular economic or political system, or with Americanism. Accordingly, we cannot accept the view that to be anticommunist is therefore necessarily to be Christian, or that to exercise Christian love toward communist persons is therefore necessarily to be procommunist.

5. That although we teach and warn against atheistic communism we cannot be involved in any anticommunist crusade which takes the form of a "holy war" and employs distortion of facts, unfounded charges against persons and organizations (particularly against fellow Christians), promotes blind fear, and creates an atmosphere which can lead to a very dangerous type of totalitarian philosophy.

6. That our word of warning must go out particularly against the current use of the pulpit, radio, and the religious press, in the name of Christianity, for this purpose.

Believing that world communism today has been permitted by God as a judgment upon an unfaithful Christendom, we confess our own past failure to proclaim as we ought the whole truth of the Gospel by word and deed. We urge the brotherhood to be more concerned to live out the Gospel fully in all areas of life, and to give itself to prayer to the end that the providence of God may overrule in the affairs of nations that peace may prevail. And we pray for the direction of the Spirit that we may faithfully perform our mission as effective witnesses for Christ in a world replete with economic greed, hate, and warfare, and struggling with competing ideologies, remembering that we are pilgrims here whose citizenship is in heaven, and who are looking for the consummation of all things in the return of our ascended Lord and in His ultimate eternal kingdom.

THE CHRISTIAN WITNESS TO THE STATE

A Statement Adopted by Mennonite General Conference, August 25, 1961

Introduction

Reaffirmation

We, the representatives of the Mennonite Church, assembled as the Mennonite General Conference at Johnstown, Pennsylvania, August 22-25, 1961, herewith reaffirm "A Declaration of Christian Faith and Commitment with Respect to Peace, War and Nonresistance," as adopted by this body at Goshen, Indiana, in 1951.

We believe this statement of a decade ago to be in harmony with the Anabaptist-Mennonite vision which speaks of civil government as ordained of God, and of resistance by the sword as forbidden to the disciple of Christ. It is our conviction that this declaration and this vision are a true expression of the teaching of the New Testament, the whole tenor of which is epitomized in the statement that "Christ . . . suffered for us, leaving us an example, that ye should follow his steps . . . who, when he was reviled, reviled not again; when he suffered, he threatened not" (1 Peter 2:21-23).

The Obligation to Witness

At this time we would give special attention and further expression to that portion of section C-8 of the 1951 Declaration in which "we acknowledge our obligation to witness to the powers-that-be of the righteousness which God requires of all men, even in government, and beyond this to continue in earnest intercession to God on their behalf."

The decade since these words were spoken has been given to search for a fuller understanding of the meaning of this obligation. What is the basis of the Christian witness to the state? What is the character of that witness? And in what manner is it to be given? In addition to its reaffirmation of our historic nonresistant faith, therefore, the present statement seeks to find helpful answers to these questions and to set forth certain positive convictions concerning the Christian obligation to witness to the state.

Biblical Foundation

This obligation we believe to be rooted both in the nature of the church itself and in the nature of the world to which the church is called to witness.

The Church Accepts the Lordship of Christ

The church is the body of Christ, the community of believers, the gathered company, identified with the stream of forces issuing from the redemptive work of Christ, whom she acknowledges as the Lord of history and as her own supreme Head, and under whose lordship she walks in obedient commitment and discipleship. The believers accept the new life in Christ as a binding imperative, as a glorious possibility, and as a blessed reality in which they live. They are laborers together with God for the redemption of the world which knows Him not. The meaning of history is to be found in the redemptive work of Christ and of His redemptive community which is the church.

Rom. 8:18-23; I Cor. 15:24; II Cor. 5:17-20; Eph. 1:20-23; Phil. 2:9-11; Col. 1:11-20; Col. 2:10; Col. 3:1; Heb. 1:3; Rev. 21:1-6.

The World Denies the Lordship of Christ

Outside the body of Christ are those who reject Christ and who stand in rebellion against God. The Scriptures speak of this non-Christian company as "the world," which is under the rule of principalities, of powers, of thrones, and of dominions, These terms suggest not only a degree of structure within the fallen social order, but also a degree of conflict among the units of the structure, and a certain rebellion against the will of God.

This world does not recognize the lordship of Christ. In His death the powers even sought to destroy Him. His victory over the powers, however, is a demonstration of that lordship to which every knee shall bow and which every tongue shall confess. Thus Christ is Lord both over the church which recognizes His lordship, and over the world which denies it.

Ps. 110; Matt. 22:44; Mark 12:36; Luke 20:42, 43; Acts 2:34, 35; Acts 13:27; Rom. 13:1; I Cor. 2:8; I Cor. 15:25; Gal. 4:3, 9; Eph. 3:10; Eph. 6:12; Col. 2:15; Heb. 1:3; Heb. 2:8; Heb. 10:13; I Pet. 3:22; Rev. 3:21.

The Ministry of Reconciliation and the Witness to the State

The love of Christ constrains us to a ministry of reconciliation which extends to all men, including those in government. This ministry includes a fourfold witness: (1) concerning saving faith in Him, that whosoever will may come; (2) concerning the meaning of true discipleship which even the nominal Christian may have failed to grasp; (3) concerning the love of God for all men, even for those who resist His will; and (4) in the case of those who continue to reject the Great Invitation, a witness which reasons with them "of righteousness, of temperance, and of judgment" to which all men, whether saint or sinner, must answer before Him who is Lord over church and world. Matt. 28:18-20; Acts 1:8; Acts 24:25; Acts 26; I Tim. 2:1, 2.

The Twofold Character of the State

The State as a Minister of God for Good

The Scriptural view of the state is a twofold one. On the one hand it is a minister of God for good, whose function is the maintenance of order in this present world. Its ultimate source of power is the God of history Himself. As such, the Christian owes the state respect, obedience, and co-operation, with prayers for its rulers to the end that the people of God may "lead a quiet and peaceable life in all godliness and honesty." The primary function of the state is the maintenance of a stable society enabling the church to pursue her divine ministry of reconciliation and of prophetic witness under the lordship of Christ.

Rom. 13:1-7; Titus 3:1; I Pet. 2:13-17.

The State as an Agent of the Powers

It is clear, on the other hand, that the state is also an institution of this present evil world, and that as such it is at times an agent of the forces arrayed against the Lord of history. For this reason the Christian cannot always submit to the demands of the state. On the contrary, he must needs on occasion be in opposition to the state, as individual rulers or their acts come under the domination of the principalities, the powers, and the spiritual hosts of wickedness who are in rebellion against the lordship of Christ.

I Cor. 2:8; I Cor. 6:1-3; I Cor. 8:5; I Cor. 15:24, 25; Eph. 6:12; Rev. 13.

The Twofold Character of the Ancient State

When the Scriptures speak of the state as a minister of God, and of the world rulers of this present darkness, they do not speak of democratic as opposed to totalitarian states, even though democracy is preferable to totalitarianism. Every state, even the most evil, is in some sense a minister of God for good. And every state; even the best, is at the same time also in some sense an agent of the rebellious powers. Because of the ambiguous and conflicting workings of these powers, and of its alignment with them, the state at its best can achieve only a partial and fragmentary order in the society of this world. In the final analysis no state is committed to Christ and His lordship, not even those states who profess a support of the Christian religion.

The demonic state of Rev. 13, making war on the saints, which calls for endurance, faith, and obedience on the part of every Christian, is the same as that of Rom. 13, which merits respect and submission because it is being used of God for providing a social structure in which the church can freely work, and for the achievement in history of the purpose of the state's unaccepted Lord.

The Twofold Character of the Modern State

The influence of Christendom upon modern society has been great. This is true even of the state, which is often characterized by relative toleration and even by encouragement of the Christian faith, by outstanding morality on the part of many statesmen, by programs of human welfare, and by democracy which recognizes the worth of the individual citizen. These values, however, are only relative, a given state being in a real sense, nevertheless, at times consciously or unconsciously an agent of the principalities and the powers of darkness, as well as a minister of God for good. The friendly state protecting the church today can tomorrow be the beast of the Revelation seeking to destroy the church.

The Christian Witness to the State

Evangel and Witness

In its labors together with God for the redemption of the world, the church is at the same time a messenger of God's grace for the salvation of men for Christian discipleship and life eternal, a witness to God's love and concern for the well-being of all men (even for those who resist His will), and a prophet proclaiming the impending doom of a world in rebellion against the Lord to whom it must bow, if not in this day of grace, then surely in the day of judgment.

Concern for the State

Although the church is not responsible for policies of state and ought not assume to dictate the same, Christians do have a concern for the good of the state and for the welfare of all who are affected by its policies. Therefore, they pray that the state may be wisely administered and used of God for His purposes in history. They pray for the salvation of all leaders of states and for the blessing of God upon them. Their witness to the state is motivated by the same love that motivates their prayer. Finding their frame of reference in the holiness, the righteousness, the peace, and the justice of God, they speak in their message to men of the state, concerning both of the need for faith in Christ, and the obligation to follow righteousness in policies and acts.

The Example of the Apostles and the Fathers

According to the Scriptures the Apostle Paul proclaimed his faith in Jesus Christ, and the hope of the resurrection, before Roman officials; and witnessed prophetically concerning righteousness and temperance and the judgment which is to come. Menno Simons, moreover, gave witness to rulers of his time, both of repentance and of righteousness and justice, admonishing them to "take heed wisely, rightly to execute your responsible and dangerous office according to the will of God."

Christians in our day must also witness to the state. The invitation to faith, including its full meaning in true discipleship, must be extended to all men, including government officials. On the other hand, ever mindful that God abandons neither the state nor its rulers, even in their rebellion against Him, the Christian must, when the response is something less than Christian faith and discipleship, hold forth the claims of Christ's lordship, even upon the sub-Christian and the pagan state.

Acts 1:8; Acts 4:23; Acts 24:25; Acts 26; II Cor. 5:17-20; Eph. 3: 8-10; I Tim. 2:1-4.

The Task for Today

No list of specific claims which we might formulate could be adequately complete or final. Even if it were such for today, the needs of tomorrow and the changing priorities of time and talent would require a continuous revision of the list. As illustrations of what is meant, however, we would mention the following as particularly significant for the day in which we live and worthy of being undertaken to the extent that priorities permit.

1. Statesmen must continually be challenged to seek the highest meanings of such values and concepts as justice, equality, freedom, and peace.

2. Even though they may reject the highest good in favor of relative and lesser values, statesmen must nevertheless be challenged to find the highest possible values within their own relative frames of reference. In so doing, the Christian may and can rightfully speak to decisions which the Christian ethic will not permit him to assist in carrying out.

3. The evils of war, particularly in this nuclear age, must ever be pressed upon the consciences of statesmen. Our previous declarations to this end need continually to be renewed.

4. Social attitudes, conditions, and practices out of harmony with the righteousness of God, and which contribute to injustice, to suffering, to weakening of mind, of body, and of character, or to the growth of crime, need ever to be witnessed against. Likewise, Christians may avail themselves of opportunities to suggest positive ways in which the state can assist in meeting social needs, as well as to warn of limits

to its rightful sphere of action.

5. The church's primary task is to be the church. This itself has implications for the state. In the course of her own work, the church creates institutions, procedural patterns, and value judgments which the state can and does imitate to a degree. In emphasizing the importance of the church, Christians may rightly regard the creation of these precedents as a significant contribution of the church to the state and to the welfare of the world which is served by the state.

The Means of the Witness

The witness herein described may be carried on by word of mouth, through oral or written conversation with officials of state, whether national or local; by means of the printed page; through works of mercy, such as feeding the hungry and clothing the naked; by a ministry of reconciliation in areas of tension, whether these be racial or social tensions in our own land, or colonial, nationalistic, or political tensions abroad; or by other means consistent with New Testament teaching and the historic Anabaptist-Mennonite vision.

Deeply conscious of the inadequacy of our own past efforts, and confessing our failure to give witness in the measure of our obligation, we nevertheless have faith to believe that Christian missions and Voluntary Service at home and abroad, and other similar ministries, have been used of God for such a witness; and that through them the church has functioned as a challenge to the conscience of the state, inspiring it to useful service of its own as a minister of God for good.

Our Commitment

Inasmuch as we have been reconciled unto God through Christ, and a ministry of reconciliation has been given unto us as a charge to keep, we would renew our commitment as ambassadors for Christ, that we may truly be used as a means for bringing the divine appeal to the hearts of men, including officials of state.

Strengthened by the firm conviction that more than ever before the world stands in need of the Gospel which we preach and that witness of peace which the Gospel enjoins, we would give ourselves anew to the task of a more effective witness to the nations of the holiness, the righteousness, and the justice of God, and of the way of peace which has been given by Christ, who in His resurrection has triumphed over all powers and principalities and whom we acknowledge as Lord of the church and of the world.

Finally, we would appeal to all Christians, particularly to those of our own congregations, that each examine his own life in view of the command, "Ye shall be my witnesses," and that each give himself to prayer and thought to the end that the opportunity which lies before us may be grasped with effectiveness, and that this great responsibility may be discharged as by true soldiers of Jesus Christ.

Index of Scripture Citations

General Index

Abel, 20
Abraham, 18
Abrams, Ray H., 78 n., 80
Absolutism, 8
Absolutists, 124, 146, 203, 206
Account of the Manners of the German Inhabitants of Pennsylvania, An, 101 n.
Acknowledgments, vi
Adams, Charles Francis, 218
Affirmation vs. oath, 100 f.
Africa, 7, 152
Agag, 25, 34
Agricola, Franz, 85
Agriculture, 126, 226; nonresistance and, 220 f.; Thomas Jefferson on, 225 f.; U.S. Dept. of, 210
Alcatraz prison, 114
Alexander the Great, 4
Alternative service, 106, 117, 119, 123, 146, 268; in Belgium, 151; in Canada, 131; in France, 151; in Germany, 151; in Holland, 149; in Russia, 93 f.; Quakers and, 105 f.
Alternative Service Camps, Canada, 131
Alternative Service Work Administration, Canada, 131
Amalekites, 34
Ambrose, 71
America, industrial conflicts in, 210 ff.; Mennonites in, 97 ff., 109, 116
American Federation of Labor, 212
American Friends Service Committee, 111, 125
American frontier closed, 212
American Indians, 3
American Labor, 234
American Relief Administration, 136
American Revolution, 97 ff., 134
American State University, The, 216 n.
Amos, 186

Anabaptists, 56, 76, 81, 84 f., 229, 243, 245 ff., 255 ff., 282; attitude to state, 157 f., 166; covenant theology, 15, 24
Anabaptists, The, 85 n., 96, 249 n.
Anabaptist View of the Church, The, 96
Ananias and Sapphira, 44
Ancient monarchs and war, 4, 11
Ancient wars, 3 ff., 9
Angell, R. C., 252 n.
Ante-Nicene Fathers, 65 ff. n., 170 n.
Appeal board, 124
Aquinas, Thomas, 74, 76 f., 261
Arabia, 3
Arizona, 119
Arles, Council of, 70
Armed forces, Mennonite men in, 204
Army experiences in camps, 111 ff., 116; is it necessary for peace, 311; service, 69
Arnobius, 68 f.
Aryans, 3
Asia, Mennonite Central Committee in, 153
Asia Minor, 3 f.
Associations, in American Revolution, 99
Assyria, 4, 34, 39
Athanasius, 70
Athenagoras, 66
Atlantic Monthly, 308
Atonement, 16 f., 59
Attitude, Christian, in wartime, 318; toward rulers, 295
Augustine, 12, 72 ff., 77, 260
Aurelius, Marcus, 65
Ausbund, 85, 98
Austria, relief work in, 138
Ayer, J. C., 73 n.
Babbitt, Irving, 216
Babylon, 41; Babylonian captivity, 40
Baer, John (and wife), 100

365

Netherlands, 247; Mennonites in, 86 ff., 134, 137, 148
See also Holland
New covenant, 15 ff., 24, 46; and kingdom of God, 43
New Testament, 342; love of God in, 17 f.; nonresistance in, 49, 291; soldiers in, 300; wrath of God in, 18 f.
New Testament Basis of Pacifism, The, 63, 310 n.
Newton, Kansas, 123, 135, 164
New York Peace Society, 172
Nicene and Post-Nicene Fathers, 73 n.
Niebuhr, H. Richard, 13 n., 14, 185 n.
Niebuhr, Reinhold, ix, 195, 207, 240 f., 252, 254
Niebuhr, Reinhold, and Christian Pacifism, 208
Nietzsche, Friedrich Wilhelm, 217
Noncombatant service, 96, 110, 248 f., 315; clarifying the issue, 116 ff.
Nonconformity and nonresistance, 277
Nonmilitary service, need for consistent policy of, 265 f.
Nonpacifists, 239 f.
Nonresistance, 15, 17 ff., 36, 81 f., 109, 134; and agriculture, 220 f.; and Christian brotherhood, 249 ff.; and economic relations, 218 ff.; and industrial conflict, 210 ff.; and nonconformity, 277; and pacifism, 172 f.; and the state, 156 f.; challenged by nonpacifists, 239 f.; Christ author and example of, 47; contribution to society, 167 f.; declaration of Christian faith and commitment with respect to, 331 f.; does it encourage evil, 312; Dutch Mennonites and, 148 ff.; for our time, 57 f.; in CPS, 203 f.; in daily life, 349 f.; in New Testament 43, 49 ff., 291; in Old Testament, 286; in practice, 308; integral part of Gospel, 58 ff., 152,

237; is it practical, 309; outreach of, 279 f.; service of to society, 236 ff., 242 ff.; sign of weakness, 312; social implications of, 209 ff.
Nonresistance in Colonial Pennsylvania, 133
Nonresistance Under Test, 133
Nonresistant Christian, 169 f.; and participation in state functions, 162 ff.; attitude of in wartime, 318; is he a parasite, 167, 169, 240 ff.; task of, 236 f.
Nonresistant Relief Organization, 122, 135
Nonviolence, 1, 186 ff., 202
Nonviolent Coercion. . . , 207
No-shooting pledge, 106
Nuclear Weapons and the Conflict of Conscience, 208
Oath, 50
Oath of allegiance, 100
Obedience, to God and man, 55, 105, 166; to government, 297
Ohio, 115
Oklahoma, 115
Old covenant, 15 ff., 24, 36, 44 ff.; and Israel's sin, 27 ff.; superseded, 17; war under, 25 f.
Oldham, J. H., 167, 263
Old Testament, 342; love of God in, 17 f.; nonresistance in, 286; on war and peace, viii f.; war in, 15 f.; wars and Israel's sin, 30; wrath of God in, 18 f.
Onesimus, 52, 188
Ontario Mennonites, 121 f.
Orders in Council, Canada, 1873 and 1898, 120 f.; of 1919, 122
Organized labor, 212 f., 216, 218, 341
Origen, 66 n., 67 f., 169, 242 f.
Origin of Species, 216
Pacifism, and nonresistance, 172 f.; and the social gospel, 180 f.; challenge of to nonresistance, 237 f.; in CPS, 203 f.; liberal Protes-

Guy F. Hershberger, professor emeritus of history at Goshen College, was educated at Hesston College and the universities of Michigan, Chicago, Basel, and Iowa. He has served as a member of the editorial boards of the *Mennonite Quarterly Review* and the *Studies in Anabaptist and Mennonite History* series, sponsored by the Mennonite Historical Society, Goshen, Indiana.

Besides his general expertise in Anabaptist-Mennonite studies, the author early in his career developed a special interest in war, peace, and nonresistance and in related aspects of Christian social ethics.

Besides numerous book reviews and articles in journals and encyclopedias his published works include: *Can Christians Fight? Essays on Peace and War* (1940); *Christian*

Relationships to State and Community (1942); *The Mennonite Church in the Second World War* (1951); and *The Way of the Cross in Human Relations* (1958). He is editor of *The Recovery of the Anabaptist Vision* (1957) and *Harold S. Bender, Educator, Historian, Churchman* (1964), and contributed the lead chapter in each of these books.

The present volume is the third edition of *War, Peace, and Nonresistance*, first published in 1944. The author spent a year in Europe making a firsthand study of European pacifism, both in England and on the continent. From 1939 to 1965 he was executive secretary of the Committee on Economic and Social Relations of the Mennonite Church and from 1959 to 1965 of its Peace Problems Committee.

An eightieth-birthday tribute to Guy F. Hershberger, *Kingdom, Cross, and Community*, was released by Herald Press in 1977. Edited by J. R. Burkholder and Calvin Redekop, its sixteen essays assess the impact of Hershberger's thought on the church.